T0138102

Communications
in Computer and Information Science   1994

Rationale

The CCIS series is devoted to the publication of proceedings of computer science conferences. Its aim is to efficiently disseminate original research results in informatics in printed and electronic form. While the focus is on publication of peer-reviewed full papers presenting mature work, inclusion of reviewed short papers reporting on work in progress is welcome, too. Besides globally relevant meetings with internationally representative program committees guaranteeing a strict peer-reviewing and paper selection process, conferences run by societies or of high regional or national relevance are also considered for publication.

Topics

The topical scope of CCIS spans the entire spectrum of informatics ranging from foundational topics in the theory of computing to information and communications science and technology and a broad variety of interdisciplinary application fields.

Information for Volume Editors and Authors

Publication in CCIS is free of charge. No royalties are paid, however, we offer registered conference participants temporary free access to the online version of the conference proceedings on SpringerLink (http://link.springer.com) by means of an http referrer from the conference website and/or a number of complimentary printed copies, as specified in the official acceptance email of the event.

CCIS proceedings can be published in time for distribution at conferences or as postproceedings, and delivered in the form of printed books and/or electronically as USBs and/or e-content licenses for accessing proceedings at SpringerLink. Furthermore, CCIS proceedings are included in the CCIS electronic book series hosted in the SpringerLink digital library at http://link.springer.com/bookseries/7899. Conferences publishing in CCIS are allowed to use Online Conference Service (OCS) for managing the whole proceedings lifecycle (from submission and reviewing to preparing for publication) free of charge.

Publication process

The language of publication is exclusively English. Authors publishing in CCIS have to sign the Springer CCIS copyright transfer form, however, they are free to use their material published in CCIS for substantially changed, more elaborate subsequent publications elsewhere. For the preparation of the camera-ready papers/files, authors have to strictly adhere to the Springer CCIS Authors' Instructions and are strongly encouraged to use the CCIS LaTeX style files or templates.

Abstracting/Indexing

CCIS is abstracted/indexed in DBLP, Google Scholar, EI-Compendex, Mathematical Reviews, SCImago, Scopus. CCIS volumes are also submitted for the inclusion in ISI Proceedings.

How to start

To start the evaluation of your proposal for inclusion in the CCIS series, please send an e-mail to ccis@springer.com.

Lei Wang · Tie Qiu · Chi Lin · Xinbing Wang
Editors

Wireless Sensor Networks

17th China Conference, CWSN 2023
Dalian, China, October 13–15, 2023
Proceedings

 Springer

Editors
Lei Wang
Dalian University of Technology
Dalian, China

Tie Qiu
Tianjin University
Tianjin, China

Chi Lin
Dalian University of Technology
Dalian, China

Xinbing Wang
Shanghai Jiao Tong University
Shanghai, China

ISSN 1865-0929   ISSN 1865-0937 (electronic)
Communications in Computer and Information Science
ISBN 978-981-97-1009-6   ISBN 978-981-97-1010-2 (eBook)
https://doi.org/10.1007/978-981-97-1010-2

This Springer imprint is published by the registered company Springer Nature Singapore Pte Ltd.
The registered company address is: 152 Beach Road, #21-01/04 Gateway East, Singapore 189721, Singapore

Paper in this product is recyclable.

Preface

The China Conference on Wireless Sensor Networks (CWSN) is the annual conference on the Internet of Things (IoT) which is sponsored by the China Computer Federation (CCF). The 17th CWSN took place in Dalian, China, in October 2023. As a leading conference in the field of IoT, CWSN is the premier forum for IoT researchers and practitioners from academia, industry, and government in China to share their ideas, research results, and experiences, and this strongly promotes research and technical innovation in these fields domestically and internationally.

The conference provided an academic exchange of research and a development forum for IoT researchers, developers, enterprises, and users. Exchanging results and experience of research and applications in IoT, and discussing the key challenges and research hotspots, is the main goal of the forum. As a high-level forum for the design, implementation, and application of IoT, the conference promoted the exchange and application of theories and technologies on IoT-related topics.

This year, CWSN received 105 submissions, including 38 English-language papers and 67 Chinese-language papers. After a careful double-blind review process, 22 revised and completed papers were selected. The high-quality program would not have been possible without the authors who chose CWSN 2023 as a venue for their publications. We are also very grateful to the members of the Program Committee and Organizing Committee, who put a tremendous amount of effort into soliciting and selecting research papers with a balance of high quality, new ideas, and new applications. We hope that you enjoy reading and benefit from the proceedings of CWSN 2023.

October 2023

Xinbing Wang
Lei Wang

Organization

Conference Chairs

Huadong Ma   CCF Internet of Things Special Committee, China
Zhongxuan Luo   Dalian University of Technology, China

Honorary Chair

Hao Dai   Chinese Academy of Engineering, China

Steering Committee Chair

Jianzhong Li   Harbin Institute of Technology, China

Program Committee Chairs

Xinbing Wang   Shanghai Jiaotong University, China
Lei Wang   Dalian University of Technology, China

Program Committee Co-chairs

Li Cui   Institute of Computing Technology, Chinese
     Academy of Sciences, China
Tie Qiu   Tianjin University, China

Outstanding Paper Award Chair

Xue Wang   Tsinghua University, China

Industrial Internet Forum Chairs

Songtao Guo   Chongqing University, China
Xiaojiang Chen   Northwest University, China

Education Forum Chairs

Juan Luo   Hunan University, China
Yuxin Wang   Dalian University of Technology, China

Enterprise Forum Chairs

Limin Sun   Institute of Information Engineering, Chinese
                                     Academy of Sciences, China
Guanhua Sun   Dalian Mizhen Technology Co., Ltd., China

Outstanding Young Scholars Forum Chair

Zheng Yang   Tsinghua University, China

Organization Committee Chairs

Liang Liu   Beijing University of Posts and
                                     Telecommunications, China
Chi Lin   Dalian University of Technology, China

Organization Committee Co-chairs

Luoyi Fu   Shanghai Jiaotong University, China
Xiaobo Zhou   Tianjin University, China

Organization Committee

Huanhuan Zhang	Beijing University of Posts and Telecommunications, China
Zichuan Xu	Dalian University of Technology, China
Fengqi Li	Dalian Jiaotong University, China
Junchao Du	Xidian University, China
Zumin Wang	Dalian University, China
Xianping Fu	Dalian Maritime University, China

Program Committee

Guangwei Bai	Nanjing Tech University, China
Ming Bao	Institute of Acoustics, Chinese Academy of Sciences, China
Yuanguo Bi	Northeastern University, China
Qingsong Cai	Beijing Technology and Business University, China
Shaobin Cai	Huaqiao University, China
Bin Cao	Harbin Institute of Technology (Shenzhen), China
An Zeng	Guangdong University of Technology, China
Deze Zeng	China University of Geosciences (Wuhan), China
Fanzi Zeng	Hunan University, China
Shan Chang	Donghua University, China
Guihai Chen	Nanjing University, China
Haiming Chen	Ningbo University, China
Hong Chen	Renmin University of China, China
Honglong Chen	China University of Petroleum (East China), China
Jiaxing Chen	Hebei Normal University, China
Liangyin Chen	Sichuan University, China
Wei Chen	Zhejiang University, China
Xiaojiang Chen	Northwest University, China
Xi Chen	Center for Intelligent and Networked Systems Research, Tsinghua University, China
Xu Chen	Sun Yat-sen University, China
Yihong Chen	China West Normal University, China
Yongle Chen	Taiyuan University of Technology, China
Zhikui Chen	Dalian University of Technology, China
Keyang Cheng	Jiangsu University, China
Xiuzhen Cheng	Shandong University, China

Hongju Cheng	Fuzhou University, China
Lianglun Cheng	Guangdong University of Technology, China
Siyao Cheng	Harbin Institute of Technology, China
Kaikai Chi	Zhejiang University of Technology, China
Li Cui	Institute of Computing Technology, Chinese Academy of Sciences, China
Xunxue Cui	Army Officer Academy, China
Haipeng Dai	Nanjing University, China
Xiaochao Dang	Northwest Normal University, China
Qingyong Deng	Xiangtan University, China
Xiaoheng Deng	Central South University, China
Wei Dong	Zhejiang University, China
Hongwei Du	Harbin Institute of Technology (Shenzhen), China
Juan Fang	Beijing University of Technology, China
Xiaolin Fang	Southeast University, China
Dingyi Fang	Northwest University, China
Guangsheng Feng	Harbin Engineering University, China
Xiufang Feng	Taiyuan University of Technology, China
Deyun Gao	Beijing Jiaotong University, China
Hong Gao	Harbin Institute of Technology, China
Ruipeng Gao	Beijing Jiaotong University, China
Jibing Gong	Yanshan University, China
Zhitao Guan	North China Electric Power University, China
Songtao Guo	Chongqing University, China
Zhongwen Guo	Ocean University of China, China
Guangjie Han	Hohai University, China
Jinsong Han	Zhejiang University, China
Yanbo Han	North China University of Technology, China
Zhanjun Hao	Northwest Normal University, China
Daojing He	Harbin Institute of Technology (Shenzhen), China
Shiming He	Changsha University of Science and Technology, China
Yuan He	Tsinghua University, China
Shibo He	Zhejiang University, China
Chengquan Hu	Jilin University, China
Pengfei Hu	Shandong University, China
Qiangsheng Hua	Huazhong University of Science and Technology, China
Zhan Xun	Changzhou University, China
Haiping Huang	Nanjing University of Posts and Telecommunications, China
He Huang	Soochow University, China

Liusheng Huang	University of Science and Technology of China, China
Longbo Huang	Tsinghua University, China
Shuqiang Huang	Jinan University, China
Jie Jia	Northeastern University, China
Riheng Jia	Zhejiang Normal University, China
Nan Jiang	East China Jiaotong University, China
Hongbo Jiang	Hunan University, China
Xianlong Jiao	Air Force Engineering University, Institute of Information and Navigation, China
Haiming Jin	Nanjing University of Posts and Telecommunications, China
Qi Jing	Peking University, China
Bo Jing	Air Force Engineering University, China
Linghe Kong	Shanghai Jiaotong University, China
Zhufang Kuang	Central South University of Forestry and Technology, China
Chao Li	Shandong University of Science and Technology, China
Deying Li	Renmin University of China, China
Fan Li	Beijing Institute of Technology, China
Fangmin Li	Wuhan University of Technology, China
Guanghui Li	Jiangnan University, China
Guorui Li	Northeastern University, China
Hongwei Li	University of Electronic Science and Technology of China, China
Jianqiang Li	Shenzhen University, China
Jianbo Li	Qingdao University, China
Jianzhong Li	Harbin Institute of Technology, China
Jie Li	Northeastern University, China
Jinbao Li	Heilongjiang University, China
Minglu Li	Shanghai Jiaotong University, China
Renfa Li	Hunan University, China
Xiangyang Li	University of Science and Technology of China, China
Yanjun Li	Zhejiang University of Technology, China
Zhetao Li	Jinan University, China
Zhiyuan Li	Jiangsu University, China
Zhong Li	Zhejiang Sci-Tech University, China
Zhuo Li	Beijing Information Science and Technology University, China
Hongbin Liang	Southwest Jiaotong University, China
Jiuzhen Liang	Changzhou University, China

Wei Liang	Shenyang Institute of Automation, Chinese Academy of Sciences, China
Chi Lin	Dalian University of Technology, China
Feng Lin	Zhejiang University, China
Chao Liu	Shandong University, China
Chi Liu	Beijing Institute of Technology, China
Dongning Liu	Guangdong University of Technology, China
Hongbo Liu	University of Electronic Science and Technology of China, China
Jiajia Liu	Xidian University, China
Kai Liu	Chongqing University, China
Liang Liu	Beijing University of Posts and Telecommunications, China
Min Liu	Tongji University/Jiangsu University, China
Peng Liu	Guangdong University of Technology, China
Tang Liu	Sichuan Normal University, China
Xingcheng Liu	Sun Yat-sen University, China
Yunhao Liu	Tsinghua University, China
Xiang Liu	Peking University, China
Jianfeng Lu	Wuhan University of Science and Technology, China
Chengwen Luo	Shenzhen University, China
Juan Luo	Hunan University, China
Junzhou Luo	Southeast University, China
Feng Lv	Central South University, China
Huadong Ma	Nanjing University of Posts and Telecommunications, China
Li Ma	North China University of Technology, China
Lianbo Ma	Northeastern University, China
Jianwei Jue	Beihang University, China
Xiaoguang Niu	Wuhan University, China
Hao Peng	Zhejiang Normal University, China
Jian Peng	Sichuan University, China
Li Peng	Jiangnan University, China
Shaoliang Peng	Hunan University, China
Yuanyuan Pu	Yunnan University, China
Wangdong Qi	PLA University of Science and Technology, China
Kaiguo Qian	Kunming University, China
Jiefan Qiu	Zhejiang University of Technology, China
Tie Qiu	Tianjin University, China
Fengyuan Ren	Tsinghua University, China
Ju Ren	Central South University, China

Yanzhi Ren	University of Electronic Science and Technology of China, China
Shikai Shen	Kunming University, China
Yiran Shen	Harbin Engineering University, China
Yulong Shen	Xidian University, China
Jian Shu	Nanchang Hangkong University, China
Xiaoxia Song	Shanxi Datong University, China
Geng Sun	Jilin University, China
Lijuan Sun	Nanjing University of Posts and Telecommunications, China
Limin Sun	Institute of Information Engineering, Chinese Academy of Sciences, China
Weifeng Sun	Dalian University of Technology, China
Fengxiao Tang	Central South University, China
Dan Tao	Beijing Jiaotong University, China
Xiaohua Tian	Shanghai Jiaotong University, China
Shaohua Wan	Zhongnan University of Economics and Law, China
Yang Wang	University of Science and Technology of China, China
En Wang	Jilin University, China
Jiliang Wang	Tsinghua University, China
Kun Wang	Nanjing University of Posts and Telecommunications, China
Lei Wang	Dalian University of Technology, China
Liangmin Wang	Southeast University, China
Pengfei Wang	Dalian University of Technology, China
Ping Wang	Xihua University, China
Qi Wang	Institute of Computing Technology, Chinese Academy of Sciences, China
Qingshan Wang	Hefei University of Technology, China
Ruchuan Wang	Nanjing University of Posts and Telecommunications, China
Rui Wang	University of Science and Technology Beijing, China
Shuai Wang	Southeast University, China
Tian Wang	Beijing Normal University, China
Xiaoming Wang	Shaanxi Normal University, China
Xiaodong Wang	Kunming University of Science and Technology/Fuzhou University, China
Xiaoliang Wang	Hunan University of Science and Technology, China
Xinbing Wang	Shanghai Jiaotong University, China

Xue Wang	Chongqing University, China
Yiding Wang	North China University of Technology, China
Yuexuan Wang	Tsinghua University, China
Zhibo Wang	Zhejiang University, China
Zhi Wang	Tsinghua University, China
Wei Wei	Xian University of Technology, China
Zhenchun Wei	Hefei University of Technology, China
Hui Wen	Guilin University of Electronic Technology, China
Zhongming Weng	Tianjin University, China
Hejun Wu	Sun Yat-sen University, China
Honghai Wu	Henan University of Science and Technology, School of Information Engineering, China
Xiaojun Wu	Northwestern Polytechnical University, China
Xingjun Wu	Tsinghua University, China
Kaishun Wu	Shenzhen University, China
Chaocan Xiang	Chongqing University, China
Deqin Xiao	South China Agricultural University, China
Fu Xiao	Nanjing University of Posts and Telecommunications, China
Liang Xiao	Hubei University of Technology, China
Ling Xiao	Hunan University, China
Kun Xie	Hunan University, China
Lei Xie	Northwestern Polytechnical University, China
Mandi Xie	Zhejiang Gongshang University, China
Xiaolan Xie	Guilin University of Technology, China
Yongping Xiong	Nanjing University of Posts and Telecommunications, China
Jia Xu	Nanjing University of Posts and Telecommunications, China
Wenzheng Xu	Sichuan University, China
Chenren Xu	Peking University, China
Guangtao Xue	Shanghai Jiaotong University, China
Geng Yang	Nanjing University of Posts and Telecommunications, China
Guisong Yang	Shanghai University of Technology, China
Hao Yang	Chongqing University, China
Panlong Yang	University of Science and Technology of China, China
Weidong Yang	Henan University of Technology, China
Zheng Yang	Tsinghua University, China
Weidong Yi	Chinese Academy of Sciences, China
Zuwei Yin	PLA Information Engineering University, China

Ruiyun Yu	Northeastern University, China
Jiguo Yu	Qilu University of Technology, China
Peiyan Yuan	Henan Normal University, China
Deyu Zhang	Central South University, China
Jiao Zhang	Nanjing University of Posts and Telecommunications, China
Lan Zhang	University of Science and Technology of China, China
Lei Zhang	Sichuan University, China
Lichen Zhang	Guangdong University of Technology, China
Lianming Zhang	Hunan Normal University, China
Shigeng Zhang	Central South University, China
Shuqin Zhang	Zhongyuan University of Technology, China
Yanyong Zhang	University of Science and Technology of China, China
Yin Zhang	University of Electronic Science and Technology of China, China
Yongmin Zhang	Central South University, China
Yunzhou Zhang	Northeastern University, China
Dong Zhao	Nanjing University of Posts and Telecommunications, China
Jumin Zhao	Taiyuan University of Technology, China
Junhui Zhao	East China Jiaotong University, China
Zenghua Zhao	Tianjin University, China
Zhiwei Zhao	University of Electronic Science and Technology of China, China
Jiping Zheng	Nanjing University of Aeronautics and Astronautics, China
Meng Zheng	Shenyang Institute of Automation, Chinese Academy of Sciences, China
Xiaolong Zheng	Nanjing University of Posts and Telecommunications, China
Ping Zhong	Central South University, China
Anfu Zhou	Nanjing University of Posts and Telecommunications, China
Jian Zhou	Nanjing University of Posts and Telecommunications, China
Ruiting Zhou	Southeast University, China
Changbing Zhou	China University of Geosciences, China
Hongzi Zhu	Shanghai Jiaotong University, China
Hongsong Zhu	Institute of Information Engineering, Chinese Academy of Sciences, China

Contents

Security and Privacy Protection on Internet of Things

Fog Computing and Wireless Computing

Intelligent Internet of Things

Theory and Technology on Wireless Sensor Network

MPR Node Selection Improvement in OLSR Based on Binary Cuckoo Search

Tong Wang, Kai Yu, Min Ouyang$^{(\boxtimes)}$, Shan Gao, and Liwei Chen

Harbin Engineering University, Harbin 150000, China
{wangtong,oym}@hrbeu.edu.cn

Abstract. Unmanned aerial vehicle (UAV) relay is an appropriate choice for emergency communications because of its good mobility and flexibility of placement. In this paper, the optimized link state routing (OLSR) based on binary cuckoo search (BCS) is proposed to improve the Multi-Point Relay (MPR) node selection efficiency and survival time of UAV relay network. The traditional OLSR uses the greedy algorithm to select the MPR set, ignoring the key factors such as node energy in the emergency communication relay scenario. In the optimization process, it is easy to fall into local optimal and generate redundancy, increasing protocol overhead and network delay. Therefore, binary Cuckoo search with energy sensing strategy are adopted to solve MPR node selection which is the discrete optimization problem by randomly finding the optimal solution through Lévy flight. The NS3 network simulator is used to simulate our proposed model. The results show that the improved OLSR based on the BCS has better MPR node search efficiency and higher energy utilization rate of nodes, which can effectively solve the survival time problem of emergency communication networks.

Keywords: Multi-Point Relay (MPR) · Optimized link state routing (OLSR) · Binary Cuckoo Search (BCS)

1 Introduction

Mobile Ad Hoc Networks (MANETs) are wireless networks, which can be composed of UAV mobile nodes. UAVs can communicate and cooperate with each other without fixed infrastructure. Therefore, MANETs are flexible, adaptive and scalable, such networks effectively support urgent communication needs for disaster recovery operations [1]. To establish an emergency communication network based on MANET, the first consideration is the energy limitation of drones, their batteries need to be frequently changed and their limited coverage range capacities constitute a big issue [2]. In this scenarios, it is not only necessary to ensure node data reachable, but also the network has a certain lifetime. Therefore, how to improve the survival time of the network is also one of the important research contents.

Optimized link state routing is a classical table-driven prior routing protocol in MANET. OLSR routes perform link detection, neighbor discovery, and selection of MPR nodes by broadcasting Hello messages between nodes [3]. After obtaining MPR node

© The Author(s), under exclusive license to Springer Nature Singapore Pte Ltd. 2024
L. Wang et al. (Eds.): CWSN 2023, CCIS 1994, pp. 3–14, 2024.
https://doi.org/10.1007/978-981-97-1010-2_1

information, establish and maintain the entire topology of the network base on Topology Control (TC) messages transfer. Finally, Dijkrastra algorithm is used to calculate the routing table. MPR is the core mechanism that reduces the broadcast overhead of routing information, updates and maintains the global routing table regularly.

OLSR has good coverage and stability, but the greedy mechanism in OLSR is easy to fall into local optimal in the process of optimization, which leads to excessive routing table and redundant routing information. In OLSR, each node needs to maintain a global routing table, including all destination nodes, the number of hops to the destination node, and the address of the next hop node. Therefore, with the expansion of the network scale, the space overhead of the routing table also increases. When the network topology changes frequently, it may be necessary to frequently re-select MPRs and routing paths. As a result, the updating delay and conflict probability of routing information will increase.

Cuckoo Search (CS) is a natural heuristic-based optimization algorithm proposed by Xin-she Yang and Suash Deb [4] in 2009, which is developed from the parasitic reproduction strategy of cuckoo. In nature, the cuckoo will secretly lay their eggs into the host nest when the host is out foraging, and the host will incubate and nurture them. Once the host finds the parasitic eggs, eggs will be removed. Cuckoos search for a suitable nest to lay eggs in a random way.

This paper aims to explore the application of BCS in OLSR and optimize the selection of MPRs by incorporating energy perception. BCS addresses the shortcomings of greedy mechanisms and improves the search efficiency of MPR nodes and survival time of MANET networks in emergency scenarios. The rest of this paper is organized as follows. Section 2 explains related work. In Sect. 3, the basic principles and characteristics of CS and BCS, as well as the implementation process of Lévy flight are introduced respectively. In Sect. 4, the selection of MPR nodes is modeled and analyzed, and the implementation process of BCS-OLSR combined with energy sensing is described in detail. Section 5 presents simulation results and Sect. 6 wraps up with conclusion.

2   Related Works

In routing protocols for mobile networks, the need of energy efficiency is a problem concerning with the constraints imposed by battery capacity and heat dissipation.In [5], the author proposed an energy aware willingness setting mechanism, which sets willingness based on the percentage of remaining energy of the node. The size of willingness affects the likelihood of the node becoming an MPR node and determines the degree of willingness of the node to forward messages from other nodes. However, such a mechanism can cause to excessive traffic being concentrated on nodes with high residual energy, resulting in message congestion. On this basis, [6] changes the path cost from hop count to weight accumulation by weighting t node residual energy, node degree, and MAC queue utilization, so as to update routes and further improve the network lifetime of OLSR protocol.

In [7], the author considered the scenario where UAVs frequently change network topology information during high-speed movement, improved OLSR-ETX, added three-dimensional information of nodes to the information frame, calculated Link Expiration Time (LET) based on location information, updated Expected Transmission Count

(ETX) metric, and further improved the MPR selection mechanism through two parameters, improving the dynamic stability of the network link and reducing the number of MPR node reselection, However, the selection of MPR nodes under this method still follows the greedy mechanism, resulting in results that are prone to falling into local optima.

For the OLSR protocol, the selection of MPR nodes is crucial [8]. In the traditional way, the Greedy algorithm is often used to select the MPR set, and the one hop node with the most two hop neighbors covering the source node is preferred. This can cause significant redundancy, leading to increased protocol overhead and increased latency between networks. Many scholars have improved the MPR selection algorithm from different perspectives to address this issue.

The author proposes a set operation based MPR set Selection algorithm in [9], which sorts the one hop node set by the number of two hop node connections, deletes the one hop node with the smallest coverage and has no impact on the two hop node set, effectively reducing the redundancy of the MPR set, but increasing the delay. In [10], after the route is obtained using the Djikstra algorithm, the Minmax algorithm based on the signal strength is used to select the MPR node. However, the MPR node is selected after the route is calculated, so the performance in terms of delay and throughput is not ideal.

In [11], the author proposes a new method called WRE-OLSR, which introduces the weight ratio calculation of node residual energy and node accessibility, achieving an extension of network survival time. On this basis, the authors of [12] improved the MPR selection mechanism of WRE-OLSR by measuring the energy dissipation of the one hop neighbor, significantly increasing the time delay of WRE-OLSR. In [13], the author applied Differential Evolution (DE) and Non-dominated Sorting Genetic Algorithm II (NSGA II) to the parameter design of OLSR, solving the problem of resource allocation. This article demonstrates the superiority of biomimetic algorithms and has an enlightening effect on the research of combining biomimetic algorithms with OLSR.

3   Cuckoo Search and Binary Cuckoo Search

3.1   Cuckoo Search

Choosing the optimal MPR set is an NP hard problem [14]. In response to this issue, heuristic algorithms demonstrate excellent performance. Among them, CS has fewer parameters and stronger global optimization ability compared to other algorithms, which can be flexibly combined with other algorithms and has wider applicability. CS defines the solution in the search space as the nest of a cuckoo. As the unit of algorithm iteration, set the population size to n, the number of iterations to $MaxGeneration$ and the probability of cuckoo eggs being discovered to p_a. $x_i^{(t)}$ represents the position of the i th nest in the t th generation, it corresponds to a *fitness*, which is the value of the $f(x)$, $x = (x_1, x_2,..., x_d)^T$ corresponding to the solution. The basic steps of cuckoo search can be summarized as the following Pseudocode:

Algorithm 1: Cuckoo Search algorithm
1、 **begin**
2、   Objective function $f(x), x = (x_1, x_2, ... x_d)^T$
3、   Generate initial population of n ,host nests $x_i (i = 1, 2, ... n)$
4、   **While** ($t < MaxGeneration$) or (stop criterion) **do**
5、   Get a cuckoo randomly by Lévy fights and evaluate its *fitness$_i$*
6、   Choose a nest among n (say, j) randomly
7、   **if** (*fitness$_i$* > *fitness$_j$*) **then**
8、   replace j by the new solution
9、   **end if**
10、   A fraction (p_a) of worse nests are abandoned and new ones are built
11、   Keep the best solutions (or nests with quality solutions)
12、   Rank the solutions and find the current best
13、   **end while**
14、 **end**

Cuckoo Search algorithm uses Lévy flight search mode with strong randomness, the new position obtained through Lévy flight can be calculated as:

$$x_i^{(t+1)} = x_i^{(t)} + \alpha \otimes Lévy(\lambda) \tag{1}$$

where α is the scaling factor for step, the step size generated directly by Lévy flight is often larger than the size of the problem, so it needs to be multiplied by coefficient α to adjust it. And $\otimes$ means entry-wise multiplications. $Lévy(\lambda)$ is a jump path for flight random search. This path follows the Lévy distribution:

$$Lévy \sim u = t^{-\lambda} \ (1 < \lambda \le 3) \tag{2}$$

However, Lévy flight is difficult to satisfy. Mantegna [15] proposed a method of solving random numbers with normal distribution in 1994, which generates random steps obeying Lévy distribution:

$$s = \frac{u}{|v|^{\frac{1}{\beta}}} \tag{3}$$

where s is equivalent to $Lévy(\lambda)$, $\beta = 1.5$, u and v are Normal distribution random numbers, $u \sim N(0, \sigma^2)$, $v \sim N(0,1)$, the standard deviation of u can be calculated as:

$$\sigma = \{ \frac{\Gamma(1 + \beta) \sin(\frac{\pi\beta}{2})}{\Gamma[\frac{1+\beta}{2}\beta \cdot 2^{\frac{\beta-1}{2}}]} \}^{\frac{1}{\beta}} \tag{4}$$

$$\Gamma(x) = \int_0^\infty \frac{t^{x-1}}{e^t} dt \tag{5}$$

The proposal of Mantegna method greatly simplifies the implementation difficulty of Lévy flight, and the movement step obtained through this method can be calculated as:

$$Step = \alpha \otimes Levy = \alpha \otimes s \qquad (6)$$

where *Step* is the path experienced during random search, Lévy flight is a global exploratory random walk, so the Cuckoo algorithm can jump out of the local optimal and get closer to the global optimal solution.

3.2 Binary Cuckoo Search

The original CS is very good at solving continuous optimization problems, but it can not be used to solve discrete optimization problems like knapsack problem. Binary Cuckoo Search (BCS) is adopted to solve the knapsack problem in [16], the results show that BCS is very good at solving the knapsack problem. In [17], the *Lévy* flight path is transformed by the binary code according to the Kennedy and Eberha formulas and the Liu Jianhua formulas. BCS represents the location of the nest in binary code, $x^t_{i,j} = (0,1)$ represents the *kth* digit of the d-dimensional variable of the *i* nest of the *t* generation, corresponding to the binary code representing the node selection. BCS needs to perform binary code transformation on the step size of Lévy flight update according to Kennedy and Eberha formulas:

$$Sig(Step) = \frac{1}{1 + \exp(-Step)} \qquad (7)$$

$$x^{m+1}_{i,j,k} = \begin{cases} 1 & rand() \leq Sig(Step) \\ x^m_{i,j,k} & other \end{cases} \qquad (8)$$

If the above formula is used for binary encoding updates, the algorithm has strong global search ability, but convergence is not guaranteed. Therefore, the following is an explanation of Liu Jianhua's formula:

When $Step \leq 0$:

$$Sig(Step) = 1 - \frac{2}{1 + \exp(-Step)} \qquad (9)$$

$$x^{t+1}_{i,j} = \begin{cases} 0 & rand() \leq Sig(Step) \\ x^t_{i,j} & other \end{cases} \qquad (10)$$

When $Step > 0$:

$$Sig(Step) = \frac{2}{1 + \exp(-Step)} - 1 \qquad (11)$$

$$x^{t+1}_{i,j} = \begin{cases} 1 & rand() \leq Sig(Step) \\ x^t_{i,j} & other \end{cases} \qquad (12)$$

The Liu Jianhua formula has strong convergence. The above two methods, one with strong global search ability and the other with strong convergence, introduce binary encoding control coefficients $p_r \in [0, 1][0, 1]$ to perform binary encoding hybrid updates on Lévy flight position. By adjusting the p_r parameter, the global search ability and convergence degree of hybrid encoding can be set.

4   Proposed Protocol

First analyze the MPR set selection problem. For a given node k, N_1 and N_2 are one-hop and strictly two-hop neighbor set. Suppose that the MPR set is M, because the elements of M are selected from N_1, the MPR node selection problem can be regarded as 0–1 knapsack problem (KP). Numbered the nodes in N_1 in order, and used binary coding $x = (x_1, x_2, \ldots, x_d)$ to indicate whether the nodes were selected. The encoding length d is the number of nodes contained in the N_1 set. When the i th bit is coded as 1, it means that the i th node in the N_1 set is selected as an MPR node; otherwise, it means the node is not selected. At this point, each binary coded string represents a choice of MPR nodes.

4.1   Weight of Candidate Nodes

In order to improve the survival time of nodes in OLSR, this section uses a weight function composed of the remaining energy of nodes E and the node degree D, to optimize the selection of MPR. Achieve the acquisition of node residual energy E by adding the node residual energy to the Hello and TC message frame. The modification of frames is shown in Fig. 1 and Fig. 2.

0										1										2										3	
0	1	2	3	4	5	6	7	8	9	0	1	2	3	4	5	6	7	8	9	0	1	2	3	4	5	6	7	8	9	0	1
Remain Energy																Htime								Willingness							
Link Code								Reserved								Link Message Size															
Neigubor Interface Address N1																															
Neigubor Interface Address N2																															
......																															

Fig. 1. HELLO message format

0										1										2										3	
0	1	2	3	4	5	6	7	8	9	0	1	2	3	4	5	6	7	8	9	0	1	2	3	4	5	6	7	8	9	0	1
ANSN																Remain Energy															
Link Code								Reserved								Link Message Size															
Advertised Neigubor Main Address A1																															
Advertised Neigubor Main Address A2																															
......																															

Fig. 2. TC message format

When a Hello or TC message is generated, the remaining energy value of node is included, and then periodically broadcast. When a node receives a message, it reads the latest remaining energy of the neighboring nodes included in the message, and records it in the neighbor table to achieve energy perception of the surrounding neighbors. In order to achieve efficient utilization of node energy, choose the node degree as another factor in the weight function, which is the size of neighbors in one hop of the node. The node degree to some extent indicates the degree of overhearing, which is one of the main reasons for energy dissipation. Use the weight function describes the selection value of node i, which is a one hop neighbor of a certain node:

$$W_i = \alpha_1 (1 - \frac{E_i}{E_{max}}) + \alpha_2 \frac{D_i}{D_{max}} \qquad (13)$$

where $\sum_{i=1}^{2} \alpha_i = 1, 0 < \alpha_i < 1$, E_{max} represents the initial energy of node i, D_{max} is the total number of nodes present in the network. α_1 and α_2 are the proportion coefficients, which will set as $\alpha_1 = \alpha_2 = 0.5$.

According to the above method, the weight values of any one hop neighbor node i can be obtained. Node i is considered as an item, and the weight value is the value of the item. The reachability of node i is considered as the volume of the item. The reachability R_i refers to the number of nodes in N_2 which are not yet covered by at least one node in the MPR set, and which are reachable through node i. Therefore, the selection of MPR can be described as the 0–1 Knapsack problem that obtains the minimum value under the restriction that the total volume is equal to the size of N_2, its mathematical description is as follows:

$$\min \sum_{i=1}^{d} W_i x_i \qquad (14)$$

$$s.t. \ \sum_{i=1}^{d} R_i x_i = d_2 \qquad (15)$$

where $x_i = \{0, 1\}; i = 1, 2, \ldots, d$ is the i th bit in binary encoding, indicating whether the i th hop node is selected as the MPR node in this scheme, d and d_2 are the sizes of N_1 and N_2. Formula 14 serves as the objective function of the optimization problem, while Formula 15 serves as the limiting condition.

4.2 The MPR Node Selection Based on BCS

In this section, the BCS is used to solve the problem. The specific steps of BCS to select MPR nodes are as follows:

(1) Start with an MPR set made of all members of N_1 with willingness equal to WILL_ALWAYS and remove those node from N_1.
(2) Add to the MPR set nodes in N_1, which are the only nodes to provide reachability to a node in N_2, and remove those node from N_1. Remove the nodes from N_2 which are now covered by a node in the MPR set.
(3) While there exist nodes in N_2 which are not covered by at least one node in the MPR set, calculate the reachability R and the weights W for each node in N_1.

(4) Determine probability p_a and p_r, set the population size to n host nests, and initialize the population *nest* by randomly generating binary codes for each nest value. The binary code length is the size of the processed N_1 set. Each nest is a randomly generated binary code that represents the selected nodes in N_1. The number of algorithm iterations is controlled by Formula 15.

(5) Decode the current population, calculate the *fitness* of each individual in the *nest* using Formula 14 based on the weight value W of each selected node, and find the nest position with the highest *fitness* value as the current optimal solution *Bestnest*.

(6) If the current optimal solution does not meet the constraint conditions, it enters the loop. Retain the optimal nest position of the previous generation and use Lévy flight to update the binary encoding positions of other nests to obtain a new set of nest positions *newnest*. Repeat step (5).

(7) Based on *fitness*, the position of the *newnest* is compared with that of the previous generation *nest*. The better nest position will replace the worse nest position, resulting in a new optimal population for updating *nest* and *Bestnest*.

(8) Update the nest that was found to be a foreign egg and remove it from the population. Select two individuals as the mother from the current population *nest*. Randomly select several points from the binary encoding positions of the two mothers for multi-point crossing to update new positions *newnest*. Repeat step (7).

(9) Determine whether the *Bestnest* meets the constraint requirements. If it meets the requirements, stop searching, output the *Bestnest* and the corresponding value *fitness*. Otherwise, return to step (6).

5   Performance Evaluation

Based on practical application scenarios, the performance of the proposed protocol was evaluated using the NS3 simulator. The simulation environment parameters were set in reference [11] to achieve a performance comparison between WRE-OLSR and the proposed protocol called BCS-OLSR. Set the simulation range to 1000 m × 1000 m area, nodes will be randomly distributed in the area, and the simulation time will last for 300 s. In order to observe the performance of BCS-OLSR in dynamic scenarios, chose end-to-end time delay and the number of dead nodes as performance parameters, and selected RandomWalk2dMobilityModel as the mobile model of the protocol. Conducted group simulations by increasing the number of UAV nodes from 20 to 100. The simulation parameters are shown in Table 1.

In order to verify the effectiveness of BCS-OLSR in improving network survival time, set simulation parameters according to Table 1, where the number of drone nodes is set to 30 and the movement speed is set to 8 m/s. Compare the average remaining energy of nodes with OLSR under the same conditions. To ensure the stability of the results, collected data from 100 s after the start of the simulation. Figure 3 shows that BCS-OLSR significantly reduces the rate of decay of average node residual energy over time, which is approximately 15% higher than the OLSR average node residual energy value. This is due to the node is more inclined to choose one hop neighbor nodes with higher residual energy and lower degree of node as MPR nodes to forward control messages.

Table 1. Simulation parameters

Parameters	Description
Simulation time	300 s
Transmission area	1000 m × 1000 m
Number of nodes	20, 40, 60, 80, 100
Traffic type	CBR
Packet rate	2
Initial energy	100 J
Rx power	1.1 W
Tx power	1.65 W
Idle Power	0.3 W
MAC Layer	802.11

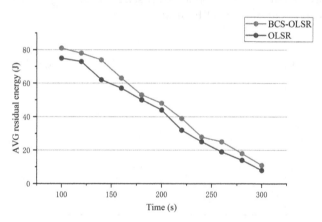

Fig. 3. Comparison of average residual energy between OLSR and BCS-OLSR

In the second setup, compared BCS-OLSR with WRE-OLSR under the same conditions. Firstly, with different node densities, compared the number of dead nodes between the two protocols. Figure 4 shows that as the node density increases, BCS-OLSR outperforms WRE-OLSR in extending network survival time. This is because as the node density increases, one-hop neighbor set N1 for node will expand, and BCS uses Lévy flight to update the search path, which can jump out of local optima and find the global optimal solution of the MPR set when the search space is large.

In addition, we also considered the end-to-end delay of BCS-OLSR. Figure 5 shows the average end-to-end delay of BCS-OLSR. In scenarios with sparse nodes, BCS-OLSR has significantly higher latency than WRE-OLSR. This is because in cases where the MPR candidate set is small, the greedy mechanism converges faster, and the negative impact of the complexity of BCS algorithm is stronger than its positive impact. However, when the number of nodes exceeds 60, the global search capability of BCS can reduce

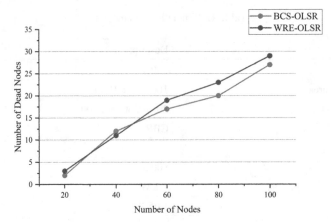

Fig. 4. Comparison of the number of dead nodes under different node densities

retransmissions caused by inappropriate MPR selection, and significantly reduce the average time delay compared to WRE-OLSR.

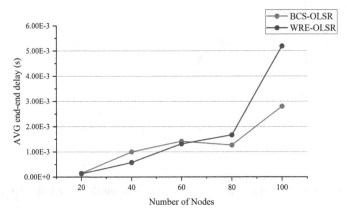

Fig. 5. Comparison of average end-end delay between BCS-OLSR and WRE-OLSR

6 Conclusions

Traditional OLSR protocol adopts greedy algorithm to solve MPR and does not consider node energy and other factors, so it cannot adapt to the current emergency communication relay scenario. To solve this problem, this paper regards MPR selection problem as 0–1 knapsack problem, and adopts binary coding of node selection scheme as the nest. By introducing residual energy and the node degree to construct node weight function, Lévy flight binary is implemented to solve the MPR selection problem with BCS. The experimental results show that when the number of nodes in the network is large, BCS-OLSR has obvious improvement compared with the traditional algorithm in reducing the network delay and improving the survival time of the UAV network has been greatly. Therefore, BCS-OLSR proposed in this paper can effectively improve the MPR node selection efficiency and enhance the network lifetime.

Acknowledgements. This article is supported by the National Natural Science Foundation of China (62372131).

References

1. Aliyu, U., Takruri, H., Hope, M., Halilu, A.G.: DS-OLSR – disaster scenario optimized link state routing protocol. In: 2020 12th International Symposium on Communication Systems, Networks and Digital Signal Processing (CSNDSP), Porto, Portugal, pp. 1–6 (2020). https://doi.org/10.1109/CSNDSP49049.2020.9249639
2. . Cheriguene, Y., et al.: SEMRP: an energy-efficient multicast routing protocol for UA V swarms. In: 2020 IEEE/ACM 24th International Symposium on Distributed Simulation and Real Time Applications (DS-RT), pp. 1–8. IEEE (2020)
3. Qayyum, A., Viennot, L., Laouiti, A.: Multipoint relaying: an efficient technique for flooding in mobile wireless networks. Institut National De Recherche En Informatique Et En Automatique, Technical report (2000)
4. Yang, X.S., Deb, S.: Cuckoo Search via Lévy flights. World Congress on Nature & Biologically Inspired Computing IEEE (2010)
5. Suhaimi, S., Mamat, K., Wong, K.D.: Enhancing the willingness on the OLSR protocol: methodology on experimenting the real testbed. In: Proceedings - 5th International Conference on Wireless Communications, Networking and Mobile Computing, WiCOM 2009 (2009)
6. Sahnoun, A., Abbadi, J.E., Habbani, A.: Increasing network lifetime by energy-efficient routing scheme for OLSR protocol. In: 2016 International Conference on Industrial Informatics and Computer Systems (CIICS), Sharjah, United Arab Emirates, 2016, pp. 1–5, doi: https://doi.org/10.1109/ICCSII.2016.7462412
7. Gangopadhyay, S., Jain, V.K.: A position-based modified OLSR routing protocol for flying Ad Hoc networks. In: IEEE Transactions on Vehicular Technology. https://doi.org/10.1109/TVT.2023.3265704
8. Boushaba, A., Benabbou, A., Benabbou, R., et al.: Multi-point relay selection strategies to reduce top ology control traffic for OLSR protocol in MANETs. J. Netw. Comput. Appl. **53**, 91–102 (2015)
9. Dong, S., Zhang, H.: An MPR set selection algorithm based on set operation. In: 2021 IEEE 5th Advanced Information Technology, Electronic and Automation Control Conference (IAEAC), Chongqing, China, pp. 5–8 (2021). https://doi.org/10.1109/IAEAC50856.2021.9390719
10. Alamsyah, A., Purnama, I.K.E., Setijadi, E., Purnomo, M.H.: Minmax algorithm for MPR selection in improving the performance of OLSR protocol on MANET. In: 2018 International Conference on Intelligent Autonomous Systems (ICoIAS), Singapore, pp. 136–140 (2018). https://doi.org/10.1109/ICoIAS.2018.8494131
11. Belkhira, S.A.H., Hacene, S.B., Lorenz, P., et al.: WRE-OLSR, a new scheme for enhancing the lifetime within ad hoc and wireless sensor networks. Int. J. Commun. Syst. (2) (2019). https://doi.org/10.1002/dac.3975
12. Belkhira, S.A.H., Boukli-Hacene, S., Lorenz, P., Belkheir, M., Gilg, M., Zerroug, A.: A new mechanism for MPR selection in mobile ad hoc and sensor wireless networks. In: ICC 2020 - 2020 IEEE International Conference on Communications (ICC), Dublin, Ireland, pp. 1–6 (2020). https://doi.org/10.1109/ICC40277.2020.9148633

13. Harrag, N., Harrag, A.: Bio-inspired OLSR routing protocol. In: 2019 6th International Conference on Control, Decision and Information Technologies (CoDIT), Paris, France, pp. 1763–1767 (2019). https://doi.org/10.1109/CoDIT.2019.8820369
14. Qayyum, A., Viennot, L., Laouiti, A.: Multipoint relaying: an efficient technique for flooding in mobile wireless networks. HAL - INRIA (2006)
15. Mantegna, R.N.: Fast, accurate algorithm for numerical simulation of Lévy stable stochastic processes. Phys. Rev. E Stat. Phys. Plasmas Fluids Related Interdiscip. Top. **49**(5), 4677 (1994)
16. Bhattacharjee, K.K., Sarmah, S.P.: A binary cuckoo search algorithm for knapsack problems. In: 2015 International Conference on Industrial Engineering and Operations Management (IEOM), Dubai, United Arab Emirates, pp. 1–5 (2015)
17. Feng, D., Ruan, Q., Du, L.: Binary cuckoo search algorithm. J. Comput. Appl. **33**(06), 1566–1570 (2013)

Research on Energy Consumption Optimization Using a Lyapunov-Based LSTM-PSO Algorithm

Sheng Pan, Rui Zhao, Chenbin Huang, Hui Wang$^{(\boxtimes)}$, and Zheyan Shi

School of Computer Science and Technology, Zhejiang Normal University, Jinhua 321004, China
hwang@zjnu.cn

Abstract. As the Internet of Things (IoT) proliferates, there's a growing demand for efficient task processing and top-tier service. This paper introduces a Lyapunov-based LSTM-PSO (LLPSO) predictive offloading algorithm, tailor-made to optimize both user task and computation node resource allocation in rechargeable networks. Simulations reveal that our method eclipses conventional strategies, including the original, First-Come-First-Serve (FCFS), and Greedy algorithms, in terms of energy optimization. Notably, our approach adeptly predicts user task attributes and offloads tasks based on these insights, promoting a more judicious resource allocation. This not only trims down energy expenditure but also amplifies system performance. Taking into account the unique characteristics of rechargeable networks, we leverage Lyapunov functions for dynamic resource tuning, effectively curbing energy usage and bolstering resource efficiency. Experimental benchmarks underscore our algorithm's edge in harmonizing computation node load, augmenting energy conservation, and refining task processing efficiency. In essence, our LLPSO predictive offloading algorithm stands out as a pivotal tool for elevating resource allocation prowess and user experience within IoT frameworks.

Keywords: Predictive offloading · resource allocation · Internet of Things (IoT) · System Stability · LLPSO

1 Introduction

The proliferation of the Internet of Things (IoT) in recent years has led to the emergence of a vast number of smart mobile devices [1]. The introduction of 5G technology has further accelerated the surge in edge devices. However, this rapid expansion places immense pressure on the IoT infrastructure. Current statistics show that the number of connected devices has surpassed 9 billion, with an annual growth rate of 50%. In comparison, the backbone network's transmission speed is increasing at a rate of less than 10% per year [2]. As a result, public cloud servers often experience latencies exceeding 100 ms [3], which can be detrimental for latency-sensitive applications [4].

L. Wang et al. (Eds.): CWSN 2023, CCIS 1994, pp. 15–28, 2024.
https://doi.org/10.1007/978-981-97-1010-2_2

Fog computing offers a paradigm shift from traditional cloud computing, by shifting computational, storage, and network resources to edge nodes near IoT devices. Recognizing that not all user tasks necessitate the formidable computing power of cloud computing, conducting data processing and analysis at edge nodes proves a pragmatic strategy. This approach facilitates the integration and utilization of existing devices and provides real-time decision-making support and intelligence for IoT applications, optimizing latency, bandwidth, security, and privacy.

Task offloading, the process of redirecting computational tasks from end devices or edge nodes to more potent edge or cloud servers, provides a solution when the computing resources of end devices or edge nodes are insufficient or inadequate for a specific task. However, while enhancing task processing capacity, it may also inadvertently increase latency due to task stacking.

Emphasizing fog offloading and resource allocation, fog computing systems are equipped to optimize task processing and resource utilization, thereby enhancing system performance and user experience. Two key considerations are:

1) Effective resource management of fog nodes or cloud servers in a fog computing system, as there will invariably be nodes with idle resources or suboptimal resource utilization. Consequently, judicious resource scheduling management can enable the fog nodes to achieve more with less.

2) Task prioritization, factoring in the time sensitivity of tasks, is essential in the current application scenario. Reasonable decision-making measures are required to prevent task stacking and augment task processing efficiency.

The main contributions of this paper are presented as follows.

- For the first time, we introduce the concept of predictive resource allocation grounded in fog federation, considering the system's long-term nature and incorporating the notion of system stability to enhance the user experience and quality on edge devices. To achieve this, we propose the Lyapunov-based Long Short-Term Memory Predictive PSO algorithm (LLPSO) for managing and forecasting task and resource allocation.

- We illustrate our model in Fig. 1. Fog nodes that are geographically close to each other form a fog cluster, managed by a central fog server.

- We use the LLPSO policy to predict the computational task size of fog nodes. Given the limited computational resources of the device and the need for low latency transmission, we assign task priorities based on latency constraints. The central fog server determines workload distribution among fog servers and fog nodes. High-priority tasks are assigned to a central fog server for processing, while medium-priority tasks are distributed to fog nodes.

The rest of this paper is organized as follows. Section 2 describes the related work and research motivations. Section 3 introduces the system model including transmission model, predict model, priority assessment and algorithm design. Section 4 presents simulation results and analyses the performance of our proposed allocating protocol compared with other allocating protocols. Section 5 concludes the paper.

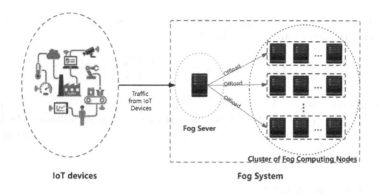

Fig. 1. Fog computing system architecture

2   System Model

2.1   System Basic Elements

In the proposed fog computing architecture, the infrastructure is hierarchically organized into a two-tiered fog layer catering to data processing demands from K Internet of Things (IoT) devices, represented $I_1, I_2, \ldots, I_k$. These devices generate and transfer data to the fog layer for requisite computation.

1) Fog Layer 1: This layer exclusively comprises the Fog Server (FS), a centralized node that plays a pivotal role in orchestrating task allocation and scheduling. The FS is adeptly equipped with knowledge about the status, power consumption, and computational capabilities of each Cluster of Fog Computing Nodes (CFCNs) in the subsequent layer. As data from IoT devices reaches this layer, the FS is entrusted with the responsibility of efficiently distributing it to appropriate CFCNs for processing.

2) Fog Layer 2: This layer is structured into N distinct CFCNs, each denoted as , where i ranges from 1 to N. A single CFCN encapsulates m Fog Nodes (FNs) which are individual computing units. Thus, a fog node within the i cluster can be symbolized as $N_{j,i}$, where j ranges from 1 to m.

It's noteworthy to emphasize that the pivotal nexus between these two layers is the Fog Server (FS). The FS not only maintains an overarching view of the entire fog layer's status but also determines the optimal distribution of tasks across the CFCNs, ensuring efficient utilization of computational resources and power.

2.2   Transmission Model

When an IoT device interacts with a server in Fog Layer 1, it is hypothesized that the length of each time slot of its wireless channel is τ, which remains stable during time slot t and can vary from time slot to time slot. The gain of the wireless channel decays with time assuming that its decay power is $S_k(t)$.

According to Shannon's capacity formula, the transmission capacity between devices in time slot t can be calculated as:

$$C(t) = W\tau \log_2 \left(1 + \frac{P_{k(t)} S_{k(t)}}{W\sigma}\right) \tag{1}$$

where W denotes the wireless bandwidth, $P_k(t)$ represents the transmitted power of the IoT device $k(k \in 1, 2, 3, ..., k)$ when in time slot t. $S_k(t)$ indicates the fading gain of the wireless channel used by IoT device $k(k \in 1, 2, 3, ..., k)$. σ signifies the noise power.

2.3   Task Queue Model

In our system, there is a many-to-one relationship between user devices and fog servers. The time intervals between task requests sent by user devices are random and follow an exponential distribution. This means that the service time provided by fog servers to user devices is also random and follows an exponential distribution. For instance, when an IoT device sends a data packet to a fog server and no ongoing tasks are being processed by the server, it will immediately handle the task. The main function of fog server nodes is allocation and management. At this node, task arrivals and processing are independent, unaffected by other factors that may impact task queuing and processing. Therefore, it follows the queuing theory M/M/1 model.

Between time slots t, we assume $I_i(t)$ ($T_i(t) \leq$ Tmax for some constant Tmax) for the IoT device Ik that arrives at the FS. Usually, this task arrives at different time slots and the processing size is different. Based on this condition, the information sent by the task is recorded by the FS, which has an LSTM model algorithm to predict the future workload within a prediction window of size, i.e., the workload will arrive in the next time slot. Thus, FS will deploy the assigned tasks in advance based on the prediction result so there are two types of queues on FS:

1) Prediction queue, $\{P_{i,0}(t), ..., P_{i,W_{i-1}}(t)\}$
2) Arrival queue, $\{T_i(t)\}$

The actual tasks arriving at the FS will be arranged in the arrival queue and forwarded to the fog processor at any time to process the tasks, with local processing resources prioritized for the management of CFCNs. Prediction Queue:

$$P_{i,W_{i-1}}(t+1) = P_i(t+W_i) \tag{2}$$

$$Q_c^{(p)}(t+1) = [Q_c^{(p)}(t) - Q_i^{(I(i))}(t)]^+ + P_i(t+W_i) \tag{3}$$

2.4   Energy Model

The total power consumptions P(t) of fog tiers in time slot t consist of the processing power consumption and wireless transmit power consumption, Where the processing work number in turn contains the distribution power consumption of the fog server and the computational power consumption of the fog processor. Given a local CPU with frequency f .

In the previous section, the task queue in the energy consumption model for task processing follows the M/M/1 pattern. The local computational delay τ_i can be expressed using the following formula:

$$\tau_i = \frac{\lambda_i(t)(\sigma_i^{F^2} + \mathcal{D}_i^2)}{2(\mathcal{F}_i^2 - \lambda_i(t)\mathcal{F}_i D_i)} + \frac{\mathcal{D}_i}{\mathcal{F}_i} \tag{4}$$

Herein, λ denotes the probability of task arrival, σ represents the standard deviation of the task size, and F_i denotes the computational resources of i. The total energy consumed in performing a task is therefore represented as P_i^l:

$$P_i^l = \sum_{i=1}^{N} p_i(t) \tag{5}$$

Here $p_i(t) = \tau_i \varsigma (F_i(t))^3$ denotes the energy consumption of edge devices i at time slot t, and ζ depends on the parameters of the deployed hardware, which can be measured in practice [5].

Therefore, in our system, delay-sensitive tasks are allocated processing based on computational requirements: a perception of the current local resources is made, and if there is the capacity to handle them, computational offloading is not considered. Otherwise, the task data that needs to be processed is allocated according to the current resource status of the fog node by the control node, and offloaded to the fog processor layer for processing, as shown in Fig. 1.

The total energy consumption of delay tasks can be expressed as:

$$P(t) = \sum_{s=1}^{S} p_s(t) + \sum_{i=1}^{N} p_{i,j}^c(t) + \sum_{i=1}^{N} (1 - \alpha) p_i(t) \tag{6}$$

Here $p_i(t)$ represents the energy consumed by fog node s, which can be expressed as

$$p_s(t) = \tau_s \zeta (F_s(t))^3 \tag{7}$$

where ζ is a parameter depending on the deployed hardware and is measurable in practice [6].

In this paper, $P_{i,j}^c(t) = \tau_c p_i^c(t)$ is defined as the energy consumption of the device i transmitting tasks to j. M represents the set of IoT nodes, and N represents the set of fog nodes (Table 1).

3   Problem Formulation

The optimization of total energy consumption is a key concern in this study. We adopt the Lyapunov approach to optimize total energy consumption. Ensuring the condition that the queue is stable, the entire optimization problem can be

Table 1. Key Notations

Notations	Meanings
F_i, F_j, F_s	The computing power of devices i, c and s, respectively
K	Num of IoT nodes
c	Central of fog layer :(fog server node)
N	Set of fog computing nodes(CFCNs)
$F_{i,c}(t)$	Computing power allocated to i by device c in time slot t
$F_{i,s}(t)$	Computing power allocated to i by device s in time slot t
τ_c	Transmission delay
τ_t	Delay at time slot t
τ	Each time slot of its wireless channel
P_c	Consumption of fog server node
$\lambda_i(t)$	Arrival rate of tasks for time slot t
σ	Device i computes the standard deviation of the task size
D_i	Mean value of task size for device i
C_j	Device j's downstream bandwidth
L_s	Local processing task delay
$P_a(t)$	Total energy consumption of time slot t
$P_i(t)$	Energy consumed by fog node i
$P_c(t)$	Energy consumed by fog node c
$P_s(t)$	Energy consumed by fog node s
$P_{i,j}^c$	Energy consumption of device i to transfer tasks to j
F_i^c	Transmit power of device i
$C_{i,j}$	Device i to j transfer rate
α	Offload rate
P_i^b	Device i's battery

transformed into a Lyapunov optimization problem. That is, to guarantee the minimum average energy consumption per time slot, it can be represented as:

$$p1:\& \lim_{T \to \infty} \frac{1}{T} \sum_{t=0}^{T-1} P_a(t) \tag{8}$$

$$s.t. \quad \lim_{T \to \infty} \frac{1}{T} \sum_{t=0}^{T-1} \sum_{i=1}^{N} \mathcal{F}_{i,s}(t) < \mathcal{F}_s \tag{9}$$

$$\lim_{T \to \infty} \frac{1}{T} \sum_{t=0}^{T-1} \sum_{i=1}^{N} \mathcal{C}_{i,j}(t) < \mathcal{C}_j \tag{10}$$

$$0 \le p_i(t) \le P_i^b \tag{11}$$

$$0 \le \mathcal{F}_{ij}(t) \le \mathcal{F}_s \tag{12}$$

$$0 \le \mathcal{C}_{ij}(t) \le \mathcal{C}_j \tag{13}$$

The objective of P1 is to minimize the long-term average energy consumption of all IoT devices [7], where F_a implies that if tasks are offloaded to the fog network, they must be entirely offloaded to the computing nodes. The decision variables include the computational resources of the offloading fraction $\alpha_i(t)$, $F_i(t)$, the transmission power at each time slot $P_i(t)$, and the computational resources of the computing layer nodesF_s, where $i \in N$. In the problem P1, the decision variables are influenced by the task size, processing delay required for the task . The objective function is constrained by the channel bandwidth, the computational resources of P1, the computational resources of F_s, and the transmission power of the IoT nodes. In this paper, it is assumed that all time slot lengths are the same.

In the problem P1, the constraints in limit the computational resources allocated to the tasks from the device i (9), the transmission speed of the device i (10). In the long term, constrained by computational resources F_s, the computational resources allocated to the device i should be less than its own computational resources. Restricted by the device's own transmission speed, in the long term, the size of the channel bandwidth occupied by the task should be less than the total channel bandwidth, and the energy consumption is always less than the total battery energy. If the task can be processed locally, only the energy consumption is calculated.

3.1   Setting up Lyapunov Virtual Pairs of Columns

In Lyapunov optimization, the satisfaction of long-term average constraints is equated to the rate stability of the virtual queue. To be more precise, a virtual queue is introduced to replace the computation resource constraint at edge node(9), $G_{(}t)$ represents the random process of the virtual queue length at time slot t [8]. The channel constraint is denoted by $C_{(}t)$, $G_{(}t)$and $C_{(}t)$ explicit form can be represented as follows:

$$\mathcal{G}\left(t+1\right) - \mathcal{G}\left(t\right) = \max\left(\sum_{i=1}^{N}\mathcal{F}_{i,s}\left(t\right) - \mathcal{F}_s, -\mathcal{G}\left(t\right)\right) \qquad (14)$$

$$\mathcal{H}\left(t+1\right) = \max\left(\mathcal{H}\left(t\right) + \sum_{i=1}^{N}\mathcal{C}_{i,j}(t) - \mathcal{C}_j, 0\right) \qquad (15)$$

This study assumes a stable environment, with consistent transmission power from the charging device. The estimated value of the charging amount $P_i^{opt}(t)$ can be expressed as:

$$P_i^{opt}(t) = \frac{1 - e^{-\psi(t)d}}{(\psi(t)d)^2} \qquad (16)$$

Here, d denotes the distance between the sender and the receiver, ψ denotes the decay factor, often determined by signal frequency and medium characteristics. If the virtual queue is rate-stable, it must only $\lim_{T\to\infty} \frac{A(T)}{T}$ can meet the constraint (9) according to the definition in [9]. Similarly, we can derive the channel backlog virtual queue B, delay backlog virtual queue C, and edge node energy backlog virtual queue D. The proof is as follows:

First, we prove the stability of the virtual queue:

$$\mathcal{G}\left(t+1\right) - \mathcal{G}\left(t\right) = \max\left(\sum_{i=1}^{N} \mathcal{F}_{i,s}(t) - \mathcal{F}_s, -\mathcal{G}\left(t\right)\right) \tag{17}$$

For $t \in (0, 1, 2, ..., T-1)$ exists

$$\lim_{\mathbb{T}\to\infty} \frac{\mathcal{G}(T) - \mathcal{G}(0)}{T} \geq \lim_{T\to\infty} \frac{1}{T} \sum_{t=0}^{T-1} \sum_{i=1}^{N} \mathcal{F}_{i,s}(t) - \mathcal{F}_s \tag{18}$$

If $A(0) = 0$, then

$$\lim_{\mathbb{T}\to\infty} \frac{\mathcal{G}(T)}{T} = 0 \tag{19}$$

Hence, there is:

$$\lim_{T\to\infty} \frac{1}{T} \sum_{t=0}^{T-1} \sum_{i=1}^{N} \mathcal{F}_{i,j}(t) \leq \mathcal{F}_j \tag{20}$$

Therefore, the queue A is stable, and similarly, the virtual queue B(t) is stable, yielding:

$$\lim_{T\to\infty} \frac{1}{T} \sum_{t=0}^{T-1} \sum_{i=1}^{N} C_{i,j}(t) \leq C_j \tag{21}$$

After proving the above, we can translate the problem P1 into problem P2 .

3.2   Constructing the Lyapunov Function

In this subsection, the specific Lyapunov derivation process and the translation of the problem P1 into the problem P2 will be shown, as represented by the following equations:

$$P2: \quad \lim_{T\to\infty} \frac{1}{T} \sum_{t=0}^{T-1} \mathbb{P}_a(t) \tag{22}$$

$$\text{s.t. } G\ (t) \text{ is rate stable} \tag{23}$$

$$H\ (t) \text{ is rate stable} \tag{24}$$

$$(11)–(13) \tag{25}$$

Equations (11)–(13) set up the virtual queue vector, with the system state represented as $\theta(t)$:

$$\Theta(t) = [\mathcal{G}(t), \mathcal{H}(t)] \tag{26}$$

$$\mathcal{L}(\theta(t)) = \frac{1}{2} \sum_{i=1} Q_i(t)^2$$

$$= \frac{1}{2}(\mathcal{G}(t)^2 + \mathcal{H}(t)^2)$$

(27)

$$\varDelta\theta(t) = E(\mathcal{L}(\theta(t+1)) - \mathcal{L}(\theta(t)) \mid \theta(t))$$

(28)

When the rate in each queue is stable, the problem P2 can be transformed into the problem P3 , because the original problem with long-term average objectives and constraints can be approximately transformed into a problem with drift plus penalty. In this paper, it is assumed:

$$P(t) = \sum_{t=0}^{T-1} P_a(t)$$

(29)

Based on the Lyapunov drift plus penalty algorithm, it can be converted into the problem P3 as shown below:

$$\text{P3:} \quad \min \varDelta\theta(t) + VE(P(t) \mid \theta(t))$$
$$s.t. \quad (10), (11), (12)$$

(30)

Here, V represents the weight of the objective function, and $\varDelta\theta(t)$ represents the drift of the queue, i.e., the stability of the queue. The following shows the specific form of A to prepare for the upper bound of P4. First, we show $\mathcal{G}(t+1)^2 - \mathcal{G}(t)^2$:

$$G(t+1)^2 - G(t)^2$$

$$= \max(G(t) + \sum_{i=1}^{N} F_{i,s}(t) - F_s, 0)^2 - G(t)^2$$

$$\leq 2G(t)(\sum_{i=1}^{N} F_{i,s}(t) - F_s) + \left(\sum_{i=1}^{N} F_{i,s}(t) - F_s\right)^2$$

$$\leq 2G(t) \sum_{i=1}^{N} F_{i,s}(t) - 2G(t)F_s + (\sum_{i=1}^{N} F_{i,s}(t))^2$$

$$- 2F_s \sum_{i=1}^{N} F_{i,s}(t) + F_s^2$$

(31)

$$\leq 2(G(t) - F_s) \sum_{i=1}^{N} F_{i,s}(t) + \left(\sum_{i=1}^{N} F_{i,s}(t)\right)^2 + F_s^2$$

$$\leq 2(G(t) - F_s) \sum_{i=1}^{N} F_{i,s}(t) + (N+1)F_s^2$$

$$= D_1 + 2(G(t) - F_s) \sum_{i=1}^{N} F_{i,s}(t)$$

Here the fixed value is represented by , where

$$\mathcal{D}_1 = (\mathcal{N} + 1)\mathcal{F}_s^2 \tag{32}$$

Similarly, the virtual queue B under bandwidth constraints can be represented as:

$$\mathcal{H}(t+1)^2 - \mathcal{H}(t)^2 = D_2 + 2(\mathcal{H}(t) - \mathcal{C}_j)\sum_{i=1}^{N} C_{i,j}(t) \tag{33}$$

D_2 represents a fixed constant and is expressed by the following formula:

$$\mathcal{D}_2 = (\mathcal{N} + 1)\mathcal{C}_j^2 \tag{34}$$

The problem P3 can be expanded to problem P4:

$$\text{P4}: \quad \min \ VP(t) + (\text{G }(t) - \text{F}_s)\sum_{i=1}^{N} \text{F}_{i,s}(t) + (\text{H }(t) - C_j)\sum_{i=1}^{N} C_{i,j}(t) \tag{35}$$

$$s.t. \ (13),(14),(15),(16)$$

Assume P4 has an upper bound, and the upper bound is a constant C. First, this paper will prove that the virtual queue A and virtual queue B are stable. The proof is as follows:

$$\mathcal{L}(\theta(t+1)) - \mathcal{L}(\theta(t)) + VP(t) \leq C$$
$$\mathcal{L}(\theta(t+1)) - \mathcal{L}(\theta(t)) \leq C \tag{36}$$
$$\mathcal{L}(\theta(T)) - \mathcal{L}(\theta(0)) \leq TC$$

Next, we can use approximate analysis to explore the upper bound of problem P4.

4   Algorithm Design

In this section, we design and analyse the algorithm. First, the data is preprocessed and then an LSTM model is built using Pytorch, we take 90% of the data to train test models and finally predict the size of subsequent tasks using the trained model. We take the remaining 10% to verify the effectiveness of our model. Since this paper focuses on how to set up an LSTM model for the prediction of the impact on task assignment efficiency. The specific algorithm is as follows:

5   Numerical Results

In this section, we evaluate the performance of the proposed LLPSO algorithm through numerical simulations. The simulations are conducted on a Windows 10 with a 2.3 GHz Intel Core i5 processor, and 24 GB 2667 MHz DDR4 memory, and the simulation program is implemented by Python 3.9. This section first describes the basic settings of our simulations and then provides the results under different latency requirement tasks, respectively.

Algorithm 1 LLSTM-PSO algorithm

Require: $P(t), F(i), F(j), F(s), P_c, P_i, P_c, P_s$

Ensure: $T_{MAX} > t > 0$

1: **for** $t = 0 to T_{MAX}$ **do**
2:     $Q(t) = Q(t-1) + \lambda i(t)$ // update queue
3:     Check if Prediction satisfied
4:     **if** $Q_i^p(t) > Q_i^a(t)$ is even **then**
5:         carry out programme
6:     **else**if for each $CFCNsi \in n$
7:         Using PSO looking for eligible CFCNs
8:         **if** resouces$(CFCNs(i)) > taskQ_i^a(t)$ is even **then**
9:             Offloading to CFCNs(i) //reallocation
10:         **end if**
11:     **end if**
12:     **for** each t **do**
13:         //get task from queue and finding the best allocation $X(t) = \alpha(t), F_{i,c}(t), F_{i,s}(t), p_i^c(t)$
14:         **for** $i = 1 to K$ **do**
15:             Initialize velocity V_i and position X_i for particle i
16:             $pBest = VP(t) + (A(t) - F_i)\sum_{i=1}^{z} F_{ij}(t) +$
                 $(B(t) - C_i)C_{i,i}(t) + \frac{1}{2}(\tau_i(t) + \tau_i(t) +$
                 $\sum_{s=1}^{z} \tau_s(t))(2C(t) + \tau_s(t) + \tau_s(t) + \sum_{s=1}^{z} \tau_s(t))$
17:             Evaluate particle i and set pBest
18:             parameters = Xi
19:         **end for**
20:         predict next slot and make a programme
21:         enter predicte and Update $T_i^p(t+1), A_i^p = PSO((X(t+1)))$
22:     **end for**
23: **end for**

5.1 Basic Settings

We simulated a fog computing system with 20 users and 50 computing nodes, and 10 control nodes. Each control node corresponds to computing nodes, all nodes are active, and their total resources vary. The amount of resources available to each node is different. When the node offloads a task, the available memory and CPU available memory and CPU for processing dynamically change.

We randomly generated a one-hour task volume and took its first 54 min as the training set for the prediction model, and the last 6 min as the prediction volume. The bandwidth between users and computing node are both set to 10Mb/s, the initial processing capacity of the cpu of users is 500 Mhz and the RAM is 500M. The initial processing power of the cpu of computing node is 300 Mhz and the RAM is 300M. The communication interference and distance between users and computing node are constant. The noise between users and cloud would changes randomly. All tasks volume are between 1-10M.

5.2 Evaluation with Different Delay Requirement Task

We have evaluated the performance of various algorithms for tasks with different latency requirements. Specifically, we evaluated tasks with the same number of nodes but different arrival rates, tasks with different numbers but the exact arrival rate, and tasks with different arrival rates resulting in different completion conditions.

Here, we observe the total energy consumption of different algorithms at different times. Among them, the improved LLPSO algorithm performs the best, followed by the original PSO algorithm, the First-Come-First-Serve (FiFs)algorithm, and the Greedy algorithm. The reason for this phenomenon is that our proposed LLPSO algorithm takes into account the stability of the entire system queue. In particular, the dynamic adjustment strategy for reserved resources dramatically improves the speed of resource allocation. On the other hand, the unimproved PSO algorithm requires dynamic resource allocation for each incoming task, resulting in increased energy consumption. The FiFs strategy leads to increased queue congestion and task latency, requiring higher investment in computing and communication resources to meet deadlines, thus increasing energy consumption. Lastly, the Greedy algorithm consumes more energy to complete all tasks as quickly as possible (Figs. 2 and 3).

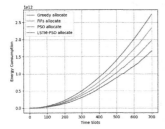

Fig. 2. Total time consumption of various tasks.

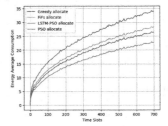

Fig. 3. Average energy consuming graph of time slots.

In Fig. 4, we present the energy consumption of tasks under different arrival rates. Here, we can see that our proposed LLPSO algorithm still performs the best even when the arrival rates are the same. This is because the combination of Lyapunov-based system control and LSTM-based task prediction, while maintaining queue stability, significantly reduces queuing time and decreases system energy consumption. In contrast, the other three algorithms only focus on resource allocation without dynamic optimization (Fig. 5).

In addition, we also compared the performance of different algorithms under different task arrival rates with the same number of user nodes. In these comparisons, the Greedy algorithm outperforms the LLPSO algorithm. This is because the Greedy algorithm invests significant resources and energy, resulting in a higher task completion rate. On the other hand, the other two algorithms perform relatively poorly in terms of task completion rate compared to LLPSO. LLPSO utilizes available resources efficiently and prioritizes optimal task allocation to ensure timely task completion. It allocates a substantial amount of resources and energy to task execution, thereby improving the task completion

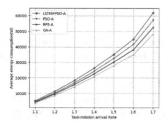
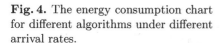
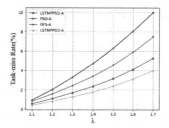

Fig. 4. The energy consumption chart for different algorithms under different arrival rates.

Fig. 5. The task-miss rate for different algorithms under different arrival rates.

rate. However, the other two algorithms are less flexible in resource utilization and task allocation, thus unable to fully utilize available resources to meet task demands, leading to a lower task completion rate.

6 Conclusion

This paper introduced a Lyapunov-based predictive offloading algorithm, LLPSO, optimized for rechargeable scenarios. Through comparative experiments, we found that the LLPSO algorithm outperforms the other three algorithms in terms of task completion rate, yielding satisfactory results. However, despite the outstanding performance of the LLPSO algorithm in task completion rate and energy consumption optimization, there remain some limitations and areas for improvement. We did not consider the mobility issue of user nodes. In actual scenarios, user nodes may move to different locations, which could affect task distribution and resource utilization. Therefore, in future research, we need to consider how to adapt to the mobility of user nodes to enhance the algorithm's performance further.

In conclusion, further improvements are required despite the effective optimization results achieved by the LLPSO algorithm in this paper. We are committed to addressing the issue of user node mobility and further enhancing resource utilization efficiency to advance research in this field and improve the performance and applicability of the algorithm.

Declarations

This research was supported by the National Natural Science Foundation of China under Grant Nos. 62171413.

The public welfare research project of Jinhua City of Zhejiang Province of China under Grant 2022-4-063.

References

1. Gao, X., Huang, X., Bian, S., et al.: PORA: predictive offloading and resource allocation in dynamic fog computing systems. IEEE Internet Things J. **7**(1), 72–87 (2020). https://doi.org/10.1109/JIOT.2019.2945066

2. Li, Z., Qian, Y., Tang, F., Zhao, M., Zhu, Y.: H-BILSTM: a novel bidirectional long short term memory network based intelligent early warning scheme in mobile edge computing (MEC). IEEE Trans. Emerg. Top. Comput. **11**(1), 253–264 (2023). https://doi.org/10.1109/TETC.2022.3202266

3. Gao, Y., Tang, W., Wu, M., Yang, P., Dan, L.: Dynamic social-aware computation offloading for low-latency communications in IoT. IEEE Internet Things J. to be published. https://doi.org/10.1109/JIOT.2019.2909299

4. Zhang, D., et al.: Near-optimal and truthful online auction for computation offloading in green edge-computing systems. IEEE Trans. Mob. Comput. to be published. https://doi.org/10.1109/TMC.2019.2901474

5. Jiang, Z., Mao, S.: Energy delay tradeoff in cloud offloading for multi-core mobile devices. IEEE Access **3**, 2306–2316 (2015)

6. Gao, X., Huang, X., Bian, S., Shao, Z., Yang, Y.: PORA: predictive offloading and resource allocation in dynamic fog computing systems. IEEE Internet Things J. **7**(1), 72–87 (2020). https://doi.org/10.1109/JIOT.2019.2945066

7. Lin, R., et al.: Energy-efficient computation offloading in collaborative edge computing. IEEE Internet Things J. **9**(21), 21305–21322 (2022). https://doi.org/10.1109/JIOT.2022.3179000

8. Ren, C., Lyu, X., Ni, W., et al.: Distributed online optimization of fog computing for internet of things under finite device buffers. IEEE Internet Things J. **7**(6), 5434–5448 (2020)

9. Lin, R., et al.: Distributed optimization for computation offloading in edge computing. IEEE Trans. Wirel. Commun. **19**(12), 8179–8194 (2020). https://doi.org/10.1109/TWC.2020.3019805

Attitude-Aware Based Geographical Opportunity Routing Protocol for Floating Wireless Sensor Network

Yuting Wang[1]([✉]), Chaoyi Zhou[1], XiangWei Liu[2], and Yong Yang[1]

[1] Tiangong University, Tianjin, China
{wangyuting,yangyong}@tiangong.edu.cn
[2] ByteDance, Beijing, China
15399881529@163.com

Abstract. Wireless sensor devices are increasingly deployed in both terrestrial and aquatic environments. In wireless sensor networks, routing protocols are responsible for establishing data forwarding paths between source and sink nodes. Unlike terrestrial environments, sensor devices deployed in aquatic environments are floating, which can cause routing path failures. Most of the existing routing protocols ignore the effect of attitude change on routing connectivity. In this paper, we propose Polar-Routing, an attitude-aware geographical opportunity routing protocol for floating wireless sensor networks. PolarRouting divides the network topology into zones delineated by geographic information, according to the correlation between attitude and geographic information, to determine forward candidate areas. And PolarRouting selects an attitude-aligned relay node based on the attitude information of candidate nodes to reduce the routing interruptions introduced by the floating node. Simulation results show that compared to the traditional attitude-oblivious routing protocols, PolarRouting can prioritize reliable data transmission and further reduce the end-to-end delay of the network.

Keywords: Wireless sensor network · Geographical opportunity routing protocol · Attitude-aware · Forwarding area

1 Introduction

Wireless Sensor Network (WSN), with its advantages of low power consumption, flexible structure, and high data security, has been widely used in agriculture, ecological monitoring, industry, intelligent transportation, and other fields [1,2]. Although WSNs performs well in land applications, its application in aquatic environments, which covers 70% of the earth's total surface area, is still rare [3,4]. Unlike land, sensor nodes deployed in aquatic environments will float with the waves. Therefore, as the popularity of WSNs increases, it has become an urgent need to deploy WSN according to the characteristics of aquatic environments.

As an integrated intelligent network that combines data collection, processing, and transmission, the key to WSN is to establish multiple reliable routing

L. Wang et al. (Eds.): CWSN 2023, CCIS 1994, pp. 29–41, 2024.
https://doi.org/10.1007/978-981-97-1010-2_3

paths from the source node to the sink node to complete efficient data transmission tasks and maximize the network's life cycle [5]. Although existing wireless sensor routing protocols, such as table-driven routing, on-demand routing, and geographic routing methods, enable reliable communication of networks in terrestrial environments. However, in the aquatic environment, the floating nature of sensor nodes can lead to polarization alignment of transceiver antennas, which results in signal strength degradation. In contrast, existing attitude-oblivious routing protocols ignore the effect of attitude on link quality and allow nodes to transmit data according to pre-established routing paths [6,7]. In terrestrial networks, such attitude-oblivious routing protocols are unproblematic because the nodes in the network usually do not have drastic attitude changes. However, for floating nodes, the constantly changing attitude can lead to dynamic degradation of the wireless link quality or even to transceiver link disruption. Hence, the traditional attitude-oblivious routing protocols are not applicable to the aquatic environment.

An opportunistic routing protocol for data transmission appears to be a viable solution as it obviates the need for a priori path construction and enables the dynamic selection of next-hop nodes based on current link conditions [8]. Compared with traditional fixed routing protocols, opportunity routing protocols do not require forwarding lists to be inserted into packet headers in advance but dynamically maintain their next-hop relay node for each node to adequately address routing voids resulting from node floatability that impede relay transmissions, and ensure effective routing between source and destination node. However, existing opportunistic routing protocols that only consider factors such as inter-node distance and energy consumption cannot be directly applied to the aquatic environment because of ignoring the variation of node attitude [9,10]. The most intuitive idea is to retransmit data after a link break is detected, but blind retransmissions dissipate excessive amounts of energy while only achieving marginal performance gains given that the misaligned attitude orientations can nonetheless enable retransmissions. In a nutshell, attitude-oblivious routing protocols are proved inefficient as they depend upon an attitude-insensitive link paradigm and fail to consider ephemeral link quality fluctuations engendered by sharp attitude changes.

However, designing an attitude-aware based opportunity routing protocol faces the following challenges. First, although the node attitude is known to have an impact on the performance of the communication link, it is difficult to obtain the attitude information of all adjacent nodes. Second, even if the attitude information of the adjacent nodes is obtained, it is challenging to precisely determine the best relay node because due to the floating nature of the nodes in the aquatic environment, the attitude of the nodes is likely to oscillate by a large magnitude within a second, resulting in high dynamics of the communication link.

By settling these challenges, we propose PolarRouting, an attitude-aware based geographic opportunity routing protocol for floating wireless sensor networks. The main technical highlight of PolarRouting is to select attitude-aligned relay nodes based on the attitude information of candidate nodes, thereby reducing the routing interruptions introduced by node float ability and achieving reliable transmission of floating wireless sensor networks. To the best of our knowledge, this paper is the first work to discover and solve the failure of the routing protocol of floating WSNs due to dynamic attitude in aquatic environments.

The main contributions of PolarRouting can be summarized within the following domains:

- Given the correlation between attitude and geographic information, PolarRouting divides the network topology into zones delineated by geographic information to determine forward candidate areas. Consequently, only the attitude parameters of nodes within the forwarding areas need to be obtained, which can reduce communication overhead.
- To choose the optimal relay node, PolarRouting maintains prioritized next-hop relay information for each node by incorporating both geographic and attitude metrics. Then, PolarRouting selects attitude-aligned relay nodes based on the attitude information of candidate nodes.
- We implement PolarRouting on NS-3 and evaluate its performance from end-to-end reliability and delay. Our evaluation results show that compared to the traditional attitude-oblivious routing protocols, PolarRouting can prioritize reliable data transmission and further reduce the end-to-end delay of the network.

The rest of this paper is organized as follows. In Sect. 2, we introduce the background to motivate this work. Then, we present the design of PolarRouting in Sect. 3 and the evaluation results in Sect. 4. The related works are discussed in Sect. 5. Finally, we conclude this paper in Sect. 6.

2 Background and Motivation

2.1 Attitude-Aware Based Link Model

In practice, deploying existing routing protocols directly in aquatic environments can significantly degrade network performance. In [9,10], it is known that the dynamic polarization alignment state caused by an ever-changing attitude is the root cause of the reliability degradation of the floating networks. Normally, with maximum antenna gain pointing to alignment, the receiving antenna can only receive electromagnetic waves with the same polarization as the transmitting antenna, i.e. polarization alignment. Only when the transceiver antenna polarization state is aligned, the maximum energy can be received, otherwise, there will be a loss of received power, i.e. polarization loss. Therefore, the establishment of the link model based on attitude awareness should consider the polarization of the transceiver antenna.

For this reason, the signal strength received at the receiver side can be expressed by the Friis formula [11] as follows.

$$P_r\left(\theta_p\right) = P_t \frac{G_t G_r \lambda^2}{(4\pi \mathrm{d})^2} p \tag{1}$$

where λ is the signal wavelength, d represents the transceiver distance, and G_r and G_t represent the gain of the antenna at the receiver and transmitter, respectively. It is worth noting that, unlike the traditional Friis Transmission Formula, a transmission factor p is added to denote the Polarization Loss Factor (PLF). As defined in [9,10], PLF can be represented as:

$$p = |(\cos\theta_p \, \overrightarrow{x} + \sin\theta_p \, \overrightarrow{z}) \cdot \overrightarrow{z}|^2 = \sin^2\theta_p \tag{2}$$

where θ_p is the polarization angle between transmitter antenna and the X-axis and $(.)^*$ indicates the complex conjugate. In practice, the value range of p is $(0°, 180°)$.

2.2 Geographical Opportunity Routing Protocol

The geographic opportunity routing requires each node to select the most suitable relay node for data forwarding according to the geographic information of candidate nodes to improve the success rate of forwarding packets [12]. Unlike routing protocols based on topological information, geographic routing protocols use geographic information rather than topological connectivity information to gradually approach and eventually reach the intended destination.

Geographic environment encompasses not only terrestrial areas but also aquatic spheres. Typical characteristics of water waves exist in the aquatic environment and water waves are commonly fluctuations on the surface of aquatic environments generated by the straightforward action of wind on the aqueous exterior. Therefore, in aquatic environments, water waves are very closely related to wind. For instance, changes in wind speed and direction have a direct effect on water wave floatation, and changes in wind time and wind area also affect water wave propagation. Furthermore, wind waves propagating to the near shore will form near-shore waves. And the near-shore waves can produce a series of physical processes such as reflection, refraction, and bypassing, due to the impacts by topography, shoreline, and shallow water depth, which will further affect the distribution of wave height, wave direction, and other changes in wave elements. Thus, the spatial and temporal variation and evolution of near-shore waves are closely related to the geographical location compared with those in offshore waters.

In summary, attitude parameters should be considered a critical factor when constructing geographic opportunity routing protocols to ensure the precision and dependability of routing paths. This is because the geographic location has an impact on attitude information. For example, there is a high probability that nodes in horizontal or vertical positions will have different attitude information. And the best link performance often occurs when the polarization states between the transceiver antennas are aligned. For this reason, in practice, the transmission performance of WSN will be improved if the attitude information of nodes can be obtained and good transmission opportunities are utilized.

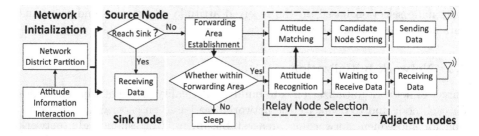

Fig. 1. The overview of PolarRouting.

3 Design

3.1 Overview

The design goal of PolarRouting is to select the attitude-aligned relay nodes in the forwarding area for data forwarding based on the polarization and geographic information of the candidate nodes, to achieve reliable transmission of floating wireless sensor networks. However, although we already know the theoretical link model from [9,10], it is not easy to select the attitude-aligned relay nodes from the sets of adjacent nodes because the attitude information of adjacent nodes is difficult to determine. Besides, the probing-based approach exclusively depends on the probed connectivity quality within the network domain whilst overlooking the cardinal elements engendering the physical occurrence. Since the attitude of nodes in the aquatic environment can change rapidly within a second, in floating WSNs, it is difficult to get the attitude information of all the nodes in a timely and efficient manner.

To reduce the overhead of exchanging attitude information between all nodes, PolarRouting utilizes geographic information to quickly delineate the network area. Based on the network area and destination address, PolarRouting proposes the concept of path guidance points to identify forwarding areas. Then, PolarRouting combines the attitude information of the nodes with geographical information to schedule the attitude-aligned node to transmit data.

Figure 1 presents the overview of PolarRouting, which consists of three main modules: network initialization and the processing flow of current and adjacent nodes. Note that the current node here is the node where the route is established to reach. Initially, during the network initialization, all nodes in the network broadcast their own attitude and geographic information, and each node builds a link quality model regarding [9,10]. Then, PolarRouting divides the network area based on the geographic information of the nodes deployed in the network, and all nodes know the geographic location of the sink node. Based on the network division, the current node that cannot reach the sink node after one hop determines the forwarding area in combination with the distance to the sink node and the communication radius and broadcasts the forwarding area address. Once in the forwarding area, adjacent nodes capture attitude information via inertial sensors and send it to the current node. The current node then performs relay node selection based on the received attitude information and transmits data according to a priority list.

3.2   Network Initialization

Target of network initialization is to build a link quality model of adjacent nodes for each node and to delineate the network area based on geographical information for subsequent forwarding area establishment. Correspondingly, network initialization consists of two modules: attitude information interaction and network district partition.

Attitude Information Interaction. Initially, all nodes employ inertial measurement units (IMUs) to obtain physical attitude information and broadcast captured attitude and geographic information in turn. Note that IMUs are extensively harnessed in floating applications to collect hydrological statistics such as flow velocity and trajectory [97, 98]. Consequently, reutilizing IMU data incurs neither supplementary hardware nor energy overhead. Even if a node lacks an IMU, supplementing an IMU confronts a negligible hardware cost and an extremely constrained energy overhead.

At the same time, as shown in [9,10], the attitude-aware link model can be constructed by the received attitude information from the adjacent nodes and the corresponding Received Signal Strength (RSS). Furthermore, it has been shown that the link models with an error of less than 1dBm can be constructed using a few measurements.

Network District Partition. After the attitude-aware link model is constructed, the network area is divided according to geographic location. Assume that N nodes are randomly deployed in a two-dimensional plane in the aquatic environment. All nodes have the same transmission range and the communication radius is r. Each node can use GPS or other positioning systems to know its location and the geographic location information of the sink node. PolarRouting uses the node as the center of a circle, the geographical coordinate system

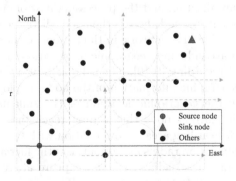

Fig. 2. Network district partition.

as the axis, and the communication radius r as the edge length to divide the area, as shown in Fig. 2. Each node knows the location information within its communication range.

3.3 Forwarding Area Establishment

When sending data, based on the partition of the network topology, the current node ascertains the relay forwarding area in conjunction with the distance from the sink node and the communication range. Firstly, as shown in Fig. 3, Polar-Routing connects the current node to the sink node with a line as expounded in [13]. Next, PolarRouting makes a square at the angle of this line and connects the current node to the square vertex. Then, the sector that is split is called the initial forwarding area, such as the sector SAB in Fig. 3.

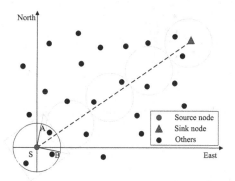

Fig. 3. The initial forwarding area establishment.

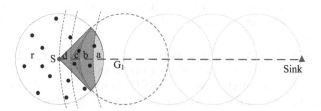

Fig. 4. Forwarding area establishment when $n \neq 0$.

After determining the initial forwarding area, a convex mirror circle is made from the destination node to the current node to determine the forwarding area. Assume that the distance from the current node to the destination node is L and the distance from the current node to the convex mirror circle on the transceiver link is $n = \mod(L, r)$. Further, the center of the convex mirror circle is on this line and the distance R to the current node satisfies

$$\begin{cases} R = r + n, n \neq 0 \\ R = \frac{3}{2}r, n = 0 \end{cases} \tag{3}$$

Here the center of the convex mirror circle dividing the sector SAB is the path guidance point G, where the first hop path guidance point is labelled G_1. The two cases of $n \neq 0$ and $n = 0$ are depicted in Fig. 4 and Fig. 5, respectively. In the figures, the initial forwarding area is divided into four regions by a circle centered on G_1 and a circle centered on the sink, notated as a, b, c, and d, respectively. Moreover, the priorities of the four regions are in the sequential order of a, b, c, and d. That is to say, PolarRouting first performs relay node selection in region a. The wake-up nodes within the forwarding region are called candidate relay nodes.

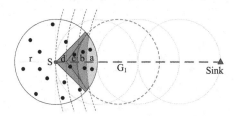

Fig. 5. Forwarding area establishment when $n = 0$.

3.4   Relay Node Selection

Upon ascertaining the forwarding area, the nodes deployed within the area constitute the initial candidate set. Concurrently, the current node apprises these nodes of the relay contention. To select the optimal relay node among them, the initial candidate set must be prioritized. In prioritizing the initial candidate set, we propose a weighting metric, W_{ar}, that takes into account attitude parameters and range gain.

Initially, as delineated in Fig. 1, if the current node is not the destination node and cannot be reached directly after one hop, a forwarding area is established, and a routing request message (RREQ) is broadcast, otherwise the data is transmitted directly to the adjacent node that can reach the destination node directly. Upon receiving the RREQ from the previous hop node, the candidate node will harness the IMU to sense its inherent attitude information and compute the Euclidean distance, d_i, and the distance gain D_i to the path guidance point. Specifically, the Euclidean distance, d_i, and the distance gain, D_i, can be expressed as $d_i = \sqrt{(x_i - x_g)^2 + (y_i - y_g)^2}$ and $D_i = \frac{d_i}{r}$. The attitude information and the distance gain are then packed into the routing response message (RREP) sent to the previous hop node. Note that the attitude information refers to the polarization angle as expounded in [9,10].

After receiving a RREP from an adjacent node in the forwarding area, the node starts the relay node selection, i.e. selects the node with the highest weight from the candidate nodes in the forwarding area to transmit data based on attitude and geographical information. Specifically, the weight of each node is calculated as follows:

$$W_{ar} = \alpha P_i + (1 - \alpha)D_i, \tag{4}$$

where α denotes a factor between 0 and 1, which can be fine-tuned pursuant to the pragmatic scenario. P_i denotes the packet reception rate between competing node i and the sending node. Note that P_i is deduced by the current node predicated on the perceived attitude statistics of the adjacent nodes and the corresponding RSS, combined with the known attitude-aware link model. If all nodes within the forwarding area are asleep and no RREP is received, the previous node broadcasts the RREQ again in the subsequent time slot.

4   Evaluation

In this section, we implement PolarRouting on NS-3 and evaluate its performance from end-to-end reliability and delay. We present the experiment settings and then show the evaluation results in detail.

4.1   Experiment Setup

The network area of 2000 m × 2000 m with 200 nodes randomly deployed is considered for the simulation. To emulate the floating devices in a real aquatic environment, we collect half-hourly attitude samples of sensor devices using IMUs on the sea surface. Without loss of generality and to match the real environment, we set the maximum transmission distance of each sensor to 30m. To preclude the repercussions of stochastically engendered network topologies, we conduct 10 iterations and derived the mean values. In each experiment, we randomly select transceiver nodes to establish multi-hop routes. For each source node, a new packet is generated every second and transmitted to the sink node via this path. To compare with traditional attitude-oblivious routing protocols, we also implement AODV [6], a typical representative of fixed routing protocol, and ExOR [8], a typical representative of opportunity routing protocol.

4.2   Attitude Angle in Real Scenario

Figure 6 shows the collected attitude angle of the floating node using IMUs on the sea surface. Note that IMUs are widely used as high-precision dynamic marine measurement instruments to measure the spatial position and attitude information of the devices, as well as to obtain the tilt angle of the pitch, roll, and vertical axes. Once the above Eulerian angles are obtained, the IMU coordinate relative to the geographical coordinate can be calculated using the method described in [9,10]. From the figure, we can find that the attitude angle of the node varies between −65° and 65°, showing a periodicity. This means that we can predict the attitude information for the next moment based on the attitude change model.

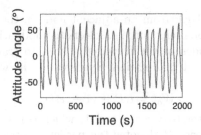

Fig. 6. The attitude angle of node floating.

4.3 End-to-End Reliability

We investigate the end-to-end reliability of PolarRouting in terms of packet loss rate. The topology of our experiment is shown in Fig. 7. The experiment runs ten times. Figure 8 presents the average packet loss rate of different methods. From the results, we can find that the average packet loss rate of PolarRouting is lower than the others. Specifically, as the number of packets increases, the advantages of PolarRouting become increasingly apparent. When the number of packets to be transmitted is 700, the packet loss rate of PolarRouting is only 0.25, while the other two methods are as high as 0.4 and 0.5. The reason behind this result is that AODV requires a pre-established route before forwarding packets, and AODV is likely to be ineffective when the node attitude changes frequently, making the routing protocol more susceptible to packet loss. Moreover, while ExOR with opportunistic routing performs better than fixed routing, it ignores the floating nature of the nodes and only achieves a limited performance improvement. PolarRouting can bring out higher reliability by considering the node attitude information.

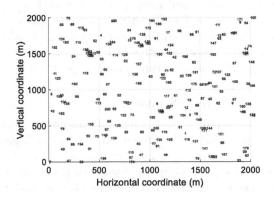

Fig. 7. Network simulation topology.

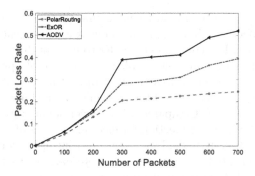

Fig. 8. Average packet reception rate.

4.4 End-to-End Delay

We evaluate the end-to-end delay of different methods in terms of average delay. Average delay refers to the ratio of the total time to send all packets to the number of packets. As shown in Fig. 9, the average delay increases with increasing the number of transmitted packets, and the latency of PolarRouting is lower than the other two methods. This is because as the number of packets increases, attitude-oblivious routing protocols require more packets to be transmitted during attitude mismatches, requiring more retransmissions. Moreover, while Polar-Routing requires extra time for attitude awareness, the average latency is also lower than the other two methods.

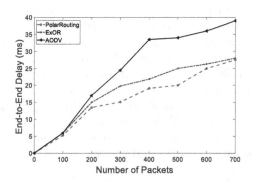

Fig. 9. Average delay.

5   Related Work

The study of routing protocols in WSNs focuses on how to make the nodes in the network choose an optimal forwarding path to the destination node when sending data. Due to traditional routing protocols, such as Ad-hoc On-Demand Distance Vector(AODV) [6] or Dynamic Source Routing (DSR) [7] request the availability of contemporaneous end-to-end connectivity, these routing protocols can not perform effectively in a changing network environment.

The capricious wireless connections render routing protocol in WSNs a challenging problem. To surmount this problem, the notion of opportunity routing was proposed. ExOR [8] introduces the first opportunity routing, which takes advantage of the broadcast nature of the transmission medium to create multiple transmission opportunities. Compared with conventional static routing, opportunistic routing exhibits a predilection for electing a series of viable relay candidates rather than a discrete node. Heterogeneous routing protocols with discrete priorities are implemented by harnessing discrete parameters to compute routing expenditures. In [14], opportunity routing based on geolocation information is proposed to balance single-hop forwarding delay and transmission rate. An approximate solution-optimal algorithm with multiple constraints is proposed in [15] and a game-theory based opportunity routing is proposed in [16]. Moreover, there are routing protocols [17,18] focus on cross-layer design, taking into account the impact of the underlying protocol on the higher layer protocols. However, these routing protocols did not consider the effect of dynamic attitude for electing the apposite forwarding list.

6   Conclusion

To remedy the quandary of routing protocol failure in floating WSNs in aquatic environments, this paper proposes PolarRouting, an attitude-aware geographical opportunity routing protocol for floating WSNs. To expeditiously glean the attitude information of the most promising adjacent node, PolarRouting determines the forwarding area by partitioning the network nodes predicated on the correlation between attitude information and geographical location. The source node needs only capture and sustain the attitude-aware link model of the candidate node within this area. Subsequently, the attitude information of the current node itself and the candidate nodes, PolarRouting opts for the relay node with an aligned attitude for data transmission. Simulation results show that compared with attitude-oblivious routing protocols, PolarRouting can prioritize reliable data transmission in floating WSNs and further curtail the end-to-end delay of the network. Prospectively, we will construct a physical testbed to evaluate PolarRouting for realistic scenarios and perform further optimization.

Acknowledgements. This work is supported in part by the National Natural Science Foundation of China (No. 62302334).

References

1. Kandris, D., Nakas, C., Vomvas, D., Koulouras, G.: Applications of wireless sensor networks: an up-to-date survey. Appl. Syst. Innov. **3**(1), 14 (2020)
2. Gulati, K., Boddu, R.S.K., Kapila, D., Bangare, S.L., Chandnani, N., Saravanan, G.: A review paper on wireless sensor network techniques in Internet of Things (IoT). Mater. Today Proc. **51**, 161–165 (2022)

3. Shahanaghi, A., Yang, Y., Buehrer, R.M.: On the stochastic link modeling of static wireless sensor networks in ocean environments. In: IEEE Conference on Computer Communications, pp. 1144–1152 (2019)
4. Shahanaghi, A., Yang, Y., Buehrer, R.M.: Stochastic link modeling of static wireless sensor networks over the ocean surface. IEEE Trans. Wirel. Commun. **19**(6), 4154–4169 (2020)
5. Shafiq, M., Ashraf, H., Ullah, A., Tahira, S.: Systematic literature review on energy efficient routing schemes in WSN-a survey. Mob. Netw. Appl. **25**, 882–895 (2020)
6. Perkins, C., Belding-Royer, E., Das, S.: RFC3561: Ad hoc on-demand distance vector (AODV) routing. USA (2003)
7. Johnson, D.B., Maltz, D.A.: Dynamic source routing in ad hoc wireless networks. In: Imielinski, T., Korth, H.F. (eds.) Mobile Computing. SECS, vol. 353, pp. 153–181. Springer, Boston (1996). https://doi.org/10.1007/978-0-585-29603-6_5
8. Biswas, S., Morris, R.: Opportunistic routing in multi-hop wireless networks. ACM SIGCOMM Comput. Commun. Rev. **34**(1), 39–74 (2004)
9. Wang, Y., Zheng, X., Liu, L., Ma, H.: PolarTracker: attitude-aware channel access for floating low power wide area networks. In: IEEE Conference on Computer Communications, pp. 1–10 (2021)
10. Wang, Y., Zheng, X., Liu, L., Ma, H.: PolarTracker: attitude-aware channel access for floating low power wide area networks. IEEE/ACM Trans. Netw. **30**(4), 1807–1821 (2022)
11. Johnson, R.C., Jasik, H.: Antenna Engineering Handbook. McGraw-Hill Book Company, New York (1984)
12. Kim, B.S., Ullah, S., Kim, K.H., Roh, B., Ham, J.H., Kim, K.I.: An enhanced geographical routing protocol based on multi-criteria decision making method in mobile ad-hoc networks. Ad Hoc Netw. **103**, 102–157 (2020)
13. Kumar, V., Kumar, S.: Position-based beaconless routing in wireless sensor networks. Wirel. Pers. Commun. **86**, 1061–1085 (2016)
14. Zeng, K., Yang, Z., Lou, W.: Location-aided opportunistic forwarding in multirate and multihop wireless networks. IEEE Trans. Veh. Technol. **58**(6), 3032–3040 (2008)
15. Fang, X., Yang, D., Gundecha, P., Xue, G.: Multi-constrained anypath routing in wireless mesh networks. In: IEEE Conference on SECON, pp. 1–9 (2010)
16. Zhang, X., Li, B.: Dice: a game theoretic framework for wireless multipath network coding. In: ACM Conference on MobiHoc, pp. 393–302 (2008)
17. Pavkovic, B., Theoleyre, F., Duda, A.: Multipath opportunistic RPL routing over IEEE 802.15. 4. In: ACM Conference on MSWIM, pp. 179–186 (2011)
18. Ghadimi, E., Landsiedel, O., Soldati, P., et al.: Opportunistic routing in low duty-cycle wireless sensor networks. ACM Trans. Sens. Netw. (TOSN) **10**(4), 1–39 (2014)

Dynamic Liveness Detection Based on Fusion of mmWave Radar and Vision

Chongyang Song[1], Luoyu Mei[1,2], Borui Li[1], and Xiaolei Zhou[3(✉)]

[1] School of Computer Science and Engineering, Southeast University,
Nanjing 210096, China
{chongyangsong,lymei-,libr}@seu.edu.cn
[2] Department of Computer Science, City University of Hong Kong,
Hong Kong 999077, China
[3] The Sixty-Third Research Institute, National University of Defense Technology,
Nanjing 210007, China
zhouxiaolei@nudt.edu.cn

Abstract. Liveness detection is critical to various scenarios such as autonomous vehicles. A remaining challenge of this topic is accurately identifying liveness from other visual disruptions, such as distinguishing persons from printed characters in billboard advertisements or LED screens in real-world scenarios. To address this problem, we leverage multi-model information, i.e., millimeter wave (mmWave) and vision, to improve the accuracy and robustness of liveness detection. We propose a feature fusion network grounded on the attention mechanism, which amalgamates mmWave radar features with visual features to augment live object detection. To validate our approach, we collect a multi-model liveness detection dataset using commercial-off-the-shelf mmWave radar and camera. We then evaluate the effectiveness and robustness via this real-world dataset. Results show that our approach could achieve 13.5%–45.6% improvement on the mAP metric compared with the state-of-the-art vision-based techniques.

Keywords: mmWave radar · Vision · Rider detection · Multi-modal fusion · Attention mechanism

1 Introduction

The growing problems of traffic congestion and air pollution have driven a shift in transportation preferences, with autonomous driving technology emerging as a vital aspect of future mobility. According to Statista, a market research firm, the global autonomous vehicle market is projected to rise from \$6 billion in 2021 to \$80.9 billion in 2030, highlighting the substantial potential and market demand for this technology.

Although numerous research institutions are developing higher-level autonomous driving systems, real-world road tests often take place in low-traffic

© The Author(s), under exclusive license to Springer Nature Singapore Pte Ltd. 2024
L. Wang et al. (Eds.): CWSN 2023, CCIS 1994, pp. 42–55, 2024.
https://doi.org/10.1007/978-981-97-1010-2_4

areas with simpler road conditions, occasionally resulting in safety issues and fatal accidents, such as the Uber incident in March 2018 [1].

Moreover, real-world road environments introduce various interferences, such as pedestrians, roadside billboards, cyclists, and LED screens, posing significant challenges for autonomous driving systems [2]. Existing vision-based object detection techniques struggle to accurately differentiate unconventional human forms, like cyclists or individuals using wheelchairs. Therefore, there's an urgent need for an accurate living entity detection system.

In this context, mmWave radar technology is instrumental. It employs electromagnetic waves reflected from objects to detect their position and velocity [3]. Compared to cameras [17,26], LiDAR [22], and traditional wireless sensors [21,23–25,28–32], mmWave radar excels at detecting obstacles and living entities in complex environments [21].

To address these challenges, this paper proposes an attention-based feature fusion network that combines mmWave radar with dynamic computer vision to enhance living entity detection's accuracy and robustness. Specifically, the paper extracts radar cross-section (RCS) features from mmWave radar signals to distinguish dynamic liveness from other visual interferences. The features from mmWave radar and vision are fused using an attention mechanism, enabling precise living entity detection.

2   Motivation

2.1   Limitation of Existing Solutions

Significant advancements occur in the field of object detection using mmWave radar and cameras [29–31]. Several mmWave radar datasets, including CRUW [4], CARRADA [5], nuScenes [6], and RadarScenes [7], are available. However, most of these studies primarily focus on general object detection, relying on object location or intensity as features. This approach limits their effectiveness in distinguishing between dynamic liveness and visual obstructions like portrait billboards. Simply relying on object position does not offer sufficient information about the object's type, and dynamic liveness and visual interferences may display similar absolute intensity levels.This research introduces a novel method to improve the robustness of the cyclist detector against visual obstructions [27,28,33–36].

2.2   Opportunity

The integration of vision-based object detection and mmWave radar-based cyclist detection presents a distinctive opportunity within the autonomous driving field. Vision and mmWave radar sensors are extensively deployed in autonomous vehicles, each offering complementary capabilities [22]. Vision sensors enable object detection and pose recognition, providing abundant visual information to identify various objects on the road. Conversely, mmWave radar sensors excel in cyclist detection, remaining impervious to environmental factors and functioning adeptly in challenging lighting and weather conditions [24,25].

By harnessing the strengths of both vision and mmWave radar sensors and utilizing the RCS as a discriminative feature, it becomes feasible to develop a robust system capable of accurately detecting dynamic liveness while mitigating the impact of visual interference [17,26].

3 mmWave Radar Feature Extraction Mechanism for Live Cyclist

The aim of this paper is to explore the use of mmWave radar features for cyclist detection. In this section, we present a comprehensive explanation of how mmWave radar operates. We propose a method for preprocessing raw signal data to generate three-dimensional point clouds that represent observed targets from the mmWave radar's perspective. Additionally, we introduce a mechanism for extracting radar reflectivity cross-section features specifically tailored for cyclists. This mechanism utilizes energy calibration techniques applied to the mmWave radar signals, enabling effective feature extraction from observed targets [8]. Through experimental comparisons, we demonstrate the effectiveness of this feature extraction approach for cyclist detection.

3.1 Radar Data Collection and Processing

Radar data collection was performed in outdoor environments, including static obstructions such as trees and the ground, as well as portrait billboards and cyclists. These environments exhibit significant multipath noise, a common challenge in RF technologies. mmWave signals propagate through multiple paths between objects and transceivers due to ambient object reflections and beam spreading. Consequently, unwanted points, referred to as ghost points, often appear in the radar point cloud [10]. To address the influence of these noisy points and distinguish portrait billboards from cyclists, we employed a clustering-based point segmentation approach.

We applied the DBScan algorithm [11] for cluster identification of points corresponding to billboards and cyclists, effectively suppressing noise. Since DBScan does not require a predefined number of clusters and can automatically detect outliers as noise, it has been widely utilized for separating individual objects from mmWave radar point clouds. Our implementation segregates radar points into distinct clusters and selects relevant objects based on the number of points within each cluster. Regarding the hyperparameter settings of DBScan, we empirically set the maximum distance (radius) between two points within the same cluster to 1 and the minimum point number in a cluster to 3.

3.2 Radar Cross Section (RCS)

Radar Cross Section (RCS) [12] is a physical parameter that characterizes a target's ability to reflect radar waves and represents the target's scattering strength in a specific direction. The magnitude of RCS determines the detectability and recognizability of a target in a radar system.

In the context of active cyclist detection in this experiment, the mmWave radar scene includes not only active cyclists but also visual interferences such as roadside billboards. However, these targets exhibit distinct differences in shape, size, and material composition, leading to variations in their RCS. As billboards or vehicle advertisements typically consist of large amounts of metal and mmWave signals cannot penetrate through metal, the billboards exhibit significantly higher RCS compared to the active cyclists. This discrepancy in RCS can serve as a crucial feature for active cyclist detection.

The fundamental equation that influences radar detection range is as follows:

$$P_r = \frac{P_t G_{TX}}{4\pi r^2} \sigma \frac{1}{4\pi r^2} A_{eff} \tag{1}$$

In this equation, P_t represents the transmitting power of the radar (unit: watts, W), G_{TX} represents the gain of the radar antenna (unit: decibels, dB), r represents the distance from the radar to the detected target (unit: meters, m), σ represents the RCS of the target (unit: square meters, RCS m^2), A_{eff} represents the effective area of the receiving antenna (unit: square meters, m^2), and P_r represents the received radar power (unit: watts, W).

The formula for the effective receiving area A_{eff} in the above equation is, where G_{RX} represents the gain of the radar receiving anten1na (unit: decibels, dB):

$$A_{eff} = \frac{G_{RX}\lambda^2}{4\pi} \tag{2}$$

However, this is not the final result. Considering various losses, clutter, and noise present in practical environments, the representation of P_r becomes more complex. The final expression for σ is:

$$\sigma = \frac{(4\pi)^3 r^4 kTFSNR}{P_t G_{TX} G_{RX} \lambda^2 T} \tag{3}$$

Here, k denotes the Boltzmann constant, T represents the antenna temperature, F is the receiver noise factor, SNR indicates the signal-to-noise ratio, and T represents the measurement time. The key challenge lies in obtaining SNR, which is the ratio of the average signal intensity received by the RX to the average noise intensity. Specifically, the noise primarily comprises background noise from the radar circuit. Although the average noise intensity can be considered constant, it is difficult to measure directly from the integrated radar device.

3.3   Building Signal Strength Reference Database

Our approach is based on the assumption that the RCS is directly proportional to the received signal intensity when other parameters are fixed. To establish a reference database, we utilize a corner reflector [13], which is a commonly utilized type of radar target. The corner reflector has a triangular shape resembling an equilateral triangle and possesses a specific geometric structure. The RCS of the corner reflector can be determined by its side length L using the formula $\frac{4\pi L^4}{3\lambda^2}$.

Specifically, we collect the received signal intensity of the corner reflector at various distances d and construct a benchmark database $\mathcal{B}(d)$. With the reference database $\mathcal{B}(d)$, we can obtain the RCS σ_p of an object at a spatial Cartesian coordinate (x, y, z) with a corresponding received signal intensity P_{r_t} using the equation:

$$\sigma_p = \frac{P_{r_t}}{\mathcal{B}\left(\sqrt{x^2 + y^2 + z^2}\right)}\sigma_r \tag{4}$$

3.4   RCS Value: Cyclists vs. Visual Interference

To validate the effectiveness and stability of the proposed mmWave radar feature extraction mechanism for detecting cyclists, we conducted four sets of controlled experiments. Each experimental scenario was measured three times, and the average of the valid values was taken as the final result. The four experimental objects included a humanoid billboard, a cyclist (side view), a cyclist (front view), and a pedestrian. The implementation results are presented in Table 1.

By comparing the RCS values of the same target at different radial distances, we observe overall stability, which is consistent with the characteristic of the target's RCS remaining relatively unchanged under radar far-field conditions. This observation indicates that the RCS feature extraction mechanism based on energy-calibrated mmWave radar signals performs as expected. Furthermore, when comparing the RCS values of the live cyclist targets and the billboard targets, we observe significant differences in the range of fluctuations. This suggests that the RCS can effectively serve as an mmWave radar feature for distinguishing live cyclist targets from billboard targets.

Since cyclists are not always positioned directly in front of the radar, their movements result in changes in the angle of arrival of the radar-reflected signal. To investigate the impact of this angle change on the RCS value, we have designed an experiment. Figure 1 illustrates the experimental setup, which includes two cyclist targets. The first cyclist moves away from the radar in the normal direction of the radar plane, while the second cyclist follows a trajectory that is 2 m to the left of the horizontal direction of the mmWave radar.

Table 1. Experimental Results of RCS Feature Extraction Mechanism Validation

Target Group	Target Object	RCS
1	Portrait billboard	220–270
2	Cyclist Side	47–51
3	Cyclist Front	17–22
4	Pedestrian	1–12

Fig. 1. Experimental scenarios of stability of RCS at different angles.

This experiment aims to verify how the change in the angle of arrival influences the RCS value for cyclist targets. By observing the RCS values under different moving paths, we can assess the stability of the RCS in the presence of varying body angles of the cyclists.

The results displayed in Fig. 2 depict the RCS values obtained for the cyclist targets moving along the two designated paths. Despite the variations in the angles of arrival of the radar signals, which consequently modify the areas exposed to the mmWave radar, both groups of RCS values exhibit consistent fluctuations. This consistency suggests that the RCS of cyclist targets, even with different body angles, demonstrates robust stability within the road environment.

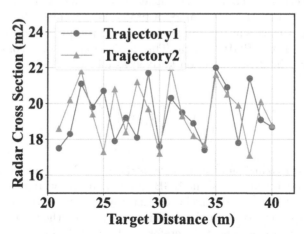

Fig. 2. Experiment result of stability of RCS at different angles.

3.5   Summary

The empirical measurements provide evidence of the consistent behavior of RCS across different distances and angles, as well as its ability to differentiate between cyclists and other objects present in the road environment. These findings serve as a motivation to develop a framework that combines radar RCS with an image-based cyclist detector, aiming to achieve robust and reliable detection capabilities.

4   mmWave Radar and Vision Fusion Mechanism

In the previous chapter, we successfully extracted the mmWave radar features of dynamic cyclists. Our next objective is to integrate these radar features with the computer vision features to achieve an effective fusion mechanism. The primary goal is to distinguish dynamic cyclist targets and accurately provide their bounding boxes within the image. This chapter presents a detailed explanation of the mmWave radar and vision fusion mechanism.

Firstly, we conduct a joint calibration process to establish the spatial coordinates of the mmWave radar and the camera. This calibration aligns the two distinct feature datasets within a unified coordinate system. Subsequently, we design a fusion module that incorporates residual networks and attention mechanisms to combine the two sets of features. This fusion module creates a comprehensive fusion model that merges the radar and vision features.

4.1   mmWave Radar Pixel Image

Our RCS calculation algorithm generates an RCS value for each voxel in the 3D space, resulting in a 3D heatmap of RCS values. However, the radar point cloud is sparse, leading to numerous voxels that do not contain relevant information for cyclist detection. To enhance the efficiency of extracting multi-scale features from radar RCS data [14], we employ a projection technique to map the RCS from the radar's Cartesian coordinate system to the pixel coordinate system, which aligns with the RGB camera. This projection involves compressing the RCS data along the depth direction (y-axis) as follows:

$$
\begin{bmatrix} u \\ v \\ 1 \end{bmatrix} = \frac{1}{y} M_1 M_2 \begin{bmatrix} x \\ y \\ z \\ 1 \end{bmatrix}
\tag{5}
$$

where M1 is the 3×3 internal parameter matrix of the RGB camera, M2 is the 3×4 external parameter matrix of the RGB camera, and (u, v) represents the pixel location in the RGB camera's pixel coordinate system. Since the mmWave radar and RGB camera are fixed on the autonomous vehicle, their relative positions remain static during movement. Therefore, M1 and M2 can be pre-calculated.

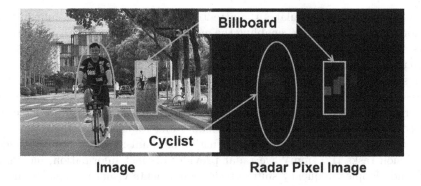

Fig. 3. Image and radar pixel image.

After the transformation, a 3-channel radar pixel image is generated, having the same height and width as the RGB image. Initially, all pixel values are set to 0. However, each pixel's value is determined based on the corresponding RCS value of the radar point it is projected from. Figure 3 illustrates an RGB image and a radar pixel image captured simultaneously. Since the RCS value of the cyclist is lower compared to that of the billboard, the pixel blocks representing the cyclist appear less bright in contrast to the pixel blocks representing the billboard. This contrast in brightness enables differentiation between the cyclist and the billboard in the radar pixel image.

4.2 Multi-modal Feature Extraction

Darknet53 [15] is a widely used deep convolutional neural network architecture for object detection and image recognition, particularly in YOLOv3. In the context of extracting features from mmWave radar and vision data, Darknet53 can be employed to extract features from both sensor modalities [37,38].

Visual images and radar pixel images have distinct complexities and feature distributions. Therefore, different sequences of residual units are utilized in the computer vision data feature extraction module and the mmWave radar data feature extraction module, adapting to their respective characteristics. The sequences are (1, 2, 4, 4, 4) for computer vision data and (1, 2, 8, 8, 4) for mmWave radar data. The features extracted from the last three layers, from shallow to deep, represent features at three different scales with sizes of 52×52, 26×26, and 13×13. In other words, each pixel in the deeper layer captures features at a larger scale. These three features are utilized for multi-modal feature fusion.

4.3 Feature Fusion Module Based on Attention Mechanism

The attention mechanism plays a crucial role in models by selectively focusing on different parts or features of the input to enhance the processing and utilization of key information. It emulates the attention allocation process in human perception and cognitive tasks, enabling the model to learn and prioritize important parts automatically.

In the domain of computer vision, attention mechanism is widely employed in tasks such as image classification, object detection, and image generation [16]. By leveraging attention mechanism, models can autonomously determine the most relevant and significant regions or features in an input image for effective task-solving, leading to improved performance and robustness.

In the context of mmWave radar, attention mechanism can be applied to feature fusion tasks [17]. mmWave radar provides distinct information, including RCS and Doppler frequency shift, which complements visual images. By incorporating attention mechanism, the features from computer vision and mmWave radar can be weighted and fused, enabling the model to leverage the strengths of both information sources and achieve enhanced performance.

Specifically, this paper adopts the following form of attention mechanism to aggregate features:

$$\delta\left(x_i, y_i\right) = \varphi\left(x_i\right) \odot \Psi\left(y_i\right) \tag{6}$$

The attention operations are applied to features at different scales. Additionally, we incorporate the concept of a feature pyramid network by propagating features captured at a global scale back to those at a local scale, providing additional contextual information. Specifically, the fusion feature from Layer 5 is up-sampled and concatenated with the fusion feature from Layer 4 to generate the final fusion feature for Layer 4. The new fusion feature of Layer 4 is then up-sampled and concatenated with the fusion feature from Layer 3, resulting in the final fusion feature for Layer 3. Finally, we utilize these fusion features from the three layers to generate prediction results for detecting cyclists.

5 Evaluation

5.1 Dataset and System Environment

The implementation of the dynamic liveness detection system in this study is based on the previously mentioned mmWave radar extraction mechanism for live cyclists and the dynamic fusion mechanism of mmWave radar with computer vision. The data used for this study is proprietary data collected from the internal roads of Southeast University's Jiulonghu Campus.

The system's working environment consists of the following: Linux data acquisition platform with Ubuntu 20.04 as the operating system, IWR6843 mmWave radar operating at 6 frames per second, Aoni A31 camera with a frame rate of 30 frames per second, NVIDIA GeForce RTX 3090.

5.2   Evaluation Methodology

5.2.1   Evaluation Metrics

In the domain of object detection, the performance of object detection algorithms is evaluated using key metrics such as precision, recall, F1 score, and mAP (Mean Average Precision).

- Precision: Precision refers to the ratio of correctly predicted positive samples to the total number of samples predicted as positive by the model.
- Recall: Recall is the ratio of correctly predicted positive samples to the total number of actual positive samples.
- F1 score: The F1 score is the harmonic mean of precision and recall. It provides a balanced measure of the model's accuracy and completeness, serving as a comprehensive performance metric.
- mAP (Mean Average Precision): mAP is a metric used to evaluate the accuracy of object detection algorithms. It calculates the average precision for each object category and computes the mean of all category-specific average precisions. mAP takes into account the model's performance across different categories, offering a comprehensive evaluation metric. It measures the area under the Precision-Recall curve, where Precision is plotted as a function of Recall. The mAP value is derived from the average precision obtained from the Precision-Recall curve.

5.2.2   Competing Approaches

1. **YOLOv3:** YOLOv3 (You Only Look Once v3) is an advanced real-time object detection algorithm, succeeding the YOLOv2. It balances speed and accuracy through parallelization and has excelled in object detection competitions and practical applications, including autonomous driving, video surveillance, and security.
2. **Faster R-CNN:** Faster R-CNN (Region-based Convolutional Neural Network) improves upon the R-CNN, prioritizing both speed and accuracy in object detection. By implementing key modifications, it achieves significant advancements in detection tasks while maintaining high accuracy.

5.3   Overall Performance

Our method achieves an mAP of 97.27% in the cyclist detection, surpassing all other methods and demonstrating the best performance.

In comparison, the Faster-RCNN method achieves an mAP of 51.64%, which is 45.63% lower than our proposed approach. These results illustrate the limitations of two-stage approaches for object detection in autonomous driving scenarios, particularly their inaccuracy in detecting distant cyclists with small scales in the image.

In summary, the evaluation results demonstrate the superior performance of our proposed method in detecting and recognizing living cyclists. It outperforms other methods in terms of mAP, indicating its effectiveness in accurately identifying cyclists while mitigating the impact of visual interference. The weaknesses of alternative approaches further validate the advantages of our proposed framework for cyclist detection in autonomous driving applications.

5.4 Sensitivity Analysis

5.4.1 Precision, Recall, and F1 Score

We break down the overall accuracy and compare precision, recall, and F1 score of our method with baselines. The results in Fig. 4 that our method outperforms baselines in all metrics. As can be seen from Fig. 4a, due to the replacement of RCS with intensity, No-RCS loses the unambiguous metrics for distinguishing living cyclists and thus is prone to false positive errors, resulting in a Precision reduction of more than 13% compared to the our method. Furthermore, Fig. 4b shows that due to the lack of multi-scale feature extraction, Faster R-CNN is prone to miss detection, which leads to a relatively low Recall.

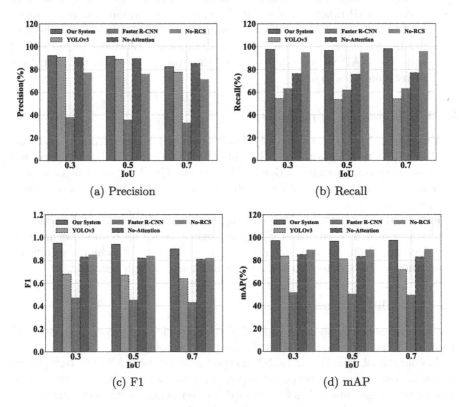

Fig. 4. Performance of proposed and baselines in different IoU thresholds

5.4.2   Impact of IoU Threshold

In our evaluation, we calculate the IoU (Intersection over Union) of predicted bounding boxes and ground truth boxes. The cyclist is detected when the IoU is higher than the predefined threshold. Thus, we set IoU thresholds to various values to observe its impact on evaluation results.

When the IoU threshold increases, bounding boxes of small-scale objects are more likely to be lost. Figure 4d shows that the mean Average Precision (mAP) of the Proposed method is always above 97% and remains optimal, which proves its robustness. The performance of the method based on a two-stage detector is lower than that of the method based on a one-stage multi-scale detector, which proves that the multi-scale method can detect small-scale objects in long-distance scenes.

6   Conclusion

This paper introduces a novel system design for detecting living cyclists using data captured by mmWave radar and RGB camera. Our approach leverages radar RCS as the fundamental feature for cyclist detection. To address the challenge of detecting small-scale objects at long distances, we have developed a global multi-scale feature extraction network. Moreover, our system proposes a multi-modal feature fusion method based on an attention mechanism to effectively combine the features from multiple sensor modalities. We believe that our research holds significant theoretical and practical value, providing valuable insights and references for the advancement and adoption of autonomous driving technologies.

References

1. Sacks, E.: Self-driving uber car involved in fatal accident in Arizona. NBC News (857941) (2018). https://www.nbcnews.com/tech/innovation/self-driving-uber-carinvolved-fatal-accident-arizona
2. Tesla's self-driving technology fails to detect children in the road, group claims.   https://www.theguardian.com/technology/2022/aug/09/tesla-self-driving-technology-safety-children
3. Gao, X., Xing, G., Roy, S., et al.: Experiments with mmWave automotive radar test-bed. In: 2019 53rd Asilomar Conference on Signals, Systems, and Computers, pp. 1–6. IEEE (2019)
4. Wang, Y., Jiang, Z., Li, Y., et al.: RODNet: a real-time radar object detection network cross-supervised by camera-radar fused object 3D localization. IEEE J. Sel. Top. Signal Process. 15(4), 954–967 (2021)
5. Ouaknine, A., Newson, A., Rebut, J., et al.: CARRADA dataset: camera and automotive radar with range-angle-doppler annotations. In: 2020 25th International Conference on Pattern Recognition (ICPR), pp. 5068–5075. IEEE (2021)
6. Caesar, H., Bankiti, V., Lang, A.H., et al.: nuScenes: a multimodal dataset for autonomous driving. In: Proceedings of the IEEE/CVF Conference on Computer Vision and Pattern Recognition, pp. 11621–11631 (2020)

7. Schumann, O., Hahn, M., Scheiner, N., et al.: RadarScenes: a real-world radar point cloud data set for automotive applications. In: 2021 IEEE 24th International Conference on Information Fusion (FUSION), pp. 1–8. IEEE (2021)

8. Li, H., Liu, R., Wang, S., et al.: Pedestrian liveness detection based on mmWave radar and camera fusion. In: 2022 19th Annual IEEE International Conference on Sensing, Communication, and Networking (SECON), pp. 262–270. IEEE (2022)

9. Seddon, N., Bearpark, T.: Observation of the inverse Doppler effect. Science **302**(5650), 1537–1540 (2003)

10. Bansal, K., Rungta, K., Zhu, S., et al.: Pointillism: accurate 3D bounding box estimation with multi-radars. In: Proceedings of the 18th Conference on Embedded Networked Sensor Systems, pp. 340–353 (2020)

11. Schubert, E., Sander, J., Ester, M., et al.: DBSCAN revisited, revisited: why and how you should (still) use DBSCAN. ACM Trans. Database Syst. (TODS) **42**(3), 1–21 (2017)

12. Fuhs, A.E.: Radar cross section lectures. Naval Postgraduate School Monterey CA (1982)

13. Sarabandi, K., Chiu, T.C.: Optimum corner reflectors for calibration of imaging radars. IEEE Trans. Antennas Propag. **44**(10), 1348–1361 (1996)

14. Singh, A.D., Ba, Y., Sarker, A., et al.: Depth estimation from camera image and mmWave radar point cloud. In: Proceedings of the IEEE/CVF Conference on Computer Vision and Pattern Recognition, pp. 9275–9285 (2023)

15. Redmon, J., Farhadi, A.: YOLOv3: an incremental improvement. arXiv preprint arXiv:1804.02767 (2018)

16. Sun, J., Jiang, J., Liu, Y.: An introductory survey on attention mechanisms in computer vision problems. In: 2020 6th International Conference on Big Data and Information Analytics (BigDIA), pp. 295–300. IEEE (2020)

17. Wang, S., Cao, D., Liu, R., et al.: Human parsing with joint learning for dynamic mmWave radar point cloud. Proc. ACM Interact. Mob. Wearable Ubiquit. Technol. **7**(1), 1–22 (2023)

18. Redmon, J., Divvala, S., Girshick, R., et al.: You only look once: unified, real-time object detection. In: Proceedings of the IEEE Conference on Computer Vision and Pattern Recognition, pp. 779–788 (2016)

19. Ren, S., He, K., Girshick, R., et al.: Faster R-CNN: towards real-time object detection with region proposal networks. In: Advances in Neural Information Processing Systems, vol. 28 (2015)

20. Palieri, M., Morrell, B., Thakur, A., et al.: Locus: a multi-sensor lidar-centric solution for high-precision odometry and 3D mapping in real-time. IEEE Robot. Autom. Lett. **6**(2), 421–428 (2020)

21. Jiang, W., Li, F., Mei, L., et al.: VisBLE: vision-enhanced BLE device tracking. In: 2022 19th Annual IEEE International Conference on Sensing, Communication, and Networking (SECON), pp. 217–225. IEEE (2022)

22. Song, P., Mei, L., Cheng, H.: Human semantic segmentation using millimeter-wave radar sparse point clouds. In: 2023 26th International Conference on Computer Supported Cooperative Work in Design (CSCWD), Rio de Janeiro, Brazil, pp. 1275–1280 (2023)

23. Mei, L., Yin, Z., Zhou, X., Wang, S., Sun, K.: ECCR: edge-cloud collaborative recovery for low-power wide-area networks interference mitigation. In: Liu, Z., Wu, F., Das, S.K. (eds.) WASA 2021. LNCS, vol. 12937, pp. 494–507. Springer, Cham (2021). https://doi.org/10.1007/978-3-030-85928-2_39

24. Qin, P., Mei, L., Jing, Q., Wang, S., Yin, Z., Zhou, X.: Edge-cloud collaborative interference mitigation with fuzzy detection recovery for LPWANs. In: 2022 IEEE 25th International Conference on Computer Supported Cooperative Work in Design (CSCWD), pp. 792–797. IEEE (2022)
25. Mei, L., Yin, Z., Wang, S., Zhou, X., Ling, T., He, T.: ECRLoRa: LoRa packet recovery under low SNR via edge-cloud collaboration. ACM Trans. Sen. Netw. (TOSN) **20**, 1–25 (2023)
26. Cao, D., Liu, R., Li, H., et al.: Cross vision-RF gait re-identification with low-cost RGB-D cameras and mmWave radars. Proc. ACM Interact. Mob. Wearable Ubiquit. Technol. **6**(3), 1–25 (2022)
27. Guo, B., Zuo, W., Wang, S., et al.: WePos: weak-supervised indoor positioning with unlabeled WiFi for on-demand delivery. Proc. ACM Interact. Mob. Wearable Ubiquit. Technol. **6**(2), 1–25 (2022)
28. Sun, K., Yin, Z., Chen, W., et al.: Partial symbol recovery for interference resilience in low-power wide area networks. In: 2021 IEEE 29th International Conference on Network Protocols (ICNP), pp. 1–11. IEEE (2021)
29. Qin, Z., Cao, F., Yang, Y., et al.: Cell Pred: a behavior-aware scheme for cellular data usage prediction. Proc. ACM Interact. Mob. Wearable Ubiquit. Technol. **4**(1), 1–24 (2020)
30. Wang, S., Yin, Z., Li, Z., et al.: Networking support for physical-layer cross-technology communication. In: 2018 IEEE 26th International Conference on Network Protocols (ICNP), pp. 259–269. IEEE (2018)
31. Tu, L., Wang, S., Zhang, D., et al.: ViFi-MobiScanner: observe human mobility via vehicular internet service. IEEE Trans. Intell. Transp. Syst. **22**(1), 280–292 (2019)
32. Wang, S., Kim, S.M., Liu, Y., et al.: CorLayer: a transparent link correlation layer for energy efficient broadcast. In: Proceedings of the 19th Annual International Conference on Mobile Computing & Networking, pp. 51–62 (2013)
33. Wang, S., Kim, S.M., He, T.: Symbol-level cross-technology communication via payload encoding. In: 2018 IEEE 38th International Conference on Distributed Computing Systems (ICDCS), pp. 500–510. IEEE (2018)
34. Hu, B., Yin, Z., Wang, S., et al.: SCLoRa: leveraging multi-dimensionality in decoding collided LoRa transmissions. In: 2020 IEEE 28th International Conference on Network Protocols (ICNP), pp. 1–11. IEEE (2020)
35. Chae, Y., Wang, S., Kim, S.M.: Exploiting WiFi guard band for safeguarded ZigBee. In: Proceedings of the 16th ACM Conference on Embedded Networked Sensor Systems, pp. 172–184 (2018)
36. Kim, S.M., Ishida, S., Wang, S., et al.: Free side-channel cross-technology communication in wireless networks. IEEE/ACM Trans. Netw. **25**(5), 2974–2987 (2017)
37. Guo, B., Wang, S., Wang, H., et al.: Towards equitable assignment: data-driven delivery zone partition at last-mile logistics. In: Proceedings of the 29th ACM SIGKDD Conference on Knowledge Discovery and Data Mining, pp. 4078–4088 (2023)
38. Xia, K., Lin, L., Wang, S., et al.: A predict-then-optimize couriers allocation framework for emergency last-mile logistics. In: Proceedings of the 29th ACM SIGKDD Conference on Knowledge Discovery and Data Mining, pp. 5237–5248 (2023)

LMCRA: A Reliable Satellite Internet Routing Method with Low Maintenance Cost

Yihu Zhou[1,2], Haiming Chen[1,2(✉)] ⓘ, and Zhibin Dou[3]

[1] Faculty of Electrical Engineering and Computer Science, Ningbo University,
Ningbo 315211, Zhejiang, China
`chenhaiming@nbu.edu.cn`
[2] Zhejiang Key Laboratory of Mobile Network Application, Ningbo 315211, China
[3] The 54th Research Institute of China Electronics Technology Group Corporation,
Shijiazhuang 050081, China

Abstract. The current shortest path-based satellite routing algorithms do not consider the periodicity and persistence of links, resulting in high costs and unreliable maintenance of routing tables. In this regard, we propose a novel approach that leverages the periodicity and predictability of satellite constellation movements to rid repetitive route calculations and associated maintenance overheads across periods. Furthermore, within each period, we design a routing algorithm, named LMCRA (A Low Maintenance Cost and Reliable Routing Algorithm), which takes into account both the persistence and latency of inter-satellite links. Compared to traditional shortest path algorithms, LMCRA reduces the frequency of path switching caused by neighboring satellites moving out of communication range, thereby enhancing path stability, reducing maintenance costs, and maintaining low path latency. Additionally, a fast rerouting mechanism is considered to enhance the reliability of the routing algorithm. Simulation results demonstrate that, across various network configurations, time spans, and constellation densities, LMCRA significantly improves path stability compared to the conventional Dijkstra algorithm, while maintaining low latency costs.

Keywords: Satellite Internet · Routing algorithm · Path stability · Latency · Simulation experiments

1 Introduction

With the rapid development of communication technology, the demand for network communication is growing exponentially among people. In this information era, an efficient and reliable communication network is a crucial infrastructure for social development, personal life, and work. In many places, the lack of reliable network connectivity restricts the scope of people's activities and opportunities. The emergence of satellite internet offers a new way of connectivity, overcoming geographical limitations. It utilizes satellites operating in space and ground

L. Wang et al. (Eds.): CWSN 2023, CCIS 1994, pp. 56–71, 2024.
https://doi.org/10.1007/978-981-97-1010-2_5

infrastructure to provide high-bandwidth, low-latency, extensive coverage, and highly reliable network services to users globally.

In satellite internet, routing algorithms play a crucial role in network performance. Satellite routing algorithms can be categorized into centralized routing, distributed routing, and hybrid routing based on the differences in routing decision-making entities. Centralized routing involves the central node calculating the routing table and distributing it to the satellite nodes in the network for ease of management. However, as the scale of satellite networks grows and mega-constellations emerge, centralized routing relying on satellite nodes as central nodes faces challenges of high routing computation complexity and significant signaling overhead due to the limited processing and computing capabilities of individual satellites. Distributed routing makes each satellite node the decision-making entity, independently calculating the optimal next-hop node and forwarding data packets. Distributed routing algorithms offer advantages in satellite networks, such as reducing the computational burden on satellite nodes and being sensitive to changes in network traffic. It can promptly update routes to adapt to changes in network conditions. However, distributed routing algorithms also have certain drawbacks. Since satellite nodes independently choose the next hop, they lack global traffic information, resulting in suboptimal path selection. Moreover, routing decisions require satellite nodes to interact with link states and control information, which may lead to early data packets being forwarded through non-optimal paths and increase signaling overhead. Hybrid routing combines the characteristics of centralized routing, involving centralized computation, and distributed routing, involving independent decision-making. Hybrid routing algorithms have higher complexity and impose greater requirements on the robustness of satellite-to-ground links and on-board processing capabilities.

This paper proposes a low maintenance and reliable routing method for satellite internet, ensuring low maintenance overhead from multiple perspectives. First, from the perspective of cycles, satellite network cycles are very long. Running the routing algorithm continuously during this period incurs significant computational overhead. Based on the periodic nature of satellites, we infer that after completing a cycle, the topology and routing table will be exactly the same. Therefore, we run the routing algorithm for one cycle and save the routing table for reference in subsequent cycles, thereby reducing computation and maintenance overhead. Next, from the perspective within a cycle, we propose an algorithm that combines path stability and latency, taking into account the periodic and predictable characteristics of satellite networks. By integrating the shortest path algorithm, we reduce the frequency of path switches caused by satellite operations, thereby improving path stability while maintaining low path latency. This is a centralized routing algorithm, where the central node is responsible for computing the routing table and distributing it to individual satellite nodes for ease of management. Lastly, to ensure the reliability of the routing algorithm, we employ a fast rerouting strategy to deal with node failures. In the event of a node failure in the satellite network, a backup path is reconstructed and switched to, thereby avoiding the impact of network failures on service quality and reliability.

2   Related Work

Currently, research in the field of routing methods for satellite internet can be categorized into three types: centralized, distributed, and hybrid. Table 1 provides a list of representative algorithms, comparing and summarizing their optimization objectives, considered factors, and computation and maintenance costs.

Table 1. Comparison of Three Different Satellite Internet Routing Strategies

Routing Strategy	Algorithm	Optimization objectives	Latency	Packet loss rate	Throughput	Path stability	Calculate and maintain costs
Centralized Routing	Dijkstra	Shortest Path	✓				high
	FD [1]	Shortest Path	✓				high
	MPQR [2]	Qos Optimization Based on Genetic Algorithm and Simulated Annealing	✓	✓	✓		high
	MO-DNN [3]	Multi-objective routing based on neural networks	✓	✓	✓		high
	FSA [4]	Optimizing Link Load Based on Simulated Annealing		✓	✓	✓	high
Distributed Routing	DORA [5]	Load Balancing Based on Multipath	✓		✓		high
	ELMDR [6]	Load Balancing Based on Machine Learning	✓			✓	high
	LBRA-SR [7]	Load Balancing Based on Traffic Density Region Partitioning		✓	✓	✓	high
	TNDR [8]	Temporal Netgrid Model-based Dynamic Routing	✓	✓	✓		high
	SDTAMR [9]	Multipath Routing Algorithm Based on Service Demand and Traffic Awareness	✓	✓	✓		high
Hybrid Routing	WSDRA [10]	Shortest Path Based on Semi Distributed Decision-Making	✓				high
	GURA [11]	Reduce Computational Overhead Based on the Combination of Global and Local Information	✓			✓	lower
	ESCBR [12]	Energy Sensitive and Congestion Balance Routing Scheme	✓	✓	✓		high
	HGLBRS [13]	Load Balancing Based on a Combination of Global and Local Policies	✓	✓		✓	high

2.1   Centralized Routing

Centralized routing is a routing strategy in which the central node is responsible for computing and forwarding the routing table. The most common centralized routing algorithm is the shortest path algorithm, such as Dijkstra's algorithm and Bellman-Ford algorithm. In satellite networks, ground stations are responsible for computing and controlling the routing tables. Once the globally optimal paths are computed, the routing table information is distributed to individual satellite nodes. Gragopoulos et al. proposed an adaptive routing strategy [1], which includes the FD routing algorithm based on shortest paths. In the FD routing algorithm, nodes update their local node information by periodically broadcasting routing information (such as distance, neighbor lists, etc.) and use this information to construct routing tables. Differing from traditional routing algorithms, nodes in the FD algorithm do not attempt to acquire global network topology information but focus on node information within their local view.

Rao et al. utilized genetic algorithms to optimize QoS-based route selection to meet different quality of service requirements [2]. They considered multiple QoS parameters such as latency, bandwidth, packet loss rate, and used the optimization capability of genetic algorithms to find the best routing path, improving service quality in LEO satellite networks. Liu and Zhang optimized the traditional SO-DNN using neural networks [3], transforming the single-objective routing problem into a multi-objective routing problem. They proposed the MO-DNN model, considering multiple optimization objectives, and achieved good results. Chang et al. introduced the Finite State Automata (FSA) routing algorithm [4], modeling the satellite network as a static topology. However, the applicability and computational complexity of the FSA algorithm have limitations.

2.2   Distributed Routing

Liu et al. investigated an adaptive routing algorithm called DORA for latency-sensitive services in multi-hop Low Earth Orbit (LEO) satellite networks [5]. DORA selects the optimal routing path based on real-time network state and traffic load, considering factors such as link quality, congestion, and service type to make the best routing decisions. However, this algorithm may have limitations in terms of maintenance costs. Na et al. studied a machine learning-based distributed routing strategy for LEO satellite networks [6]. This strategy utilizes machine learning algorithms to train models that predict the optimal routing paths by collecting and analyzing extensive network data and historical routing information. Liu and Tao proposed a segment routing-based load balancing routing algorithm called LBRA-SR [7] for traffic steering in LEO satellite networks. The algorithm divides the routing paths into multiple segments and dynamically distributes traffic to different segments based on destination nodes and network states to achieve load balancing. It considers factors such as node load status and link congestion and selects the optimal segment routing using appropriate routing policies to achieve balanced traffic distribution and efficient transmission. Li et al. focused on the effective management and optimization of data transmission in small satellite networks. They proposed a dynamic routing method based on a temporal netgrid model to enhance the efficiency and performance of data transmission [8]. Xing et al. proposed a more effective multipath routing strategy for improving routing decisions [9] in satellite networks by considering service demand and traffic conditions, aiming to enhance performance and efficiency.

2.3   Hybrid Routing

Guo et al. [10] proposed a weight-based semi-distributed LEO satellite network routing algorithm, named WSDRA. This algorithm selects the optimal path by considering node weights and link state through two stages: global route selection and local route update. However, the algorithm may suffer from the limitation of high computational and maintenance costs. Zhang and Zhou et al. [11] presented an effective method to generate and update routing tables in satellite networks based on the idea of distributed routing. This algorithm enables each satellite node to independently generate and update routing tables according to its own state and network information, thereby reducing the computational burden of satellite nodes. Jiang et al. [12] proposed an energy-sensitive and congestion-balanced routing scheme for Non-Terrestrial Satellite Networks (NTSN). The aim was to consider energy consumption and network congestion in satellite networks, with the goal of enhancing network performance and reliability. Liu and Li et al. [13] studied a hybrid global-local load balancing routing scheme, named HGLBRS, for connecting IoT through satellite networks. This scheme optimizes routing decisions by combining global and local load balancing mechanisms. At the global level, a global load balancing strategy is established by collecting the load information of various devices in the IoT, and the optimal global path is selected in the satellite network. At the local level, local load balancing and path optimization are achieved by considering direct communication between devices and the assistance of neighboring devices.

From the above analysis, it can be seen that each algorithm has its own characteristics and optimization indicators to consider, but almost all algorithms suffer from the problem of high computational and maintenance costs. These algorithms need to constantly run routing algorithms during the operation of satellite networks. Except for the GURA algorithm, which considers the link state and control information between satellite nodes and uses this information to make routing decisions, and enables each satellite node to independently generate and update routing tables according to its own state and network information, distributing the computational burden of the central node in centralized routing to various routing nodes, thereby reducing the computation and signaling overhead of satellites. However, this strategy still requires routing algorithms to be constantly running, resulting in considerable maintenance costs. Therefore, this paper will propose a routing algorithm with low maintenance costs, considering multiple optimization indicators, and with high reliability.

3   System Architecture

The architecture of satellite networks differs significantly from that of ground networks, as shown in Fig. 1. The entire network system can be divided into three segments: the space segment, the ground segment, and the user segment. The space segment consists of different types of satellites, mainly including Geostationary Earth Orbit (GEO), Middle Earth Orbit (MEO), and Low Earth Orbit (LEO) satellites. The ground segment mainly consists of ground stations. The routing method proposed in this paper is mainly focused on centralized routing for LEO, i.e., there is a ground station responsible for controlling routing (network control center) in the ground station.

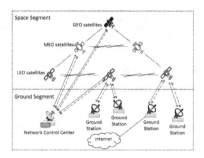

Fig. 1. Satellite Network Architecture.

4   Algorithm Design

4.1   Calculation of Satellite Network Period and Design of Low Maintenance Cost Routing

To avoid the maintenance and update costs of continuously running the routing algorithm during satellite operation, this paper leverages the periodic and predictable nature of satellite networks. The orbital period of a satellite refers to the time it takes to complete one revolution around its orbit. By using Kepler's third law, we can calculate the value of the satellite's orbital period using other parameters. Kepler's third law states that the square of the orbital period of a planet or satellite is proportional to the cube of its semi-major axis, and their ratio is a constant. In other words, if we know the semi-major axis of the satellite's orbit, we can use Kepler's third law to calculate its orbital period. This process can be represented by $T^2 = \frac{4\pi^2 a^3}{GM}$. In this formula, T represents the orbital period, a represents the semi-major axis of the satellite's orbit, G represents the universal gravitational constant, and M represents the mass of the satellite's orbiting body, which is the mass of the Earth. By solving this equation, we can determine the value of the satellite's orbital period. Taking a satellite constellation with 10 orbital planes, each containing 10 satellites (10×10), with an inclination angle of $60°$ and an altitude of $1200\,\text{km}$ as an example, we can approximate the satellite orbits as circles, where the semi-major axis can be considered as the radius, which is equal to the satellite's orbit altitude. The orbital period of the mentioned Walker constellation is $6556\,\text{s}$. However, ground stations move along with the rotation of the Earth, which has a rotation period of $86400\,\text{s}$. The least common multiple of these two periods is $141609600\,\text{s}$ (approximately 4.5 years). Based on this characteristic, we only need to run the routing algorithm for one orbital period to determine the shortest path at each moment. From the second orbital period onwards, there is no need to run the routing algorithm or maintain the routing table. Instead, we can refer to the situation of the first orbital period, thus reducing the computational overhead. The details of the Calculation of Satellite Orbital Period are presented in Algorithm 1.

Algorithm 1. Calculation Method of Satellite Orbital Period

Input: $semi\_major\_axis, GM$
Output: p //Period
1: //According to Johannes Kepler's third law:$T^2 = \frac{4\pi^2 a^3}{GM}$
2: $tmp = \frac{semi\_major\_axis^3}{GM}$
3: $p = 2\pi\sqrt{tmp}$
4: **return** p

4.2 A Routing Algorithm Considering Latency and Path Stability During a Cycle

It is well known that Dijkstra is a classic algorithm used to solve the single-source shortest path problem in weighted graphs. Its main idea is to start from the source node and iteratively expand the closest node to the source, and updating the distances of its neighboring nodes. In the context of the satellite internet problem mentioned above, we can transform the entire satellite network into a weighted topology graph, where the nodes represent satellite nodes and ground station nodes, and the edge weights represent the link distances. Therefore, we can also use Dijkstra to solve the communication problem in the satellite network and obtain the shortest path between any two ground stations.

Due to the continuous movement of satellites, the connections between satellites are constantly changing over time. For example, at time t, there may exist a link between satellite A and satellite B, but at time $t+1$, the distance between satellite A and satellite B may exceed the maximum communication range, resulting in the absence of the link at $t+1$. Due to this characteristic, the shortest paths obtained using Dijkstra, although having the shortest distance, often do not meet the requirements for path stability. In other words, the paths frequently experience switching. Therefore, to improve path stability, we combine the predictable nature of satellite movement with the routing algorithm and propose a routing algorithm that takes into account both latency and path stability.

The predictable nature of satellite movement allows us to predict the position of any satellite at any given time [14]. Therefore, based on the current state of the satellite network, we can predict the positions of all satellites after N time steps (e.g., 10 s), where N is an integer greater than zero. The main idea of the algorithm is as follows: when selecting the next hop at a node, among the candidate neighbors, we prioritize choosing a neighbor with a longer duration of connectivity. The criterion for selecting the neighbor with a longer duration is based on checking the existence of the connection between the current satellite and the neighbor satellite after N time steps. If there are multiple candidate neighbors that meet this criterion, we choose the closest neighbor as the final next hop, ensuring minimal latency.

In practical implementation, we can define a constant λ, where $0 < \lambda < 1$. For the candidate neighbors of the current node, if a candidate neighbor remains within communication range after N time steps, the corresponding edge weight is set to the normal distance. If a candidate neighbor is no longer within communication range after N time steps, it is considered unstable, and the corresponding edge weight is amplified by setting it as distance$/\lambda$. Consequently, Dijkstra, which prioritizes selecting edges with smaller weights or shorter distances, is less likely to select the unstable edge. If there are multiple stable candidate neighbors, the algorithm chooses the neighbor with the smallest weight as the next hop. The details of the algorithm mentioned above are presented in Algorithm 2.

Algorithm 2. Low Maintenance Cost and Reliable Routing Algorithm(LMCRA)

Input: $G, Source, Target, Weight, N$
Output: $path, length$

1: //Initialize $G, groundpoints\_array, groundpoints\_array2, satellites\_array,$
    $satellites\_array2.$ $groundpoints\_array$ and $satellites\_array$ store the coordinates
    of the current time, while $groundpoints\_array2$ and $satellites\_array2$ store the
    coordinates after N steps
2: //Set weights for satellite_to_ground links
3: **for** g_i in $ground\_node\_counter$ **do**
4:     **for** s_i in $satellites\_counter$ **do**
5:         $d =$ The distance between two nodes at the current moment
6:         $d1 =$ The distance between two nodes after N steps
7:         **if** $d <$max_stg_range and $d1 <$max_stg_range **then**
8:             $weight = d$
9:         **else if** $d <$max_stg_range and $d1>$max_stg_range **then**
10:             $weight = d/\lambda$
11: //Set weights for inter-satellite links
12: **for** s_i in $satellites\_counter$ **do**
13:     **for** s_i in range($s_{i+1}, satellites\_counter$) **do**
14:         $d =$ The distance between two nodes at the current moment
15:         $d1 =$ The distance between two nodes after N steps
16:         **if** $d <$max_isl_range and $d1 <$max_isl_range **then**
17:             $weight = d$
18:         **else if** $d <$max_isl_range and $d1>$max_isl_range **then**
19:             $weight = d/\lambda$
20: // Run the bidirectional Dijkstra algorithm
21: $length, path =$ nx.bidirectional_dijkstra($G, source = Source, target = Target, weight =' distance')$
22: **return** $path, length$

4.3   Fast ReRouting Mechanism

Fast ReRoute (FRR) is a network fault recovery technique. In satellite networks, FRR can be implemented using either backup paths or local repair mechanisms. In the backup path-based FRR mechanism, when the primary path fails, data traffic is switched to the backup path. On the other hand, the local repair-based FRR mechanism involves computing multiple local paths to quickly repair the route near the point of failure. In this paper, we adopt the Backup Path-based Fast ReRoute mechanism (FRR-BP) in the satellite network. In FRR-BP, when a node in the satellite network fails, the network control center removes the failed node from the network topology and recalculates the backup path from the source to the destination. To ensure the stable operation of the satellite network, it is essential to trigger the recalculation of the backup route and swiftly switch to the backup path when a network failure occurs, minimizing the impact of network failures on service quality and reliability. The details of the FRR-BP are presented in Algorithm 3.

Algorithm 3. Fast Rerouting Method Based on Backup Path (FRR-BP)

Input: $G, Source, Target, Weight, path, length, fault\_node$
Output: new_path, new_length

1: $length, path$ = nx.bidirectional_dijkstra($G, source$ = $Source, target$ = $Target, weight =' distance')$
2: **if** $fault\_node$ in $path$ **then**
3:     //A node failure occurred, causing the path to be unreachable
4:     G.remove_node($fault\_node$)
5:     $length, path$ = nx.bidirectional_dijkstra($G, source$ = $Source, target$ = $Target, weight =' distance')$
6:     print(new_path, new_length)
7: **else**
8:     //If there is no disconnection in the path, output the original path
9:     print($path, length$)

---

5   Simulation Experiment Evaluation

5.1   Simulation Environment

We utilized the SILLEO-SCNS simulator proposed by B. S. Kempton [15], which is a simulation tool designed for studying routing in large-scale satellite networks. This tool enables the simulation of various satellite network architectures and routing schemes, allowing for performance evaluation. The architecture of this simulator primarily consists of a graphical user control interface, constellation class, and simulation class, as shown in Fig. 2. The constellation class serves as the core component responsible for generating satellites, ground stations, and network structures. The simulation class handles the visualization of the satellite network and all associated animations. The GUI provides a user control interface that allows users to configure constellation parameters, set the source and destination for path planning, and specify satellite connectivity options. Communication between the GUI and Simulation is facilitated through interprocess communication for information exchange.

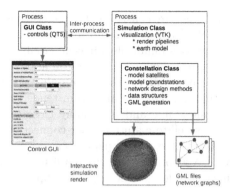

Fig. 2. Simulator Class Diagram.

5.2   The Impact of Networking Methods on Algorithm Performance

Different networking methods have a crucial impact on the density of inter-satellite connections. Common networking methods include Ideal, +Grid, and Sparse. Under the Ideal scheme, satellites can establish connections with all visible satellites without any restrictions. Under the +Grid scheme, each satellite can only establish four connections, including the adjacent satellites in the same orbit and the nearest satellites in the adjacent orbits. The Sparse scheme is a special case of the +Grid scheme, where each satellite can only maintain two connections with the adjacent satellites in the same orbit. To investigate the impact of networking methods on the LMCRA algorithm, we tested the LMCRA algorithm under the three networking methods (Ideal, +Grid, and Sparse) and compared it with traditional algorithms.

The experimental setup is as follows. We constructed a satellite constellation consisting of 10×10 (10 orbit planes, with 10 satellite nodes per plane) satellites with an inclination of $60°$ and an orbit altitude of $1200\,km$. The ground stations include well-known stations from various locations around the world. The step size was set to $10\,s$, and the time span was also set to $10\,s$, i.e., $N = 1$, which means that during the selection of the next hop, we checked if the candidate neighbors were still within communication range after one step. To ensure reliable results, we set the total runtime to $100000\,s$, equivalent to 10000 steps. We evaluated the path stability based on the average duration of each path and the path latency as the path length divided by the speed of light (c). We compared the performance of the LMCRA algorithm and the traditional Dijkstra algorithm for the Beijing to Los Angeles link under different networking methods.

The comparison results for path stability are shown in Fig. 3(a), while the comparison results for path length are shown in Fig. 3(b). Under the Ideal scheme, the satellite network topology has the highest number of connections, resulting in the lowest latency, followed by the +Grid scheme. In the Sparse scheme, the satellite network topology is generally sparser, often exhibiting higher network latency and larger variance, indicating poorer path stability. Both the +Grid and Sparse schemes are constrained to connections between neighboring satellites. In the Ideal scenario, there are numerous selectable neighboring nodes, and connections can span multiple adjacent satellites, reducing the number of hops. However, better neighboring nodes will appear soon. In the Sparse scenario, due to the sparser topology, there are only two selectable neighboring nodes, and the traditional Dijkstra algorithm tends to choose the shortest path, missing out on some stable and reasonably close neighboring nodes. In the +Grid scenario, each satellite maintains four connections, resulting in more stable paths compared to the Ideal and Sparse scenarios. Therefore, from a stability perspective, LMCRA algorithm exhibits more significant improvements in stability under the inherently less stable Ideal and Sparse schemes than under the +Grid scheme.

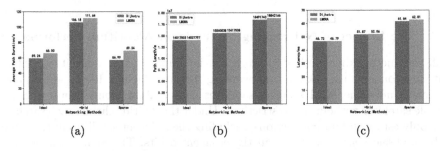

(a)   (b)   (c)

Fig. 3. The Impact of Different Networking Methods on (a) Path Stability, (b) Length, and (c) Latency.

The conversion of length to latency is calculated using $latency = \frac{length}{c}$, where $latency$ represents path delay, $length$ represents path length, and c represents the speed of light, i.e., $3 * 10^8$ m/s. The comparison results for latency are shown in Fig. 3(c).

From Fig. 3, it can be observed that achieving higher stability often comes at the cost of increased path length. However, the length increase caused by the new algorithm is not significant and falls within an acceptable range. Among the three schemes, Sparse scheme exhibits a significant improvement in path stability, but it also incurs a higher latency cost compared to the other two schemes. Under the Ideal scheme, the average duration of paths increased by 11.41%, with a 0.15% increase in latency. Under the +Grid scheme, the average duration of paths increased by 5.14%, with a 0.37% increase in latency. Under the Sparse scheme, the average duration of paths increased by 21.49%, with a 1.90% increase in latency. This is because there are enough available satellites to choose from under the Ideal and +Grid scheme. However, under the Sparse scheme, there are not enough options. The improvement of stability will inevitably bring greater latency.

5.3   The Impact of Time Spans (Parameter N) on Algorithm Performance

In the above-mentioned routing method, LMCRA, we prioritize connections that can maintain at least one time step of connectivity. In this experiment, we further investigate the effect of prioritizing connections that can maintain at least N time steps on the performance of the routing algorithm. We refer to N as the time span parameter. As shown in Fig. 4, when using Dijkstra, the stability of the +Grid scheme is significantly better than the other two schemes. When using the LMCRA algorithm proposed in this paper, a peak in path stability is observed for the +Grid scheme when $N = 3$, while the stability of the Sparse scheme generally decreases with increasing time span. In the Ideal scheme, the stability remains relatively stable with little variation as N changes. By appropriately increasing the value of N, the duration of the selected connections can be extended, thereby improving path stability. However, if N is too large, it may lead to the loss of originally stable connections. For example, when N is 5, only neighboring nodes with a duration of connectivity of at least 5 time steps are considered stable, while those with a duration of 4 time steps are considered unstable. Especially for the Sparse scheme, where the available neighbors are limited, the larger N value may lead to situations where no neighbor meets the criteria, thereby reducing path stability. In the Ideal scheme, there are enough available neighbors, so the path stability is not greatly affected by N values between 10 and 50.

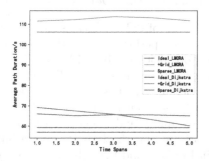

Fig. 4. The Impact of Time Spans on Path Stability.

To investigate the impact of the parameter N on path latency, we compared the LMCRA algorithm proposed in this paper with the traditional Dijkstra algorithm using different time span values ($N = 1, 2, 3, 4, 5$) in the Ideal, +Grid, and Sparse schemes. The results are shown in Fig. 5. In the Ideal scheme, the LMCRA algorithm showed only a small increase in latency for each corresponding time span. In the +Grid scheme, the LMCRA algorithm showed a slightly larger increase in latency for $N = 4$ and $N = 5$, but only a small increase for other cases. In the Sparse scheme, the LMCRA algorithm showed a very small increase in latency for $N = 1$ and $N = 2$, but a slightly larger increase for $N = 3, 4$, and 5. This is because appropriately increasing the value of the parameter N can improve the duration of the path, but when N is too large, there may be routing failures due to the inability to find the next hop that satisfies the conditions. For the Ideal scheme, where the nodes have numerous connections and available neighbors, the effect is not significant. However, for the Sparse scheme, where the network connections are sparse, a large N value leads to lower stability and greater latency costs. The +Grid scheme is somewhere in between.

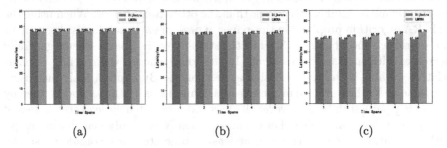

(a)   (b)   (c)

Fig. 5. The Impact of Time Spans on Latency under (a) Ideal, (b) +Grid, and (c) Sparse Scheme.

5.4   The Impact of Constellation Density on Algorithm Performance

We use satellite constellations of different scales to study the effect of different constellation densities on the performance of the routing algorithm. Figure 6 shows the constellation topologies for 10×10, 30×30, and 50×50, and the +Grid scheme is used for network formation. The starting and ending points of the paths are set to Beijing and Los Angeles, respectively. The time span parameter N for the new algorithm is set to 1, and the simulation is run for a total of 100,000 s. The stability and latency of the paths obtained from the traditional Dijkstra algorithm and the LMCRA algorithm are compared, and the results are shown in Fig. 7(a) and Fig. 7(b), respectively.

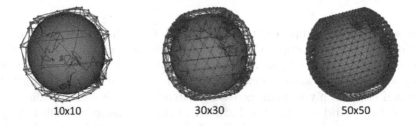

10x10   30x30   50x50

Fig. 6. Constellation Topology with Different Densities under the +Grid Scheme.

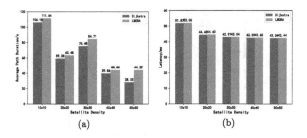

Fig. 7. The Impact of Constellation Density on (a) Path Stability and (b) Path Latency.

In general, higher constellation density increases the number of neighboring satellites, leading to more frequent path switching. Therefore, from the perspective of path stability, the overall trend shows a decrease with an increase in constellation density. With regard to path latency, the trend shows a decrease overall with an increase in satellite constellation density. However, a local maximum appears at a constellation density of 30×30, which means that the satellite constellation with specific simulation characteristics (30×30, altitude of 1200 km and inclination of $60°$) may be a good compromise between stability and latency.

5.5   Evaluation of FRR-BP

We evaluated the Fast Reroute with Backup Path (FRR-BP) mechanism based on the time required to rebuild backup paths. The time required for fast rerouting to rebuild backup paths depends on various factors, the most important of which is the network topology. In this experiment, we artificially caused satellite node failures to break the paths. We used satellite constellations of 10×10, 20×20, 30×30, 40×40, and 50×50, with a height of 1200 km and an inclination of $60°$, to investigate the effect of constellation density on the time required to rebuild backup paths. We conducted 100 simulations using the LMCRA algorithm with $N = 1$ under the Ideal, +Grid, and Sparse networking methods, respectively, and recorded the time required to rebuild backup paths and took the average. The results are shown in Fig. 8. As the constellation density increases, the number of satellites and connections also increase significantly, and it is necessary to traverse the neighboring satellites when rebuilding paths, leading to an increase in the required time. Especially under the Ideal scheme, there is no limit to the number of satellite connections, and a satellite can establish connections with any other satellite within its visible range. Therefore, under the Ideal scheme, the increase in the time required to rebuild paths is particularly significant with an increase in constellation density.

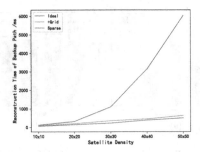

Fig. 8. The Impact of Constellation Density on the Reconstruction Time of Backup Paths.

6   Conclusion

Based on the periodicity and predictability of LEO satellite networks, we propose a reliable satellite internet routing method with low maintenance overhead while enhancing path stability and reliability. This method uses various strategies to reduce routing table maintenance overhead while enhancing path stability and reliability. These strategies include avoiding redundant calculations by utilizing the periodicity and predictability of the satellite network, selecting neighboring nodes with longer-lasting connections and minimum latency as the next hop, and using the Fast Reroute with Backup Path mechanism to handle network failures. Through simulation experiments, the results show that the LMCRA algorithm proposed in this paper is very effective in improving path stability and can maintain a relatively low latency cost. In addition, our Fast Reroute with Backup Path mechanism can maintain a short backup path rebuilding time in almost all network settings (except for the Ideal networking method with high constellation density). However, we have not yet taken into account factors such as service demands and load balancing, which might be a potential area for future research.

Acknowledgements. This work was supported by the Natural Science Foundation of Ningbo City (2021J090) and Ningbo Manicipal Commonweal S&T Project (2022S005).

References

1. Gragopoulos, I., Papapetrou, E., Pavlidou, F.N.: Performance study of adaptive routing algorithms for LEO satellite constellations under self-similar and Poisson traffic. Space Commun. **16**(1), 15–22 (2000)
2. Rao, Y., Wang, R.: Performance of QoS routing using genetic algorithm for polar-orbit LEO satellite networks. AEU-Int. J. Electron. Commun. **65**(6), 530–538 (2011)
3. Liu, D., Zhang, J., Cui, J., Ng, S.X., Maunder, R.G., Hanzo, L.: Deep learning aided routing for space-air-ground integrated networks relying on real satellite, flight, and shipping data. IEEE Wirel. Commun. **29**(2), 177–184 (2022)

4. Chang, H.S., et al.: FSA-based link assignment and routing in low-earth orbit satellite networks. IEEE Trans. Veh. Technol. **47**(3), 1037–1048 (1998)

5. Liu, L., Zhang, T., Lu, Y.: A novel adaptive routing algorithm for delay-sensitive service in multihop LEO satellite network. KSII Trans. Internet Inf. Syst. (TIIS) **10**(8), 3551–3567 (2016)

6. Na, Z., Pan, Z., Liu, X., Deng, Z., Gao, Z., Guo, Q.: Distributed routing strategy based on machine learning for LEO satellite network. Wirel. Commun. Mob. Comput. **2018** (2018)

7. Liu, W., Tao, Y., Liu, L.: Load-balancing routing algorithm based on segment routing for traffic return in LEO satellite networks. IEEE Access **7**, 112044–112053 (2019)

8. Li, J., Lu, H., Xue, K., Zhang, Y.: Temporal netgrid model-based dynamic routing in large-scale small satellite networks. IEEE Trans. Veh. Technol. **68**(6), 6009–6021 (2019)

9. Xing, Z., et al.: A multipath routing algorithm for satellite networks based on service demand and traffic awareness. Front. Inf. Technol. Electron. Eng. **24**(6), 844–858 (2023)

10. Guo, Z., Yan, Z.: A weighted semi-distributed routing algorithm for LEO satellite networks. J. Netw. Comput. Appl. **58**, 1–11 (2015)

11. Yi, Z., Quan, Z., Jun, L., Wei, L.: The generation and update algorithm of routing table in satellite network. In: 2015 IEEE International Conference on Communication Problem-Solving (ICCP), pp. 619–622. IEEE (2015)

12. Jiang, Y., Wu, S., Mo, Q., Liu, W., Wei, X.: An energy sensitive and congestion balance routing scheme for non-terrestrial-satellite-network (NTSN). Remote Sens. **15**(3), 585 (2023)

13. Liu, Z., Li, J., Wang, Y., Li, X., Chen, S.: HGL: a hybrid global-local load balancing routing scheme for the internet of things through satellite networks. Int. J. Distrib. Sens. Netw. **13**(3), 1550147717692586 (2017)

14. Chen, J., Jamalipour, A.: An adaptive path routing scheme for satellite IP networks. Int. J. Commun. Syst. **16**(1), 5–21 (2003)

15. Kempton, B.S.: A simulation tool to study routing in large broadband satellite networks. Christopher Newport University (2020)

Application on Internet of Things

WiHI: Indoor Human Identification with WiFi Signals

Ping Wang[1,2]([envelope]), WenKai Wang[1,2], Zhenya Zhang[1,2], Tao Yin[1,2], and Jiaojiao Gao[1,2]

[1] Anhui Province Key Laboratory of Intelligent Building and Building Energy Saving, Anhui Jianzhu University, Hefei 230022, China
wangping@ahjzu.edu.cn
[2] School of Electronics and Information Engineering, Anhui Jianzhu University, Hefei 230601, China

Abstract. The rapid development of human identification technology based on WiFi sensing has demonstrated immense application potential in the fields of security and smart homes. However, existing WiFi sensing methods have certain limitations, including inadequate denoising, susceptibility of selected features to environmental influences, and low recognition accuracy. In this paper, we propose a WiFi-based Human Identification method called WiHI, which utilizes the Channel State Information (CSI) of WiFi signals to extract human gait information. Firstly, antenna and subcarrier selection, along with low-pass filtering, are employed to eliminate noise in the CSI that is unrelated to walking activities. To derive unique human walking patterns from CSI, we propose an effective feature extraction algorithm based on Discrete Wavelet Transform (DWT) and Principal Component Analysis (PCA) techniques. Based on the extracted features, we have designed a two-stage human identification system consisting of stranger detection followed by target human identification. We have carried out extensive experiments on the existing publicly available dataset Widar 3.0 for method evaluation. The results indicate that WiHI can effectively detect unknown users and achieve higher recognition accuracy compared to similar approaches.

Keywords: Human identification · WiFi sensing · Channel State Information · Feature extraction

1 Introduction

Human identification is a crucial prerequisite for the convenience and security of many applications and has garnered sustained attention from researchers in recent years [1, 2]. Existing identification technologies rely on individuals' unique and stable biometric features, such as fingerprints [4], faces [5], voices [8], etc. These methods are relatively mature and have a high accuracy rate. However, they inevitably require the close and active cooperation of individuals for identification, which poses an unacceptable risk of privacy leakage. Compared to static biometrics, gait characteristics [6, 7] are more unique because visual recognition can differentiate individuals based on differences in

L. Wang et al. (Eds.): CWSN 2023, CCIS 1994, pp. 75–87, 2024.
https://doi.org/10.1007/978-981-97-1010-2_6

height, weight, and walking posture. For instance, we can identify a friend walking towards us from a great distance. Due to these characteristics, gait-based methods can perform recognition tasks at greater distances, enabling identification as humans walk in environments such as offices or homes.

Different sensor modalities, including cameras [6], Radio Frequency Identification (RFID) devices [10, 11], Ultra Wide Band (UWB) [7, 9], and commercial Wi-Fi equipment [13], have been demonstrated to extract users' gait for human identification. However, camera-based methods are prone to occlusion and privacy concerns. UWB-based methods require the deployment of dedicated sensing devices, which can be costly and challenging to widely adopt in typical home applications. RFID-based methods necessitate users to wear specific tags. In comparison, the method based on WiFi devices is more appealing due to the ubiquitous presence of WiFi infrastructure and the absence of any requirement for users to wear specific tags [2].

In recent years, researchers have proposed several WiFi-based human identification, such as WiDIGR [3], WiTraj [13], and WiHF [14]. These systems enable individuals to interact seamlessly with various smart devices through WiFi, thereby enhancing the level of building intelligence and improving human quality of life. When humans walk within a WiFi environment, their distinct body shape and walking posture lead to diverse effects on the WiFi signals, thereby facilitating the process of personnel identification. With knowledge of the user's identity, the intelligent home assistant allows authorized users to access rooms and proactively adjusts temperature, humidity, and lighting conditions based on their preferences. Furthermore, it restricts child users from operating hazardous electrical appliances. Therefore, researching human identification based on WiFi signals contributes to unlocking the potential of smart homes.

Nevertheless, human identification faces three fundamental challenges in practice.

1. **Inadequate treatment of noise in raw WiFi CSI**

    WiFi signals are typically noisy, including variations caused by human movement as well as device and environmental noise. WiFi-ID [15] and WiTraj [13] filter design based on experience may not be convincing enough and could potentially filter out waveforms related to walking, thus requiring in-depth analysis with real data to determine a reliable range for denoising. Furthermore, different receiving antennas and subcarriers exhibit significant variations in their ability to perceive human movement, and not all of them contribute equally to the identification task. Researchers often choose to use all the data or arbitrarily select data from a single antenna [12, 16]. This coarse-grained CSI contains numerous redundant information unrelated to human movement, ultimately leading to reduced recognition accuracy and robustness. Therefore, it is necessary to adequately process the raw CSI data by removing signals unrelated to walking and eliminating redundant information introduced by the MIMO system itself.

2. **Lack of effective feature extraction methods**

    Some researchers have attempted to use features such as the maximum value, variance, and signal energy of CSI waveforms as a starting point [15, 17]. However, these methods often yield unsatisfactory results due to the similarity of these values for individuals with similar body types and their dependence on the specific experimental environment. Furthermore, when humans walk, the reflections of signals from different parts of the body are superimposed in the CSI waveform. It is known that the movement speeds of the torso and limbs differ during walking, resulting in different reflection frequencies in the wireless signal. Although some researchers have utilized deep learning models to extract gait features from CSI streams [19–21], achieving higher performance in identity recognition, these methods often require longer recognition time and rely on high-performance computing devices. Additionally, they often demand the cooperation of participants to walk more than 100 times, which is challenging to achieve in practical applications. Therefore, it is necessary to perform more refined processing of CSI to extract more effective signal fluctuation features that reflect human gait.

3. **Neglecting the recognition of Unknown users**

Current WiFi-based human identification methods primarily focus on improving the accuracy of identifying target individuals, while paying little attention to the scenario involving unfamiliar individuals [20]. Wii [18] utilizes a threshold-based algorithm that is sensitive to environmental changes for detecting unknown users. For such a system, when unknown users walk within the WiFi area, their gait data may be mistakenly identified as that of a specific target individual. This phenomenon can potentially cause unnecessary complications in practical applications.

In this paper, we propose WiHI, which aims to tackle three main challenges. We employed a more refined signal processing technique to eliminate various types of noise and redundant information from the raw CSI. Capture personalized motion patterns caused by humans walking through WiFi signals. Furthermore, we designed a two-stage human identification system to facilitate the detection of unknown users, thereby achieving a more robust human identification. The contribution of this work can be summarized as follows:

- We propose an effective CSI data preprocessing method. It first helps us select antenna pairs and subcarriers from the MIMO communication system that are most sensitive to walking activities. Then, time-frequency analysis and low-pass filtering are used to remove signal perturbations that are not related to people walking.
- We implement a feature export method using DWT and PCA. The signal fluctuations of the torso reflection were separated from the mixed CSI waveforms of signal reflections from different body parts by multiple discrete wavelet decomposition. Then, the walking patterns of different people are generated by PCA.
- We add unknown human detection for more robust recognition. It recognizes strangers who are outside the target members with higher human identification accuracy compared to existing methods.

2   Preliminary

In this section, we will provide a brief overview of WiFi CSI. Mainstream WiFi communication systems typically employ MIMO (Multiple-Input Multiple-Output) technology for data transmission between multiple antenna pairs. Specifically, data packets are carried in parallel by multiple orthogonal subcarriers. This transmission method enhances communication quality while also capturing subtle variations in the environment. We can easily obtain CSI from this method and analyze the patterns of signal variations, thereby inferring human behavior. When humans walk, unique waves are generated in the ocean of WiFi signals.

For a WiFi system with M transmits antennas, N receives antennas and K subcarriers. If a total of NT moments of sampled values are obtained by sampling over some time. Then the CSI matrix representing the amplitude attenuation and phase shift can be expressed as $H \in C^{M*N*K*N_T}$. The CSI at an arbitrary moment can be described as:

$$H(f_k) = \|H(f_k)\|e^{j\angle H(f_k)}, k \in [1, K] \qquad (1)$$

where $H(f_k)$ denotes the CSI value of the kth subcarrier, $\|H(f_k)\|$ and $\angle H(f_k)$ represents the amplitude and phase, respectively.

3 System Design

3.1 System Architecture

The designed WiHI can be utilized for effective personnel identification using commercial Wi-Fi devices. As shown in Fig. 1, the data collection module serves as the input to the WiHI and the result of the identification serves as the output. WiHI consists of four main core modules: Data Collection, Data Processing, Feature Extraction, and Human Identification. When humans are walking, we collect CSI signals from WIFI devices. Antenna and subcarrier selection, as well as low-pass filtering, are conducted as preparatory work for identity identification. The DWT and PCA techniques are employed to extract motion change patterns, capturing signal variations that are highly correlated with the human body's movement. A two-stage classification module is utilized to classify and generate identification results, enabling the recognition of humans engaged in walking activities.

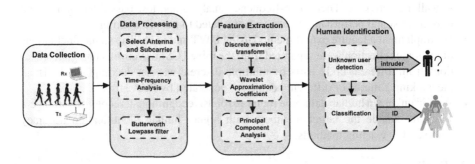

Fig. 1. Overview of WiHI

3.2 Data Collection

The data collection device consists of one transmitting antenna and three receiving antennas, with each antenna containing 30 subcarriers, so the collected CSI data sequence contains 30 * 1 * 3 = 90 CSI streams. The testing area allows for human walking for a duration of five steps while collecting CSI at a sampling frequency of 1000 Hz. Each walking sample has a duration of 2.5 s, resulting in a CSI size of 90 * 2500 for each sample. In the CSI amplitude matrix, each column represents a CSI stream that records the variation in the amplitude of the channel as the person travels.

3.3 Data Processing

Antenna and Subcarrier Selection. The full OFDM subcarriers have a strong linear correlation, which also brings a lot of redundant information. To reduce the impact of redundant information, we propose a parameter to select antenna pairs with stronger dynamic responses. We consider antenna symbols with both smaller amplitudes and larger variances to be more suitable for our requirements, and we provide detailed experimental explanations in Sect. 4.2. This coefficient is obtained from the following equation:

$$\gamma_n = \frac{1}{K} \sum_{k=1}^{K} \frac{\text{var}(\|H(f_k, t)\|)}{mean(\|H(f_k, t)\|)}, n \in \{1, 2, 3\} \tag{2}$$

where $\text{var}(\|H(f_k, t)\|)$ and $mean(\|H(f_k, t)\|)$ denote the variance and mean of the amplitude data on the Kth subcarrier of the Nth antenna. Based on this equation, we chose the antenna pair with the supreme proportion coefficient.

On this basis, we discarded the first two and the last two subcarriers that are susceptible to non-deterministic noise [18] and selected the CSI streams on the 3–17 path subcarriers as the data source. The above operation largely mitigates the weak CSI reflected on the other paths and focuses on the CSI most relevant to walking. After processing, the size of each sample is 15 * 2500.

Time and Frequency Analysis. In order to analyze the effect of walking on WiFi signals more intuitively and accurately, thereby retaining the most significantly perturbed frequency band. We applied Short-Time Fourier Transform (STFT) to the CSI data of two users, and the transformed results are shown in Fig. 2. From the spectrogram, we can observe that the impact of the WiFi signal on the two individuals is distinctly different, which is sufficient for personnel identification. Additionally, although the disturbances during walking are different, the frequency band primarily affected remains consistent, with the most significant fluctuations occurring in the 0–80 Hz range. We believe that disturbances in other frequency bands are unlikely to be caused by walking. Therefore, we will design filters to remove these disturbances.

Lowpass Filter. We designed a Butterworth lowpass filter to remove signals outside the 0–80 Hz range. The effect before and after filtering is shown in Fig. 3. It can be seen that the raw data is more chaotic, with jagged noise interspersed in the waveform. The denoised CSI data becomes smoother and the signal fluctuation characteristics are more obvious, which will be used for feature extraction next.

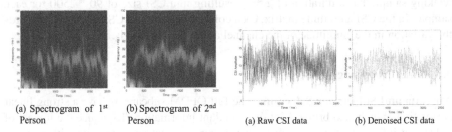

(a) Spectrogram of 1st   (b) Spectrogram of 2nd
     Person   Person

(a) Raw CSI data   (b) Denoised CSI data

Fig. 2. Comparison between spectrograms of two persons.

Fig. 3. Raw and filtered CSI sequences.

3.4 Motion Change Pattern Extraction

After the Data Processing module, we have initially overcome the influence of noise. The remaining challenge is how to effectively extract motion patterns from the overlapping CSI. Specifically, the torso, limbs, and other parts of the body move at different speeds during walking, which will perturb the signal in different frequency bands. Based on our experimental observations, the influence of trunk movement is the most pronounced and contains more effective individual walking patterns. In order to isolate the walking patterns, we designed the motion change pattern extraction algorithm. The specific algorithm description is shown in Algorithm 1.

Algorithm 1 Motion Change Pattern Extraction

Input: $X_i[n], (i = 1, 2, ..., s)$,the Processed CSI sequence.

       $db5$,the selected wavelet function.

       L ,the number of transformation layers.

       M ,the number of principal components retained by PCA.

Output: *Features* ,Walking characteristics of the current person

       // Performing wavelet decomposition:

1: **for** i=1:s **do**

2:      **for** j=1:L **do**

3:        $A_0 = X_i[n]$

4:        $c_j[n] = \sum_{k=0}^{L-1} A_{j-1}[n-k] \otimes h[k]]$

5:        $A_j = c_j[2n]$

6:      **end for**

7:      $\Bbbk(i,:) = A_j$

8: **end for**

       // Feature Dimensionality Reduction:

9: $H_{norm}[s,n] = (\Bbbk(:,:) - mean[n]) \div std[n]$

10: $H_{cov} = \frac{1}{s} \times H'_{norm} * H_{norm}$

11: $[E_g, D] = eig(H_{cov})$

12: $Features = E_g(M \times s) * H_{norm}(s \times n)$

13: **return** *Features*

The algorithm is divided into two steps. Firstly, Daubechies (db5) wavelets are used for decomposing the discrete CSI sequence into 4 layers, retaining the components in the frequency range of 0–30 Hz, which contain more information about the gait. Secondly, the PCA technique is applied to extract the most representative first principal component from the coefficients obtained after decomposing multiple subcarriers. Specifically, we input the 15 * 2500 CSI data into the feature extraction module, which outputs a 1 * 164 feature vector. The resulting walking pattern can be considered as the variation caused by trunk movement, which is theoretically unaffected by the environment.

To demonstrate the effectiveness of feature extraction, we generated 164-dimensional features for five individuals walking and visualized these features using the t-SNE algorithm. The results are shown in Fig. 4. It can be observed that the feature points of the 1–5 target users are tightly clustered, with only a few samples overlapping. This indicates that the features we extracted are highly effective and can be well utilized for subsequent personnel identification.

3.5 Human Identification

Our human identification is a two-stage process. The walking person is first subjected to unknown person detection, and a specific human identification procedure is triggered only if the walking human is a target user.

Unknown User Detection. Unknown user detection is an important issue in personnel identification. Even if we haven't collected walking instances of unknown users, it is crucial to differentiate between unfamiliar individuals and target users. Although we were only able to obtain a small number of samples from strangers, however, we had enough samples from the target members. According to Fig. 4, we find that the feature

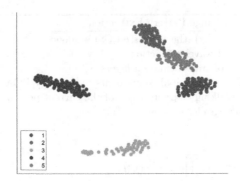

Fig. 4. t-SNE visualization of target user distribution

points of different humans are distributed in different regions of the feature space, and we are clear about the distribution of features of all target users. Therefore, we consider a person to be a stranger when their feature points are distributed outside a specific region. The unknown user detection algorithm is described in detail in Algorithm 2.

Algorithm 2 Unknown user detection algorithm

Input: $\Psi[i], (i = 1, 2..., N)$,the feature data from the samples of N target users.

   $\Theta[j]$,the feature data of the current test user.

   K ,the nearest neighbor parameter.

   σ ,the threshold parameter.

Output: ϑ ,The recognition result ;unknown user or target user.

   //Calculate the neighborhood density of each target user:

1: **for** i=1:N **do**

2:    For each sample $\varphi[j]$ in Ψ,Calculate the average distance of the nearest K neighbors d_j

3:    $density[i]$ =average(d)

4: **end for**

   //Diagnostic test user identity

5: Calculate the average distance of the nearest K neighbors D_j

6: **if** $D_j > \sigma \bullet density[i]$ **then**

7:    ϑ= unknown user

8: **else**

9:    ϑ= target user

10: **end if**

11: **return** ϑ

The algorithm is divided into two steps. Firstly, during the training phase, WiHI calculates the average neighbor distance for each target user and considers it as the class density. Secondly, during the testing phase, WiHI calculates the average distance to the nearest K samples. If this distance is greater than the weighted class density, the test sample is considered an unknown user; otherwise, it is classified as a target member. Although our algorithm can effectively identify unknown users, the overlapping regions of feature points among different target members can lead to a decrease in the accuracy of target member identification. When a test individual is detected as an unknown user, the identification system terminates the current task. Only when the walking human is detected to be the target user, the identification process is activated for human identification.

Identity Classification. Target classification is the second step in personnel identification, and we have confirmed that the test sample belongs to a target member. We achieve the classification recognition of target persons by finding more effective hyperplanes with the help of SVM's superior high-dimensional feature mapping capability. To identify an individual from a set of N users, we feed the extracted features into an SVM classifier with a linear kernel function and optimize the hyperparameters. We trained an optimized SVM classifier using N-member training data (N ranging from 2–6) using standard ten-fold cross-validation and analyzed the performance with test data.

4 Experiments and Evaluation

We have implemented WiHI and evaluated its performance through extensive experiments. The detailed settings are as follows:

Dataset: We leverage a public dataset from Widar3.0 [22], which comprises the walking patterns of 11 users collected in typical residential settings. Each user walked along four trajectories, and the raw CSI measurements were recorded at a sampling rate of 1000 Hz. Due to the non-uniform distribution of user walking samples, we selected trajectories where users approached the transmitting and receiving devices. We further selected 6 users as target users, while the remaining 5 users were considered unknown users for overall performance evaluation. A total of 300 target person data and 150 unknown person data were provided for the dataset. This selection adequately represents normal smart home scenarios.

Metrics: To characterize the performance of WiHI, two metrics, namely average recognition accuracy and confusion matrix, are employed for person identification. We randomly selected 70% of the total data as the training dataset, and each experiment was repeated 50 times to calculate the average accuracy. And the percentages of correct identification and misidentification in matrix form.

4.1 Overall Performance

We initially evaluated the performance of WiHI in human identification on the public dataset, including its ability to detect unknown users and recognize target users.

By incorporating walking data from multiple unknown users into the target users dataset, Fig. 5 depicts the outcomes of detecting unknown users. When only the walking data of one unknown user was included, a correct detection rate of 94.79% was achieved. This indicates that when an unknown user walks within the WiFi sensing area, they can be effectively detected. However, as the number of unknown users increases, the recognition performance declines, possibly due to more feature points of unknown users appearing at the edges of the target users. As the size of the target person group ranges from 2 to 6 individuals, the average recognition accuracy varies between 96.51% and 89.9%. We believe that as the number of individuals increases, the likelihood of encountering similar body types and gaits between individuals also increases, thereby leading to a decline in recognition performance. Figure 7 shows the confusion matrix for 6 people. It can be seen that the recognition accuracy of most of the people is over 88.9% and most of the individuals can be uniquely identified with a high probability, which shows the effectiveness of WiHI for identifying people in indoor environments with few people such as homes and offices (Fig. 6).

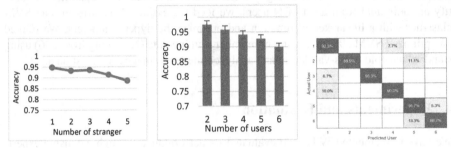

Fig. 5. Performance of stranger recognition   **Fig. 6.** Accuracy for user diversity   **Fig. 7.** Confusion matrix

4.2 Performance Evaluation

Performance Comparison. To fully verify the superiority of the identification model proposed in this paper, the classical WiFi-ID [15], FreeSense [17], and GaitSense [20] identification models are compared in the same dataset. The recognition performance from 2 to 6 individuals is depicted in Fig. 8. All average accuracies tend to decrease as the group size increases. The fact that WiHI still exhibits good recognition performance even with a larger number of users indicates that we have successfully identified patterns that effectively capture variations in human walking behavior.

Impact of Antenna and Subcarrier Selection. To validate the role of antenna and subcarrier selection, we compare the performance of the total subcarrier data and the selected subcarrier data during identification. The identification accuracy of the two types of data at different cluster sizes is shown in Fig. 9. From this difference, we can conclude that removing noise and redundant information from the raw CSI data contributes to achieving higher recognition accuracy.

Impact of Different Classifiers. We compare WiHI with two other typical classification models to analyze their accuracy of person identification for different group sizes. The results are shown in Fig. 10. It can be seen that when there are only two members to be recognized, both WiHI, KNN, and decision tree classifiers have high recognition accuracy. However, when the cluster size becomes large, WiHI still has a high recognition accuracy.

Impact of Walking Distance. To evaluate the impact of walking distance on recognition accuracy, we extracted walking data ranging from one step to four steps from the dataset. We conducted experiments with four volunteers, and Fig. 11 illustrates the recognition accuracy at different numbers of walking steps. From walking 5 steps to walking 1 step,

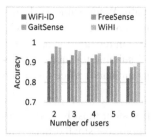

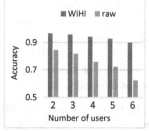

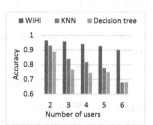

Fig. 8. Compared with the gait recognition systems.

Fig. 9. Impact of antenna and subcarrier selection

Fig. 10. Performance of different classification models

the average recognition accuracy of the system dropped from 94.73% to 76.12%, but the accuracy was still 89.98% when walking 2 steps. This suggests that a complete gait consists of at least two consecutive steps. A complete and reliable identity cannot be obtained from a single-step walk, and adding more steps to the walk does not result in a significant performance gain. We recommend that the actual deployment requires the target member to walk 4 steps, which consists of two full gait cycles, while most indoor environments have the space to walk 4 steps.

Impact of Walking Sample Data. To evaluate the effect of the number of walking samples per member on the system performance, 4 volunteers were randomly selected and multiple sets of data from 5 to 50 walks each were randomly selected from their 50 walks data for a controlled trial. From Fig. 12, the average recognition accuracy of the system increased from 79% to 94.73% when the number of training samples was increased from 5 to 50 times. It is difficult for us to capture the complete signature of signal fluctuations from the perturbed CSI when volunteers walk only a few times. When each volunteer walks 25 times in the sensing area, the system is already better able to distinguish the unique perturbation patterns caused by each member, and we suggest that the target members be required to walk 25 times when deployed.

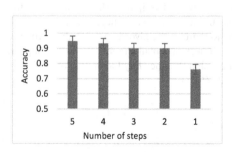

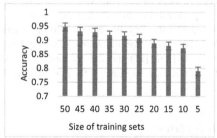

Fig. 11. Impact of walk steps

Fig. 12. Impact of walk number

4.3 Limitations and Discussion

The WiHI system shows the feasibility of using commercial WiFi for human identification. However, the current implementation of WiHI has three limitations.

Walking Path: The subjects must walk along a straight path. When subjects do not walk along a straight path, the CSI produces a different pattern of variation and fails to indicate the same gait information. This can lead to a decrease in recognition accuracy. Therefore, the current implementation of the WiHI system is suitable for indoor places where walking is along a straight line. For example, entering an indoor place through a corridor, only the target member is allowed to enter.

Application Sites: To ensure better recognition, the WiHI system must be applied in indoor environments with a small number of people, such as homes or small offices. The classification effect gradually decreases as the number of categories increases. This is a common problem of current learning-based recognition methods. This limitation will motivate us to seek solvable solutions in the future.

Multi-person Coexistence: Our research focuses on the recognition problem of single-person walking and does not explore the actual recognition capability of multi-person walking systems. When more than one person walks in the sensing area, they will cause additive effects on the receiver. To solve this problem, the gait information of each walker needs to be separated from the mixed CSI. In future work, we plan to explore the possibility of multiple signal separation using multiple WiFi devices.

5 Conclusion

In this paper, we propose a WiFi-based human identification framework called WiHI, which effectively removes various noises from the raw CSI and extracts meaningful walking patterns for human identification. WiHI also can detect unknown users, which gives the system stronger robustness in practical deployment. We have carried out extensive experiments on the existing publicly available dataset Widar 3.0 for method evaluation. The results demonstrate that WiHI is capable of effectively identifying unknown users with high accuracy in settings such as homes or small office environments.

Acknowledgement. This work is partially supported by the Discipline (Major) Top-notch Talent Academic Funding Project of Anhui Provincial University and College (gxbjZD2021067, gxyq2022030), Key Project of Natural Science Research of Universities of Anhui Province (KJ2020A0470), the Innovative Leading Talents Project of Anhui Provincial Special Support Program ([2022]21), the director foundation of the Anhui Province Key Laboratory of Intelligent Building & Building Energy Saving (No. IBES2022ZR01).

References

1. Li, C., Cao, Z., Liu, Y.: Deep AI enabled ubiquitous wireless sensing: a survey. ACM Comput. Surv. (CSUR) **54**(2), 1–35 (2021)
2. Ma, Y., Zhou, G., Wang, S.: WiFi sensing with channel state information: a survey. ACM Comput. Surv. (CSUR) **52**(3), 1–36 (2019)
3. Zhang, L., Wang, C., Ma, M., Zhang, D.: WiDIGR: direction-independent gait recognition system using commercial Wi-Fi devices. IEEE Internet Things J. **7**(2), 1178–1191 (2019)

4. Li, Y., Guo, J., Zhang, Q.: Methods and technologies of human gait recognition. J. Jilin Univ. (Eng. Technol. Ed.) **50**(01), 1–18 (2020)
5. Yan, C., et al.: Age-invariant face recognition by multi-feature fusion and decomposition with self-attention. ACM Trans. Multimedia Comput. Commun. Appl. (TOMM) **18**(1s), 1–18 (2022)
6. Fan, C., Liang, J., Shen, C., Hou, S., Huang, Y., Yu, S.: OpenGait: revisiting gait recognition towards better practicality. In: Proceedings of the IEEE/CVF Conference on Computer Vision and Pattern Recognition, pp. 9707–9716 (2022)
7. Zhou, J.H., Wang, Y.C., Tong, J.P., et al.: Ultra wide band radar gait recognition based on slow-time segmentation. J. Zhejiang Univ. (Eng. Sci.) **54**(2), 283–290 (2020)
8. Li, Z., Li, Y., Xiong, W., Chen, M., Li, Y.: Research on voiceprint recognition technology based on deep neural network. In: Proceedings of the 2021 International Conference on Bioinformatics and Intelligent Computing, pp. 412–417 (2021)
9. Abdulatif, S., Aziz, F., Armanious, K., Kleiner, B., Yang, B., Schneider, U.: Person identification and body mass index: a deep learning-based study on micro-Dopplers. In: 2019 IEEE Radar Conference (RadarConf), pp. 1–6. IEEE (2019)
10. Ding, H., et al.: RFnet: automatic gesture recognition and human identification using time series RFID signals. Mob. Netw. Appl. **25**, 2240–2253 (2020). https://doi.org/10.1007/s11036-020-01659-4
11. Zhao, C., et al.: RF-Mehndi: a fingertip profiled RF identifier. In: IEEE INFOCOM 2019-IEEE Conference on Computer Communications, pp. 1513–1521. IEEE (2019)
12. Qian, K., Wu, C., Zhou, Z., Zheng, Y., Yang, Z., Liu, Y.: Inferring motion direction using commodity Wi-Fi for interactive exergames. In: Proceedings of the 2017 CHI Conference on Human Factors in Computing Systems, pp. 1961–1972 (2017)
13. Wu, D., et al.: WiTraj: robust indoor motion tracking with WiFi signals. IEEE Trans. Mob. Comput. **22**(5), 3062–3078 (2023)
14. Li, C., Liu, M., Cao, Z.: WiHF: enable user identified gesture recognition with WiFi. In: IEEE INFOCOM 2020-IEEE Conference on Computer Communications, pp. 586–595. IEEE (2020)
15. Zhang, J., Wei, B., Hu, W., Kanhere, S.S.: WiFi-ID: human identification using WiFi signal. In: 2016 International Conference on Distributed Computing in Sensor Systems (DCOSS), pp. 75–82. IEEE (2016)
16. Lu, Y., Lu, S., Wang, X.: Research review of human behavior sensing technology based on WiFi signal. Chin. J. Comput. Sci. **42**(2), 3–23 (2019)
17. Xin, T., Guo, B., Wang, Z., Wang, P., Yu, Z.: FreeSense: human-behavior understanding using Wi-Fi signals. J. Ambient. Intell. Humaniz. Comput. **9**, 1611–1622 (2018). https://doi.org/10.1007/s12652-018-0793-4
18. Shah, S.W., Kanhere, S.S.: Smart user identification using cardiopulmonary activity. Pervasive Mob. Comput. **58**, 101024 (2019)
19. Wang, X., et al.: Placement matters: understanding the effects of device placement for WiFi sensing. Proc. ACM Interact. Mob. Wearable Ubiquit. Technol. **6**(1), 1–25 (2022)
20. Zhang, Y., Zheng, Y., Zhang, G., Qian, K., Qian, C., Yang, Z.: GaitSense: towards ubiquitous gait-based human identification with Wi-Fi. ACM Trans. Sens. Netw. (TOSN) **18**(1), 1–24 (2021)
21. Bu, Q., Ming, X., Hu, J., Zhang, T., Feng, J., Zhang, J.: TransferSense: towards environment independent and one-shot wifi sensing. Pers. Ubiquit. Comput. **26**, 555–573 (2022). https://doi.org/10.1007/s00779-020-01480-6
22. Zhang, Yi., Zheng, Y., Zhang, G., Qian, K., Qian, C., Yang, Z.: Gaitid: robust wi-fi based gait recognition. In: Yu, D., Dressler, F., Yu, J. (eds.) WASA 2020. LNCS, vol. 12384, pp. 730–742. Springer, Cham (2020). https://doi.org/10.1007/978-3-030-59016-1_60

Age of Information-Based Channel Scheduling Policy in IoT Networks Under Dynamic Channel Conditions

Chao Wang[✉], Lu Jiang, Yunhua He, Guangcan Yang, and Ke Xiao

Information Science and Technology, North China University of Technology, Jinyuanzhuang Street, Beijing 100144, China
wangchao.andy@gmail.com

Abstract. IoT networks are comprised of multiple terminal devices and control centers, where the increasing amount of connected IoT devices have led to a drastic data growth. The generated data from multiple terminals needs to be transmitted to the control center through public wireless channels that undergoes real-time changes. To ensure the timeliness of the data forwarded to the control center, this paper introduces the concept of AoI as a metric to quantify the timeliness of data delivery with throughput considered either. We propose two transmission scheduling policies, namely the Priority-based Scheduling Policy considering AoI and Throughput (PSP-AT) and the Dynamic Classification-based Priority Scheduling Policy (DCP-AT). Both of them aim to schedule channels to maximize the throughput and minimize the AoI and they are compared with existing scheduling policies. Experimental results show that our proposed algorithms outperform existing scheduling policies in terms of AoI and throughput.

Keywords: Age of Information · Scheduling · Wireless network · Dynamic channel

1 Introduction

The proliferation of connected Internet of Things(IoT) devices have led to a drastic growth on data. In the IoT system scenario, remote devices generate a significant amount of shared data and forward them to the control center. In fact, the timeliness of data transmission is of great concern, since outdated information may be useless. However, due to the limitation of communication resource, control center may not receives all the generated data in real-time. Therefore, it is necessary to allocate communication resources in a reasonable manner to ensure that the control center receive up-to-date status information for each remote device.

The conception of Age of Information (AoI) has been introduced in [1] and it is commonly used to quantify the freshness of data from remote devices [2].

L. Wang et al. (Eds.): CWSN 2023, CCIS 1994, pp. 88–98, 2024.
https://doi.org/10.1007/978-981-97-1010-2_7

Many works have made significant contributions to the scheduling problem on minimizing system AoI. Some of the work focused on the theoretical discussion of the AoI model (e.g., [3,4]), the other part explored scheduling policies to minimize AoI [5–13].

First, majority of them focused on AoI analysis and optimization under different network setting [5]. Subsequently, authors extended the models to simulate scheduling policies for multiple remote devices in different network structures. A broadcast network is considered in [6,7,10], and authors proposed three low-complexity scheduling policies to minimizing the expected weighted sum AoI of broadcast network in [7]. Some other works have begun to consider the impact of channel quality on scheduling policies. Authors in [8] proposed two scheduling policies on the scenario where the channel states are unknown, and the scheduling results are close to the optimal. Then, in [11–13] authors proposed a multi-source system, where the channel conditions were changing in real-time.

Although many scheduling policies have been proposed to optimize the average AoI in the special network scenarios they are set up for, scheduling policies primarily emphasize enhancing information freshness from the receiver's perspective. There is a lack of studies which consider the system throughput and the AoI together. In order to minimize the average weighted AoI while maximizing timely throughput, this paper proposes two scheduling policies for heterogeneous IoT networks with dynamical channel conditions. Then the proposed policies are verified by experiment simulation and the results demonstrate the validation of the policies.

The rest of this paper is organized as follows. In the second section, the system model is described, and the optimization objective of this paper is proposed. In the third part, the priority-based scheduling policies are proposed. In the fourth section, the experimental results are given and related discussions are carried out, with the conclusion in the last part.

2   System Model

The system model presented in this paper is based on [12], which proposed a 5G-based IoT network comprising a base station (BS) and N source nodes (SNs). The SNs collect the time-sensitive information, which is subsequently transmitted to the BS through shared channels, as show in Fig. 1(a).

In the depicted IoT network communication technology illustrated in Fig. 1(b), the transmission resources are meticulously gridded in the time-frequency domain, forming B resource blocks (RBs) in a slot. A channel is established by utilizing one or more RBs to cater to the requirements of a specific SN. With consideration for the dynamic variations in the channel conditions, the primary objective of our proposed algorithms is to effectively allocate RBs and determine the appropriate modulation and coding scheme (MCS) m for each SN.

To ensure the transmission of samples at a higher rate while maintaining an adequate number of RBs, as show in Eq. 1, we utilize $h_i(t)$ to denote the maximum m that SN i can use at slot t. If SN i selects $m \leq h_i(t)$ at slot t, the corresponding data transmission rate $u_i^m(t)$ is r_m; otherwise, $u_i^m(t)$ is 0.

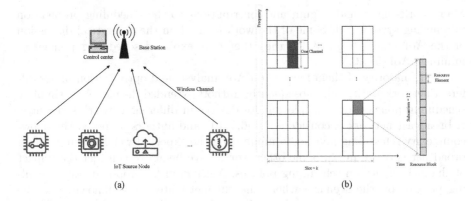

Fig. 1. System Model and Time-Frequency Structure

$$u_i^m(t) = \begin{cases} r_m, & if\ m \le h_i(t) \\ 0, & other \end{cases}.$$

(1)

We denote the set of RBs as $B_i(t)$, which is allocated to SN i at slot t, and the number of elements in $B_i(t)$ is $x_i(t)$. Therefore, we use $D_i(t)$ to represent the amount of data, as show in 2, that the SN i can transmit with all allocated RBs in the slot t.

$$D_i(t) = x_i(t) \cdot u_i^m(t).$$

(2)

2.1 AoI and Throughput Model

In this system, each different SN i periodically generates samples at a pried of T_i. The size of the sample data is represented by L_i. We denote $A_i^s(t)$ and $A_i^B(t)$ as the AoI of the latest sample generated by SN i at the SN and the BS, respectively. Due to the limitation of communication resources, a certain delay occurs in the reception of samples at the BS, leading to disparities between $A_i^s(t)$ and $A_i^B(t)$ within the slot t.

Therefore, we express the average AoI of source node i as:

$$\overline{A}_i^B = \lim_{T \to \infty} \frac{1}{T} \sum_{t-i}^{T} A_i^B(t).$$

(3)

In the case of having N SNs, the BS assigns a weight ω_i to each SN based on the time sensitivity of their respective information. Subsequently, the BS computes the average weighted AoI according to the following equation:

$$\overline{A} = \frac{1}{N} \sum_{i=1}^{N} \omega_i \cdot \overline{A}_i^B.$$

(4)

For a single SN, the throughput $Th_i(t)$ can be classified into the following three cases: 1) **a RB is allocated to SN i in slot t.** We consider that whether it can completely transmit the sample data before the end of slot t. If it successes, $Th_i(t)$ can be directly calculated by L_i. Otherwise, it is calculated by $D_i(t)$. 2) **SN i has incomplete sample transmission in slot $t-1$.** Its throughput is represented as $L_i - D_i(t-1)$. 3) **RBs can not be allocated to SN i in slot t.** So its throughput is 0. Therefore, the throughput of SN i is formulated as Eq. 5 in slot t.

$$Th_i(t) = \begin{cases} min\{L_i, D_i(t)\}, & i \quad complete \; transmission \; in \; slot \; t-1 \\ L_i - D_i(t-1), & i \quad incomplete \; transmission \; in \; slot \; t-1 \\ 0, & other \end{cases}.$$

(5)

Then, the average throughput of the system within a given time period T is denoted as

$$Th = \frac{1}{T} \sum_{t=1}^{T} \sum_{i=1}^{N} Th_i(t).$$

(6)

2.2   Problem Definition

Our goal is to develop an appropriate scheduling policy that effectively addresses the optimization of both system throughput and AoI in the context of dynamically changing channel conditions. To accomplish this, we introduce the primary challenge in our work by precisely defining AoI and throughput:

$$OPT \quad min \frac{1}{N} \sum_{i-1}^{N} \omega_i \cdot \overline{A}_i^B$$

$$max \frac{1}{T} \sum_{t=1}^{T} \sum_{i=1}^{N} Th_i(t)$$

(7)

$$s.t. \quad 0 < A_i^s(t) \leq T_i \tag{8a}$$

$$A_i^s(t) \leq A_i^B(t) \tag{8b}$$

$$B_i(t) \cap B_{(i-1)}(t) = \varnothing \tag{8c}$$

where the optimization problem is subject to three constraints that impose certain limitations: 1) constraint 8a governs the AoI of the sample at the SNs, mandating it to be greater than 0 or less than the SN's sampling interval T_i. 2) constraint 8b states that, for a given SN i, the AoI of the most recent sample at the SN must not exceed the AoI of the latest sample at the BS. 3) constraint 8c stipulates that a RB can only be allocated to a single SN within one slot.

3　Scheduling Policy

In this section, we propose two enhancements of the current Kronos scheduling policy aimed at increasing Th of the system. Firstly, a more effective weight function is introduced. Secondly, a scheduling policy is proposed to show improved performance when combining with dynamic threshold classification. These policies can improve the performance of communication in IoT system, according to reduce $\overline{A}$ and increase Th.

From the perspective of AoI optimization, it is evident that minimizing the AoI of each SN is crucial. Since the BS can only update the AoI once receiving the complete samples, minimizing the number of partial transmission samples can have a significant impact on the overall AoI of the system. According to [5], it has demonstrated that the Max-Weighted policy outperforms other methods. Therefore, we propose the utilization of the Max-Weighted policy to determine the priority of SN scheduling, aiming to achieve effective AoI reduction.

3.1　Priority-Based Scheduling Policy Considering AoI and Throughput, PSP-AT

In order to reduce the average weighted AoI and increase the average system throughput, we introduce the PSP-AT algorithm, which serves as a proposed greedy policy that leverages a priority function to minimize the average weighted AoI while maximizing the maximum average throughput. Our algorithm 1 is designed to accommodate real-time channel variations effectively.

Within a slot, our PSP-AT entails the following crucial steps:

Step one: Remove three types of SNs. 1) SN i has no new sample arriving at time t while $A_i^B(t) = A_i^s(t)$. 2) The AoI in slot t for SN i is less than its sampling period, indicated by $A_i^s(t) < T_i$. 3) SN i has RBs already allocated during previous iterations in slot t.

Step two: Determining whether there is a SN for partial transmission in the previous slot $t-1$. $RD_i(t-1)$ denotes the size of SN i's untransmitted data in the slot $t-1$. If $RD_i(t-1) > 0$, the RBs are allocated to SN i firstly.

Step three: The appropriate MCS m is selected for each SN based on the real-time channel conditions, and their corresponding priority functions are derived based on the following specific factors:

Step three-a: As the first impacting factor, we think about the SN's weight ω_i.

Step three-b: Secondly, we takes into account the difference in the freshness of sample as seen from the BS and the SNs $A_i^B(t) - A_i^s(t)$.

Step three-c: In the slot t, we utilize $p_i^m(t)$, $n_i^m(t)$ to represent the number of RBs that satisfy the channel requirements and the number of selected RBs, respectively.

Step three-d: Finally, considering the amount of data contained in each sample of the SN as the last measurement factor, we define L_i, L_{max} to denote the amount of data generated by samples of various SNs and generated by the largest sample among various SNs respectively.

Algorithm 1. Priority-based Scheduling Policy considering AoI and Through-put

---

Input: $C_{N \times B}$, ω_i, $A_i^s(t)$, $A_i^B(t)$, L_i, $RD_i(t-1)$, l_{max}
Output: $A_i^s(t)$, $A_i^B(t)$, $RD_i(t-1)$
1: **initialize:** RBs set $RB(t)$, RBs allocation set $dRB(t)$, RBs available Allocation set $aRB(t)$, temporary record set r_t
2: **while** $RB_i(t).size() > 0$ **do**
3:     Skip the SN i that have been assigned in the previous iteration or have not been updated
4:     **for** remaining SNs **do**
5:         **if** $RD_i(t) > 0$ **then**
6:             Select appropriate MCS m and allocate RBs $dRB_i(t)$
7:             $dRB(t) \Leftarrow dRB(t) \bigcup dRB_i(t)$
8:             $aRB(t) \Leftarrow RB(t) - dRB(t)$
9:             *Break*
10:         **end if**
11:         Select appropriate MCS m
12:         Calculate $n_i^m(t)$, $P_i^m(t)$ and $W_i(t)$
13:         allocate RBs $dRB_i(t)$
14:         append to r_t
15:     **end for**
16:     Select SN i that $W_i(t)$ is the largest in r_t
17:     $dRB(t) \Leftarrow dRB(t) \bigcup dRB_i(t)$
18:     $aRB(t) \Leftarrow RB(t) - dRB(t)$
19: **end while**
20: Update $A_i^s(t)$, $A_i^B(t)$, $RD_i(t-1)$

Therefore, the priority function can be formulated as follows:

$$W_i(t) = \omega_i \cdot \left(A_i^B(t) - A_i^s(t) \right) \cdot \left(1 - \frac{n_i^m(t)}{p_i^m(t)} \right) \cdot \frac{L_i}{l_{max}}. \qquad (9)$$

Among all the updated SNs, we select the SN with the highest value of $W_i(t)$ and allocate a corresponding number of RBs, denoted as $n_i^m(t)$. In the event that multiple SNs possess the same value of $W_i(t)$ within a slot, we prioritize the assignment of RBs to the SN with the largest value of L_i/l_{max}. This selection criterion aims to maximize the average throughput. Subsequently, the RB allocation set $dRB_i(t)$ and the available RBs set $aRB(t)$ are updated accordingly.

Step four: In the scenario that there are no available RBs in the set $aRB(t)$ or all the SNs requiring transmission in slot t have completed their transmissions, we update the information of the $SN(A_i^B(t), A_i^s(t), RD_i(t-1))$ before entering the slot $t+1$.

Complexity Assessments: We now discuss the complexity of PSP-AT. The primary time-consuming tasks involve RB allocation and the selection of the corresponding MCS m. The time complexity for RB allocation and MCS m selection for partial transmission nodes is given by $O(|B| \times |M|)$. Subsequently, the calculation of $W_i(t)$ for each SN, the determination of RB allocation and MCS m selection exhibit a time complexity of $O(|N| \times |B| \times |M|)$. In a slot, our algorithm iteratively considers N SNs, resulting in a time complexity of $O(|N|^2 \times |B| \times |M|)$. Hence, the overall time complexity of PSP-AT for each slot is expressed as $O(|N|^2 \times |B| \times |M|)$.

3.2 Dynamic Classification-Based Priority Scheduling Policy, DCP-AT

In order to further improve the optimization efficiency of the AoI, we introduce the concept of Dynamic classification based on the aforementioned algorithm. Recognizing that AoI tends to increase over time, the objective is to reduce the average weighted AoI within each slot. Therefore, our Algorithm 2, namely DCP-AT, classifies SNs solely based on their AoI levels.

Algorithm 2. Dynamic Classification-based Priority Scheduling Policy

---

Input: $C_{N \times B}$, ω_i, $A_i^s(t)$, $A_i^B(t)$, L_i, $RD_i(t-1)$, l_{max}, $\overline{A}$
Output: $A_i^s(t)$, $A_i^B(t)$, $RD_i(t-1)$, $\overline{A}$
1: initialize: RBs set $RB(t) = \mathbf{B}$, RBs allocation set $dRB(t)$, RBs available Allocation set $aRB(t)$, temporary record set r_t
2: **for** SN **do**
3:     **if** $RD_i(t) > 0$ **then**
4:         append SN i to classification I
5:     **else if** $A_i^B(t) + 1 \geq \overline{A}$ **then**
6:         append SN i to classification II
7:     **else**
8:         append SN i to classification III
9:     **end if**
10: **end for**
11: **for** I, II, III **do**
12:     Allocate RBs to SN in the classification according to Algorithm 1
13: **end for**
14: Update $A_i^s(t)$, $A_i^B(t)$, $RD_i(t-1)$, $\overline{A}$

Our algorithm DCP-AT consists of three main steps: SN classification, RB allocation and SN Information update.

SN Classification: We define a threshold $v(t)$, which is used to categorize SNs at the beginning of each slot. There are three categories: 1) the samples of SNs were partially transmitted in the slot $t-1$. 2) the AoI of SNs at the BS in the slot $t+1$ is greater than or equal to $v(t)$, denoted as $A_i^B(t) + 1 \geq v(t)$. 3) the AoI of SNs at the BS in the slot $t+1$ is less than $v(t)$, represented by $A_i^B(t) + 1 \leq v(t)$.

RB Allocation: The BS assigns the highest priority to the first category of SNs, which comprises only one SN. Once the RB allocation for this category is completed, the remaining RBs are allocated to the second and third categories sequentially. However, as the second and third categories may consist of multiple SNs, the DCP-AT employs the priority function $W_i(t)$ as the criterion for RB allocation.

SN Information Update: In RB allocation, RBs are allocated to each SN according to the determined RB allocation scheme. Then, the updates are made to the changes generated by the SNs, including the updates of $A_i^B(t)$, $A_i^s(t)$ and $RD_i(t)$.

Complexity Assessments: The time complexity of DCP-AT is similar to PSP-AT. On the basis of PSP-AT, the time overhead the SN classification is increasing, denoted as $O(|N|)$. Therefore, in each slot, the time complexity of DCP-AT is
$$O(|N|)+O(|B|*|M|)+O(|N|*|B|*|M|)+O(|N|^2*|B|*|M|) = O(|N|^2*|B|*|M|).$$

4   Experiment and Result

In this section, we present the experimental setup and results. In the first part, we describe the experimental equipment and parameter settings. In the second part, we compare the performance of PSP-AT and DCP-AT with Kronos using the same source node configurations, focusing on $\overline{A}$ and Th.

4.1   Experiment Setup and Parameter Settings

We set the sample size uniformly, with specific values shown in Table 1, and classify the SNs into 10 types. The MCS for each SN is evenly distributed within the range of $M = 0, 1, 2, ..., 25$, and the corresponding modulation and coding rates can be calculated based on 3GPP standards.

Table 1. Sampling Parameters For Different Types of Source Nodes

SN Type	ω_i	L_i (bits)	T_i
1	1	5300	6
2	6	5900	6
3	3	8400	1
4	9	7300	6
5	4	6800	3
6	7	6500	1
7	8	8300	5
8	2	9700	5
9	5	6100	2
10	10	5100	4

The experiment assumes an uplink transmission consisting of 100 RBs, denoted as $B = 100$. The experiment is designed to run for 500 slots, and $\overline{A}$

and Th are calculated at the end of the experiment. During the initialization phase, each SN is assigned a random value of AoI within the range of 0 to $2T_i$.

Environment: This experiment is run on a PC, that the CPU of the PC is AMD Ryzen 9 5900HS with Radeon Graphics, 3.30 GHz; the memory is 16.0 GB; the window 10 64-bit operating system. The experimental codes are written by Matlab 2020a.

4.2 Result

4.2.1 PSP-AT

This section, we compare the PSP-AT with the Kronos under different numbers of SNs. Due to the constant channel capacity, the results of the two scheduling policies may differ. Hence, we consider scenarios with different levels of channel congestion by setting the number of SNs to 100, 120, and 150. The evolution of $\overline{A}$ and Th over time is illustrated in Fig. 2.

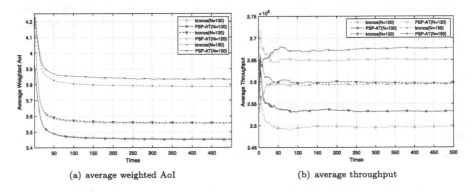

(a) average weighted AoI   (b) average throughput

Fig. 2. The evolution of average weighted AoI and average throughput

Figure 2(a) illustrates that $\overline{A}$ is decreasing with time and tends to stabilize around 50 slots. We also can observe that when the number of RBs is fixed, the lower the number of SNs, the lower their $\overline{A}$ is. When the number of SNs is 100 or 120, both the PSP-AT and Kronos exhibit similar performance in the early slots. However, after 30 slots, the PSP-AT outperforms Kronos slightly. This is due to both policies can generally satisfy the transmission of samples in scenarios with relatively abundant channels. When the number of SNs is 150, Kronos performs better than PSP-AT. The main reason is that in highly congested channels, some samples lose their scheduling qualifications since low priority. Considering the priority factors, PSP-AT gives priority to samples with a large amount of data, it requires more RBs for transmission under the same channel conditions. Therefore, in terms of $\overline{A}$, the performance of the Kronos is superior in this case.

Regarding Th, as show in Fig. 2(a), in all three scenarios($N = 100$, $N = 120$, and $N = 150$), PSP-AT outperforms Kronos. When the channel becomes more congested ($N = 120$ changes to $N = 150$), the performance of Th of the Kronos is hardly improved while PSP-AT showing an improvement in Th.

4.2.2   DCP-AT

In this section, we evaluate the performance of the DCP-AT and the Kronos by comparing their results across different numbers of SNs. To gain a deeper understanding of the impact of channel congestion on these two algorithms, we specifically set the number of SNs to large values, respectively $N = 100$, $N = 150$, and $N = 200$.

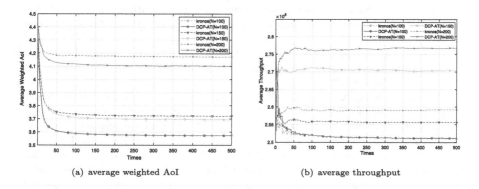

(a) average weighted AoI   (b) average throughput

Fig. 3. The evolution of average weighted AoI and average throughput

Figure 3 illustrates the temporal evolution of $\overline{A}$ and Th for three different scenarios. According to the result, the DCP-AT is superior to the Kronos. In the case of an idle channel with $N = 100$, there is minimal disparity in the effects observed in terms of both $\overline{A}$ and Th. This is due to the ample availability of channel resources at time t, which enables the provision of all the required samples. However, comparing the scenarios with $N = 150$ and $N = 200$, it's evident that our DCP-AT outperforms the Kronos significantly.

When comparing channel congestion at $N = 200$ and $N = 150$, it is obvious that $\overline{A}$ of two algorithms increases rapidly due to insufficient RBs. The value of Th obtained by the Kronos at $N = 150$ is smaller than that at $N = 200$, indicating that in the case of channel congestion, the channel conditions is a key factor affecting Th.

5   Conclusion

In this paper, we propose two priority scheduling policies that take into account both AoI and throughput considerations for different channel conditions. Both of them can allocate RBs and select MCS for each SN under the varying channel conditions in real-time. The analysis of experimental results shows that in the case of limited channel capacity, the policies proposed in this paper have better performance in terms of average weighted AoI and average throughput.

References

1. Kaul, S., Gruteser, M., Rai, V., Kenney, J.: Minimizing age of information in vehicular networks. In: 2011 8th Annual IEEE Communications Society Conference on Sensor, Mesh and Ad Hoc Communications and Networks, pp. 350–358. IEEE (2011)
2. Yates, R.D., Sun, Y., Brown, D.R., Kaul, S.K., Modiano, E., Ulukus, S.: Age of information: an introduction and survey. IEEE J. Sel. Areas Commun. **39**(5), 1183–1210 (2021)
3. Kaul, S., Yates, R., Gruteser, M.: Real-time status: How often should one update? In: 2012 Proceedings IEEE INFOCOM, pp. 2731–2735 (2012)
4. Yates, R.D., Kaul, S.: Real-time status updating: multiple sources. In: 2012 IEEE International Symposium on Information Theory Proceedings, pp. 2666–2670 (2012)
5. Jiang, Z., Krishnamachari, B., Zheng, X., Zhou, S., Niu, Z.: Decentralized status update for age-of-information optimization in wireless multiaccess channels. In: Isit, pp. 2276–2280 (2018)
6. Wang, C., Cheng, X., Li, J., He, Y., Xiao, K.: A survey: applications of blockchain in the internet of vehicles. EURASIP J. Wirel. Commun. Netw. **2021**, 1–16 (2021)
7. Talak, R., Karaman, S., Modiano, E.: Optimizing information freshness in wireless networks under general interference constraints. In: Proceedings of the Eighteenth ACM International Symposium on Mobile Ad Cast Networking and Computing, Mobihoc 2018, pp. 61–70. Association for Computing Machinery, New York (2018)
8. Talak, R., Kadota, I., Karaman, S., Modiano, E.: Scheduling policies for age minimization in wireless networks with unknown channel state. In: 2018 IEEE International Symposium on Information Theory (ISIT), pp. 2564–2568 (2018)
9. Wang, C., Wang, S., Cheng, X., He, Y., Xiao, K., Fan, S.: A privacy and efficiency-oriented data sharing mechanism for IoTs. IEEE Trans. Big Data **9**(1), 174–185 (2022)
10. Ren, Q., Chan, T.-T., Pan, H., Ho, K.-H., Du, Z.: Information freshness and energy harvesting tradeoff in network-coded broadcasting. IEEE Wirel. Commun. Lett. **11**(10), 2061–2065 (2022)
11. Sombabu, B., Moharir, S.: Age-of-information aware scheduling for heterogeneous sources. In: Proceedings of the 24th Annual International Conference on Mobile Computing and Networking, MobiCom 2018, pp. 696–698. Association for Computing Machinery, New York (2018)
12. Li, C., et al.: Minimizing Aoi in a 5g-based IoT network under varying channel conditions. IEEE Internet Things J. **8**(19), 14543–14558 (2021)
13. Ye, H., Hao, W., Huang, F.: Link resource allocation strategy based on age of information and sample extrusion awareness in dynamic channels. IEEE Access **9**, 88048–88059 (2021)

Underwater Target Detection Based on Dual Inversion Dehazing and Multi-Scale Feature Fusion Network

Lian-suo Wei[1][✉], Long-yu Ma[2], and Shen-hao Huang[2]

[1] School of Information Engineering, Suqian University, Suqian 223800, Jiangsu, China
weiliansuo@squ.edu.cn
[2] College of Computer and Control Engineering, Qiqihar University, Qiqihar 161006, Heilongjiang, China

Abstract. In response to the insufficient small-scale feature extraction capabilities of traditional SSD object detection algorithms, which lead to missed detections and false alarms in the detection of small underwater targets, this paper proposes a new underwater object detection algorithm. The algorithm first uses a Dual Reverse Dehazing (DRDM) module for image enhancement. Then, on the basis of the backbone network of the SSD algorithm, a channel attention mechanism and feature extraction convolution are introduced to construct a SE-Feature-Enhancement Module (SFEM) to integrate high-resolution shallow feature maps and deep feature maps with high semantic information. This fusion method preserves the context information of the feature maps, learns the necessary features, and suppresses redundant information, thereby improving the network's learning ability. The experimental results show that the proposed algorithm achieves a detection accuracy of 94.62% on the Wilder_fish_new dataset. Compared with the current commonly used SSD (VGG) and SSD (Mobilenetv2) algorithms, the proposed algorithm improves the accuracy by 2.7 and 3.13 percentage points, respectively.

Keywords: Underwater object detection · dehazing algorithm · SSD · feature enhancement

1 Introduction

In recent years, with the continuous development of ocean exploration, real-time and accurate detection of underwater targets has become increasingly important and has been applied in a wide range of fields. Because water absorbs different wavelengths of light to different extents, with red light having the longest wavelength and blue and green light relatively shorter wavelengths, the attenuation of red light is relatively fast, while the attenuation of blue and green light is relatively slow, resulting in underwater images having a blue-green tint.

At the same time, the detection information of small underwater targets accounts for a low proportion and can be lost after multiple convolutions, which not only causes color

L. Wang et al. (Eds.): CWSN 2023, CCIS 1994, pp. 99–112, 2024.
https://doi.org/10.1007/978-981-97-1010-2_8

distortion and contrast reduction in underwater images but also increases the difficulty of underwater target detection [1–10]. Therefore, improving underwater target detection's accuracy, robustness, and efficiency has been a research hotspot in this field.

In 2021, [11] Yeh et al. proposed a lightweight deep neural network for joint learning of underwater target detection and color transformation. To address the issue of color distortion in underwater images and save computational resources, RGB color images were converted to grayscale, which improved the situation under certain conditions. However, in more complex and diverse underwater environments such as chaotic waters, it may affect the performance of target detection. In the same year, [12] Zhao et al. proposed an underwater target detection algorithm based on attention mechanisms and used cascaded attention mechanisms to obtain multi-scale contextual features to improve detection accuracy. However, the color attenuation and insufficient illumination in underwater optical images still affect the network's detection ability. In 2022, [13] Li et al. proposed an underwater target detection algorithm based on an improved SSD convolutional block attention. They replaced the VGG16 backbone network of the original SSD algorithm with ResNeXt-50 to enhance feature extraction capabilities by increasing network depth. However, as the network depth increases, more detection information for small targets is lost. In the same year, [14] Shi et al. proposed an underwater target detection algorithm that combined data augmentation and an improved YOLOv4 algorithm. They used convolutional block attention mechanisms to improve the model's feature extraction ability and the PredMix algorithm to simulate underwater biological overlap, occlusion, and other situations. This enhances the robustness of the network model. However, they did not consider the low proportion of small targets in underwater target detection, which makes them difficult to detect.

Deep learning technology has significantly improved the accuracy of underwater image target classification and detection through the use of Convolutional Neural Networks (CNNs). In 2014, Girshick et al. proposed the R-CNN (Region-Convolutional Neural Networks) object detection algorithm, which has led to the widespread use of deep learning in object detection. Currently, there are two types of object detection algorithms, two-step and one-step detection. Two-step detection separates object localization and classification into separate steps, while one-step detection combines both steps into a single process. Common one-step detection algorithms include YOLO [15] and SSD [16]. YOLO, proposed by Redmon et al., is a representative algorithm that performs poorly in detecting small objects. Liu et al. then proposed the SSD (Single Shot Multi-Box Detector) object detection algorithm, which combines YOLO's regression concept with the anchor box concept of Faster-R-CNN [17]. The SSD algorithm uses VGG16 as the backbone neural network but also improves it by replacing VGG's fully connected layers with convolutional layers, significantly reducing training parameters. The SSD algorithm extracts six effective feature layers from VGG16 and performs object localization and classification on these six feature maps. However, the algorithm still struggles with detecting small objects.

This article combines image enhancement algorithms and object detection algorithms. Before using deep learning object detection networks, the article uses a dual-reverse dehazing algorithm for image preprocessing. In addition, the article proposes a multiscale feature fusion deep learning object detection network based on the SSD object detection network and the dual-reverse dehazing algorithm. This network enhances and fuses the feature maps output from different feature layers in VGG16 for object detection. Based on these enhancements, deep networks can obtain contour features and other information that shallow networks cannot acquire, thereby improving detection accuracy.

The rest of the article is as follows. Section 2 presents the multiscale feature fusion deep learning object detection network. In Sect. 3, simulation experimental results are presented. Finally, Sect. 4 provides the conclusion.

2 Multiscale Feature Fusion Deep Learning Object Detection Network

This article proposes a deep-learning object detection network, the structure of which is shown in Fig. 1. The input image is first subjected to image enhancement through a dual dehazing and inversion module and then passed through a convolutional layer for feature extraction. Next, a feature map of size 38×38 is extracted and the channel weights are adjusted through channel attention mechanisms. Five rounds of feature extraction are performed using the feature extraction module. The feature map processed by the channel attention mechanism is concatenated with the extracted feature map to obtain the processed feature map, which is then used as the input for the next round of feature extraction. The same processing method is then used for size 19×19 and 10×10 feature maps. Finally, the processed feature maps of size 38×38, 19×19, 10×10, 5×5, and 1×1 are sent to the classification and detection module for classification regression and localization regress.

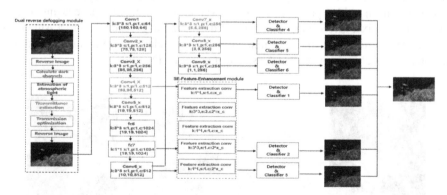

Fig. 1. Network structure of multi-scale feature fusion target detection network.

The purpose of this article is to improve the performance of the SSD network and to incorporate a dual dehazing and inversion algorithm for more accurate object detection. Before object detection, the image is preprocessed using the dual dehazing and inversion algorithm to reduce image haze. Through multiple experiments of network layer fusion, it was found that fusing the first three layers of the network and performing detection on each feature layer improved the accuracy of small object detection. Therefore, the shallow convolutional layers in the SSD object detection algorithm were enhanced with feature fusion with the deep convolutional layers to improve feature extraction capabilities. In the experiment, the article borrowed the idea of a feature pyramid network (FPN) [18] and fused conv4_3 with fc7 and conv6_2 layers to propose a multiscale feature fusion deep learning object detection algorithm.

2.1 Dual Inverted Dehazing Module (DRDM)

After collecting the dataset, we found that underwater images often suffer from problems such as insufficient light sources or overexposure. We used methods such as histogram equalization to improve the quality of the images, but the results were not satisfactory. Issues such as whitened edges and insufficient color restoration not only existed but also had a negative impact on the subsequent object detection results. To solve these problems, we conducted research and found that the dehazing algorithm proposed by Dr. Kaiming He [19] can be widely applied to dark environments and other low-light environments. This method can make dark images clearer. Considering that underwater images have some similarities with low-light images in terms of pixels, we decided to improve the dehazing algorithm and apply it to the dataset collected in this article to improve the problem of low light in underwater images.

Underwater images are RGB three-channel color images. After observation and research, we used the dehazing algorithm on underwater images by first performing a pixel inversion on the RGB three channels, and then performing another inversion on the dehazed image, resulting in a relatively clear and color-restored image. First, we perform pixel inversion on the original underwater image of the three channels of RGB. An example of inverting an image is shown in Group A in Fig. 2. Using the dark channel prior dehazing algorithm proposed by Dr. He Kaiming, we can obtain a dehazing image. Then, another pixel inversion is applied to the dehazing image, and after processing with the double inverted dehazing algorithm, an underwater clear image optimized in terms of color and brightness is produced, as shown in Group D in Fig. 2.

a. Original image   b. Inverted image   c. Dehaze image   d. Double inverted dehazing image

Fig. 2. Image preprocessing using dual inverted dehazing module

In theory, the expression formula for any input hazy image can be represented as:

$$I(x) = J(x)t(x) + A(1 - t(x)) \tag{1}$$

In the formula, represents the image to be processed (hazy image), represents the real image (dehazed image) that we want to obtain, represents the transmission rate, and denotes the global atmospheric light value. After derivation, the expression formula for the dehazed image can be obtained:

$$J(x) = \frac{I(x) - A}{\max(t(x), t0)} + A \tag{2}$$

Compared with the original pictures group A and the image group in D after the dual inversion and dehazing algorithm, it can be observed that after the above operations, the images after the dual inversion and dehazing algorithm have improved in color and brightness, enabling more accurate detection of targets during object detection.

After digitizing the pixel values of the original image and the image enhanced by the double inversion deghazing algorithm, and the total number of pixels corresponding to the corresponding pixel values, the plot is carried out as follows:

a. Original Image

b. Image enhanced by dual inversion dehazing algorithm

c. Pixel values of the original image and the number of corresponding pixel points

d. Pixel values and the number of corresponding pixel points for each pixel value in the dual inversion dehazing image

Fig. 3. Comparison between original and enhanced images

In the above figure, the pixel distribution of the original image in Group C of Fig. 3 is around 0–200. Meanwhile, the number of pixels with a 0-pixel value in the image is significantly higher, while the distribution of other pixel values is more scattered and uneven. After the dual inversion dehazing module, the distribution of pixel values in the image becomes more uniform. The number of pixels at 0-pixel value is significantly lower than the number of pixels at 0-pixel value in the original image. This indicates that the image enhanced by the dual inversion dehazing module has improved in both color and brightness, which helps to improve the accuracy of underwater object detection.

The above dual inversion dehazing algorithm can be used to process underwater images, which helps to restore the pixel values of underwater targets and improve the accuracy of underwater target detection. It is worth noting that the image generated by the proposed dual inversion dehazing algorithm is suitable for anchor box-based deep learning network object detectors. The detector relies on anchor boxes to describe the position and category of the target. The generated image can effectively distinguish the target and background at the pixel level. Therefore, based on the experimental results of this article, it can be concluded that the proposed image enhancement method indeed helps to improve the final detection results.

2.2 Feature Enhancement Module (SFEM)

Considering the small size of small targets, the relatively small number of pixels, and the poor anti-interference ability, multiple convolutions and pooling will result in the loss of a large amount of feature information, leading to a decrease in the accuracy of small target detection. To solve this problem, we were inspired by the feature pyramid network and the analysis of the VGG network structure and designed a feature enhancement module. At the same time, we embed the SE attention mechanism module into the network to improve its anti-interference ability and accuracy in detecting small targets. We name this module Feature Enhancement Module (SFEM). The network structure diagram of the feature enhancement module is shown in Fig. 4.

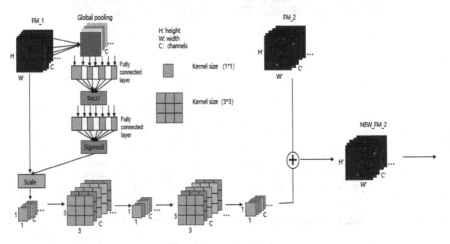

Fig. 4. SFEM Module

The SFEM module is a top-down structure that consists of three parts. Firstly, it adds an SE attention mechanism module to the upper convolutional network layer, in order to clearly express the interdependence between channels and adaptively adjust the feature response of channels. The SE attention mechanism module assigns weights to each channel, allowing multiple channels to have an impact on the results. These weights represent the influence of each channel on feature extraction. When the weight is greater, the value of the channel feature map will be smaller, and the impact on the final output will also be smaller. This means that when extracting image features, some feature maps output by convolutional layers have a significant impact on the final result, while others have a small impact on the final result. Therefore, applying the weights obtained from the channel itself to these feature maps can adaptively give channel weights based on the features extracted from the convolutional layer, allowing feature maps that have a greater impact on the final result to have a greater impact.

Secondly, after the SE attention mechanism module further strengthens the feature map processed by the previous layer of convolutional network, the convolution kernel of the previous layer is first carried out with a convolution kernel of 1*1, and the number of channels is adjusted, and then the convolution kernel is 3*3 and the convolution with a step size of 2 is carried out, the width and height of the feature map are adjusted, and the calculation amount is simplified, and the feature extraction is further entered into the convolutional layer with the next convolution kernel of 1*1 and the convolutional layer with a convolution kernel of 3*3 for enhanced feature extraction. Finally, the convolutional layer with a convolution kernel of 1*1 is adjusted to adjust the number of channels. By downsampling of convolution operations, deep features can have larger receptive fields, resulting in better capture of important features in the image. Secondly, compared with the weighting and operation of the pooling layer, the point-by-point operation of the 1*1 convolution operation is more conducive to the optimization solution. Therefore, the pooling layer after the convolutional layer with the first convolution kernel of 1*1 and the convolutional layer with a convolution kernel of 3*3 in the original sense is cancelled and replaced with a convolutional layer with a convolution kernel of 1*1, thereby reducing the risk of effective information being lost, improving information fusion, and strengthening feature extraction.

Finally, by using the add method, the convolutional network layer that has been enhanced for feature extraction is concatenated with the next layer's feature extraction convolutional network layer, and the channel is adjusted to the corresponding size. Compared to the concat method, the add method overlays the information extracted multiple times, which highlights the proportion of correct classification and is beneficial for the final target classification, achieving high activation of correct classification.

3 Simulation Experiment Results

3.1 Wilder_ Fish_ New Dataset and Environment

This article selects 1914 images of underwater fish schools from the wilder fish dataset and annotates them using labelimg dataset annotation software. Finally, a VOC format dataset is generated for recognition. Divide the dataset into training and testing sets through a dataset partitioning program. Among them, 1548 underwater images were input into the network as training sets for training, and the remaining 366 were used for testing the dataset.

The experimental platform configuration for this article is: Windows 11 operating system, AMD Ryzen 7 5800H with Radeon Graphics 3.20 GHz processor. The graphics card model is NVIDIA GeForce RTX 3060, using the TensorFlow framework.

3.2 Comparison of Output Feature Maps

The left column in Group A in Fig. 5 and Group B in Fig. 5 shows the feature maps output by the original SSD, while the right column shows the feature maps output by the multi-scale feature fusion target detection network after feature enhancement and the introduction of attention mechanism. From the figure on the left, we draw a conclusion: the deeper the network, the finer the information obtained from the output feature map, but the Semantic information is also more abundant, limited to specific areas or adjacent areas. From the graph on the right, we can see that combining the feature maps output by shallow networks with the feature enhancement and attention mechanisms of deep networks can obtain more detailed information, making the network more fine-grained, and also improving the ability of small object detection, as it can capture information about contours and other information in shallow networks.

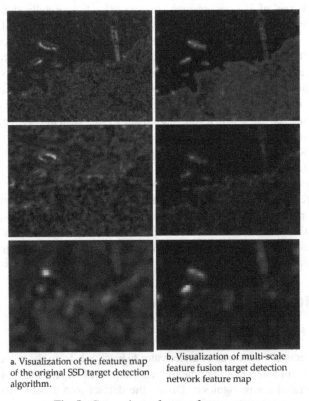

a. Visualization of the feature map of the original SSD target detection algorithm.

b. Visualization of multi-scale feature fusion target detection network feature map

Fig. 5. Comparison of output feature maps

3.3 Comparison of Loss Function

The loss function is an algorithm to measure the consistency between network model and data. The loss function describes the difference between the measured true value and the predicted value. The higher the value, the more the prediction deviates from the true value. On the contrary, the lower the value, the closer the predicted value is to the true value. In this paper, the multi-scale feature fusion target detection network uses the loss calculation function of the SSD network to compare with the original SSD target detection algorithm. The overall loss function of the SSD target detection network is:

$$L(x, c, l, g) = \frac{1}{N}\left(L_{conf}(x, c) + \alpha L_{loc}(x, l, g)\right) \tag{3}$$

In the equation, c is the predicted value of category confidence, l is the predicted value of the bounding box corresponding to the prior box, and g is the positional parameter of the real box. The total loss function is the weighted sum of classification and regression. α represents the weight of both, and N represents the number of matches to the initial box.

The SSD location loss function (using Smooth l1 loss) is:

$$L_{lco}(x, l, g) = \sum_{i \in Pos}^{N} \sum_{m \in \{cx,cy,w,h\}} x_{ij}^{k} smooth_{L1}(l_i^m - \hat{g}_j^m) \tag{4}$$

where x_{ij}^k represents whether the i -th predicted box matches the j-th true box for category k, with matching values of 0, 1. l_i^m represents a prediction box and $\hat{g}_j^m$ represents a real box.

$$smooth_{L1}(x) = \begin{cases} 0.5x^2 & \text{if } |x| < 1 \\ |x| - 0.5 & \text{otherwise} \end{cases} \tag{5}$$

When $x_{ij}^k = 1$, it indicates that the i-th prior box matches the j-th real box, and the category of the real box is k.

The SSD classification loss function (softmax loss) is:

$$L_{conf}(x, c) = -\sum_{i \in Pos}^{N} x_{ij}^P \log(\hat{c}_l^P) - \sum_{i \in Neg}^{K} \log(c_l^o) \tag{6}$$

$$\text{where } \hat{c}_i^P = \frac{\exp(c_i^P)}{\sum_P \exp(c_i^P)} \tag{7}$$

where $x_{ij}^P \log(\hat{c}_i^P)$ represents the degree of matching between the predicted box i and the real box j for category p. The more matched, the higher the probability of P and the smaller the loss. $\hat{c}_i^0$ represents there is no target in the prediction box, the higher the probability of predicting as the background, the smaller the loss.

According to the above formula, the loss function diagram of the multi-scale feature fusion network and the loss function diagram of the original SSD target detection algorithm are drawn as follows:

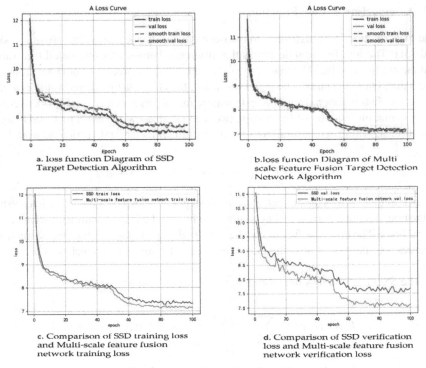

Fig. 6. Comparison of loss functions

Group B of Fig. 6 The loss function of the multi-scale feature fusion target detection network algorithm Group A of Fig. 6 and Group B of Fig. 6 show that compared with the original SSD target detection algorithm, the loss function of the multi-scale feature fusion target detection network converges faster and fits better.

From Group C of Fig. 6 and Group D of Fig. 6, it can be seen that compared to the SSD object detection algorithm, the multi-scale feature fusion object detection network has lower training and validation loss values, proving that the multi-scale feature fusion object detection network can better detect targets, and the improved model is more robust.

3.4 Comparison of Algorithm Detection Effects

Simulation testing experiment using Wilder_ Fish_ Perform model pre training on the New dataset and extract two images with dark backgrounds and mixed small and large fish from the test set for detection. The experimental results are shown in the Fig. 7.

It can be seen from the Fig. 7 that no matter whether VGG or Mobilenetv2 is used as the SSD target detection of the backbone network, there are problems of missing and false detection when detecting underwater images. When using YOLOv3 for testing, there may also be missed detections. However, when the deep learning object detection network with feature enhancement module detects the same image, its detection ability is improved while reducing missed and false detections.

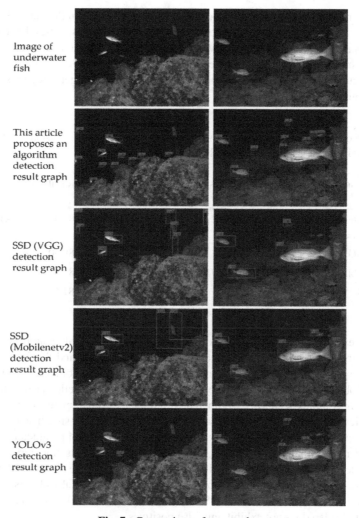

Fig. 7. Comparison of test results

The performance of the model is evaluated using Precision, Recall, and the average precision value mAP. The calculation formula is as follows:

$$P = \frac{TP}{TP + FP} \tag{8}$$

$$R = \frac{TP}{TP + FN} \tag{9}$$

$$mAP = \frac{1}{C} \sum_{K=1}^{c} J(P, R, K) \tag{10}$$

where TP represents the number of positive samples predicted in the network; FP represents the number of negative samples in the predicted positive samples; FN represents the number of positive samples that violate the network prediction; J () represents the precision mean function, which is the area enclosed by the curve and abscissa formed by the accuracy P and recall R; C is the number of detected target categories; K is the category number (Table 1).

Table 1. Comparison of evaluation indicators between multi-scale feature fusion target detection network and other target detection algorithms

Detection network	Precision (score threshold set to 0.5)	Recall (%)	mAP (%)
Multi-scale feature fusion target detection network	94.62	89.95	41.83
SSD (VGG)	92.35	88.30	40.19
SSD (Mobilenetv2)	91.49	87.57	40.74
YOLOv3	89.63	81.58	38.85

After experimental comparison, it is found that the multi-scale feature fusion deep learning object detection network model using DRDM module and SFEM module can identify targets in complex underwater scenes more accurately. Compared with the original SSD object detection network, the network has multiple detection errors and missed detection in complex scenarios. Compared with the 23.75M parameters of SSD (VGG), the deep learning object detection network proposed in this paper significantly improves the accuracy, recall and average accuracy with an increase of 9M parameters. After the same underwater image detection test, the proposed model detects more targets and will not miss detection in the same scenario. Compared with the false alarms of the original SSD target detection network, the proposed model does not have false alarms. Compared to the false positives in the original SSD target detection network, the model proposed in this article also does not exhibit any false positives.

4   Conclusion

Underwater image object detection has important theoretical research value and practical application significance. This article proposes a novel deep cascading learning object detection network, which combines the DRDM module and SFEM module, and applies it to underwater fish school detection. Theoretical analysis and simulation experiments show that this method has high precision detection and strong small target detection capabilities. This model combines a dual inversion dehazing algorithm to better cope with color shift and insufficient lighting in underwater images. At the same time, SFEM module is added to improve the detection ability of small targets in underwater object detection.

The next research focus for underwater image object detection is: (1) researching attention mechanisms that are more suitable for underwater image object features; (2) Research on feature extraction modules that are more suitable for underwater image targets.

Funding. This work is supported by the National Natural Science Foundation of China under Grant No.61872204 and Heilongjiang Province Natural Science Foundation (LH2019F037), Key topics of Jiangsu Provincial Education Science "14th Five-Year Plan (B/2022/01/166), Social Science Research Topics in Suqian City, Jiangsu Province (23SYB-12).

Data Availability Statement. All data generated or analyzed during this study are included within the article. Further details can be obtained from the corresponding author on request.

Conflicts of Interest. The authors declare that they have no conflicts of interest.

References

1. Li, H., Zhuang, P., Wei, W., Li, J.: Underwater image enhancement based on dehazing and color correction. In: 2019 IEEE Intl Conf on Parallel & Distributed Processing with Applications, Big Data & Cloud Computing, Sustainable Computing & Communications, Social Computing & Networking (ISPA/BDCloud/SocialCom/SustainCom), Xiamen, China, pp. 1365–1370 (2019). https://doi.org/10.1109/ISPA-BDCloud-SustainCom-SocialCom48970.2019.00196
2. Li, R., Dong, H., Wang, L., Liang, B., Guo, Y., Wang, F.: Frequency-aware deep dual-path feature enhancement network for image dehazing. In: 2022 26th International Conference on Pattern Recognition (ICPR), Montreal, QC, Canada, pp. 3406–3412 (2022). https://doi.org/10.1109/ICPR56361.2022.9955635
3. He, L., Yan, Y., Cai, C.: Underwater image enhancement based on light attenuation prior and dual-image multi-scale fusion. In: 2022 Global Conference on Robotics, Artificial Intelligence and Information Technology (GCRAIT), Chicago, IL, USA, pp. 478–482 (2022). https://doi.org/10.1109/GCRAIT55928.2022.00105
4. Berman, D., Levy, D., Avidan, S., Treibitz, T.: Underwater single image color restoration using haze-lines and a new quantitative dataset. IEEE Trans. Pattern Anal. Mach. Intell. **43**(8), 2822–2837 (2021). https://doi.org/10.1109/TPAMI.2020.2977624
5. Desai, C., Tabib, R.A., Reddy, S.S., Patil, U., Mudenagudi, U.: RUIG: realistic underwater image generation towards restoration. In: 2021 IEEE/CVF Conference on Computer Vision and Pattern Recognition Workshops (CVPRW), Nashville, TN, USA, pp. 2181–2189 (2021). https://doi.org/10.1109/CVPRW53098.2021.00247
6. Yang, H.Y., Chen, P.Y., Huang, C.C., Zhuang, Y.Z., Shiau, Y.H.: Low complexity underwater image enhancement based on dark channel prior. In: 2011 Second International Conference on Innovations in Bio-inspired Computing and Applications, Shenzhen, China, pp. 17–20 (2011). https://doi.org/10.1109/IBICA.2011.9
7. Wang, Y., Yu, X., Wei, Y., An, D., Bai, X.: Three-channel cascade network for underwater image enhancement. In: 2022 International Conference on High Performance Big Data and Intelligent Systems (HDIS), Tianjin, China, pp. 136–140 (2022). https://doi.org/10.1109/HDIS56859.2022.9991369
8. Han, M., Lyu, Z., Qiu, T., Xu, M.: A review on intelligence dehazing and color restoration for underwater images. IEEE Trans. Syst. Man Cybern. Syst. **50**(5), 1820–1832 (2020). https://doi.org/10.1109/TSMC.2017.2788902

9. Yeh, C.-H., Huang, C.-H., Kang, L.-W.: Multi-scale deep residual learning-based single image haze removal via image decomposition. IEEE Trans. Image Process. **29**, 3153–3167 (2020). https://doi.org/10.1109/TIP.2019.2957929

10. Lin, C.-Y., Tao, Z., Xu, A.-S., Kang, L.-W., Akhyar, F.: Sequential dual attention network for rain streak removal in a single image. IEEE Trans. Image Process. **29**, 9250–9265 (2020). https://doi.org/10.1109/TIP.2020.3025402

11. Yeh, C.-H., et al.: Lightweight deep neural network for joint learning of underwater object detection and color conversion. IEEE Trans. Neural Netw. Learn. Syst. **33**(11), 6129–6143 (2022). https://doi.org/10.1109/TNNLS.2021.3072414

12. Zhao Xiaofei, Y., Shuanghe, L.Q., et al.: Underwater object detection algorithm based on attention mechanism. J. Yangzhou Univ. (Nat. Sci. Edit.) **24**(01), 62–67 (2021). https://doi.org/10.19411/j.1007-824x.2021.01.011

13. Li, Q., Er, M.J., Li, L., Chen, J., Wu, J.: Underwater object detection based on improved SSD with convolutional block attention. In: 2022 5th International Conference on Intelligent Autonomous Systems (ICoIAS), Dalian, China, pp. 37–42 (2022). https://doi.org/10.1109/ICoIAS56028.2022.9931319

14. Pengfei, S., Song, H., Jianjun, N., et al.: Underwater target detection algorithm based on data augmentation and improvement of YOLOv4. J. Electron. Meas. Instrum. **36**(03), 113–121 (2022). https://doi.org/10.13382/j.jemi.B2104168

15. Redmon, J., Divvala, S., Girshick, R., Farhadi, A.: You only look once: unified, real-time object detection. In: 2016 IEEE Conference on Computer Vision and Pattern Recognition (CVPR), Las Vegas, NV, USA, pp. 779–788 (2016). https://doi.org/10.1109/CVPR.2016.91

16. Liu, W., Anguelov, D., Erhan, D., et al.: SSD: single shot multibox detector. In: Leibe, B., Matas, J., Sebe, N., Welling, M. (eds.) Computer Vision – ECCV 2016. ECCV 2016. LNCS, vol. 9905, pp. 21–37. Springer, Cham (2016). https://doi.org/10.1007/978-3-319-46448-0_2

17. Ren, S., He, K., Girshick, R., Sun, J.: Faster R-CNN: towards real-time object detection with region proposal networks. IEEE Trans. Pattern Anal. Mach. Intell. **39**(6), 1137–1149 (2017). https://doi.org/10.1109/TPAMI.2016.2577031

18. Lin, T.Y., Dollar, P., Girshick, R., et al.: Feature Pyramid Networks for Object Detection. IEEE Computer Society (2017)

19. He, K., Sun, J., Tang, X.: Single image haze removal using dark channel prior. In: 2009 IEEE Conference on Computer Vision and Pattern Recognition, Miami, FL, pp. 1956–1963 (2009). https://doi.org/10.1109/CVPR.2009.5206515

Security and Privacy Protection on Internet of Things

Honeynet Module Simulation and Dynamic Configuration of Honeypots Based on Online Learning

Yuanyuan Zhang[1] , Xingyi Xia[1], Zhiwen Pan[2], Cheng Dai[1],
Liangyin Chen[1] , and Yanru Chen[1(✉)]

[1] Sichuan University, Chengdu 610065, China
yuanyuanzhang@stu.scu.edu.cn,
{daicheng,chenliangyin,chenyanru}@scu.edu.cn
[2] Institute of Information Engineering, Chinese Academy of Sciences, Beijing 100085,
China
panzhiwen@iie.ac.cn

Abstract. With the emergence of various attack techniques, defending against malicious behavior and attacks is very important for industrial control systems. Unlike defenses such as firewalls, intrusion detection, and anti-virus software, honeynet is a more proactive and deceptive defense. This paper addresses the specific design and implementation challenges of honeynets by proposing an innovative approach that leverages a dynamic Human-Machine Interface (HMI) interface for virtual honeypots. This approach enables active trapping of attackers and enhances the overall effectiveness of the honeynet. Additionally, the paper introduces a realistic and dynamic physical process simulation to enhance the functionality of physical honeypots within the honeynet. To achieve dynamic configuration of the honeypots, an online prediction model based on the Follow-the-Regularized-Leader (FTRL) algorithm is presented. The proposed solution is evaluated through the deployment and testing of a high interaction hybrid honeypot system called Baggage Handling System (BHS). The experimental results demonstrate that the honeynet presented in this paper exhibits exceptional concealment, camouflage capability, and interaction capability, while maintaining a high level of cost effectiveness.

Keywords: Industrial control system security · honeynet · physical process simulation · online Learning · dynamic configuration

1 Introduction

In recent years, industrial control systems have emerged as prime targets for malicious attacks. As a result, honeynets have gained considerable attention as an

Supported in part by the National Natural Science Foundation of China under Grant 62302324 and 62072319; the Sichuan Science and Technology Program under Grant 2023YFQ0022 and 2022YFG0041; the Luzhou Science and Technology Innovation R&D Program (No. 2022CDLZ-6).

L. Wang et al. (Eds.): CWSN 2023, CCIS 1994, pp. 115–130, 2024.
https://doi.org/10.1007/978-981-97-1010-2_9

active defense technique and complementary approach for protecting industrial control systems. Honeynets involve the deployment of multiple honeypots within the industrial control network to entice and divert potential attackers, thereby safeguarding the actual system from direct threats. To ensure the effectiveness of honeynets in the industrial control domain, it is crucial to design and implement high-quality honeynets.

Despite ongoing efforts by researchers to create more sophisticated and realistic industrial control honeynets to attract attackers, existing honeynets exhibit several shortcomings. Firstly, virtual honeypots within these honeynets lack adequate interaction capabilities, failing to effectively engage with attackers. Secondly, current honeypots within honeynets do not sufficiently simulate real physical processes. The degree of realism in physical process simulation directly impacts the level of attraction for attackers, the sophistication of their interaction, and the overall effectiveness of the honeypot. Consequently, attackers entering these honeypots are unable to perceive the same physical and control processes as those in authentic systems. Moreover, industrial control honeypots also need to simulate unique industrial control processes. Currently, there is a lack of focus on simulating physical processes in some research on industrial control honeypots, for instance, Conpot [1], S7commTrace [2], HoneyPLC [3] and HoneyVP [4]. Some industrial control honeypot research has focused on physical process simulation, such as Mimepot [5], GasPot [6], HoneyPhy [7], and ICSpot [8], but they cannot be migrated to other industrial control scenarios. Consequently, the development of honeypots specifically tailored for simulating industrial control physical processes is urgently needed to effectively deploy honeypots in the industrial control domain.

In addition, the majority of honeypots within honeynets are configured and deployed by security personnel in a predetermined manner. This static nature of honeynet configuration and deployment renders the honeypots easily detectable by attackers during network scans, compromising the overall deception strategy. Additionally, static honeynets lack the ability to adapt and respond in real-time to network events, thereby limiting their effectiveness. In contrast, dynamic honeynets possess the capability to adjust their configuration and topology in response to changes in the network environment or network events. Hence, dynamic honeynets hold significant importance for the industrial control systems, deceiving potential attackers and fortifying system security. Existing research approaches for dynamic deployment of honeynets primarily revolve around intelligent agent-based [9], machine learning-based [10], and distributed-based methods [11]. Despite the advancements in dynamic deployment strategies, it is noteworthy that the honeypot configuration within these dynamically deployed honeynets remains static, requiring further attention and improvements.

In summary, the main contributions of this paper are as follows:

- This paper presents a comprehensive design of both virtual and physical honeypots within the Honeynet framework. The virtual honeypot is enhanced with a dynamic Human-Machine Interface (HMI) interface, building upon the foundation of HoneyPLC. This interface significantly enhances the inter-action capabilities of the virtual honeypot, enabling effective interference and trapping of attackers.

- To address the limitation of existing honeypots in adequately simulating real physical processes, a detailed design of the physical honeypot is provided in this paper. Specifically, the design focuses on simulating the airport baggage sorting control process and data processing process, ensuring a high level of interaction and camouflage capability within the honeynet.

- This paper tackles the challenge of dynamic honeypot configuration by proposing an innovative online learning model. This model combines cap-tured attack features with honeypot environment features to predict attack-ers' attack protocols. Based on the prediction results, the honeypot protocols and ports are dynamically configured, enabling effective adaptation to emerg-ing attack scenarios.

- Real-time collection and organization of log data within the honeynet are addressed, with the data being written to MySQL for further analysis and support in the subsequent chapters. Leveraging the comprehensive design, a complete BHS (Baggage Handling System) high-interaction hybrid honeynet system is built and deployed using IMUNES. This system not only supports dynamic and scalable deployment but also offers the necessary foundation for designing visual user interfaces in future work.

2   Background

2.1   Virtual Honeypot Module Simulation

The virtual honeypot module in this study focuses on simulating subsystems beyond the baggage sorting system. It is implemented using the HoneyPLC framework, which primarily handles initial interactions with network attackers during reconnaissance and detection activities. The virtual honeypot module provides essential protocols and service responses to the attackers, serving as a foundation for further engagements.

To enhance the interactivity and camouflage capabilities of the virtual hon-eypot, this section extends the development of the Human-Machine Interface (HMI) page specifically designed for the virtual honeypot. The extended HMI offers a dynamic display, incorporating rich interactive features and realistic sim-ulation of Siemens S7-1500 PLC device data. The dynamic HMI interface actively interferes with the attacker, trapping their packets and capturing keystroke behaviors, among other information. This functionality enables the honeypot to gain insights into the behavioral patterns of the attackers. The provided HMI panel supports various functions, including CPU status operations, display of PLC device parameters and operational data, as well as log and file reading and uploading. These features contribute to a comprehensive and interactive experi-ence within the virtual honeypot environment. The panel mainly consists of the following parts, which correspond to the five numbers in Fig. 1:

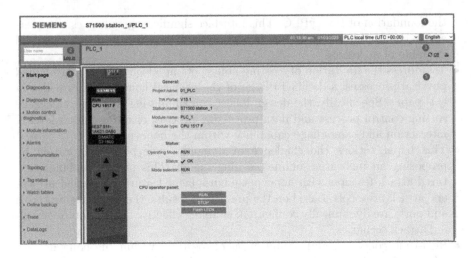

Fig. 1. Standard page layout example of Siemens S7-1500 PLC.

- Web service title: brand name, name, PLC local time and language selection.
- Login or Logout: Login and permission verification templates.
- Marker page: it contains the title of the standard page being viewed, and the module information section displays the navigation path here.
- Navigation bar: switch the current page to the next page.
- Content: The content of the particular Web page to be viewed is displayed.

2.2 Physical Honeypot Module Simulation

The existing honeypots for industrial control systems generally lack realistic simulation of actual physical processes. In this work, our physical honeypot module focuses on providing comprehensive physical process simulation specifically tailored for baggage sorting systems. Its primary objective is to engage in deep interaction with attackers and gather crucial information regarding their basic profiles, penetration techniques, and attack tactics. The physical honeypot module is built upon a genuine Programmable Logic Controller (PLC) device, and the entire sorting process control program is scripted to replicate the control and data processing functionalities of a real-world PLC device operating within an authentic environment. The inclusion of physical honeypots and their associated process simulations significantly enhances the realism and interaction capabilities of honeynets, expanding the range of attack scenarios available to potential attackers. Moreover, by collecting valuable information such as the attacker's fundamental details, penetration skills, and attack techniques, security personnel can promptly identify and address vulnerabilities and weaknesses in actual PLC devices, thus improving overall system security and resilience.

2.3   Data Collection Module

The data collection module plays a critical role in capturing and organizing incoming traffic and interaction logs within the honeynet. In real-time, it gathers and imports this data into a MySQL database. The collected data serves as the foundation for developing a visual interface that enables users to monitor honeypot activities within the honeynet in real-time. For physical honeypots, the TIA Portal software provides robust monitoring and debugging tools, allowing users to monitor the real-time status of physical honeypots. Additionally, the Siemens S7-1500 PLC supports a specialized table data flow protocol that establishes connections and facilitates communication with the MySQL database. This communication enables the retrieval of pertinent operation logs and device data from the PLC. In the case of virtual honeypots, log collection is facilitated through the utilization of Honeyd, the underlying framework for HoneyPLC. By employing the Honeyd2MySQL tool, logs from HoneyPLC can be extracted and seamlessly imported into the MySQL database. The process involves creating a dedicated database named "honeyPLC-logs" and a corresponding table named "logs" within MySQL to store the collected logs. Furthermore, a new MySQL user is created and granted full permissions to operate on the database. The running configuration of Honeyd2MySQL is adjusted to save the captured data into the designated database. The output format is set to "log-tcpdump", enabling HoneyPLC to generate log data in TCPdump format. Subsequently, the TCPdump-formatted log data is directed to Honeyd2MySQL's input pipeline by specifying the path of Honeyd2MySQL. Once the configuration is completed, initiating HoneyPLC and Honeyd2MySQL ensures real-time synchronization of virtual honeypot logs with MySQL.

3   Dynamic Honeypot Configuration Based on Online Learning

To achieve dynamic honeypot configuration and enhance authenticity, security, and adaptability, this section employs the Follow-the-Regularized-Leader (FTRL) online learning optimization algorithm to dynamically update parameters of the Factorization Machine (FM) model. The process involves capturing attack features and honeypot environment features during the attacker scanning honeypot phase. Subsequently, the attacker's attack protocol is predicted, enabling dynamic honeypot configuration based on the prediction results. In the context of our work, the honeynet deployed in the airport baggage handling scenario lacks a sufficient volume of malicious traffic data to train an accurate machine learning model beforehand. Furthermore, the attack data is constantly changing and incrementing over time, making online learning more suitable for systematic attack prediction. By leveraging online learning, the model can analyze and learn from real-time evolving attacker data while actively functioning, effectively addressing dynamic network environments and emerging attack types. Once a honeypot within the honeynet is targeted, the online model can provide corresponding protocol configurations for other honeypots, enticing attackers and acquiring additional real-time attack information.

Our approach involves determining the attacker's intended attack protocol by examining the scan traffic features and honeypot environment features during reconnaissance probing. This essentially becomes a multi-classification problem, with honeynet-supported industrial control protocols divided into nine distinct classes. To express the combined features of attack and honeypot environment, we utilize the Factorization Machine (FM) model as the underlying learner. The FM model adapts well to sparse features resulting from One-hot encoding.

Specifically, the FM model represents each feature vector as a low-dimensional latent vector. The pairwise combinations of these features are then computed as the dot product of the low-dimensional vectors, as modeled by the following objective function:

$$\hat{y}(x \mid \Theta) = \omega_0 + \sum_{i=1}^{d} \omega_i x_i + \sum_{i=1}^{d} \sum_{j=i+1}^{d} \langle v_i, v_j \rangle x_i x_j \tag{1}$$

The probability of a sample belonging to category "c" is calculated using the softmax function, yielding the following expression:

$$P(y = c|x, \Theta) = \frac{e^{\hat{y}_c(x|\Theta)}}{\sum\limits_{j=1}^{9} e^{\hat{y}_j(x|\Theta)}} \tag{2}$$

To address the challenges of the stochastic gradient descent algorithm, such as the manual adjustment of learning rates and slow convergence, we introduce the FTRL optimization algorithm for our online learning approach. The FTRL algorithm efficiently updates model parameters while processing data in real time. Unlike traditional approaches, the FTRL algorithm only needs to track the weights and historical gradients of each feature, resulting in improved efficiency when processing online data. At each iteration, a learning rate is calculated based on the current gradient and historical gradient information, enabling effective parameter updates. Additionally, the FTRL algorithm incorporates regularization techniques to prevent overfitting. Moreover, the FTRL algorithm incorporates gradient truncation during the gradient descent process, preventing gradient explosions and ensuring that model parameters do not deviate excessively.

The formula for updating the weights of each feature in the FTRL algorithm is as follows.

$$\omega_{t+1,i} = \begin{cases} 0, if \, |z_i| < \lambda_1 \\ -(\lambda_2 + \sum\limits_{s=1}^{t} \sigma_s)^{-1} (z_{t,i} - sgn(z_{t,i})\lambda_1), otherwise \end{cases} \tag{3}$$

where z_i and σ_s are intermediate values to assist in the calculation, and λ_1 and λ_2 are regularization parameters. In FTRL, the learning rate is defined as follows:

$$\eta_{t,i} = \frac{\alpha}{\beta + \sqrt{\sum\limits_{s=1}^{t} g_{s,i}^2}} \tag{4}$$

where α and β are custom parameters, $\sum_{s=1}^{t} g_{s,i}^2$ is the cumulative value of the historical gradient, and the adaptive learning rate is calculated from the historical gradient information of the ith feature and the current gradient information. Thus we have:

$$\sum_{s=1}^{t} \sigma_s = \frac{1}{\eta_{t,i}}, \sigma_i = \frac{1}{\eta_{t,i}} - \frac{1}{\eta_{t-1,i}} \tag{5}$$

Let $n_i = \sum_{s=1}^{t} g_{s,i}^2$, which denotes the cumulative sum of gradients g_i. The final weight update formula is obtained as follows:

$$\omega_{t+1,i} = \begin{cases} 0, if \ |z_i| < \lambda_1 \\ -(\lambda_2 + \frac{\beta+\sqrt{n_i}}{\alpha})^{-1}(z_i - sgn(z_i)\lambda_1), otherwise \end{cases} \tag{6}$$

The updated weights are incorporated into the formula to calculate the predicted value "p" for a given sample. Following this, the algorithm updates the variables g_i, $sigma_i$, z_i, and n_i based on the actual feedback value "y". The update formula is as follows.

$$\begin{aligned} g_i &= (p - y)x_i \\ \sigma_i &= \frac{1}{\alpha}(\sqrt{n_i + g_i^2} - \sqrt{n_i}) \\ z_i &= z_i + g_i - \sigma_i \omega_i \\ n_i &= n_i + g_i^2 \end{aligned} \tag{7}$$

The specific flow of the algorithm is as follows:

3.1 Specific Implementation

In this work, we present an online learning model based on the FTRL algorithm to achieve real-time prediction of the attacker's attack protocol and enable dynamic configuration of the honeypot. This is achieved through the analysis and extraction of attack features and honeypot environment features. The proposed methodology can be summarized in the following steps:

- Data collection: Simultaneous collection of scan attack data and honeypot environment data received by the honeypot.
- Feature extraction and processing: The honeypot environment data, encompassing deployment information such as OS version, hardware resources, network conditions, and open protocol services, serves as honeypot environment features. Attack features are extracted from the attacker's scan packets using the CICFlowMeter tool. The extracted features are pre-processed and converted to numeric types, serving as input features for the model.
- Model training: The aforementioned features are utilized to train the model and obtain the initial model weights.

Algorithm 1: FTRL-based online FM model update algorithm

Input: value$\alpha^\omega, \alpha^v, \beta^\omega, \beta^v, \lambda_1^\omega, \lambda_1^v, \lambda_2^\omega, \lambda_2^v, \sigma$

1 initialize $\omega_0 = 0; n_0^\omega = 0; z_0^\omega = 0 \ \forall i, \forall f, \omega_i = 0; n_i^\omega = 0; z_i^\omega = 0; v_{i,f} \sim$
$N(0, \sigma); n_{i,f}^v = 0; z_{i,f}^v = 0;$

2 **for** $t = 1$ **to** T **do**

3   get the feature vector x_t, includes attack characteristics and honeypot environment characteristics$I = \{i | x_i \neq 0\}$;

4   **for** *classification vectors1* **to** *9* **do**

5   if $|z_0^\omega| \leq \lambda_1^\omega$, $\omega_{t+1,0} \leftarrow 0$ else

         $\omega_{t+1,0} \leftarrow -(\frac{\beta^\omega + \sqrt{n_0^\omega}}{\alpha^\omega} + \lambda_2^\omega)^{-1}(z_0^\omega - sgn(z_0^\omega)\lambda_1^\omega)$ for an
         arbitrary$i \in I$calculate;

6   if $|z_i^\omega| \leq \lambda_1^\omega$, $\omega_{t+1,i} \leftarrow 0$ else

         $\omega_{t+1,i} \leftarrow -(\frac{\beta^\omega + \sqrt{n_i^\omega}}{\alpha^\omega} + \lambda_2^\omega)^{-1}(z_i^\omega - sgn(z_i^\omega)\lambda_1^\omega)$

7   **for** $f = 1$ **to** k **do**

8   if $\left|z_{i,f}^v\right| \leq \lambda_1^v$, $v_{i,f} \leftarrow 0$ else

           $v_{i,f} \leftarrow -(\frac{\beta^v + \sqrt{n_{i,f}^v}}{\alpha^v} + \lambda_2^v)^{-1}(z_{i,f}^v - sgn(z_{i,f}^v)\lambda_1^v)$

9   **end**

10   use $\omega_{t,i} v_{i,f}$ calculate the predicted value $p(x|\Theta)$;

11   get real tags$y \in \{0, 1\}$;

12   g_0^ω calculating gradient loss; $\sigma_0^\omega = \frac{1}{\alpha^\omega}(\sqrt{n_0^\omega + (g_0^\omega)^2} - \sqrt{n_0^\omega})$;

13     $z_0^\omega \leftarrow z_0^\omega + g_0^\omega - \sigma_0^\omega \omega_0; n_0^\omega \leftarrow n_0^\omega + (g_0^\omega)^2$;

14   **for** $i = 1$ **to** d **do**

15        $g_i^\omega = (p - y)x_i$ calculating gradient loss;

         $\sigma_i^\omega = \frac{1}{\alpha^\omega}(\sqrt{n_i^\omega + (g_i^\omega)^2} - \sqrt{n_i^\omega})$;

16        $z_i^\omega \leftarrow z_i^\omega + g_i^\omega - \sigma_i^\omega \omega_i; n_i^\omega \leftarrow n_i^\omega + (g_i^\omega)^2$;

17   **for** $f = 1$ **to** k **do**

18          $g_{i,f}^v$ calculating gradient loss;

           $\sigma_{i,f}^v = \frac{1}{\alpha^v}(\sqrt{n_{i,f}^v + (g_{i,f}^v)^2} - \sqrt{n_{i,f}^v})$;

19          $z_{i,j}^v \leftarrow z_{i,j}^v + g_{i,j}^v - \sigma_{i,j}^v \omega_{i,j}; n_{i,j}^v \leftarrow n_{i,j}^v + (g_{i,j}^v)^2$;

20   **end**

21   **end**

22   **end**

23 **end**

- Prediction of attack protocols: When the honeypot detects scanning traffic from an attacker, the model in conjunction with honeypot environment data predicts the potential attack protocols for the honeypot. A network architecture, as depicted in Fig. 2, is employed where the current honeypot environment features, combined with the attack features, are input into the network after undergoing feature preprocessing. The weighted sums of the nine classification categories are computed using the current weights, followed by the application of the softmax function to derive the probabilities for each classification. The final comparison is made to obtain the output results, representing the predicted attack protocols.

- Dynamic configuration of honeypots: The honeypots are dynamically configured based on the predicted attack protocols, enabling the opening of corresponding protocols and ports to enhance honeypot interactivity. Additionally, when a honeypot encounters an unknown attack, the online model can provide real-time protocol configuration information to other honeypots, attracting attackers and gathering additional attack information.
- Model parameter update: Employing the concept of online learning, the results obtained from a real attack are fed back into the model, and the FTRL algorithm is utilized to update the model parameters in real time. This ensures the adaptation and refinement of the model. The overall process is depicted in Fig. 3.

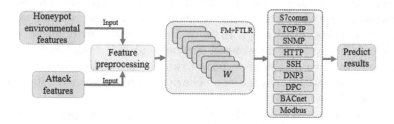

Fig. 2. Protocol prediction network diagram

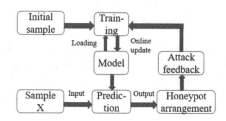

Fig. 3. Dynamic honeypot configuration process based on online learning

3.2 Experiment and Analysis

In the Python development environment, this study employs numpy and pandas libraries to preprocess the captured malicious traffic data and honeypot environment data. Additionally, pytorch is utilized for algorithm modeling, training, and prediction experiments. The experiments involve six different configurations of honeypots interacting with various protocols. A small sample dataset of 1000 simulated attack data instances is used to input into the model, and the accuracy of the online model's prediction results is assessed.

The experimental findings reveal that when the dataset size is 100, the prediction accuracy is relatively low. However, as the dataset size increases to 500, the accuracy improves to 96.84%. When the dataset size further expands to

1000, the prediction accuracy reaches 98.77%. These results indicate that the online model demonstrates stability and possesses the ability to effectively predict attack protocols. Furthermore, as the dataset volume gradually increases, the model's prediction accuracy exhibits an upward trend, thereby confirming its online learning capability.

By leveraging online learning algorithms, we achieve dynamic opening of protocols and ports for honeypots. This approach enables the prediction of potential attack protocols for honeypots, yielding the following outcomes:

- Enhanced security: The dynamic adjustment of open protocols and ports on honeypots significantly enhances the security of the honeynet. By modifying these configurations in real-time, the external behavior of the honeypot can be altered at any given moment, effectively thwarting potential attacks.
- Improved adaptivity: The flexible configuration of open protocols and ports enables honeypots to adapt to both the network environment and the attacker's behavior. If an attacker attempts to target protocols and ports that are not open on the honeypot, it can automatically adjust its configuration to align with the attacker's behavior, thereby enhancing its resilience and adaptability.
- Mislead attackers: Through the dynamic adjustment of open protocols and ports, honeypots can effectively mislead attackers, preventing them from accurately discerning the actual behavior of the honeypot. By consuming additional time and resources attempting to breach the honeypot, the attacker's progress is slowed down, subsequently reducing the likelihood of an attack on the genuine system.

In summary, the dynamic adjustment of open protocols and ports on honeypots represents a robust security defense strategy. This approach effectively bolsters the security and efficiency of honeypots, especially in scenarios where deployment environments and attacker behaviors undergo dynamic changes.

4   Honeynet System Deployment and Testing

4.1   Honeynet System Construction

To construct a comprehensive honeynet system, it is imperative to combine both virtual and physical honeypots. In this section, we utilize the IMUNES network simulator for the development of the honeynet system. The topology of the honeynet can be dynamically modified to accommodate varying demands and network changes, ensuring the achievement of dynamic honeynet deployment. Additionally, IMUNES streamlines the deployment overhead, making it feasible to meet the requirements of honeynet deployment within a single virtual machine. Furthermore, we introduce a scripting language that enables the seamless one-click deployment of HoneyPLC virtual honeypots, significantly reducing deployment costs and providing an out-of-the-box honeynet experience (Fig. 4).

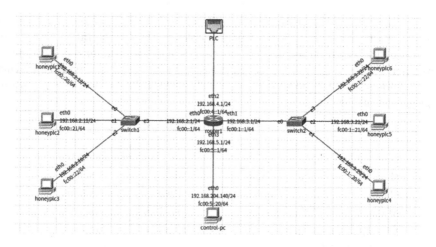

Fig. 4. Topology of honeynet

In our study, we employ IMUNES to simulate a complex honeynet system on a virtual machine running Ubuntu 18.04. Within the honeynet, the virtual honeypots operate as Docker containers. The scalability of the IMUNES model is noteworthy, as it can accommodate over 10,000 nodes on a medium-powered workstation. However, when employing HoneyPLC as an IMUNES network node, considerations such as memory consumption, CPU utilization, network traffic, as well as the size and complexity of the network topology, must be taken into account. Based on the system requirements of HoneyPLC, each Honey-PLC instance exhibits low memory and CPU consumption, allowing it to run efficiently with 256MB of memory and a single core CPU. Considering the hardware parameters of the experimental virtual machine, an optimal configuration of six HoneyPLC virtual honeypots is established within the honeynet. Following the principle of minimizing the degree of each honeypot node, the topology of the honeynet is meticulously designed in this study, yielding the following structure:

In the depicted honeynet topology, a network layer node called "pc" is designated as the control host, serving as the engineer station within the honeynet. Additionally, six new pc nodes are introduced as HoneyPLC virtual honeypots. To facilitate this setup, a HoneyPLC image is constructed using Dockerfile, and the configuration of a Docker image for the virtual pc node in IMUNES enables it to function as a HoneyPLC virtual honeypot. For the physical honeypots, i.e., PLC devices, an external interface is required as a link layer node to establish connectivity between the PLC devices and IMUNES. Upon completing the network configuration via IMUNES, the honeynet is initiated, with all nodes operating as Docker containers.

Our constructed honeynet system adopts a hybrid honeynet scheduling mechanism, employing a one-to-many approach to optimize hardware costs. Specifically, a single Siemens S7-1500 PLC device supports up to 31 concurrent queries, thereby maximizing the utilization of limited resources and enhancing cost effectiveness. Furthermore, the development, deployment, and operation and maintenance of the entire honeynet system can be efficiently managed by a single developer. A cost comparison between the BHS high-interaction hybrid honeynet and the honeypots and honeynets commonly utilized in real-world applications is presented in Table 1.

Table 1. Comparison of input costs .

Honeypot/Honeynet	Hardware Costs	Development	Maintenance
Hilt	High	High	Medium
Gaspot	Low	High	Medium
Mimepot	High	Medium	Low
BHS High Interaction Hybrid Honeynet	Medium	Low	Low

4.2 Honeynet System Deception Test

The first step in deceiving attackers with the honeypot in our Honeynet system is to mislead the search and scanning tools they employ. Among these tools, Shodan is specifically designed to search for information about Internet-connected industrial control devices. By searching for open ports and service banners, Shodan obtains device information and offers a search engine-like interface to assist users in finding devices of interest. Attackers can exploit Shodan to identify vulnerabilities and weaknesses in industrial control devices. Notably, Shodan provides an API called Shodan Honeyscore, which assigns a probability score ranging from 0.0 to 1.0 to determine whether a device is a honeypot. A score of 0.0 indicates that the host is a genuine system, while a score of 1.0 indicates that the host is a honeypot.

In our implementation, we configure HoneyPLC as a Siemens S7-1500 PLC, achieving a Shodan Honeyscore of 0.3. This score is comparable to that obtained by a genuine Siemens S7-1500 PLC indexed by Shodan. Additionally, our physical honeypot, constructed using real PLC devices, obtains a Shodan Honeyscore of 0.0. These results demonstrate the effectiveness of our proposed honeynet in maintaining stealth against advanced reconnaissance tools. Consequently, the honeynet successfully accomplishes the first step of deceiving the attacker's search tool.

The second step involves evaluating the comprehensive disguise capabilities of our honeynet system, specifically assessing whether the attacker can trust the honeynet and engage in extensive interaction with it once introduced. The disguise capabilities of the honeynet system are assessed across various dimensions, including network service simulation, physical interaction simulation, HMI interface, and programmability. A comparison table is presented to demonstrate the disguise capabilities of existing honeypots or honeynets relative to our proposed BHS high-interaction hybrid honeynet.

The provided table concludes that our proposed highly interactive hybrid honeynet exhibits the most realistic system simulation capabilities. This encompasses web service simulation, physical interaction simulation, HMI interface simulation, and the ability to program the honeynet to enhance functional simulation.

4.3   Honeynet System Interactivity Test

To evaluate the interaction capabilities of our proposed honeynet, we conducted tests focusing on the S7comm protocol and SNMP protocol. Among these protocols, the S7comm protocol plays a crucial role in the communication between PLC devices within the airport baggage handling system and represents a prime target for attacks within the honeynet environment. The S7comm protocol, developed by Siemens, facilitates communication between industrial automation products and operates on a default port of 102. It serves as a primary communication protocol for PLCs, remote I/O and other industrial automation devices. In our experimentation, we utilized the Snap7 Client Demo to establish interactions with the honeynet system via the S7comm protocol, thereby assessing the interactivity of our proposed honeynet. Snap7 is an open-source S7 communication library that enables the implementation of read and write operations using the S7 protocol. The Snap7 Client, built upon the Snap7 library, serves as a client for communication with S7 series PLCs, facilitating data reading and writing operations.

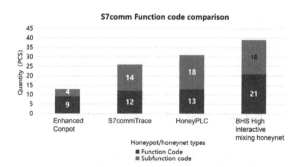

Fig. 5. Comparison of the number of S7comm function codes supported

During the experiment, we tested various honeynet interaction functions, including upload, download, start, and stop functions. Furthermore, we conducted a comparative analysis between our proposed honeynet system and existing honeypots in terms of the number of simulated S7comm function codes. Figure 5 illustrates the comparison, demonstrating that our honeynet system supports the highest number of S7comm service function codes and sub-function codes. This comprehensive support for a wide range of S7comm functions further strengthens the capabilities of our proposed honeynet in simulating realistic interactions within the context of the airport baggage handling system.

To evaluate the effectiveness of our honeynet system, we conducted experiments to measure the response time of various functions, including read, write, upload, and download functions. A comparison was made between the response times of our proposed honeynet, an enhanced Conpot virtual honeypot, and a real PLC device. The results show that our proposed honeynet exhibits response times similar to those of a real PLC device, further confirming its ability to deceive attackers effectively (Fig. 6).

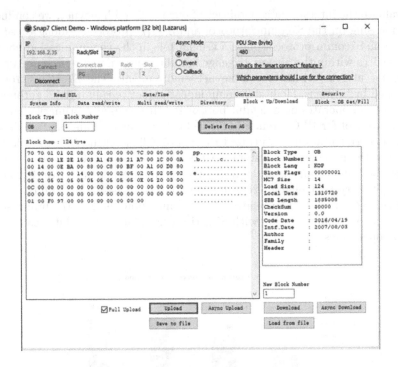

Fig. 6. Upload & Download function test

In addition, we tested the SNMP protocol, which is utilized for managing and monitoring network devices on the default port 161. This experiment involved using the Net-SNMP tool as a management site to simulate an attacker conducting a remote scanning attack on the honeypot using the SNMP protocol. By accessing the management information repository of the SNMP agent simulation within the honeypot, we obtained information such as the honeypot's simulated PLC name, type, firmware version, operating system, as well as details about connections between honeypots and the network topology. This evaluation enabled us to validate the capabilities of our honeynet system in responding to SNMP-based attacks and maintaining the illusion of being a genuine industrial control system.

5   Conclusion

In our investigation of existing industrial control honeypots, we identified several shortcomings in their design and implementation. To address the lack of interaction between virtual honeypots and attackers, we introduced HMI pages to enable trapping and interference with attackers. Furthermore, in order to enhance the realism of the honeynet by simulating real physical processes, we incorporated real PLC devices as physical honeypots and developed PLC ladder logic code to simulate the airport baggage sorting process. To tackle the limited dynamic expressiveness of the honeynet, we employed an online learning approach based on the FTRL optimization algorithm to predict the attacker's attack protocol and dynamically configure the honeypot accordingly. By integrating these advancements, we constructed a BHS (Baggage Handling System) high-interaction hybrid honeynet system that optimizes honeynet deployment, maximizes resource utilization, and reduces cost investment. Subsequently, a series of experiments were conducted to evaluate the deceptive and interactive capabilities of the honeynet. The results confirmed the honeynet's exceptional stealth against state-of-the-art reconnaissance tools. Additionally, the honeynet effectively responded to attacker requests and recorded their behavior, demonstrating its remarkable deception and interaction capabilities.

References

1. Conpot [EB/OL] (2013). http://conpot.org/. Accessed 05 Mar 2023
2. Xiao, F., Chen, E., Xu, Q.: S7commTrace: a high interactive honeypot for industrial control system based on S7 protocol. In: Qing, S., Mitchell, C., Chen, L., Liu, D. (eds.) ICICS 2017. LNCS, vol. 10631, pp. 412–423. Springer, Cham (2018). https://doi.org/10.1007/978-3-319-89500-0_36
3. López-Morales, E., Rubio-Medrano, C., Doupé, A., et al.: HoneyPLC: a next-generation honeypot for industrial control systems. In: Proceedings of the 2020 ACM SIGSAC Conference on Computer and Communications Security, pp. 279–291 (2020)
4. You, J., Lv, S., Sun, Y., et al.: HoneyVP: a cost-effective hybrid honeypot architecture for industrial control systems. In: ICC 2021-IEEE International Conference on Communications, pp. 1–6. IEEE (2021)
5. Bernieri, G., Conti, M., Pascucci, F.: MimePot: a model-based honeypot for industrial control networks. In: 2019 IEEE International Conference on Systems, Man and Cybernetics (SMC), pp. 433–438. IEEE (2019)
6. Wilhoit, K., Hilt, S.: The GasPot experiment: unexamined perils in using gas-tank-monitoring systems. Trend Micro **6**, 3–13 (2015)
7. Litchfield, S., Formby, D., Rogers, J., et al.: Rethinking the honeypot for cyber-physical systems. IEEE Internet Comput. **20**(5), 9–17 (2016)
8. Conti, M., Trolese, F., Turrin, F.: ICSpot: a high-interaction honeypot for industrial control systems. In: 2022 International Symposium on Networks, Computers and Communications (ISNCC), pp. 1–4. IEEE (2022)
9. Zarca, A.M., Bernabe, J.B., Skarmeta, A., et al.: Virtual IoT HoneyNets to mitigate cyberattacks in SDN/NFV-enabled IoT networks. IEEE J. Sel. Areas Commun. **38**(6), 1262–1277 (2020)

10. Tan, L., Yu, K., Ming, F., et al.: Secure and resilient artificial intelligence of things: a HoneyNet approach for threat detection and situational awareness. IEEE Consum. Electron. Mag. **11**(3), 69–78 (2021)
11. Lu, X.X., Yu, X.N., Liu, Y.Z., et al.: Dynamic deployment model of lightweight honeynet for internet of things. In: 2022 International Conference on 6G Communications and IoT Technologies (6GIoTT), pp. 30–34. IEEE (2022)

Fog Computing and Wireless Computing

Edge-Assisted Multi-camera Tracking for Digital Twin Systems

Tianyi Zhang, Weichen Liu, Juntong Luo[✉], Zhuoliu Liu, and Zhiwei Zhao

School of Computer Science and Engineering, University of Electronic Science and
Technology of China, Chengdu 610097, Sichuan, China
lance_tong0324@163.com, zhuoliu@mobinets.org, zzw@uestc.edu.cn

Abstract. The digital twin system combines physical entities or processes with their digital representations, which are marked by real-time data acquisition, processing, and simulation. Object tracking, as a fundamental service to map the physical and digital entities, faces new challenges in the digital twin systems: positioning in 3D space can be affected by object blocking, multi-camera conflicts, and lack of computing resources for real time restore of the object positions in the digital space. To address the challenge, we propose an edge-assisted multi-camera tracking (eMT) approach, which consists of three building blocks: 1) We devise a position calibration scheme to aggregates the 2D coordinates from multiple cameras into unified and accurate 3D coordinates; 2) To deal with the impact of camera view blocking, we propose an adaptive method to adjust the detection boxes according spatial-temporal box traces; 3) To meet the real-time requirements, we utilize edge computing and adopt a person re-identification algorithm based on the 3D coordinates and appearance features. We implemented eMT and embed it into a real digital twin system for real time indoor monitoring. Both trace-driven and real experiment results show that eMT can effectively and accurately restore the 3D coordinates at a low latency for the digital twin systems.

Keywords: Digital twin · Multiple camera tracking ·
Re-identification · Blocked camera views · Edge computing

1 Introduction

In recent years, with the continuous development of the new generation of information technology, digital twins, as the integration of various information technologies such as the Internet, Internet of Things (IoT), artificial intelligence (AI), and big data, are thriving. They have been applied in various fields such as intelligent manufacturing, logistics management, and smart cities. By employing various data collection methods and processing techniques, it maps physical

---

T. Zhang and W. Liu—These authors contributed equally to this work.

L. Wang et al. (Eds.): CWSN 2023, CCIS 1994, pp. 133–149, 2024.
https://doi.org/10.1007/978-981-97-1010-2_10

entities from the real world to the virtual world, enabling spatial observation and management.

Since the digital twin system needs to utilize a large amount of real-time information collected from physical devices. If we use traditional cloud computing to process huge raw data, there will be many problems such as insufficient computing power, high latency, high energy consumption, and privacy leaks. Edge computing is a distributed computing architecture. It uses an open platform near the source of data to provide the closest services directly. Edge nodes are closer to user terminal devices, which can speed up data processing and transmission, shorten response times, reduce delays, and are more suitable for processing massive data generated by physical equipment. At the same time, it also provides a better privacy protection mechanism for sensitive data, effectively reducing network pressure and reducing energy consumption.

Therefore, this paper builds a complex indoor digital twin system based on edge computing technology, relying on edge nodes to provide system computing power support to achieve efficient, accurate, and real-time digital twins. At the same time, since edge nodes often have limited computing power, the algorithm we propose is lightweight to meet the needs of edge computing scenarios.

In digital twin systems, there is often a challenge in personnel management. When dealing with the tracking of complex human movements, the system needs to assign an ID to each individual and continuously track their activities indoors until they exit the observation space. The methods to address personnel management issues can be broadly categorized into three aspects: target tracking, person re-identification, and occlusion handling.

Target tracking is a well-established field that has been studied for a long time, and many algorithms have achieved excellent results. They typically annotate the positions of multiple individuals in a video based on shape, color, and other information, providing trajectory information in a 2D video. However, in a digital twin system, the positions of individuals are required in a 3D coordinate system, and these existing algorithms do not directly calculate specific 3D coordinates, making them unsuitable for direct application in the implementation of digital twins.

Complex indoor environments often require multiple cameras to extract the necessary information. However, using multiple cameras can introduce inconsistencies in assigning identities to the same individual captured by different cameras. Existing approaches generally extract person-specific features and calculate the differences in these features to assign identities. This process is computationally intensive and may consume significant computing resources, potentially compromising the real-time performance of the digital twin system.

In complex indoor environments, occlusions of individuals can occur. When there are no additional means to gather more information, we need to process the detection boxes of the target recognition to obtain relatively accurate coordinates during coordinate calculations.

We utilize camera calibration principles to determine the position of a person's feet using the bottom edge of the detection box. Firstly, we perform distortion correction on the image to obtain the real-world coordinates of the person.

Then, using camera calibration principles, we transform the image coordinate system to the camera coordinate system, and subsequently, convert it to the virtual coordinate system. Finally, by incorporating the ground plane equation, we obtain the 3D coordinates of the person in the virtual space. This completes the coordinate transformation from the image's 2D plane to the virtual 3D space. We consider the person's coordinates as the primary factor for determining their identity. By matching identities based on the relationship between coordinates, we address situations where the coordinate relationship is not accurate by using a lightweight identity matching algorithm based on person appearance features. In cases where occlusion occurs, we attempt to reconstruct the occluded parts based on the normal proportion relationship of the person. If the resulting trajectory significantly deviates from the estimated trajectory, we employ a Kalman filtering method to calculate the potential coordinates of the person. We term the method as edge-assisted multi-camera tracking (eMT) approach.

This article focuses on utilizing limited edge computing power and employing multi-camera multi-object tracking techniques to accomplish the digital twin task of tracking personnel movement in complex indoor environments. Specifically, we explore multi-camera multi-object tracking method and algorithm for mapping 2D coordinates to 3D space. We have made the following contributions.

1) Proposed a real-time multi-object tracking algorithm that provides 3D spatial coordinates of individuals.
2) Proposed a multi-camera object re-identification algorithm based on 3D spatial coordinates and appearance features.
3) Proposed a method to handle occlusions and loss of individuals during multi-object tracking in indoor environments.

The remainder of this paper is summarized as Related work. We conducted a comprehensive discussion on the currently popular object tracking algorithms that can be used for digital twinning. We analyzed their advantages and disadvantages and highlighted the unique aspects of our approach, Proposed Method: We provide an overview of the overall design framework of the digital twinning system, including the proposed object tracking algorithm, person re-identification algorithm, and occlusion handling algorithm. Evaluation: We conduct performance evaluation of our algorithms and analyze the changes in accuracy under different scenarios.

2   Related Work

Multiple Object Tracking (MOT) refers to the identification, tracking, and association of multiple targets across multiple video frames to achieve complete tracking of the targets. It has been applied in various fields such as video surveillance, autonomous driving, and sports event analysis.

Before conducting target tracking, it is necessary to perform object detection. Currently, mainstream object detection algorithms utilize deep learning techniques. For instance, the SSD network [1] predicts bounding boxes and class information of different scales on feature maps at various levels, enabling multi-scale object detection. There is also a series of CNN networks, such as $R - CNN$ [2], $Faster R - CNN$ [3], $Mask R - CNN$ [4], which mainly achieve object detection by performing classification and bounding box regression on candidate regions. We adopted $YOLOv5$ [5], a member of the $YOLO$ series that performs object detection directly at the image level using a single network, demonstrating good real-time performance.

Several viable solutions have been proposed for multi-object tracking, which can be broadly categorized into two forms: single-camera and multi-camera tracking. In the single-camera domain, approaches such as [6,7] extract color features of the objects to accomplish object tracking, yielding good tracking performance. [8,9] utilize 360-degree panoramic cameras or fisheye cameras to achieve multi-object tracking, expanding the scope of multi-object tracking but constrained by special equipment and limited tracking range. [10] incorporates not only color information but also material and shape features, establishing a reference set for each camera to determine individuals with similar characteristics. The approach we primarily employ is based on the deepsort algorithm [11], which combines target feature vectors with motion models (e.g., Kalman filters). This combination enables more accurate object association and trajectory inference in multi-object tracking tasks.

On the other hand, [12–16] utilize person re-identification methods and multiple camera collaboration for multi-object tracking. They extract features such as color, shape, and trajectory for person re-identification but do not utilize 3D information. In [17,18], neural network methods are employed to extract 3D spatial features from images for person re-identification. However, these approaches are more complex and cannot provide unified 3D coordinates for individuals in the context of digital twinning. [19,20] have explored learning specific body parts to extract features of the human body. They treat the re-identification task as a pairing problem and have achieved high accuracy in their approaches.

Regarding the occlusion issue in multi-object tracking, [21,22] employ the concept of person segmentation, while [23] utilizes reverse epipolar constraints to match human feature points across multiple cameras, enhancing tracking accuracy during occlusion and ensuring continuity in person tracking. [24] adopts a multi-hypothesis tracking algorithm, which tracks objects based on a set of hypotheses and generates new hypotheses at each time step. The algorithm updates the trajectory of the target by evaluating and updating the weights of each hypothesis. These algorithms have shown promising results in terms of accuracy, but they require high computational resources and processing time, which may not meet real-time requirements. [25] uses an online multi-feature fusion approach based on geometric and shape cues, achieving good results even with a simple association framework.

Although there are many different algorithms in the field of multi-object tracking with good performance, the task of multi-object tracking in the context of digital twin systems has unique characteristics and requirements. Currently, there is no single multi-object tracking algorithm that can fully meet these requirements. In the single-camera multi-object tracking domain, while many algorithms exhibit good performance in terms of accuracy and real-time capabilities, they only accomplish object tracking in the 2D plane of the video stream and cannot provide the 3D spatial coordinates required by digital twin systems.

In indoor digital twin scenarios, multiple cameras often need to collaborate for multi-object tracking, and these cameras often have overlapping coverage areas. Existing person re-identification research relies on features such as target color, shape, and trajectory to ensure accuracy, but it does not utilize the deterministic confirmation of the same individual's identity across different cameras at the same spatial position and time, which is crucial in indoor digital twin scenarios.

Moreover, when a person is occluded, while general object tracking algorithms ensure that the person is not lost and maintain trajectory continuity, they do not provide an estimation of the person's true position in the image. However, digital twin systems rely on the accurate determination of a person's 3D coordinates based on their true position in the image.

In comparison to previous related work, our research differs in the following aspects.

1) We prioritize the real-time performance of the multi-camera multi-object tracking algorithm in the context of limited edge computing power.
2) In the digital twinning scenario, our target tracking provides 3D coordinates for individuals.
3) We utilize camera height, angle, and calibration principles for target tracking and person re-identification, achieving better speed and accuracy.
4) To address occlusions, we estimate the real positions of individuals to ensure the accuracy of 3D coordinates.

3   Proposed Method

3.1   Design Overview

In the digital twin system, edge nodes mainly provide computing power for the core algorithm. We will not discuss too much about edge computing here, but mainly explain the core algorithm we proposed for target tracking in the system. Our work consists of three main aspects: coordinate-based object tracking, multi-camera person re-identification, and occlusion handling. Firstly, in the object tracking module, we preprocess the camera images and establish the transformation relationship between the 2D image coordinate system and the camera coordinate system using camera calibration principles. We then utilize known camera parameters to establish the transformation relationship between the camera coordinate system and the virtual target coordinate system. With these two transformations, we can calculate the coordinates of individuals using geometric relationships. In the multi-camera person re-identification module, we primarily use person coordinates and person features to determine the identities of the targets. We perform matching based on the coordinates obtained in the previous step. When the reliability of coordinate matching is high, we directly assign the identity. When the reliability is low, we consider using a trained triplet network model for identity matching, thus balancing speed and reliability. In the occlusion handling module, our main idea is to restore the occluded parts of the person's bounding box based on the aspect ratio of the human body. We then perform coordinate calculation and utilize the Kalman filtering method to provide the optimal estimation of person coordinates under occlusion.

As shown in Fig. 1, our digital twin system is divided into two parts: the 3D coordinate tracker and the central controller. Among them, the 3D coordinate tracker will be assigned to each camera in the room, while there is only one central controller in the digital twin system.

The 3D coordinate tracker first obtains the video stream captured by the camera, and then runs the target tracking algorithm to obtain the position of the characters in the video. Considering that the characters in the video may be occluded, the image coordinates need to be processed by the occlusion handler to estimate the real coordinates of the characters in the picture. After obtaining the real coordinates of the person in the image, the system uses the coordinate conversion module to convert the image coordinates into 3D coordinates in the virtual space, and calls the person re-identifier to determine the identity information of the person in the image. If a person appears in the camera for the first time, since his identity information is unknown, the person re-identifier needs to send the 3D coordinates and appearance feature of the person to the central controller, and at the same time issue a person re-identification request. The central controller will allocate identity information from the personnel database to the requesting tracker based on the person's coordinate information and appearance feature. If the person's identity information is known, the tracker only needs to pass its identity information, 3D coordinates and appearance feature to the central controller.

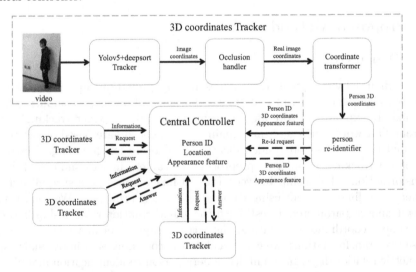

Fig. 1. Framework of the digital twin system

The central controller stores real-time character information in the entire digital twin system, including the character's identity information, 3D coordinates, appearance features, etc. It is mainly used to respond to character re-identification requests sent by trackers and unify the character information collected by all tracker.

Figure 2 shows the operation of the digital twin system in the laboratory. It depicts a simulated indoor scene, showcasing the approximate positions and poses of individuals.

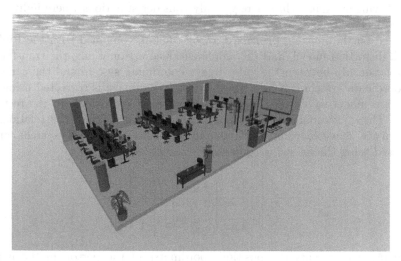

Fig. 2. The diagram of digital twin system

3.2   Target Tracking in 3D Coordinate System

In traditional object tracking tasks, the focus has typically been on tracking targets on a 2D video plane. This means that only information such as detection bounding boxes and identification labels are provided within the video. However, in the context of digital twinning, where simulation of the real world is required in a virtual 3D space, the core task of object tracking in digital twinning scenarios involves the conversion of 2D coordinates of individuals in the video to their corresponding 3D coordinates in the virtual space.

We employ the $YOLOv5 + DeepSORT$ approach to accomplish traditional target tracking, which demonstrates good performance in terms of detection accuracy and real-time capabilities. Considering that ordinary RGB cameras are commonly used in practical monitoring setups, which can only provide 2D information and lack depth information which can only given by depth cameras, obtaining 3D coordinate information in the virtual space from the 2D coordinate information in the video stream requires certain reasonable assumptions. Given that most individuals in indoor digital twin scenarios move on the ground without jumping and traditional target detection algorithms are able to give the bounding box of the entire body of a person in the absence of occlusion, we make the following two assumptions based on real-world situations: 1) individuals only move on the ground, and 2) the bottom edge of the bounding box provided by the traditional target detection algorithm is considered as the position of the person's feet. However, the second assumption may lead to errors when individuals are occluded, especially when the lower half of their bodies is occluded. To address this issue, appropriate occlusion handling is necessary to ensure the accuracy of the algorithm. This aspect will be discussed further in the following sections, while here we only consider situations where individuals are not occluded.

Based on the imaging principles of the camera, combined with the Pinhole model, distortion model, and the aforementioned assumptions, the transformation relationship between the video image coordinate system and the camera's 3D coordinate system can be derived. Firstly, the image is corrected using the distortion model to obtain the true coordinates of individuals in the rectified image. Then, according to the camera calibration principles, the relationship between the image coordinate system and the camera coordinate system can be expressed using the following equation.

$$
z_c \begin{bmatrix} x \\ y \\ 1 \end{bmatrix} = \begin{bmatrix} f & 0 & 0 & 0 \\ 0 & f & 0 & 0 \\ 0 & 0 & 1 & 0 \end{bmatrix} \begin{bmatrix} x_c \\ y_c \\ z_c \\ 1 \end{bmatrix}
\tag{1}
$$

where (x, y) represents the position coordinates of the person in the image, specifically the coordinates at the midpoint of the bottom edge of the bounding box. (x_c, y_c, z_c) is the coordinate of individual in the camera coordinate. By solving the matrix equation, we can obtain the equation of a line in the camera coordinate system that passes through the origin of the camera coordinate system. Let's assume z_c is equal to 1, which allows us to obtain the coordinate information $(x_c, y_c, 1)$ of a point P on this line in the camera coordinate system.

In the context of the digital twin scenario, it is necessary to establish a 3D coordinate system in the virtual space based on the real-world scene. Each object in the real world has corresponding coordinates in the virtual space, which can be obtained by establishing the corresponding coordinate system in the real world and using a scale conversion method. By applying this method, the coordinates of the camera in the virtual coordinate system can be obtained. Furthermore, by measuring the camera's pitch angle, rotation angle, and other information in the real world, we can determine the camera's position in the virtual coordinate system. Once we have obtained this information, we can establish the camera coordinate system with the camera as the origin, thus establishing the relationship between the camera coordinate system and the virtual coordinate system. This relationship can be expressed using the following equation.

$$\begin{bmatrix} x_c \\ y_c \\ z_c \\ 1 \end{bmatrix} = \begin{bmatrix} R & T \\ 0 & 1 \end{bmatrix} \begin{bmatrix} x_w \\ y_w \\ z_w \\ 1 \end{bmatrix} \tag{2}$$

According to the transformation equation, we can obtain the coordinates (x_w, y_w, z_w) of the point P on the line in the virtual coordinate system corresponding to the previously determined camera coordinate system. By combining these coordinates with the coordinates of the camera (i.e., the origin of the camera coordinate system) in the virtual coordinate system, we can establish a line equation in the virtual coordinate system. Considering that the position of a person is always above the ground, by combining this line equation with the plane equation of the ground, we can determine the coordinates (x_v, y_v, z_v) of the person in the virtual 3D coordinate system. At this point, we have completed the coordinate transformation from the image's 2D plane to the virtual 3D space.

3.3   Multi-camera Target Identity Re-identification Algorithm

When individuals enter the premises, their identities are typically bound through identity recognition algorithms such as facial recognition. However, in complex human activities, two common situations are frequently encountered.

1. Multiple cameras capture the same object, and at least one camera has already obtained the identity of the target.
2. An object disappears within the range of a known target identity camera and reappears within the range of another camera with an unknown target identity after a certain period of time.

To achieve the complete tracking of the target, we need to perform identity re-identification on the targets in the cameras with unknown target identities. In the existing literature, based on our research, there are already many algorithms available for person re-identification. However, these algorithms often require significant computational resources, which are not feasible for edge devices with limited computational capabilities. Therefore, we propose a method based on person position coordinates and image features to achieve person identity re-identification, taking into consideration the real-time requirements of the digital twin system.

3.3.1   Based on Character Coordinates

First, it is certain that in a single photo, there is a one-to-one correspondence between individuals and their identity *ids*. Each individual should have a unique *id*, and no *id* should be assigned to multiple individuals simultaneously. We consider the position of the target person as the primary factor determining their identity. In theory, the coordinate positions of the same object captured by multiple cameras should be the same. Therefore, we iterate through all undetermined objects (x) captured by the cameras and calculate their position using the methods from the target tracking module. We then calculate the distances $(d_1, d_2, d_3, ..., dn)$ between the coordinates of x and the known identity objects $(y_1, y_2, y_3, ..., y_n)$ captured by other cameras, and sort them in ascending order.

The theoretical value of d1 should be 0, but due to computational errors, the calculated coordinates may not be reliable. We compute a ratio, d_1/d_2, and if it does not exceed a predetermined threshold (e.g., 0.5), we directly assign the ID of y_1 to x. If the ratio exceeds the threshold, it indicates that the individuals are close to each other and the coordinate calculation is unreliable. In such cases, we use the person's image features for identity re-identification.

Algorithm 1. Identity re-identification algorithm

Input: Unknown objects $X = (x_1.id = NULL, x_1.p), (x_2.id = NULL, x_2.p), ...,$
$(x_n.id = NULL, x_n.p)$; Known objects $Y = (y1.id, y1.p), (y2.id, y2.p), (y3.id, y3.p),$
$..., (y_m.id, y_m.p)$;

1: **for** i in X **do**
2:    **for** j in Y **do**
3:        Calculate the distance $d(i, j)$
4:        Store the distances in an array and sort
5:        **if** $d[0]/d[1] < c$ **then**
6:            $i.id = j.id$ corresponding to $d[0]$
7:            Remove j from Y
8:        **else**
9:            Perform identity recognition based on person's image features endif
10:       **end if**
11:   **end for**
12: **end for**

3.3.2   Based on Character Image Features

Build a triplet network composed of three sub-networks with shared weights, each handling anchor samples, positive samples, and negative samples. The triplet network aims to minimize the distance between anchor samples and positive samples, while maximizing the distance between anchor samples and negative samples. The loss function of the triplet network, called triplet loss, is represented as follows.

$$L = \max(\mathrm{d}(a, p) - \mathrm{d}(a, n) + \text{margin}, 0) \tag{3}$$

In the equation, margin is given hyperparameter typically representing the separation distance between individuals, used to adjust the model's learning process. a represents the anchor sample, p represents the positive sample, n represents the negative sample, and d represents the distance between sample features. The advantage of using a triplet network is its ability to learn discriminative feature representations, enhancing the distinguishability of individuals. It makes the features of the same individual more similar and the features of different individuals more dissimilar, thus improving the accuracy of person re-identification. The triplet network is highly scalable and can be combined with different sub-network architectures to match various types of tasks.

Each sub-network of the triplet network utilizes the MobileNet network model for feature extraction. MobileNet is chosen because, in the edge environment of a digital twin system, there are limitations on computation performance and speed. Using a conventional feature extraction network might lead to high latency and fail to meet real-time requirements. MobileNet employs depthwise separable convolution, replacing standard convolution with depthwise convolution and point-wise convolution. This significantly reduces computation and parameter count, making it well-suited for deployment on resource-constrained devices such as smartphones, embedded devices, and IoT devices.

3.4   Occlusion Processing

In practical indoor target tracking scenarios, individuals are often occluded, where using the midsection of the bounding box as the location of the feet is clearly inappropriate. To address this issue, we need some certain occlusion handling techniques to estimate the actual position of the individuals and provide corresponding 3D trajectory coordinates.

Considering that occlusion causes a significant change in the aspect ratio of the target bounding box, a simple occlusion handling approach can be achieved by restoring the original aspect ratio. When an individual is not occluded, the bounding box has a certain aspect ratio. If the aspect ratio of the bounding box changes beyond a predefined threshold, it can be considered that the occlusion situation occurs. In such cases, the bounding box can be extended along one side until it reaches the normal aspect ratio, which can represent an estimate of the individual's actual position.

When the length of the bounding box decreases, a comparison can be made between the reduced bounding box and the previous bounding box (i.e., the bounding box before occlusion occurred) to observe whether the decrease is from the bottom edge or the top edge. This helps determine if the upper or lower part of the individual is occluded. Since occlusion of the upper part does not affect the position of the feet in the image, only when the lower part is occluded, the bottom edge is extended downwards until the normal aspect ratio is reached, serving as an estimate of the individual's actual position. On the other hand, when the width of the bounding box decreases, it may be due to factors such as the individual turning sideways, which does not affect the estimation of the feet's position and there is no need to restore the bounding box.

This method provides a simple approach for occlusion handling and estimation of the actual position of individuals. However, due to the complexity of real-world scenarios, directly using the restored bounding box for estimating the actual position may have some inaccuracies. Therefore, combining it with the Kalman filtering method can be advantageous. The restored bounding box can be used as the detection value for the individual's position, and a prediction value for the individual's position can be generated by incorporating historical trajectory data. We can achieve an optimal estimation of the current position of the individual through combining the detection and prediction values. The pseudocode for the overall algorithm is as follows.

Algorithm 2. Occlusion processing algorithm

Input: Target bounding box and the previous target bounding box at time t
Output: Optimal estimation of the target position
1: **for** each one **do**
2:     $Height = Height$ of the target bounding box
3:     $Width = Width$ of the target bounding box
4:     $lowNow =$ Bottom edge of the current target bounding box
5:     $highNow =$ Top edge of the current target bounding box
6:     **if** $Height/Width <$ threshold **then**
7:         $lowBefore =$ Bottom edge of the target bounding box at time t
8:         $highBefore =$ Top edge of the target bounding box at time t
9:         **if** $lowNow - lowBefore > highBefore - highNow$ **then**
10:             $lowDetect =$ Extend $lowNow$ downward to achieve the standard aspect ratio
11:         **else**
12:             $lowDetect = lowNow$
13:         **end if**
14:     **end if**
15:     $locationDetect =$ Calculate 3D coordinates of the person based on $lowDetect$
16:     $locationReal =$ Optimal estimation of the actual person's position using Kalman filtering
17: **end for**

---

4   Evaluation

We assume that in complex indoor environments, the coordinate estimation is considered accurate when the Euclidean distance between the estimated coordinates and the true coordinates is within 0.2 m. Based on this criterion, we conducted several tests to evaluate the algorithm: Tracking and detection of a single target without occlusion. In multiple tests, the accuracy of the coordinate calculations reached 92%. Then detection of a single target with occlusion, due to the various forms of occlusion, the accuracy decreased slightly but still remained around 87%.

Figure 3 demonstrates the results of the target tracking and distance calculation.

Figure 4 illustrates the collaboration of multiple cameras. Cameras from different orientations capture the same target and give them the same id after identifying them as the same person based on the coordinate information.

In the complex environment depicted in Fig. 3, we designed two sets of experiments to assess the accuracy of our method. The first set of experiments explored the relationship between accuracy and the number of pedestrians in scenarios

Fig. 3. Results of the target tracking and coordinate calculation

(a) Orientation I

(b) Orientation II

Fig. 4. The collaboration of multiple cameras

with and without camera view blocks. Within the optimal camera range (approximately 4 to 6 m), we placed 1 to 5 individuals and conducted approximately 100 measurements for each scenario. In the obstructed environment, we simulated real-life scenarios with varying degrees of occlusion within normal ranges. Again, we measured accuracy after approximately 100 measurements for each scenario. The second set of experiments investigated the relationship between accuracy and the distance between pedestrians and cameras, considering both obstructed and unobstructed scenarios. Distances ranged from 5 to 20 m, and we performed around 100 measurements for each distance in both scenarios. And we obtained the following results.

Figure 5 depicts the relationship between tracking accuracy and the number of people with/without camera view blocks. We see that 1) For both tracking scenarios, the accuracy decreases when there are more pedestrians. The reason is that as the number of pedestrians becomes larger, the possibility of individuals overlapping in space increases. In this case, the recognition accuracy of the position of detection frame and the individual foot will decrease, and the calculated 3D coordinates will deviate as well, ultimately leading to a decrease in tracking accuracy. 2) As expected, the accuracy without view blocks is higher than that of the scenario with view blocks. However, it is worth noting that with our block handling scheme, the accuracy degradation is around 5%. Compared to many existing works that may have totally incorrect detection boxes, the tracking results are still acceptable and can support digital twin systems at a satisfactory accuracy level. For example, with four pedestrians on site, the accuracy still achieves 55% and can work properly in the digital twin systems (as it is close to the original accuracy 61%).

In Fig. 6, we can find that 1) In both tracking scenarios, the tracking accuracy gradually decreases as the distance increases. The reason is that as the human-camera distance gets farther, the error in the actual position coordinates caused by the error in each pixel point in the picture will become correspondingly larger. And the error of the person recognition algorithm is relatively fixed, so the tracking accuracy will be reduced. 2) The tracking accuracy with camera view blocks is lower than that without camera view blocks. However, it is noteworthy that when the distance is within 11 m, the accuracy degradation with camera view blocks is all within 3% under the implementation of our block handling scheme. Such accuracy degradation is negligible for practical applications in the digital twin system. Compared to the existing work, the evaluation results are at a satisfactory accuracy level. 3) When the distance is greater than 14m, we can find a sharp drop in tracking accuracy in both tracking scenarios. The reason is that when the distance gradually increases beyond the threshold of effective recognition, the camera has lost its basic ability to recognize the person, which will have a great negative effect on the following tracking.

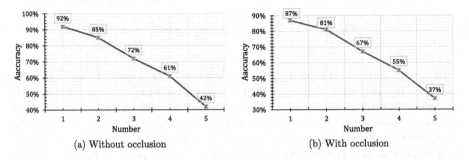

(a) Without occlusion   (b) With occlusion

Fig. 5. Relationship between the number of individuals and accuracy in pictures

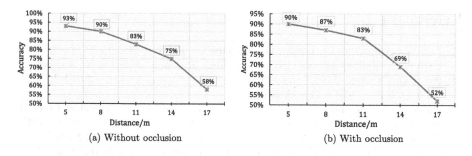

Fig. 6. Relationship between the distance and accuracy in pictures

In terms of real-time performance, we deployed our method on the $NVIDIA$ Jetson series, specifically the $Jetson\ TX2$. Under favorable network conditions, the frame rate of the video stream remained stable, ranging between 20 to 40 frames per second. Overall, this met the real-time requirements of the digital twinning system.

During experiments, we observed occasional brief frame drops when a group of individuals simultaneously exited one camera's field of view and entered the range of another camera. This occurred because performing person re-identification for these pedestrians involved extracting person features based on a triplet network, which can result in significant computational overhead. However, such situations are not frequent in real-world environments.

5   Conclusion

In this paper, we propose an edge-assisted multi-camera tracking algorithm for digital twin systems which provides 3D coordinates of individuals. We use edge nodes provide computing power for the core algorithm. Through the principle of camera calibration, we convert the traditional 2D coordinates of tracked individuals in images to 3D coordinates in space with real-time performance and accuracy, which approach effectively supports the requirements of digital twin systems. Additionally, we introduce a pedestrian re-identification algorithm for multiple cameras based on the 3D coordinates of individuals. Through a two-stage matching algorithm which first matches the 3D coordinates and then utilizes appearance features, we successfully determine the identities of the same person across different cameras, enabling collaborative tracking across multiple cameras. Moreover, we propose an occlusion handling algorithm based on bounding box ratios and Kalman filtering, which efficiently estimates the actual positions of occluded individuals in images to ensure the effectiveness of the tracking algorithm even in the presence of occluded targets. The algorithms we propose are all lightweight, which is suitable for edge computing scenarios with limited computing resources.

References

1. Liu, W., Anguelov, D., Erhan, D., Szegedy, C., Reed, S., Fu, C.-Y., Berg, A.C.: SSD: single shot multibox detector. In: Leibe, B., Matas, J., Sebe, N., Welling, M. (eds.) ECCV 2016. LNCS, vol. 9905, pp. 21–37. Springer, Cham (2016). https://doi.org/10.1007/978-3-319-46448-0_2
2. Girshick, R., Donahue, J., Darrell, T., Malik, J.: Rich feature hierarchies for accurate object detection and semantic segmentation. In: Proceedings of the IEEE Conference on Computer Vision and Pattern Recognition (CVPR) (2014)
3. Ren, S., He, K., Girshick, R., Sun, J.: Faster R-CNN: towards real-time object detection with region proposal networks. IEEE Trans. Pattern Anal. Mach. Intell. **39**(6), 1137–1149 (2017). https://doi.org/10.1109/TPAMI.2016.2577031
4. He, K., Gkioxari, G., Dollar, P., Girshick, R.: Mask R-CNN. In: Proceedings of the IEEE International Conference on Computer Vision (ICCV) (2017)
5. Redmon, J., Divvala, S., Girshick, R., Farhadi, A.: You only look once: unified, real-time object detection. In: Proceedings of the IEEE Conference on Computer Vision and Pattern Recognition (CVPR) (2016)
6. Ma, H., Lu, H., Zhang, M.: A real-time effective system for tracking passing people using a single camera. In: 2008 7th World Congress on Intelligent Control and Automation, pp. 6173–6177 (2008). https://doi.org/10.1109/WCICA.2008.4592793
7. Nguyen, H.D., Na, I.S., Kim, S.H., Lee, G.S., Yang, H.J., Choi, J.H.: Multiple human tracking in drone image. Multimed. Tools Appl. **78**, 4563–4577 (2019)
8. Nishimura, H., Makibuchi, N., Tasaka, K., Kawanishi, Y., Murase, H.: Multiple human tracking using an omnidirectional camera with local rectification and world coordinates representation. IEICE Trans. Inf. Syst. **103**(6), 1265–1275 (2020)
9. Talaoubrid, H., Vert, M., Hayat, K., Magnier, B.: Human tracking in top-view fisheye images: analysis of familiar similarity measures via hog and against various color spaces. J. Imaging **8**(4) (2022) https://doi.org/10.3390/jimaging8040115
10. Chen, X., An, L., Bhanu, B.: Multitarget tracking in nonoverlapping cameras using a reference set. IEEE Sens. J. **15**(5), 2692–2704 (2015). https://doi.org/10.1109/JSEN.2015.2392781
11. Wojke, N., Bewley, A., Paulus, D.: Simple online and realtime tracking with a deep association metric. In: 2017 IEEE International Conference on Image Processing (ICIP), pp. 3645–3649 (2017). https://doi.org/10.1109/ICIP.2017.8296962
12. Hu, W., Hu, M., Zhou, X., Tan, T., Lou, J., Maybank, S.: Principal axis-based correspondence between multiple cameras for people tracking. IEEE Trans. Pattern Anal. Mach. Intell. **28**(4), 663–671 (2006). https://doi.org/10.1109/TPAMI.2006.80
13. Chen, L., Ai, H., Zhuang, Z., Shang, C.: Real-time multiple people tracking with deeply learned candidate selection and person re-identification. In: 2018 IEEE International Conference on Multimedia and Expo (ICME), pp. 1–6 (2018). https://doi.org/10.1109/ICME.2018.8486597
14. Ristani, E., Tomasi, C.: Features for multi-target multi-camera tracking and re-identification. In: 2018 IEEE/CVF Conference on Computer Vision and Pattern Recognition, pp. 6036–6046 (2018). https://doi.org/10.1109/CVPR.2018.00632
15. Cai, Y., Medioni, G.: Exploring context information for inter-camera multiple target tracking. In: IEEE Winter Conference on Applications of Computer Vision, pp. 761–768 (2014). https://doi.org/10.1109/WACV.2014.6836026

16. Cai, Z., Hu, S., Shi, Y., Wang, Q., Zhang, D.: Multiple human tracking based on distributed collaborative cameras. Multimed. Tools Appl. **76**, 1941–1957 (2017)
17. You, Q., Jiang, H.: Real-time 3D deep multi-camera tracking. arXiv preprint arXiv:2003.11753 (2020)
18. Wen, L., Lei, Z., Chang, M.-C., Qi, H., Lyu, S.: Multi-camera multi-target tracking with space-time-view hyper-graph. Int. J. Comput. Vision **122**, 313–333 (2017)
19. Kuo, C.-H., Huang, C., Nevatia, R.: Inter-camera association of multi-target tracks by on-line learned appearance affinity models. In: Daniilidis, K., Maragos, P., Paragios, N. (eds.) ECCV 2010, Part I. LNCS, vol. 6311, pp. 383–396. Springer, Heidelberg (2010). https://doi.org/10.1007/978-3-642-15549-9_28
20. Das, A., Chakraborty, A., Roy-Chowdhury, A.K.: Consistent re-identification in a camera network. In: Fleet, D., Pajdla, T., Schiele, B., Tuytelaars, T. (eds.) ECCV 2014, Part II. LNCS, vol. 8690, pp. 330–345. Springer, Cham (2014). https://doi.org/10.1007/978-3-319-10605-2_22
21. Cai, Q., Aggarwal, J.K.: Automatic tracking of human motion in indoor scenes across multiple synchronized video streams. In: Sixth International Conference on Computer Vision (IEEE Cat. No.98CH36271), pp. 356–362 (1998). https://doi.org/10.1109/ICCV.1998.710743
22. Shu, G., Dehghan, A., Oreifej, O., Hand, E., Shah, M.: Part-based multiple-person tracking with partial occlusion handling. In: 2012 IEEE Conference on Computer Vision and Pattern Recognition, pp. 1815–1821. IEEE (2012)
23. Pan, H.-W., Li, Y., Gao, C.-M., Lei, Y.: A method for multi-cameras human tracking based on reverse epipolar line geometry. In: IEEE Conference Anthology, pp. 1–4 (2013). https://doi.org/10.1109/ANTHOLOGY.2013.6784877
24. Coraluppi, S., Carthel, C.: Track management in multiple-hypothesis tracking. In: 2018 IEEE 10th Sensor Array and Multichannel Signal Processing Workshop (SAM), pp. 11–15 (2018). https://doi.org/10.1109/SAM.2018.8448730
25. Sharma, S., Ansari, J.A., Krishna Murthy, J., Madhava Krishna, K.: Beyond pixels: leveraging geometry and shape cues for online multi-object tracking. In: 2018 IEEE International Conference on Robotics and Automation (ICRA), pp. 3508–3515 (2018). https://doi.org/10.1109/ICRA.2018.8461018

Layer-First "Cache-Rollback" Collaborative Pruning Method

Hengye Di[1,2], Runhe Chen[1], Guanchen Li[1], Jie He[1,2,3(✉)], and Yue Qi[1,2(✉)]

[1] School of Computer and Communication Engineering, University of Science and Technology Beijing, Xueyuan Road, Beijing 100083, China
m20212081202xs.ustb.edu.cn, {hejie,qiyuee}@ustb.edu.cn
[2] Shunde Innovation School, University of Science and Technology Beijing, Zhihui Road, Foshan 528399, Guangdong, China
[3] Liaoning Academy of Materials, Quanyun Road, Shenyang 110000, Liaoning, China

Abstract. With the significant enhancement of inference and storage capabilities of edge computing chips, inference speed has become the primary focus on the model compression. Existing network pruning methods, which is a classical model compression technique, face two major issues in real-time inference scenarios: firstly, a lack of differentiation in the priority of optimization objectives, leading to an overly large search space; secondly, while conventional pruning methods excel in parameter and computational compression, they do not exhibit great effects on inference acceleration. We propose a layer-first "cache-rollback" collaborative pruning method to solve them. Initially, we introduce a layer-first strategy. Subsequently, we design a layer importance evaluation method based on model recovery force, providing a reliable basis for efficient layer pruning. Finally, we design a "cache-rollback" mechanism, facilitating the efficient collaborative pruning of layers and channels, and validate its effectiveness in reducing the search space through theoretical analysis. Experimental results on mainstream edge inference chips reveal that: firstly, under the premise of within 10% decline in accuracy, our method achieves an average acceleration ratio of 2.36, an average parameter compression rate of 68%, and an average computational compression rate of 71%; secondly, compared with the currently fastest pruning algorithm, our method further increases the model acceleration ratio by 0.26 while improving the model accuracy rate by 0.47%.

Keywords: Edge Computing · Inference Speed · Model Compression · Pruning · Model Acceleration

1 Introduction

Convolutional neural networks (CNN) are increasingly used in various edge computing scenarios. In order to adapt to increasingly complex tasks, CNNs are designed to be wider and deeper to enhance their representational capabilities [1]. However, the ensuing large computational requirement and memory usage make it difficult for CNNs to fulfill various real-time requirements on resource constrained edge devices. To solve this, CNNs can be model compressed when they are actually deployed, and neural network pruning is one of the classical model compression methods, which can be seen as a multi-objective optimization of the number of model parameters, computation, and inference speed under the constraints of the task accuracy [2], by pruning away the unnecessary network parameters in order to achieve the purpose of reducing the volume of the network and enhancing the real-time inference ability of the network.

Pruning can be divided into structured and unstructured pruning. Unstructured pruning generally achieves compression of the number of model parameters by zeroing or removing unimportant weights in the network, or by removing certain neurons in the channels or filters, or certain connections in the fully connected layers. Aghasi et al. [3] converted the pruning problem into a convex optimization and sought for a sparse set of weights at each layer that kept the layer inputs and outputs consistent with the originally trained model. Lin et al. [4] proposed a dynamic allocation of the sparsity pattern and introduced a feedback mechanism for incorrect assignments to correct errors. In general, weight pruning sets the weights in the network smaller than a certain threshold and remove them in the matrix, making the network irregular. Therefore it usually requires specific hardware or software library support.

Compared with the former one, structured pruning prunes the entire redundant channels or layers at a time, which can make the pruned network maintains the original network structure. So it is more suitable for most scenarios and does not require the additional support. For channel pruning, it can be generally classified into two categories, pruning based on channel's importance or similarity. Liu et al. [5] proposed to associate a scaling factor for each channel in each convolutional layer, and use the idea of regularization to sparse these scaling factors during the model training process, so as to find the channels with small scaling factors and prune them. He et al. [6] proposed a novel filter pruning method called Filter Pruning via Geometric Median (FPGM) to compress the model regardless of those two requirements. FPGM compressed CNN models by pruning filters with redundancy, rather than those with "relatively less" importance. Although channel pruning can achieve high parameter and computational compression rates, it is not significant for actual model inference acceleration. When it comes to the layer pruning, Wang et al. [7] proposed a discrimination based block-level pruning method (DBP), which took a sequence of consecutive layers as a block and removed redundant blocks according to the discrimination of their output features, so as to accelerate inference speed by reducing the depth of CNNs. However, this method requires additional definition of the model's structure and the method performs poorly on shallow layer models.

In addition to single dimension pruning, there are several researches focusing on multi-dimensional compression methods. Wang et al. [8] proposed a multi-dimensional model pruning method, which intends to find the optimal ratios of channel pruning ratios, layer pruning ratios and input image sizes of the model, and converted this into a polynomial optimization problem. However, the algorithm needs to find a relationship between the compressible variables and the accuracy of the model, which is not easy to fit; secondly, the algorithm does not give guidance on how to take the values of the variables, which also results in not obvious acceleration effect in practice.

In conclusion, the existing pruning methods still have the following two problems in the edge real-time inference scenario:

- Lack of differentiation of target priorities: On the one hand, there is no obvious emphasis on several indicators, resulting in large search space. On the other hand, the joint pruning of layers and channels and their priorities are less considered, making it difficult to find a better trade-off between performance and efficiency.
- The actual inference speed is related to many factors such as number of parameters, computation, degree of parallelism, etc. [9]. Although the common pruning methods bring about a significant parameters and computational compression rate, they are not obvious in the inference speed improvement.

We propose a layer-first "cache-rollback" collaborative pruning method. Firstly, the advantages of layer pruning algorithm in model inference acceleration and a layer-first pruning strategy is proposed based on the priority goal of improving inference speed. Secondly, the model recovery force is designed and a layer importance evaluation method based on model recovery force is proposed. Furthermore, layer pruning is performed on the model based on the layer importance evaluation, and all the models after layer pruning that meet the accuracy requirement are cached. Finally, we use the channel pruning algorithm to further compress the model and design the "cache-rollback" mechanism to realize the collaborative layer-channel pruning, and cyclically pop up the model with the highest layer pruning rate in the cache list to perform the channel pruning, until we find the optimal model with the best speed that meets the task's requirement. Theoretical analysis verifies its effectiveness in reducing the search space. The experimental results on mainstream edge inference chips show that: 1) Our method achieves an average acceleration rate of 2.36, an average parameter compression rate of 68%, and an average computational compression rate of 71% without reducing accuracy compared to the baseline model; 2) Our method improves the model acceleration rate by 0.26 with an increase of 0.47% in the accuracy rate compared to the fastest accelerated pruning algorithm DBP.

The main contributions of this paper are as follows:

- We propose a layer-first pruning strategy based on the first goal of improving inference speed.
- We design a layer importance evaluation method based on model recovery force, which can effectively identify important layers and is explainable at the same time.
- We design a layer-first "cache-rollback" collaborative pruning method, which can solve the problem of limited inference speed of models on edge devices, and realize fast model optimization and inference acceleration under multiple constraints such as accuracy, parameter and computational compression rate.

The rest of this article is organized as follows. Section 2 introduces the layer pruning algorithm based on model recovery power. Section 3 introduces the CRCP we proposed. In Sect. 4, we verify the generality, rationality and validity of the CRCP through experiments. Finally in Secton 5, we summarize the whole paper.

2 Layer Pruning Method Based on Model Recovery Force

Most of the existing pruning methods are based on channel pruning, which make the model have a "slimming" effect, and as a result, channel pruning can bring great effect of computational and parameter compression in practice, but for the inference time, channel pruning can not bring great acceleration effect. This is because the calculation between each channel of the layer is parallel, reducing the inference time of some channels of the layer will not get a significant progress. Taking NVIDIA's GPU, which is commonly used for convolutional neural network inference, as an example, the convolutional layer requires that the number of channels in both the input and output feature maps be multiples of C due to the storage format of C channel alignment. If a layer of channels does not reach C or multiples of C, the number of channels is automatically replenished to C or multiples of C. That is, once the number of channels cut is less than C, it will have no reduction on real computation. For layer pruning, because the calculation among each layer of the model is serial, reducing one of the layers can not only reduce the number of parameters and calculation of the model, but also significantly reduce its inference time.

Convolutional Layer (Conv layer) is the core component of convolutional neural networks, and the importance of convolutional layer is the focus of most hierarchical pruning algorithms. However, in a practical application scenario, if any layer is pruned without analysis, the model may not perform forward propagation correctly due to misalignment of channels. For a Conv layer in the network, if the number of output channels in the front layer is equal to the number of input channels in the back layer, the network can still complete forward propagation after the layer is cut, that is, the layer is a prunable layer. Otherwise, the network cannot complete correct forward propagation after the layer is cut off, so it is an unprunable layer.

Layer pruning needs to focus on the design of the method of measuring the importance of each layer, that is to say, the accuracy of the model whose different layer is pruned will decrease with different importance of each layer. As a result, we propose a model recovery driven layer pruning algorithm (ReDLP) to measure the importance of layers in the network. When a layer is pruned, the accuracy of the model recovers quickly in the fine tuning process, indicating that after deleting the layer, the model does not need to spend too much time to learn its features, and it is considered that the contribution of the layer to the model is small, so the layer is "not important". Conversely, if a layer is pruned and the model accuracy recovers slowly during the fine-tuning process,

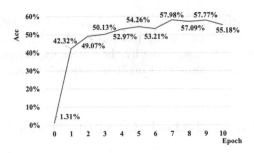

Fig. 1. Curve of the Model Recovery

Algorithm 1. Model Recovery Driven Layer Pruning Algorithm

Require: the trained model *model*, minimum accuracy requirement *min_acc*;
1: initialize *layer_impo_list*
2: **for** *sub_layer* ∈ *model* **do**
3:     **if** *sub_layer.in_channels* == *sub_layer.out_channels* **then**
4:         Empty *sub_layer*
5:         *cur_acc* ← *evaluate(model)*
6:         *layer_impo_list* ← *layer_impo_list* ∪ *cur_acc*
7:     **end if**
8: **end for**
9: *layer_impo_list.sort()*
10: *pruned_model* ← *model*
11: *pruned_acc* ← *evaluate(model)*
12: **for** *i* := 0 *to len(layer_impo_list)* − 1 **do**
13:     *cur_layer* ← *layer_impo_list[i]*
14:     *model* ← *model* − *cur_layer*
15:     *now_acc* ← *evaluate(model)*
16:     **if** *now_acc* ≥ *min_acc* **then**
17:         *pruned_model* ← *model*
18:         *pruned_acc* ← *now_acc*
19:     **end if**
20: **end for**
Ensure: the pruned model *pruned_model*, the accuracy of the pruned model *pruned_acc*

---

it means that after deleting the layer, the model needs to learn its features in more epoch, so the layer is "important". However, in practical application, if the model recovery after cutting off is judged according to the accuracy of model training convergence, the cost is extremely high. In the process of model training, with the increase of iteration epoch, the parameter search space in each iteration will also become smaller and smaller, which means the step size of gradient descent will gradually decrease. If the model's recovery is calculated with the final convergence accuracy, it cannot help the model to quickly measure the importance of the pruned layer. To quickly calculate the corresponding recovery force and order the importance of each prunable layer in the model, the train n

epoch method is proposed to accelerate the process of calculating the recovery force. Figure 1 shows the model recovery curve of VGG-16 model on CIFAR-100 after pruning a certain layer. When $epoch = 0$, the continuity of the model is destroyed by layer pruning, and the accuracy of the model is only 1.31%, which cannot be used as the indicator to judge the importance of the pruned layer. In the n subsequent rounds, the model recovers to a certain level, and the corresponding accuracy represents the recovery of the model after the layer is pruned, and the accuracy at this time can be used as an indicator to judge the importance of the layer to be pruned. The recovery force of the layer i of the model R_i is defined as follows:

$$R_i = Accuracy(finetine_n(model_{without\ i-th\ layer}))$$

where $model_{without\ i-th\ layer}$ indicates the model which the $i-th$ layer is pruned, $finetine_n(*)$ indicates the n subsequent fine-tuning round, and $Accuracy(*)$ indicates the verification of the model accuracy. Normally, the fine-tuning round n can be 1. The layer pruning algorithm based on model recovery force is shown in Algorithm 1. In generally, the minimum accuracy requirement is allowed to be within 0.1% of the baseline and the default epoch of $n = 1$ is properly set.

3   Layer-First "Cache-Rollback" Collaborative Pruning Method

3.1   Layer-Channel Collaborative Pruning Method

In this section we propose a Layer-first "Cache-Rollback" Collaborative Pruning Method (CRCP), which is shown in Fig. 2. It combines the advantages of layer pruning in inference speed acceleration and channel pruning in parameter and computational compression. Based on the first goal of improving inference speed, the optimization problem of two-dimensional variables is transformed into two one-dimensional variables by layer-first pruning strategy, and the optimization path is shortened by "cache-rollback" mechanism, thus the model inference acceleration and fast optimization under multiple constraints can be realized. The method is divided into two stages, namely cache stage and rollback stage, which is shown in Algorithm 2.

Cache Stage: By measuring the importance of the layer based on the model recovery, we get the sorted list of the importance of the model's layers. In the process of layer pruning, whether the accuracy of the current model meets the requirements is judged several times. If does, the current model is cached, and layer pruning is carried out on the model until the model cannot reach the task accuracy. Furthermore, to carry out layer pruning operation on the current model more accurately, the importance of each layer is re-judged before each layer pruning. The goal of this stage is to provide a model with a larger layer pruning rate for the next stage, so that the compression effect of the model in inference delay is more significant.

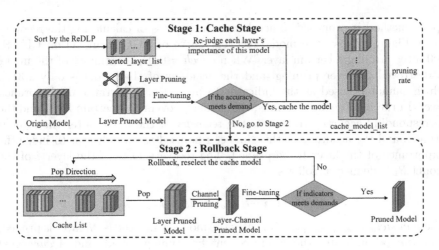

Fig. 2. Illustration of Layer-first "Cache-Rollback" Collaborative Pruning Method

---

Algorithm 2. Layer-first Cache-Rollback Collaborative Pruning Method

---

Require: the trained model *model*, task's indicators *task_indicators*, minimum accuracy requirement *min_acc*;
1: *layer_impo* ← *layer_importance_sort*(*model*)
2: *cache_model_list* ← *layer_pruning*(*model*, *layer_impo*, *min_acc*)
3: **for** *each cur_model* ∈ *reverse*(*models*) **do**
4:    *ch_impo* ← *channel_importance_sort*(*cur_model*)
5:    *pruned_model* ← *channel_pruning*(*cur_model*, *ch_impo*, *min_acc*)
6:    *cur_model_indicators* ← *evaluate*(*pruned_model*)
7:    **if** *cur_model_indicators* meets *task_indicators* **then**
8:        Empty *output_model* ← *pruned_model*
9:        **Break**
10:   **end if**
11: **end for**
Ensure: *output_model*;

Rollback Stage: The model with higher pruning rate in the cache list is preferentially pop for channel pruning and fine tuning, and the pruned model is validated by indicators and compared with the indicators requirement. If yes, the current model is directly output as the optimal output model; otherwise, the cache list pops next model and repeat the above operation until the model that meets the requirements is found. It is found through experiments that for most of the conventional tasks, when there is no extreme demand and unreasonable constraint requirements for task constraints, the target model can be found by rolling back only 0 or 1 times. Therefore, the optimization efficiency of this algorithm is very high.

At the same time, in order to further improve the feature expression and generalization ability of the pruning model, the knowledge distillation idea is introduced into each fine-tuning stage of the layer-first joint pruning algorithm based on "cache-rollback" mechanism, which is:

$$L = (1 - \alpha)CE(x, y, s(x)) + \alpha T^2 KL(p_t(x), p_s(x))$$

where $CE(*)$ represents the cross entropy loss, $KL(*)$ represents KL divergence, and $p_t(x)$ and $p_s(x)$ represent soft labels for teacher and student models, respectively. The hyper-parameter α is used to balance the contributions of the two losses, and T is used to control the "softness" of the soft label. When $T = 1$, the soft label is the standard one-hot encoding; while the soft label becomes smoother when $T \geq 1$.

3.2   Efficiency Analysis

The CRCP transforms one two-dimensional optimization problem into two one-dimensional optimization problems. The overall idea is to find the layer pruning model that meets the accuracy requirements first, and then carry on the channel pruning to the layer pruning model. Assuming that there are a total of m prunable layers with n channels in a given model, then the number of search schemes for layer pruning is $Q_{layer} = 2^m$, and the number of search schemes for channel pruning is $Q_{channel} = 2^n$. As a result, a conventional traversal optimization procedure requires the number of search spaces to be $Space\_Normal = Q_{layer} \times Q_{channel} = 2^{m+n}$.

As for the CRCP, in general, it can only use the first two cache models with the highest pruning rate that meet the accuracy requirements, and the corresponding number of channel pruning schemes are n_1 and n_2. The amount of search space required for the optimization process is: $Space_{CRCP} = 2^m + 2^{n_1} + 2^{n_2}$.

For the layer pruning model with high pruning rate, $n_1 < n_2 < n$ can be obtained because the number of channels is significantly reduced and the corresponding number of channels is smaller than the number of channels in the original model. Therefore, the CRCP algorithm has a smaller search space than the conventional optimization process, which can help the model quickly find the layer-channel pruning model that meets the task requirement with priority inference speed.

4   Simulation Experiment

4.1   Experiment Setup

We select NVIDIA Jetson AGX Orin as the edge computing chip, which is a high-performance artificial intelligence edge computing platform designed for edge computing applications and has been used in various applications such as robots and autonomous vehicles. We set the epoch of model's recovery force as 1 and the accuracy of the target pruned model is within 0.1% of the baseline

Table 1. Comparison of The Compression Effect and Performance by ReDLP and CRCP on CIFAR-100

Model	Method	D_P (%)	D_{FLOPs} (%)	Accuracy (%)	Inference Time (ms)	S_P
VGG-16	baseline	–	–	73.79	4.332	–
	ReDLP-7	38.17	53.79	73.78 (0.01↓)	2.350	1.843
	ReDLP-8	38.28	65.18	71.71 (2.08↓)	2.108	2.055
	CRCP-7	38.37	54.30	73.91 (0.12↑)	2.259	1.918
ResNet-50	baseline	–	–	72.78	13.695	–
	ReDLP-10	58.52	53.10	73.19 (0.41↑)	6.016	2.276
	ReDLP-11	59.70	58.71	72.62 (0.16↓)	5.230	2.618
	CRCP-10	76.87	73.30	72.95 (0.17↑)	6.002	2.282
MobileNet-V2	baseline	–	–	67.66	10.855	–
	ReDLP-9	45.19	47.65	68.09 (0.37↑)	5.398	2.011
	ReDLP-10	45.82	50.63	66.94 (0.72↓)	4.793	2.265
	CRCP-9	68.56	66.06	68.54 (0.88↑)	5.381	2.017

Table 2. Comparison of The Compression Effect and Performance by ReDLP and CRCP on CIFAR-10

Model	Method	D_P (%)	D_{FLOPs} (%)	Accuracy (%)	Inference Time (ms)	S_P
VGG-16	baseline	–	–	88.13	7.641	–
	ReDLP-9	9.81	58.85	90.15 (2.02↑)	4.905	1.558
	CRCP-9	34.79	86.61	88.38 (0.25↑)	2.786	2.743
ResNet-50	baseline	–	–	87.86	14.196	–
	ReDLP-13	81.11	72.53	89.98 (2.12↑)	3.856	3.682
	CRCP-13	97.15	95.37	88.00 (0.14↑)	3.824	3.712
MobileNet-V2	baseline	–	–	87.42	10.991	–
	ReDLP-9	47.80	42.12	87.28 (0.14↓)	5,247	2.095
	CRCP-9	59.54	48.49	87.71 (0.29↑)	5.354	2.053

accuracy. As for the knowledge distillation, we set the temperature parameter T of simulated loss to 1, and the equilibrium coefficient α to 0.5.

In our experiment, the comparison indexes we select include model parameter number decline rate D_P, model computational compression rate D_{FLOPs} and model inference speed acceleration ratio S_p.

4.2 Rationality and Universality Verification

In this part we verify the rationality and universality of the CRCP in different models. Three methods, ReDLP-n (layer pruning n layer only), ReDLP-n+1 (layer pruning $n + 1$ layer only) and CRCP-n (layer pruning n layer + channel pruning), are used to compare the compression effect and inference speed on the CIFAR-100 and CIFAR-10 dataset. The results are shown on Table 1 and Table 2.

As shown in Table 1, the VGG-16 model can prune up to 7 layers under the premise of only 0.01% reduction in accuracy, and the D_P reaches 1.843. When the CRCP-7 are used, not only the D_P is increased to 1.918, but also the accuracy was increased by 0.13%. The ResNet-50 model can be pruned up to 10 layers, and the accuracy is improved by 0.41% and the D_P is 2.276, while the CRCP-10 can achieve D_P of 2.282 and the accuracy is improved by 0.17%. The MobileNet-V2 model can be pruned up to 9 layers, when the D_P reaches 2.011 and the accuracy is improved by 0.43%. When the CRCP-9 is used, the D_P reaches 2.017, and the accuracy is improved by 0.43%. When these models are pruned beyond levels above, although the models get higher D_P, there accuracy cannot meet the task requirements.

Comparing the compression effect of ReDLP-n and ReDLP-n+1 methods, it can be found that the layer-first pruning strategy can bring higher acceleration benefits, but due to the limitation of task accuracy requirements, the number of pruned layers will also be limited. In this case, it is necessary to go back to the cache list and select the proper model for the next step. The experiment results show that the optimal speed model can be quickly found by CRCP method under the constraint of task index, which shows the rationality of "cache-rollback" mechanism. Comparing the compression effect of ReDLP-n and CRCP-n methods, the acceleration rate of most models is more than 2 times, and the parameter and computational compression effects are further improved. Therefore, it can be considered that the introduction of channel pruning after layer pruning can further compress the parameter and calculation amount of the model. It is worth mentioning that under lower accuracy requirements, our CRCP will have a better performance.

When it comes to the result on the CIFAR-10 dataset which is shown on Table 2, the CRCP also performs well. When using the ReDLP method, the average S_P is 2.445, the average D_P is 46.24%, and the average D_{FLOPs} is 57.83%. By further pruning with CRCP method, the average S_P is increased to 2.836, and the average D_P and D_{FLOPs} are increased to 63.83% and 76.82%. Combined with the above results, it shows that the CRCP has the universality in different tasks. It is worth noting that for the VGG-16 model, the speed improvement of the model after channel pruning is more obvious than that of other models. This is because the input feature dimension of the first layer of the fully connected layer of this model is $512 \times 7 \times 7$, and channel pruning can significantly reduce the input feature channel of this layer, thereby increasing the speed.

4.3   Comparison of Common Pruning Methods

In this part, we compare the CRCP with other existing structured pruning algorithms. We use CIFAR-10 and ResNet-56 as this experiment's dataset and model. The method of comparison is as follows: 1) Compress the dimensions of the input image, thus reducing the calculation amount of the model and improving the inference speed; 2) The classical channel pruning method based on γ values of BN layer proposed by Liu et al. [5]; 3) FPGM method based on geometric median proposed by He et al. [6]; 4) DBP layer pruning method proposed by Wang et al. [7]; 5) CPF method of multi-dimensional pruning framework based on polynomial optimization by Wang et al. [8], which is based on three dimensions of pruning. Table 3 shows the effect comparison of various pruning algorithms.

Table 3. Comparison of The Effect of Various Pruning Algorithms on ResNet-56

Method	D_P (%)	D_{FLOPs} (%)	Accuracy (%)	Inference Time (ms)	S_P
baseline	–	–	93.69	13.972	–
size compression	–	51.00	92.00 (1.69↓)	13.649	1.024
BN layer Channel Pruning [5]	50.00	50.00	92.97 (0.72↓)	13.411	1.042
FPGM [6]	–	52.00	93.26 (0.33↓)	13.415	1.041
DBP [7]	40.00	52.00	93.27 (0.42↓)	9.226	1.514
CPF [8]	40.00	50.00	93.76 (0.07↑)	12.032	1.161
CRCP	24.93	48.83	93.56 (0.13↓)	**7.874**	**1.774**

It can be seen from the result that the CRCP can achieve significantly better inference speed acceleration than other methods when the D_P is little and the D_{FLOPs} is similar. Among them, the channel pruning method can increase the S_P by 4.2% at the baseline level, the layer pruning method DBP can increase the S_P by 50.1%, and the CPF can increase the S_P by 16.1%. Compared with other methods, the CRCP can improve the S_P by 77.4% at the baseline level, and the speed improvement effect is 18 times that of channel pruning method, 1.5 times that of layer pruning method, and 4.8 times that of the CPF. At the same time, in terms of the S_P of the model, CRCP method performs just 0.2% of that of the CPF.

In a word, the parameter and computational compression rate is not equal to the practical acceleration of model inference speed, and the CRCP has a more significant improvement in model inference speed than other algorithms, which is increased by 17% compared with the current method with the best acceleration effect.

5   Conclusion

In this paper, we propose a layer-first "cache-rollback" collaborative pruning method and a model recovery driven layer pruning algorithm to achieve efficient layer importance assessment and pruning. The optimization problem of two-dimensional variables is transformed into that of two one-dimensional variables by the layer pruning priority strategy, and the fast optimization of two one-dimensional variables is realized by the "cache-rollback" mechanism, which can quickly find the speed optimal model under the multi-objective constraints. The experimental results on the edge inference chips show that the CRCP can significantly improve the inference speed of the model, and compress the parameter number and computation amount of the model efficiently. Compared with other structured pruning methods, the proposed method has significant advantages in improving inference speed and recovering model accuracy.

Acknowledgments. This work is supported by The National Key R&D Program of China, No. 2021YFB3501501, National Natural Science Foundation of China (U22A20106), National Natural Science Foundation of China (NSFC) project No. 61971031, Foshan Science and technology innovation special foundation (BK22BF001), Foshan Higher Education Advanced Talents Foundation (BKBS202203).

References

1. Liu, Z., Mao, H., Wu, C.-Y., Feichtenhofer, C., Darrell, T., Xie, S.: A convnet for the 2020s. In: Proceedings of the IEEE/CVF Conference on Computer Vision and Pattern Recognition, pp. 11976–11986 (2022)
2. Ding, X., Zhang, X., Ma, N., Han, J., Ding, G., Sun, J.: RepVGG: making VGG-style convnets great again. In: Proceedings of the IEEE/CVF Conference on Computer Vision and Pattern Recognition, pp. 13733–13742 (2021)
3. Aghasi, A., Abdi, A., Nguyen, N., Romberg, J.: Net-trim: convex pruning of deep neural networks with performance guarantee. In: Advances in Neural Information Processing Systems, vol. 30 (2017)
4. Lin, T., Stich, S.U., Barba, L., Dmitriev, D., Jaggi, M.: Dynamic model pruning with feedback. arXiv preprint arXiv:2006.07253 (2020)
5. Liu, Z., Li, J., Shen, Z., Huang, G., Yan, S., Zhang, C.: Learning efficient convolutional networks through network slimming. In: Proceedings of the IEEE International Conference on Computer Vision, pp. 2736–2744 (2017)
6. He, Y., Liu, P., Wang, Z., Hu, Z., Yang, Y.: Filter pruning via geometric median for deep convolutional neural networks acceleration. In: Proceedings of the IEEE/CVF Conference on Computer Vision and Pattern Recognition, pp. 4340–4349 (2019)
7. Wang, W., Zhao, S., Chen, M., Hu, J., Cai, D., Liu, H.: DBP: discrimination based block-level pruning for deep model acceleration. arXiv preprint arXiv:1912.10178 (2019)
8. Wang, W., et al.: Accelerate CNNs from three dimensions: A comprehensive pruning framework. In: International Conference on Machine Learning, pp. 10717–10726. PMLR (2021)
9. Ma, N., Zhang, X., Zheng, H.-T., Sun, J.: ShuffleNet v2: practical guidelines for efficient CNN architecture design. In: Proceedings of the European Conference on Computer Vision (ECCV), pp. 116–131 (2018)

The Model and Method of Electricity Consumption Data Collection Based on Producer and Consumer

Shuai Liu[1,2], Zhenya Zhang[1,2], Jun Wang[2,4(✉)], Ping Wang[1,2], and Hongmei Cheng[1,3]

[1] Anhui Province Key Laboratory of Intelligent Building and Building Energy Saving, Anhui Jianzhu University, Hefei 230022, China
[2] School of Electronics and Information Engineering, Anhui Jianzhu University, Hefei 230601, China
23958938@qq.com
[3] School of Economics and Management, Anhui Jianzhu University, Hefei 230601, China
[4] Baohe Branch, Hefei's City Police Bureau, Hefei 230051, China

Abstract. When collecting user power situation at the edge side, the collected data may be backlogged at the edge side due to the information processing capability of the collection device and the network communication overhead. To upload the collected data promptly, this paper designs a single producer and multiple consumers collaborative user electricity data collection model. The model dynamically adjusts the number of consumers by monitoring the data collection time and data upload time during the data collection process. Experiments test the performance of the electricity consumption data collection model under different numbers of consumers, and the experimental results show that the electricity consumption data collection model, which can dynamically adjust the number of consumers, can dynamically select the appropriate number of consumers, and upload the collected user power situation data promptly without significantly increasing the arithmetic burden on the edge side.

Keywords: data collection · producer · consumer · strategy · user power situation

1 Introduction

With the continuous maturity and wide application of IoT technology, it has become possible to collect data on user power situation data in different scenarios (e.g., homes and office buildings, etc.), edge side devices can collect more comprehensive data on user power situation [1, 2]. Influenced by the network communication overhead and the computing power of the equipment deployed in the data collection system, the uploading of the user power situation data collected at high frequencies may not be timely. This phenomenon undermines the user power situation data's accuracy and completeness and makes subsequent data analysis and processing difficult [3–5].

The producer/consumer model [6] has a wide range of applications in the field of data collection, and researchers have mainly focused on the usage scenarios, scheduling strategies, and other issues of this model [7–13]. To solve the problems of low

L. Wang et al. (Eds.): CWSN 2023, CCIS 1994, pp. 162–174, 2024.
https://doi.org/10.1007/978-981-97-1010-2_12

automation level, too few data channels, and limited application areas of the motor data acquisition system, a motor data acquisition and analysis system based on producer/consumer model and LabVIEW program development was designed [14]. To improve the concurrency performance of traditional servers, a thread pooling model based on the producer/consumer model is proposed to achieve high concurrency as much as possible and to optimize the operational efficiency of the server. [15] implements the producer/consumer synchronization based on the aspect-oriented programming (AOP) in both single-buffer and multi-buffer, and the execution results show that AOP can solve the producer/consumer problem effectively. [16] designed a simulator to implement the producer/consumer model, which allows the user to study the producer/consumer synchronization problem in three different scenarios: the simple producer/consumer problem, the producer/consumer problem in a uniprocessor system, and the producer/consumer problem in a multiprocessor system, and demonstrated the feasibility of the proposed simulator with experiments. [17] implemented a continuous audio signal acquisition system using LabVIEW as the development platform and a producer/consumer model combined with a sound card signal acquisition example [18]. To solve the problems of long cycle time and low execution efficiency of the program in the traditional sequential structure mode, a rail profile acquisition system is designed based on the producer/consumer mode [19]. To solve the problem of fast and large-capacity storage of data in the process of real-time data acquisition, the design of a stress wave information acquisition system is realized based on the producer/consumer design pattern, which can realize real-time updating of parameters in the acquisition process [20]. To reduce the performance overhead of CMP, an adaptive producer/consumer sharing optimization mechanism is designed to maintain cache consistency. [21] designed a producer/consumer algorithm adapted to the simultaneous localization and communication of multiple vehicles with UWB sensors. [22] discusses a thread pooling-based solution to the producer/consumer problem and the results show that the use of thread pooling makes the producer/consumer model more efficient in terms of time.

Based on the idea of linkage between a single producer and multiple consumers, the related research in this paper designs a dynamic adjustment strategy for the number of consumers to realize the data collection of user power situation. The number of consumers is dynamically adjusted to ensure timely data upload by monitoring the data upload delay.

The dynamic adjustment strategy of the number of consumers is given in the second part, the performance evaluation method of the electricity consumption data acquisition model is given in the third part, and the experimental results and analysis are given in the fourth part.

2 Strategies for Dynamic Adjustment of Consumer Numbers

When using the data acquisition device deployed on the edge side to collect user electricity consumption data, the collected data may form a data backlog on the edge side due to the influence of the acquisition device's computing power and network communication capability.

Let be a user's electricity consumption data collected at a time $t_{collect}$, then the time for s_t data to be collected is $t_{collect}$, the time for data uploading to be completed is t_{upload},

t_{delay} is the uploading delay of the user's electricity consumption data as stipulated in Eq. 1.

$$t_{delay} = t_{upload} - t_{collect} \tag{1}$$

where $t_{collect}$ and t_{upload} denote timestamps to the nearest second, respectively.

Set the data upload delay threshold as M seconds, for the user electricity consumption data s_t at time t, $\sigma(s_t)$ as stipulated in Eq. 2, $\sigma(s_t) = 0$ indicates that the data upload is timely, $\sigma(s_t) = 1$ indicates that the data upload is untimely, and $\sigma()$ is used to determine whether the user electricity consumption data collection is timely.

$$\sigma(s_t) = \begin{cases} 0, & t_{delay} \leq M \\ 1, & t_{delay} > M \end{cases} \tag{2}$$

In the specific collection process of user electricity data, as the data needs to consume a certain amount of time in carrying out the processing and uploading, M in Eq. 2 denotes the maximum total time consumed for data processing and uploading allowed by the data collection model.

When data encounters a large network delay during upload, it can cause a backlog of subsequently collected data in the buffer. This backlog will further increase the data upload latency, resulting in the collected data not being uploaded promptly.

For the phenomenon that electricity consumption data form a data backlog at the edge side, to minimize the upload delay caused by the data backlog in the buffer, under the influence of the weak information processing capability and network delay, the single producer multi-consumer model can be used to implement the collection of electricity consumption data from users. The single-producer multi-consumer model is shown in Fig. 1.

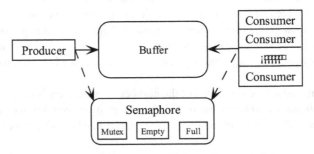

Fig. 1. Single-producer multiple-consumer model.

In this, the producer is responsible for generating data and placing it in the buffer while the consumer gets the data from the buffer and processes it, the buffer is used to store the data generated by the producer, and a semaphore is used to control the mutually exclusive access to the buffer by the producer and the consumer.

In the implementation of the single-producer multi-consumer model shown in Fig. 1, a binary semaphore *Mutex* is used to control the access to the buffer by producers and consumers. When a producer or consumer wants to access the buffer, it must first apply for the semaphore *Mutex*, if the state of the semaphore is 1, then the application will be allowed to pass, otherwise, it enters a blocking state and waits for the other producers or consumers to release the semaphore before it can continue to access the buffer.

Further, to better control the resources in the buffer, the single-producer-multi-consumer model shown in Fig. 1 also introduces the counting semaphores *Empty* and *Full*. These semaphores function as follows: the initial value of the semaphore *Empty* is set to the length of the buffer, representing the number of free positions available in the buffer; the initial value of the semaphore *Full* is 0, representing the number of data already in the buffer. When a producer produces data, it needs to request a semaphore *Empty* to indicate that it needs a free location to store the produced data, while the number of free locations in the buffer is reduced by one. Whereas, at the time when the consumer removes the data from the buffer, a semaphore *Full* needs to be requested to indicate that the amount of data in the buffer is reduced by one.

Algorithm 1 gives the workflow to be done by the producer in the single producer multiple consumer model.

Algorithm 1 Producer's workflow in the single-producer multi-consumer model

---

Input: buffer size,L; number of producers,$producerNum$
Output: write data to buffer success flag,$writeSign$
1: $Mutex = 1$
2: $Empty = L$
3: $Full = 0$
4: **if** $Empty > 0$ **then**
5:    **if** $Mutex = 1$ **then**
6:       Requesting a semaphore $Mutex$
7:       Write data to buffer
8:       Release the semaphore $Mutex$
9:       $Full = Full + 1$
10:    **else**
11:       Wait for $Mutex = 1$
12:    **end if**
13: **else**
14:    Wait for $Empty > 0$
15: **end if**
16: **return** $writeSign = true$

In Algorithm 1, the mechanism of waiting for the buffer to have a free position by step 14 can effectively control the producer's access to the buffer and avoid data writing conflicts. The producer does not cause buffer overflow problems while writing data.

Algorithm 2 gives the workflow that needs to be done by the consumers in the single producer multiple consumer-based model.

Algorithm 2 Consumer workflow in the single-producer multi-consumer model

---

Input: buffer size, L; number of consumers, $consumerNum$
Output: Remove data from buffer success flag, $readSign$

1:   $Mutex = 1$
2:   $Empty = L$
3:   $Full = 0$
4: **if** $Full > 0$ **then**
5:     **if** $Mutex = 1$ **then**
6:       Requesting a semaphore $Mutex$
7:       Getting data from the buffer and processing it
8:       Release the semaphore $Mutex$
9:       $Full = Full - 1$
10:      $Empty = Empty + 1$
11:    **else**
12:      Wait for $Mutex = 1$
13:    **end if**
14: **else**
15:    Wait for $Full > 0$
16: **end if**
17: **return** $readSign = true$

In Algorithm 2, the wait at step 13 is to ensure that the consumer performs data processing operations only when there is available data. This mechanism enables efficient utilization of resources and ensures sequential and complete data processing.

To solve the problem of how to select the appropriate number of consumers in the single-producer multi-consumer model, this study designs a dynamic adjustment strategy for the number of consumers based on this model to select the appropriate number of consumers. In the dynamic adjustment strategy of the number of consumers, whether the data is uploaded in time is calculated to determine whether the number of consumers needs to be adjusted, and if it needs to be adjusted, the number of consumers is adjusted dynamically, so that the number of consumers can meet the needs of data collection, and the algorithmic flow of the dynamic adjustment strategy of the number of consumers is given in Algorithm 3.

Algorithm 3 Strategies for dynamic adjustment of the number of consumers

Input: buffer size,L; Upload delay threshold,M
Output: Number of consumers,$consumersNum$
  1: Initialize the Queue size to L
  2: $t_{delay} = 0$
  3: $MaxDelay = M$
  4: Calculate the upload delay of the data t_{delay}
  5: **if** $t_{delay} > MaxDelay$ **then**
  6:     Producers stop generating data
  7:     Upload the remaining data in the buffer
  8:     Empty the buffer
  9:     $consumersNum + 1$
 10:     Producers start generating data
 11: **else**
 12:     does not perform any operation
 13: **end if**
 14: **return** $consumersNum$

In Algorithm 3, the uploading delay of the data is first calculated, if the uploading delay exceeds the set threshold, it means that the data collection model has experienced untimely data uploading, and it is necessary to increase the number of consumers since the producer stores the generated data in the buffer, so to prevent the data from being lost or repeatedly uploaded in the buffer, it is necessary to perform steps 7 and 8 before adjusting the number of consumers, i.e., the data in the buffer is processed, and then the buffer is emptied.

3 Evaluation of the Performance of the Dynamic Adjustment Strategy for the Number of Consumers

Let the start time of data collection be t_0, and the end time of data collection be t_{end}, and the consumer consumes a total of x pieces of data during the $[t_0, t_{end}]$ period, there is v as specified in Eq. 3, and v is said to be the rate at which the consumer consumes the data, and the unit of v is the number of pieces of data/second.

$$v = \frac{x}{t_{end} - t_0} \tag{3}$$

Using v as an evaluation metric for the dynamic adjustment strategy of the number of consumers, a higher velocity indicates that the data is consumed faster.

Let the time for data to enter the buffer is t_1, the time for data to be taken out of the buffer t_2, and there is t_{wait} as stipulated in Eq. 4, which is called the waiting time of data in the buffer, in milliseconds.

$$t_{wait} = t_2 - t_1 \tag{4}$$

Using t_{wait} as an evaluation metric for electricity consumption data collection systems, lower wait times indicate that data is consumed more quickly.

Also, considering the impact of the electricity consumption data collection system on the system load as well as the network load, the following evaluation metrics are used in this paper:

The average CPU utilization is used to estimate the overall CPU consumption of the system. The average CPU utilization avg_{cpu} is specified in Eq. 5.

$$avg_{cpu} = \frac{1}{n} \sum_{i=1}^{n} u_i \tag{5}$$

where u_i denotes the CPU utilization of the i-th acquired electricity consumption data acquisition system at runtime.

Use the maximum CPU utilization rate to estimate the maximum load capacity of the device, and the maximum CPU utilization rate M_{cpu} is specified in Eq. 6.

$$M_{cpu} = Max(u_1, u_2, ..., u_n) \tag{6}$$

Use the average memory usage index to estimate the continuous stability of the memory, and the average memory usage avg_{memory} is specified in Eq. 7.

$$avg_{memory} = \frac{1}{n} \sum_{i=1}^{n} m_i \tag{7}$$

Among them, m_i represents the memory usage rate of the power consumption data acquisition system acquired for the i-th time during operation.

Use the maximum memory usage index to evaluate the stability of the power consumption data acquisition system under high memory load conditions, and the maximum memory usage M_{memory} is as specified in Eq. 8.

$$M_{memory} = Max(m_1, m_2, ..., m_n) \tag{8}$$

Use the average sending data speed to estimate the transmission efficiency and stability of data at the sending end, and the average sending speed avg_{send} is specified in Eq. 9.

$$avg_{send} = \frac{1}{n} \sum_{i=1}^{n} sv_i \tag{9}$$

Among them, sv_i represents the data-sending speed of the data acquisition system for the i-th record during operation.

$$M_{send} = Max(sv_1, sv_2, ..., sv_n) \tag{10}$$

Use the average received data speed to evaluate the efficiency and reliability of data transmission, and the average received data speed $avg_{receive}$ is specified in Eq. 11.

$$avg_{receive} = \frac{1}{n} \sum_{i=1}^{n} rv_i \tag{11}$$

Among them, rv_i represents the data receiving speed of the data acquisition system for the i-th record at runtime.

Use the maximum transmission speed indicator to ensure that the system can still process the received data efficiently under high load conditions. The maximum receiving speed $M_{receive}$ is stipulated in Eq. 12.

$$M_{receive} = Max(rv_1, rv_2, ..., rv_n) \qquad (12)$$

4   Experimental Results and Analysis

To verify the effectiveness of the dynamic adjustment strategy of the number of consumers based on the single-producer-multiple-consumer model, the performance of the electricity data acquisition system using different numbers of consumers was compared experimentally.

The experimental device, as shown in Fig. 2, uses a TTL to RS485 module to connect the circuit breaker to the Raspberry Pi. The data collection system is deployed on the Raspberry Pi. The data collection system sends a data collection command to the circuit breaker once per second to collect the electricity consumption data in the circuit breaker. The data collection system also receives the electricity consumption data uploaded by the circuit breaker and stores it in a buffer. Consumers retrieve the electricity consumption data from the buffer and upload it to the data storage server. Since data processing and uploading to the data storage server takes a certain amount of time, a data upload threshold, denoted as M, is set to 1 s.

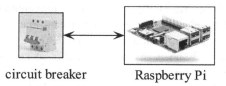

circuit breaker   Raspberry Pi

Fig. 2. The physical topology of the data collection system.

In the experiment, we collected electricity consumption data through circuit breakers to observe and record the performance of the data collection system under different numbers of consumers. The numbers of consumers used were 1, 2, 3, 4, and 5.

By analyzing Fig. 3, the following conclusions can be drawn: when increasing the number of consumers to 2, the speed of consumer consumption data increased by 0.2048 per second. And when increasing the number of consumers to 3, 4, and 5, the speed of consumer consumption data remains stable. This indicates that when the number of consumers is 2, the data in the buffer can be processed promptly, which effectively avoids the data backlog in the buffer. In addition, it is observed that there is no significant increase in the speed of consumer consumption data when using 3, 4, and 5 consumers. This is because 2 consumers are already able to process the data in the buffer promptly, and increasing the number of consumers will not further improve the speed of data processing by consumers.

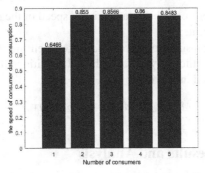

Fig. 3. Consumer consumption data rate in a user electricity data collection system with different numbers of consumers.

Analysis of Fig. 4 and Table 1 shows that when only one consumer is used, the data waiting time in the buffer shows a large range of fluctuations with a mean value of 746.17 ms and a variance of 204,444.87 ms^2. However, when increasing the number of consumers to 2, the mean value of the data waiting time in the buffer was significantly reduced by 636.07 ms with a consequent reduction in the variance of 204,441.13 ms^2. When using 3, 4, and 5 consumers, there were minor fluctuations in the mean and variance of the data waiting time in the buffer, caused by variations in the network latency as the data was uploaded to the data storage server. Therefore, using 2 consumers to process the data in the buffer is effective in reducing the data waiting time in the buffer and improving the timeliness of the data.

The analysis of Table 2 shows that as the number of consumers increases, there is no significant trend in the average CPU utilization and maximum CPU utilization of the consumer electricity data collection system, which means that increasing the number of consumers does not have a significant impact on the CPU utilization of the device.

The analysis of Table 3 shows that as the number of consumers increases, there is no significant increase in the average memory utilization as well as the maximum memory utilization of the consumer electricity data collection system, indicating that increasing the number of consumers does not have a significant impact on the memory of the consumer electricity data collection system under the current device configuration and environment.

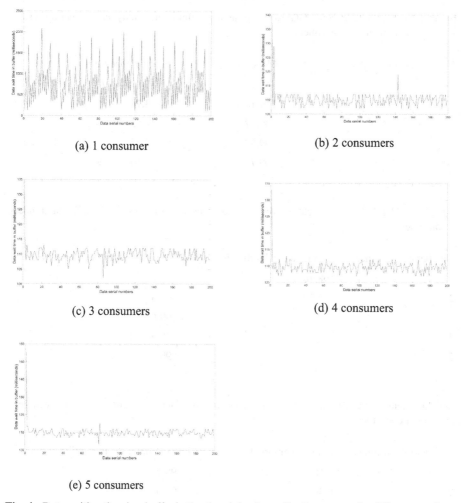

(a) 1 consumer

(b) 2 consumers

(c) 3 consumers

(d) 4 consumers

(e) 5 consumers

Fig. 4. Data waiting time in a buffer in the electricity data collection system for different numbers of consumers.

The analysis of Table 4 likewise shows that as the number of consumers increases, the indicators of average sending speed and average receiving speed of the consumer electricity data collection system do not show significant trends, indicating that increasing the number of consumers does not significantly affect the network load of the device.

Table 1. Mean and variance of data waiting time in a buffer in electricity data collection system for different numbers of consumers.

Number of consumers	Mean (*ms*)	Variance (*ms²*)
1	746.17	204444.87
2	**110.10**	**3.74**
3	109.67	4.03
4	109.67	2.24
5	109.76	4.14

Table 2. CPU utilization of electricity consumption data collection system for different numbers of consumers.

Number of consumers	Average CPU utilization (%)	Maximum CPU utilization (%)
1	98.16	99.7
2	96.30	97.5
3	97.67	99.6
4	97.30	99.5
5	96.24	99.3

Table 3. Memory utilization of electricity consumption data collection system for different numbers of consumers

Number of consumers	Average memory utilization (%)	Maximum memory utilization (%)
1	98.16	99.7
2	96.30	97.5
3	97.67	99.6
4	97.30	99.5
5	96.24	99.3

The analysis of the evaluation indexes from 1 consumer to 5 consumers shows that when using 2 consumers, the user electricity data collection system can achieve timely collection and upload of electricity consumption data, and at the same time, with the increase in the number of consumers, there is no significant impact on the load of the equipment as well as the network load.

Table 4. Impact of different numbers of consumers' electricity data collection systems on network loads.

Number of consumers	Average sending speed (KiB/Sec)	Maximum sending speed (KiB/Sec)	Average receiving speed (KiB/Sec)	Maximum receiving speed (KiB/Sec)
1	1.98	3.11	2.23	3.20
2	2.02	2.43	2.45	3.18
3	2.08	3.18	2.67	3.16
4	2.04	2.97	2.68	3.55
5	2.15	3.29	2.73	3.77

The experimental consumer electricity data collection system runs on a device model Raspberry Pi 3 Model B Rev 1.2, processor model ARMv7 Processor rev 4 (v7l), memory size 944268 kB, and operating system based on the Linux kernel with kernel version 5.15.84-v7+. The user electricity data collection system is implemented in Java language with JDK version 1.8.0.312.

5 Conclusions and Future Work

In the system based on edge computing architecture, to upload the edge side sensed user power situation data promptly, this paper designs a single-producer-multi-consumer collaborative consumer dynamic adjustment strategy and electricity data collection model and evaluates the strategy by using the metrics of "consumer consuming data speed" and "waiting time of data in the buffer zone".

Experiments show that by monitoring the uploading delay of data, the dynamic adjustment strategy of consumers is utilized to dynamically adjust the number of consumers to achieve timely uploading of collected data without significantly increasing the burden on the edge side.

In future research work, based on the strategy of dynamically adjusting the number of consumers designed in this paper, by recording and analyzing the adjustment of the number of consumers over time in the electricity consumption data collection scene, a self-learning model will be explored, which can Dynamically adjust the number of consumers for specific data collection scenarios.

References

1. Zhang, Z.Y., Fang, B., Wang, P., Cheng, H.M.: A local area network-based insect intelligent building platform. Int. J. Pattern Recogn. Artif. Intell. **37**(02), 2359004 (2023)
2. Audrito, G., Casadei, R., Damiani, F., Pianini, D., Viroli, M.: Optimal resilient distributed data collection in mobile edge environments. Comput. Electr. Eng. **96**, 107580 (2021)
3. Belli, R., Hoefler, T.: Notified access: extending remote memory access programming models for producer-consumer synchronization. In: 2015 IEEE International Parallel and Distributed Processing Symposium, Hyderabad, India, pp. 871–881 (2015)

4. Crespo Turrado, C., Sánchez Lasheras, F., Calvo-Rollé, J.L., Piñón-Pazos, A.J., de Cos Juez, F.J.: A new missing data imputation algorithm applied to electrical data loggers. Sensors **15**(12), 31069–31082 (2015)
5. Yen, S.W., Morris, S., Ezra, M.A., Huat, T.J.: Effect of smart meter data collection frequency in an early detection of shorter-duration voltage anomalies in smart grids. Int. J. Electr. Power Energy Syst. **109**, 1–8 (2019)
6. Manivannan, M., Negi, A., Stenström, P.: Efficient forwarding of producer-consumer data in task-based programs. In: 2013 42nd International Conference on Parallel Processing, Lyon, France, pp. 517–522 (2013)
7. Xu, J., Yin, J., Zhu, H., Xiao, L.: Modeling and verifying producer-consumer communication in Kafka using CSP. In: 7th Conference on the Engineering of Computer Based Systems (ECBS 2021), pp. 1–10. Association for Computing Machinery, New York (2021)
8. Maffione, V., Lettieri, G., Rizzo, L.: Cache-aware design of general-purpose single-producer–single-consumer queues. Softw.: Pract. Exp. **49**(5), 748–779 (2019)
9. Mukhin, V., Statkevych, V.: On one context-free language for producer/consumer Petri net with the unbounded buffer. In: 2020 International Conference on Development and Application Systems (DAS), Suceava, Romania, pp. 137–140 (2020)
10. Tan, H.B., Yi, J.L., Xie, S.L., Li, J., He, R.C.: Mechanical vibration fault diagnosis system based on a producer-consumer model. J. Hunan Univ. Technol. (04), 34–41 (2023)
11. Li, S.L., Zhou, Y.Y., Zhou, S.W., Yu, W.H.: The application of producer-consumer mode in earthquake early warning system. Mod. Inf. Technol. (09), 170–172+176 (2022)
12. Zhang, Y.C., et al.: Data acquisition system for fluorescence Lidar based on producer/consumer design pattern. Opt. Tech. **05**, 537–541 (2021)
13. Zhi-yu, S.: Realization of the motor data acquisition and analyzation system based on the producer/consumer model of LabVIEW. In: 2016 IEEE Advanced Information Management, Communicates, Electronic and Automation Control Conference (IMCEC), Xi'an, China, pp. 330–334(2016)
14. Wang, L., Wang, C.: Producer-consumer model based thread pool design. In: Journal of Physics: Conference Series, vol. 1616, no. 1, p. 012073. IOP Publishing (2020)
15. Zhang, Y., Zhang, J., Zhang, D.: Implementing and testing producer-consumer problem using aspect-oriented programming. In: 2009 Fifth International Conference on Information Assurance and Security, vol. 2, pp. 749–752. IEEE (2009)
16. Mehmood, S.N., Haron, N., Akhtar, V., Javed, Y.: Implementation and experimentation of producer-consumer synchronization problem. Int. J. Comput. Appl. **975**(8887), 32–37 (2011)
17. Wang, W.X., Li, Z.: Continuous sound signal acquisition system with real-time control based on producer/consumer design pattern. Mod. Electron. Tech. **7**, 129–132 (2009)
18. Wang, J., Xu, Y.J., Wang, W.P., Wang, P.: Rail profile acquisition system based on Producer Consumer model. China Railway (03), 74–76 (2014)
19. Liu, S.Z., Wu, Y.J., Zhang, C., Yang, Q.X.: Design of stress wave information acquisition system based on producer/consumer design pattern. Comput. Meas. Control **09**, 198–202 (2014)
20. Kayi, A., Serres, O., El-Ghazawi, T.: Adaptive cache coherence mechanisms with producer–consumer sharing optimization for chip multiprocessors. IEEE Trans. Comput. **64**(2), 316–328 (2015)
21. Vazquez-Lopez, R., Herrera-Lozada, J.C., Sandoval-Gutierrez, J., von Bülow, P., Martinez-Vazquez, D.L.: Sensor information sharing using a producer-consumer algorithm on small vehicles. Sensors **21**(9), 3022 (2021)
22. Sai, A.A., Reddy, D., Raghavendra, P., Kiran, G.Y., Rejeenth, V. R.: Producer-consumer problem using thread pool. In: 2022 3rd International Conference for Emerging Technology (INCET), Belgaum, India, pp. 1–5 (2022)

Design and Analysis of Service Resource Allocation Scheme Based on Mobile Edge Computing

Siyu Wang[1], Bo Yang[1(✉)], Zhiwen Yu[1], and Shuaibing Lu[2]

[1] School of Computer Science, Northwestern Polytechnical University,
Xi'an 710072, China
yang_bo@nwpu.edu.cn

[2] Faculty of Information, Beijing University of Technology, Beijing 100124, China

Abstract. With the rapid development of communication technology, the scale of user data grows exponentially. In the diversified service scenarios, the data processing speed is required more strictly in order to guarantee the service quality. Mobile edge computing technology makes the server closer to the terminal and assists the terminal to process data nearby, bringing better user experience. In mobile edge computing system, most terminal devices have strong mobility, and it is easy to cause service interruption because terminal devices are out of the service scope of the server after a few moments. In addition, the importance of the offloading task varies from one task to another, so the importance index should also be considered in the offloading request scheduling. This paper mainly studies the request scheduling problem in the field of computational offloading, and divides the problem into two stages: two-dimensional decision making and offloading. During the research, the mobility of terminal devices and the characteristics of tasks are considered, and a reward evaluation algorithm based on DDQN (Double Deep Q Network) is designed to generate scheduling strategies.

Keywords: Task offloading · Service overlapping areas · Mobility · Task priority · Task scheduling

1 Introduction

1.1 Background

In recent years, with the rapid development of information technology, there are more and more time-sensitive and computation-intensive applications. These applications have high requirements on task response speed. As computing and storage resources of terminal devices are limited, they cannot process application tasks with low latency. Therefore, they become the bottleneck of improving application service quality. In traditional Mobile Cloud Computing (MCC), terminals can access a powerful remote Central Cloud (CC) over the core network, use its

L. Wang et al. (Eds.): CWSN 2023, CCIS 1994, pp. 175–188, 2024.
https://doi.org/10.1007/978-981-97-1010-2_13

computing and storage resources. However, because the central cloud server is far away from the terminal device, various unknown errors may occur during task offloading. In order to efficiently deal with offloading tasks and improve users' service experience, the technical concept of Mobile Edge Computing (MEC) [1–3] was proposed. In mobile edge computing architecture, server nodes are placed on the edge of the network, closer to the terminal device. Precisely because of the geographical advantages of close distance, edge server can greatly reduce the processing delay of offloading tasks, making it possible to run high-demand applications on the terminal. Therefore, it is of great practical significance to conduct scientific research in the field of MEC.

1.2   Contribution and Structure

- This paper mainly studies the service resource allocation problem of mobile edge computing. And designs a scheme for offloading decision of terminal device and request scheduling of server under server overlapping service area. In the process of solving the problem, this paper considers the mobility of terminal device [4–6] and task priority.
- Considerations for mobility of terminal device: When the terminal device is located in the overlapping service area of multiple servers and has offloading requirements, the optimal offloading server will be selected for offloading request in the overlapping service area based on the predicted results of mobility and the load of server broadcast, reducing the possibility of subsequent service interruption and task forwarding and improving the user's experience.
- Considering the priority of tasks: In this paper, a reward evaluation algorithm based on Double Deep Q Network (DDQN) is designed to generate scheduling policies under such an uncertain and non-static environment of multi-user and multi-server interaction. The priority of the task [7], the computing resources required by the task and the remaining resources of the server are taken as the input of the neural network, the characteristics of the task are fully considered.

This rest of this paper is organized as follows. The System model is presented in Sect. 2, and the process of solving problem is given in Sect. 3. The DRL-based algorithm is presented in Sect. 4 and evaluate its performance in Sect. 5.

2   System Model

The scenario studied in this paper is shown in Fig. 1. The MEC system is divided into requesters and servers. Each requester can move within a certain range and can only offload tasks to the edge servers within the communication range.

Requester: A terminal device with task offloading requirements that can send task offloading requests to nearby edge servers.

Server: An edge server with certain computing and storage resources that can receive and respond to offloading requests from terminal devices within the service range. It can use its resources to process the offloading tasks and return the calculation results to terminal devices.

Service overlap area: The circled in the figure is the overlapping service area of the two servers and the blue car can send offload requests to both servers.

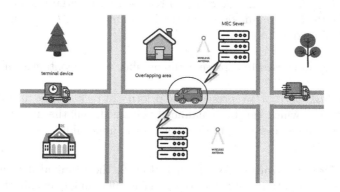

Fig. 1. System scenario.

In the whole MEC system, multiple terminal device nodes are represented by set $M = \{1, 2, ..., M\}$. The set $S = \{1, 2, ..., S\}$ indicates multiple server nodes. The current region is abstracted as a two-dimensional plane, the horizontal direction is represented by the X-axis, and the range is $(0, 40)$. The vertical direction is represented by the Y-axis, and the range is $(0, 40)$. An integer symbol $loc\_x \in (0, 40)$ represents the horizontal coordinate of a terminal device or server node on the plane, and an integer symbol $loc\_y \in (0, 40)$ represents the vertical coordinate of a terminal device or server node on the plane. The mobility of a terminal device is described by the set $\{M\_r, M\_d\}$. M_r indicates the movement rate of the terminal device [8]. $M\_d \in (0, 1, 2, 3)$ indicates the direction of movement of the terminal device, where 0 indicates east, 1 indicates west, 2 indicates south, and 3 indicates north. Because, There is no fixed pattern to human orientation preferences when driving and walking. But, People tend to move in a straight line towards their destination. So the variable M_d is randomly initialized and has seventy percent probability of not changing at the beginning of each slot. The movement rate of the terminal devices are dynamically updated at the beginning of each time slot [9]. The service radius of a server node is represented by the symbol R The set $T = \{1, 2, ..., T\}$ marks the current time slot, which is used to represent timing changes. The size of a time slot is 0.001 s.

2.1   Terminal Device

Task Parameter. At the beginning of every time slot $t \in T$ terminal device $m \in M$ produces an indivisible task J

Serial Number. Setting variable $Seq_m(t)$ represents the serial number of task J produced by the terminal device m at the beginning of the t time slot, and the serial number is equal to t.

Task Size. $S_m(t)$ is used to represent the number of bits contained in task J.

Priority of Task. $Pro_m(t)$ represents the priority of task J. The initial value of the priority is 1, which can be dynamically changed, but the upper limit is 5, and will not change after the priority reaches the upper limit.

Terminal Device Model. As shown in Fig. 2, the terminal device has two queues, one is computing queue and the other is offloading queue, both of which adopt the first-in first-out scheduling mode [10] For task J generated at the beginning of each time slot, the decision maker evaluates the payoff. The two-dimensional variable $D_m(t) \in (0, 1)$ represents the result of a decision. If the revenue evaluation is positive, $D_m(t) = 0$ then adds task J to the offloading queue for task offloading. If the revenue estimate is negative, $D_m(t) = 1$ then adds task J to the computing queue for local processing.

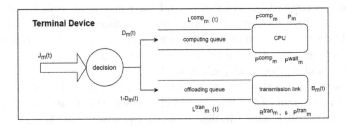

Fig. 2. Terminal device model.

The length of the computing queue at the beginning of the t time slot is expressed by $L_m^{comp}(t)$, and the length of the offloading queue at the beginning of the t time slot is expressed by $L_m^{tran}(t)$. The length of queue reflects the load of each queue.

The parameters of the processor are as follows: F_m^{comp} indicates the CPU frequency of the $m \in M$, that is the computing capacity of the terminal device m. P_m indicates the maximum number of data bits that can be processed simultaneously by a terminal device $m \in M$. In this paper, it is set to 64 bits. P_m^{comp}

and P_m^{wait} represent the computing power and standby power of processor of the device m, respectively. The computing power is used to calculate the energy loss required by processing task J, and the standby power is used to calculate the standby capacity loss in the process of waiting for offloading results. The two parameters are used for the total income assessment.

In the transmission link, the transmission rate is represented by $R_{m,s}^{tran}$, that is, how many bits of data can be transmitted per second. P_m^{tran} represents the transmission power of the device m, which is used to calculate the energy loss of the transmission task. $B_m(t) \in S$ represents the serial number of the best offloaded server selected by the terminal device m after considering its own mobility and various server loads. That is, the task $J_m(t)$ generated at the start of the t slot is uploaded to the server whose serial number is $B_m(t)$ over the transmission link.

2.2   Sever

As shown in Fig. 3, the server side has a task queue to process the offloading tasks in a first-in, first-out scheduling mode.

$L_s^{task}(t)$ indicates the length of the task queue at the start of the t time slot, which reflects the load of the server. At the beginning of each time slot, the server node broadcasts the load of the task queue to all terminal devices in the service' area for terminal devices to make offloading decisions.

F_s^{edge} represents the CPU frequency of the server node $s \in S$, which is the computing power of the server node s. P_s represents the maximum number of data bits that can be processed simultaneously by a server node s. In this paper, it is set to 64 bits.

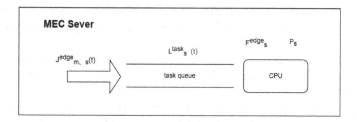

Fig. 3. Sever model.

3 Problem Solving

In this paper, the computing offloading problem is divided into two stages. The first stage is offloading decision. Terminal device makes two-dimensional decision according to the calculation result of revenue evaluation. The second is offloading stage including the selection of the optimal offloading server, the scheduling of offloading request of the server, the uploading of offloading data and the delivery of processing results. The server uses a reward evaluation algorithm to generate scheduling results.

3.1 Offload Decision

Two-Dimensional Decision. In the mobile edge system, when a new task is generated, the terminal device has to make a two-dimensional decision, that is, decide whether to process the task locally or offload it to a nearby edge server. 'The terminal device calculates the delay saving and energy saving of local processing and offloading processing respectively [11], and takes the calculation result as the basis for decision-making. If the total income is positive, the task is offloaded; otherwise, it is processed locally.

Calculation Process. Define the set of servers that can provide offloading services as $Serve\_set$. Set $Serve\_set$ is a subset of set S. Before the revenue evaluation, terminal device m must first determine the set of servers that can provide offload service at the current location.

Selecting Servers. Calculate the distance between device m and server s according to the current position parameter (loc_x, loc_y). Compare distance with the service radius R of sever s. If $distance < R$, s is added to the set $Serve\_set$. Repeating the above process until the set S has been completely traversed.

Delay Benefit. The terminal device m generates a task $J_m(t)$ at the beginning of $t \in T$ slots which the size is $S_m(t)$. The length of the computing queue is $L_m^{comp}(t)$, the clock frequency of the processor CPU is F_m^{comp}, and the number of bits that can be processed simultaneously is P_m. The transmission rate of the offload link is $R_{m,s}^{tran}$, and the transmission power is P_m^{tran}. The length of the offload queue is $L_m^{tran}(t)$. Take server node $s \in Serve\_set$, that $L_s^{task}(t)$ is the length of task queue in s. The clock frequency of the processor CPU is F_s^{edge}, and the number of bits that can be processed simultaneously is P_s. The local processing delay is calculated as follows:

$$D\_local = (L_m^{comp}(t) + S_m(t)) / (F_m^{comp} \times P_m) \tag{1}$$

W indicates offloading link bandwidth distribution channel, $|h_{m,s}|^2$ indicate the channel gain between terminal device and server nodes, σ^2 indicate noise power, P_m^{tran} indicate the transmission power of device m.

$$R_{m,s}^{tran} = W \times \log_2 \left(1 + \frac{|h_{m,s}|^2}{\sigma^2} \times P_m^{tran} \right) \tag{2}$$

The transmission rate is calculated as follows:

$$D\_tran = \left(L_m^{tran}(t) + S_m(t) \right) / R_{m,s}^{tran} \tag{3}$$

The delay of the task processing on the server is calculated as follows:

$$D\_serve = \left(L_s^{task}(t) + S_m(t) \right) / \left(F_s^{edge} \times P_s \right) \tag{4}$$

Since the amount of data returned after the task processing is usually small, the delay is not considered in this paper. Therefore:

$$D\_offload = D\_tran + D\_serve \tag{5}$$

The delay benefit is defined as:

$$D\_gain = D\_local - D\_offload \tag{6}$$

Energy Benefit. The computing power of m processor of terminal device is P_m^{comp}, standby power is P_m^{wait}, and transmission power is P_m^{tran}. The energy loss of local processing is calculated as follows:

$$P\_local = P_m^{comp} \times D\_local \tag{7}$$

The energy loss of transmission is calculated as follows:

$$P\_tran = P_m^{tran} \times D\_tran \tag{8}$$

The energy loss of Standby is calculated as follows:

$$P\_wait = P_m^{wait} \times D\_serve \tag{9}$$

The energy loss of offloading tasks to the server for processing is calculated as follows:

$$P\_offload = P\_tran + P\_wait \tag{10}$$

The energy benefit is defined as:

$$P\_gain = P\_local - P\_offload \tag{11}$$

The variable $\varepsilon \in [0,1]$ represents the preference factor [12], which determines whether the optimization objective is more focused on delay reduction or energy loss reduction. T_gain indicates the total income evaluation result.

$$T\_gain = \varepsilon \times D\_gain + (1 - \varepsilon) \times P\_gain \tag{12}$$

The variable $D_m(t) \in \{0,1\}$ represents the result of the offloading decision. The value of $D_m(t) \in \{0,1\}$ are set as follows:

$$D_m(t) = \begin{cases} 0, T\_gain > 0 \\ 1, T\_gain < 0 \end{cases} \quad (13)$$

If $D_m(t) = 1$, the task $J_m(t)$ is added to the end of the computing queue. otherwise, selecting an optimal server for subsequent offloading in the set $offload\_set$.

3.2   Offloading Stage

- When the terminal device is in the overlapping service area and has the offloading requests, the terminal device will be calculated the range of movement according to the current motion parameters. Then considering the calculation results and offloading benefits, selecting an optimal server to send the offloading request.
- Server $s \in S$ receives offloading requests from many terminal devices at the same time, and the server's computing and storage resources are also limited, which cannot meet the offloading requests of a large number of terminal devices. Therefore, offloading request scheduling is performed to maximize the benefits from limited resources.
- After the server uses the reward evaluation algorithm to generate the scheduling result, the scheduling result should be sent to the terminal device. The scheduling result generated by the server is the $\{0,1\}^N$, whose subscript starts from 1 and ends with N corresponding to the serial number of the terminal device. In the scheduling result set, 0 indicates that the offloading request is rejected and 1 indicates that the offloading request is approved. The terminal device performs operations based on the value of the subscript corresponding to the set. If the value is 1, the terminal device adds the offloading task to the end of the offloading queue for data upload. If the value is 0, the priority of the offloading task increase 1, and then a new round of processing is carried out by repeating the above two-dimensional decision-making, server selection, sending offloading request and so on.
- The server adds the tasks that received from each terminal device to the end of the task queue in turn, then takes out the tasks from the head of the task queue in turn, and allocates certain computing and storage resources for data processing and analysis. After an offloading task is completed, the server sends the processing result to the corresponding terminal device over a transmission link based on the $seq\_produce$. The terminal device respond after receiving the processing result from the server. The process of the offloading task is complete.

4   Algorithm Introduction

This section will introduce the algorithm flow and the definition of three necessary parameters in reinforcement learning algorithm, namely state space, action space and reward function.

The algorithm flow is as follows:

Algorithm 1. The reward evaluation algorithm based on DDQN

1: Initialize Memory buffer to collect experience from environment and count:=0
2: Initialize eval Neural Network with random θ_s
3: Initialize target Neural Network with random θ_s^-
4: **for** count ≤ 3000 **do**
5:     Observe the environment state S_t
6:     Input the S_t to the eval Neural Network and get the $Q(S_t, a)$, a $\in$ Action Space
7:     Based on the ϵ - greedy to choose an action a_t
8:     Get the reward r_t and Observe the next state S_{t+1}
9:     Store the experience (S_t, a_t, r_t, S_{t+1}) to the Memory buffer
10:    count:=count+1
11: **end for**
12: Initialize learn_steps:=0 and replace_steps:=0
13: **for** learn_steps ≤ 20000 **do**
14:    random select some experience from the Memory buffer
15:    Input the S_t to the eval Neural Network and get the $Q(S_t, a)$
16:    Input the S_{t+1} to the target Neural Network and get the $Q(S_{t+1}, a)$
17:    Input the S_{t+1} to the eval Neural Network and choose the action A which make
       the $Q(S_{t+1}, A)$ is the biggest
18:    Let the $r_t + \gamma \times Q(S_{t+1}, A)$ as the target Q value
19:    Compute the loss of the target Q value and the eval Q value and update θ_s
20:    **if** replace_steps%200 == 0 **then**
21:        $\theta_s^- = \theta_s$
22:    **end if**
23:    learn_steps+=1 and replace_steps+=1
24: **end for**

4.1 State Space Definition

Setting $Size\_task_s(t) = \{S_1(t), S_2(t), \ldots, S_m(t)\}$ as the set of task size which is the terminal devices offload to the server node $s \in S$ at the beginning of the slot t. If the terminal device n does not send an offloading request to server node s at the beginning of slot t, the element value of the subscript position of n in the set $Size\_task_s(t)$ is 0, otherwise, the element value of the corresponding subscript position is equal to the number of bits of the offloading task. $Pro\_task_s(t)$ is setting as set of task priority, which is the server node s received offloading tasks at the beginning of the slot t. If terminal device n does not send an offloading request to server node s at the beginning of slot t, the element value of the subscript position corresponding to n in the set $Pro\_task_s(t)$ is 0, otherwise, the element value of the corresponding subscript position is equal to the priority of the offloading task. The remaining computing resources of server s at the beginning of slot t are represented by $eval\_r$. In summary, the state space is defined as follows:

$$S(t) = \{Size\_task_s(t), Pro\_task_s(t), eval\_r\} \tag{14}$$

4.2 Action Space Definition

Based on input information, server node s generates a scheduling policy in response to offloading requests from various terminal devices. Setting the action space at the beginning of the time slot t as follows:

$$A(t) = \{0,1\}^m \tag{15}$$

$m = |M|$, which is the number of the request of the offloading tasks, the elements subscript of action space is corresponding to the terminal serial number. If the terminal device did not send offloading requests, or the server node s rejected the terminal device's offloading request, the element value whose subscript is corresponding to the terminal device's serial number is 0, otherwise, it's value equals 1.

4.3 Reward Function Definition

Variable $B\_value = 10$ is set as the base reward value, and the reward obtained by completing a single task is the task priority multiplied by the base reward value. Taking the task $J_m(t)$ produced by the task terminal device m at the beginning of the time slot t as an example, the reward value obtained by completing $J_m(t)$ is:

$$S\_r_m(t) = B\_value \times Pro_m(t) \tag{16}$$

Immediate Income. The variable $C\_r_s(t)$ is defined as the immediate benefit, that is, all rewards that can be obtained after completing multiple tasks in server node s in the time slot t. Defining set $t\_queue_s(t)$ as the task queue of server node s at the beginning of slot t.

$$C\_r_s(t) = \sum_{i=1}^{n} t\_queue_s(t)[i].pro \times B\_value \tag{17}$$

Expected Benefit. Variable $E\_r_s(t)$ is defined as the expected benefit, that is the offloading request arriving at server node s at the beginning of the time slot t and the reward brought to server node s in the future after the offloading scheduling. n is the number of slots in which the task is waiting to be processed.

$$E\_r_s(t) = \sum_{i=1}^{m} S\_r_i(t) \times \frac{A(t)[i]}{n} \tag{18}$$

Expected Loss. Variable $E\_loss_s(t)$ is defined as the expected loss, that is, the offloading request that reaches server node s at the beginning of the time slot t, and the future loss of server node s after the offloading scheduling.

$$E\_loss_s(t) = \sum_{i=1}^{m} S\_r_i(t) \times \frac{1 - A(t)[i]}{n} \tag{19}$$

The reward function is defined as follows:

$$R_s(t) = C\_r_s(t) + E\_r_s(t) + E\_loss_{s(t)} \tag{20}$$

I take into account both the effect of the decision on the present and the future payoff of the offload task. So, I define the reward function as an operation of immediate gain, expected gain, and loss, which can make the scheduling policy generated by the algorithm is more comprehensive.

5   Analysis of Experimental Results

This paper sets up such a scenario, representing a region in a two-dimensional plane. The X-axis represents the east-west direction, and the Y-axis represents the north-south direction. Both the X-axis and the Y-axis range are $[0, 40]$. In this area, there are 5 server nodes, the initial coordinates are random and do not change, and the service radius ranges from 10 to 20. With 20 terminal devices, the initial coordinates are random and dynamic, and the movement direction and speed are random. The terminal device is set to advance in a straight line, such as east, west, south and north. If it moves in one direction for a period of time and exceeds the range of the set area, it will enter the area again in the opposite direction. The coordinates of the terminal device are updated at the beginning of each time slot.

5.1   Convergence

Figure 4 shows the convergence of the network under different learning rates. Image X-axis Axis represents the number of training episodes, one episodes is 100 training steps, namely 100 time slots. The Y-axis shows the average error between the predicted value and the true value. As shown in the figure, in the first 30 rounds, the interactive information between the agent and the environment is stored in the experience buffer as experience. The agent has not yet started to learn, so the network prediction error is at a high level under different learning rates. After 30 turns, the experience buffer is full and the agent starts to learn. The network prediction errors with a learning rate of 0.005 and 0.01 begin to decrease, while the network prediction errors with a learning rate of 0.002 continue to rise. This is because when the learning rate is set at a low level, the network has a low learning ability and cannot quickly learn from the experience. As a result, in the last 50 rounds, the networks with a learning rate of 0.005 and 0.01 tend to converge, and the network prediction error has stabilized at a low value, The oscillation range of the curve is decreasing. The network prediction error with a learning rate of 0.002 is relatively high, the convergence speed is slow.

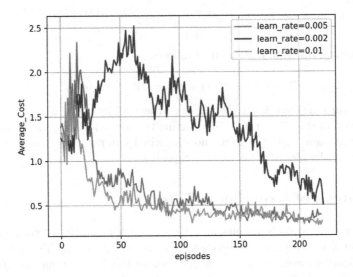

Fig. 4. Average loss.

5.2   Performance

The evaluation criterion of the performance of the algorithm is cumulative returns in each episode, the first episodes of the cumulative return value is equal to the $\sum_{t=1}^{100} r_t \times 0.99^{t-1}$, r_t defined reference Eq. (20).

Figure 5 shows the cumulative return to the agent for each of the 200 episodes. The X-axis of the Figure is the number of training episodes, and the Y-axis is the cumulative return value obtained in each episode. Each episodes contains 1,000 training steps for a total of 200,000. The first three episodes are the stored-experience phase. As can be seen from the graph, the cumulative return per episodes increases continuously from the third episodes and becomes stable after several rounds. This suggests that the agent is constantly learning from experience and adjusting the parameters of the network. In the learning process, better scheduling strategies are gradually generated, so that the cumulative return of each episodes is continuously increased.

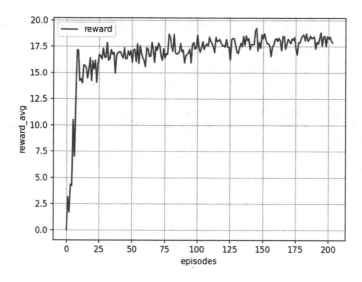

Fig. 5. Round cumulative reward.

Acknowledgements. The subject of this paper comes from Beijing University of Technology. I would like to thank Mr. Lu from Beijing University of Technology and Mr. Yang from Northwestern Polytechnical University for their guidance.

References

1. Mach, P., Becvar, Z.: Mobile edge computing: a survey on architecture and computation offloading. IEEE Commun. Surv. Tutor. **19**(3), 1628–1656 (2017)
2. Li, Z., Zhou, X., Qin, Y.: A survey of mobile edge computing in the industrial internet. In: 2019 7th International Conference on Information, Communication and Networks (ICICN), pp. 94–98 (2019)
3. Abbas, N., Zhang, Y., Taherkordi, A., Skeie, T.: Mobile edge computing: a survey. IEEE Internet Things J. **5**(1), 450–465 (2018)
4. Zhan, W., Luo, C., Min, G., Wang, C., Zhu, Q., Duan, H.: Mobility-aware multi-user offloading optimization for mobile edge computing. IEEE Trans. Veh. Technol. **69**(3), 3341–3356 (2020)
5. Jehangiri, A., Maqsood, T., uz Zaman, S.K.: Mobility-aware computational offloading in mobile edge networks: a survey. Clust. Comput. **24**(4), 2735–2756 (2021)
6. Lu, S., Wu, J., Shi, J., Lu, P., Fang, J., Liu, H.: A dynamic service placement based on deep reinforcement learning in mobile edge computing. Network **2**(1), pp. 106–122 (2022). https://www.mdpi.com/2673-8732/2/1/8
7. Gao, L., Moh, M.: Joint computation offloading and prioritized scheduling in mobile edge computing. In: 2018 International Conference on High Performance Computing & Simulation (HPCS), pp. 1000–1007 (2018)
8. Zhou, J., Tian, D., Wang, Y., Sheng, Z., Duan, X., Leung, V.C.M.: Reliability-oriented optimization of computation offloading for cooperative vehicle-infrastructure systems. IEEE Signal Process. Lett. **26**(1), 104–108 (2019)

9. Huang, B., et al.: Security and cost-aware computation offloading via deep reinforcement learning in mobile edge computing. Wirel. Commun. Mob. Comput. **2019**, 3 816 237:1–3 816 237:20 (2019)
10. Tang, M., Wong, V.W.: Deep reinforcement learning for task offloading in mobile edge computing systems. IEEE Trans. Mob. Comput. **21**(6), 1985–1997 (2022)
11. Zhou, Y., et al.: Offloading optimization for low-latency secure mobile edge computing systems. IEEE Wirel. Commun. Lett. **9**(4), 480–484 (2020)
12. Yang, B., Cao, X., Bassey, J., Li, X., Kroecker, T., Qian, L.: Computation offloading in multi-access edge computing networks: a multi-task learning approach. In: ICC 2019-2019 IEEE International Conference on Communications (ICC), pp. 1–6 (2019)

Edge Computing Task Unloading Decision Optimization Algorithm Based on Deep Reinforcement Learning

Yu Kong, Ying Li[✉], Jiandong Wang, and Shiwei Yin

College of Computer Science Technology, Qingdao University, Qingdao 266071, China
yingli_2016@163.com

Abstract. Mobile Edge Computing (MEC) is used to enhance the data processing capability of low-power networks and has now become an efficient computing paradigm. In this paper, an edge-cloud collaborative system composed of multiple terminals (Mobile Terminal, MT) and its resource allocation strategy are considered. In order to reduce the total delay of MTs, a variety of offloading modes are adopted, and an edge-cloud collaborative task offloading algorithm based on deep reinforcement learning (DDPG) is proposed. The coordinated serial task dynamic allocation processing provides approximately optimal task allocation and offloading strategies for different user equipment applications. The simulation results show that compared with the Deep Q Neural Network (DQN) algorithm and the Deep Deterministic Policy Gradient (DDPG) algorithm, the proposed algorithm significantly improves the maximum performance gain. Experiments show that the DDPG algorithm has better system performance than the traditional scheme, and improves the service quality of the application.

Keywords: Serial Tasks · Mobile Edge Computing · Deep Reinforcement Learning · Task Offloading Algorithm · Edge-cloud Collaboration

1 Introduction

With the rapid development of artificial intelligence technology and mobile applications, application services such as natural language processing, face recognition, augmented reality, and behavior analysis are widely used in various MTs [1]. Using cloud computing to offload the tasks generated by the MT in the wireless network to the cloud with super computing power can solve the problem of insufficient computing power of the MT itself. However, the cloud server is often located in the core network far away from the MT, so the data exchange process between the MT and the cloud server will generate a long delay and a large energy consumption, and it is also suitable for unmanned driving and remote surgery. In certain applications, a large delay cannot meet the system requirements. In order to improve user demand and user experience, some experts and scholars have proposed MEC technology [2]. MEC provides users with low-latency and efficient computing services by deploying computing nodes or servers at the network edge. However, the computing power, computing resources and storage capacity of the MEC server are still limited. Offloading too many tasks to the network edge will bring a heavy burden to the MEC server and the network with limited computing resources, resulting in network congestion on the backhaul link and affecting the network user experience. Therefore, using the computing method of edge-cloud collaboration to shorten the data round-trip time and reduce the delay of task offloading is an effective compromise method to alleviate cloud computing and edge computing.

In addition, machine learning algorithms are used to analyze large-scale data under multi-user and multi-task conditions in the network, and feature extraction and modeling are performed to guide resource allocation, which can solve the problems of complex networking, low transmission rate, and reliability faced by traditional resource allocation algorithms. It solves problems such as poor performance and meets the high requirements of system latency and energy consumption due to the access and data processing of a large number of devices. Task offloading and resource allocation of MEC have always been hot issues. Resource allocation includes wireless resource allocation and computing resource allocation. Wireless resources include bandwidth, transmit power, etc. Computing resources generally include the central processing unit (CPU) cycles frequency of local and MEC servers. Performance indicators optimized in task offloading and resource allocation include latency, energy consumption, throughput, etc.

In recent years, a large number of research works have proved that the use of deep reinforcement learning methods can effectively solve the problem of task offloading mode and resource allocation in MEC networks. Liang et al. [3] proposed a distributed-based deep learning algorithm, which uses multiple parallel deep neural networks for offloading decision-making training to predict the offloading decision scheme of MEC servers. Lv et al. [4] used a recurrent neural network (RNN) to model network traffic as a time-varying sequence of states to optimize resource allocation by predicting network traffic changes in future periods. In addition, many works describe the continuous state space in the optimization problem as a Markov decision process (MDP). Yu et al. [5] proposed a deep reinforcement learning method to solve the MDP high-dimensional state space problem. Optimized offloading and resource allocation strategies to maximize network performance by improving resource allocation efficiency. Shi et al. [6] obtained the optimal resource allocation strategy through a performance-aware resource allocation scheme based on the DDPG algorithm. Zhang et al. [7] proposed an improved DQN algorithm to minimize the long-term weighted sum of average completion time and average number of requested resources. Chen et al. [8] proposed a computational offloading algorithm for two-layer DQN, which effectively reduces the computational offloading failure rate under the premise of satisfying the task delay constraint. Cao et al. [9] proposed a multi-workflow scheduling method for edge computing environments based on DQN and probabilistic performance perception, which effectively improved the execution efficiency of workflows.

However, the above research still has the following shortcomings: 1) The consideration of cloud-edge collaboration is ignored; 2) The coarse-grained offloading algorithm lacks flexibility. To this end, this paper proposes an innovative algorithm based on the cloud-edge-user three-tier structure. Aiming at the task offloading resource allocation problem in the edge-cloud collaboration scenario, we use the weighted serial task offloading algorithm (DDPG) based on the DQN algorithm. The algorithm takes into account the competition of multi-user serial task offloading for MEC server and cloud computing resources, as well as the priority of different user applications. Task latency, task energy consumption, and service quality assurance are used as evaluation criteria.

The innovations and contributions of this article mainly include:

- Introducing the cloud-edge collaboration problem: Considering the importance of cloud-edge collaboration for resource allocation.
- Propose the DDPG algorithm: Based on the DQN algorithm, a flexible task offloading decision-making algorithm is provided.
- Consider multi-user competition and priorities: Weigh resource allocation and task offloading to meet user needs.
- Comprehensive evaluation metrics: Evaluate performance using task latency, task energy consumption, and service quality assurance.

2 System Model

The task offloading model in this paper consists of multiple mobile User Equipment (UE), wireless Base Station (BS) with MEC servers, and Cloud Server (CS), forming a three-layer structure, as shown in Fig. 1. The user equipment generates serial tasks [10]. The MEC server provides task resource allocation, task offloading and scheduling for the user and the cloud in the middle layer, and can also share a certain degree of computing tasks for the user. Solve complex computing problems, but will have higher network latency than edge servers [11].

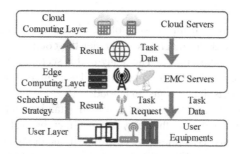

Fig. 1. Edge-cloud collaborative system model.

After the user equipment generates a task, it will send the task offloading decision request to the MEC server, and the MEC server will decide whether to execute the task locally or upload it to the MEC server or the cloud for execution according to the current system state. The uninstall policy is represented by X, where $X \in \{0, 1, 2, 3\}$, 0 means that this policy is a no-op, 1 means that the task will be executed locally, 2 means that the task will be uninstalled to the MEC server for execution, 3 means that the task will be offloaded to the cloud server for execution [12].

2.1 Serial Task Model

The task in this article is assumed to be a task composed of multiple microtasks in series, and a task application consists of multiple serial microtasks, where the start and end of the microtask represent the input and output parts of the task, and the input must be done locally. The characteristic of serial tasks lies in the dependencies between their tasks. Only when microtask $i - 1$ is completed can microtask i be executed, and until the last microtask is executed, all the serial tasks are completed [13].

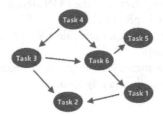

Fig. 2. Relationships between microtasks.

The basic principle of serial tasks is that when tasks are executed in a specific sequence, the execution time and resource requirements of each task may be different. As shown in Fig. 2, there is a dependency relationship between tasks, that is, subsequent tasks must wait for the completion of the previous task before starting execution. This dependency can be linear or complex, forming a chain of tasks.

2.2 Delay Model

Latency represents the time from the start of a task request to the completion of the task, and the size of the delay determines whether the completion time of a task can be satisfied application requirements. The delay in this section is the delay for the user equipment to complete its current micro-task [14]. The composition of the task delay is discussed from three parts: local, edge, and cloud.

The basic principle of the delay model is to understand the total delay of task execution by modeling and analyzing the delay process, thereby evaluating system performance and service quality. By optimizing each link in the delay model, the total delay of the task can be reduced, and the system response speed and user experience can be improved.

1) Local execution: In the local execution strategy, it means that the microtask will be calculated locally and will not transmit data to the MEC server [15], so the current task delay dT_u is expressed as:

$$dT_{local} = \frac{c_t}{f_u} \tag{1}$$

In the formula, c_t is the number of CPU cycles required by the task; f_u is the CPU frequency (Hz) of the user equipment.

2) Edge Server Execution: In the execution strategy [16] of the edge server, it means that the micro-task will be offloaded through wireless transmission, and the necessary data for computing the micro-task will be transmitted to the MEC server. In this strategy, the delay consists of calculation delay, transmission delay, and queuing delay, so the current task delay dT_u is expressed as:

$$dT_{edge} = \frac{d_t}{H_u} + \frac{c_t}{f_s} + \frac{e_t}{H_u} + T_m \tag{2}$$

In the formula, f_s is the number of CPU cycles of the edge server; e_t is the amount of data returned by the edge server; H_u is the transmission rate of the user equipment and the MEC server; T_m is the estimated completion time of the current task of the edge server.

3) Cloud Execution: In the cloud execution strategy, it means that the task will submit the data required by the task to the cloud server through wireless transmission and the backbone network [17]. In this strategy, the delay consists of calculation delay, transmission delay, propagation delay, and queuing delay, so the current task delay dT_u is expressed as:

$$dT_{cloud} = \frac{d_t + e_t}{S_u} + \frac{d_t + e_t}{S_c} + \frac{c_t}{f_c} + 2dt + T_c \tag{3}$$

In the formula, f_c is the number of CPU cycles of the cloud server; S_c is the transmission rate between the MEC server and the cloud server; dt is the propagation delay between the MEC server and the cloud; T_c is the estimated completion time of the current task of the cloud server.

2.3 Energy Consumption Model

Energy consumption is also one of the most important indicators in practical scenarios. User equipment powered by batteries will be more sensitive to the amount of energy consumption. In this scenario, energy consumption is composed of CPU calculation and idle consumption, and energy consumption during wireless transmission.

The basic principle of the energy consumption model is to understand the energy consumed by task execution by modeling and analyzing the energy consumption process, thereby evaluating the energy efficiency performance of the system. By optimizing each link in the energy consumption model, the energy expenditure of the system can be reduced and energy efficiency and sustainability improved [18].

1) Local execution: The CPU of the local user equipment will be used to perform computing tasks, so the execution energy consumption of the policy is:

$$E_{local} = \eta(f_u)^2 c_t \tag{4}$$

In the formula, η is the energy efficiency coefficient of the CPU; f_u is the number of CPU cycles of the user equipment.

2) Edge Server Execution: The computing task will be submitted to the MEC server for calculation. The energy consumption consists of the transmission energy consumption and idle energy consumption of the user equipment:

$$E_{edge} = \omega_1 \frac{d_t}{R_u} + \omega_2 \frac{c_t}{f_s} \tag{5}$$

In the formula, ω_1 is the energy consumed by the user equipment during wireless transmission; ω_2 is the energy consumed by the user equipment when it is idle.

3) Cloud Execution: The computing task data will be transmitted to the cloud server through the wireless and backbone network, and the energy consumption is composed of the transmission energy consumption and idle energy consumption of the user equipment:

$$E_{cloud} = \omega_1 \frac{d_t}{H_u} + \omega_{cloud} \frac{d_t}{H_c} + \omega_2 \left(\frac{d_t}{H_u} + \frac{d_t}{H_c} + dt \right) \tag{6}$$

The serial task model, delay model and energy consumption model are comprehensively considered. First, based on the serial task model, the dependencies and execution order between tasks are determined. Then, use the delay model to analyze the delay during task execution. Next, the energy consumption model is considered to evaluate the energy consumption during task execution. Finally, after understanding the task dependencies, latency and energy consumption, optimization strategies are used to improve system performance.

2.4 Problem Statement

In the context of task scheduling, service quality assurance is a key factor in ensuring that users with different priorities can meet their latency or energy consumption requirements. This means that users with lower latency or energy consumption requirements will gain more advantages when competing for resources. In this context, the components of service quality are:

$$Q_{S_u} = \lambda_1 + \lambda_2 q_u \tag{7}$$

In the formula, $\lambda_1 + \lambda_2 = 1, \lambda_1, \lambda_2 \geq 0$; λ_1 is the initial value; λ_2 is the service quality weight in the objective function; q_u is the priority weight of different users.

The goal of this paper is to generate decisions by applying the DDPG algorithm to reduce latency and energy consumption, reduce total task delay, and improve system performance and service quality in task scheduling scenarios. In the previous section, the delay and energy consumption models have been introduced, and a linear weighting method is used to formulate the objective function. Therefore, the original problem can be defined as:

$$F = min \sum_{u}^{N} \left(\alpha E_{local} + \beta d T_{local} - \gamma Q_{S_u} \right) \tag{8}$$

In the formula, $\alpha, \beta, \gamma \in [0, 1]$, and $\alpha + \beta + \gamma = 1$; The weights in the objective function respectively determine the relative importance of energy consumption, delay and service quality assurance in the overall goal.

3 Algorithm Model

Since the optimization problem is a complex non-convex problem, it is difficult to solve it directly, so this paper proposes a task offloading (DDPG) algorithm based on deep reinforcement learning to solve the problem.

Deep Deterministic Policy Gradient (DDPG) [19] is a deep deterministic policy gradient algorithm, which is proposed to solve the continuous action control problem. The previously learned Q-learning algorithm, Sarsa algorithm and DQN algorithm are all discrete for the action space. DDPG is an extension of the DQN algorithm, mainly to enable DQN to solve the problem of continuous action control. From Q-learning to DQN, it just maps the evaluation function of state and action from discrete space to continuous space with neural network, and does not solve the problem of discrete action, but DDPG solves this problem. DDPG can be simply regarded as the DQN algorithm plus the Actor-Critic framework. The AC framework [20] used in the DDPG algorithm is a framework based on the action value function Q. The algorithm includes an actor network and a critic network. Each network follows its own the update rule is updated so that the cumulative expected return is maximized.

This paper models an optimization problem using MDP, where the agent continuously learns and makes decisions from interactions with the environment in discrete time steps. In general, MDP [21] can be defined as a tuple $\{S, A, P, R, \gamma\}$, in this paper, S represents the state space, A represents the action space, P represents the state transition probability, R represents the reward function, and γ represents the discount factor. In a network environment, the state transition probabilities and expected payoffs of all states are usually unknown. Therefore, in the edge-cloud collaborative system considered in this paper, the task offloading mode and resource allocation problem is a model-free enhanced framework, and the MDP adapted in this paper has a continuous state and action space. The goal of MDP is to find the optimal policy and then solve the decision problem to maximize the expected return. This paper defines the state and role of the environment as $s_t \in S$, which correspond to a single $a_t \in A$ respectively, forming a state-action pair. Typically, the agent takes action a_t from the current state s_t to a new state $s_{t+1} \in S$, after which the agent will receive a scalar reward from the environment $r_t = r(s_t, a_t) \in R$, according to the transition probability $p(s_{t+1}|s_t, a_t)$ of the environment, the agent will be in the next state $s_{t+1} \in S$.

This paper adopts reinforcement learning based on policy gradient. As a kind of reinforcement learning, the core idea of DDPG is to learn parameterized policies instead of selecting actions by consulting the value function. The value function is mainly used for policy parameter learning, not for action selection. During this process, the agent's goal is to choose a strategy that maximizes the expected return. When deciding the strategy [22], data generation and strategy optimization are performed through the interaction between the agent and the environment. DDPG uses multi-step learning [23] to update the Loss function:

$$\left(R_t^{(n)} + \gamma_t^{(n)} \max_{a'} q_{\overline{\theta}}\left(S_{t+n}, a' \right) - q_{\theta}(S_t, A_t) \right)^2 \tag{9}$$

where A and S are the system state and action, respectively; γ is the discount factor; R is the reward function; $\overline{\theta}$ is the target network parameter; θ is updated according to the loss; S_t is the observation of the action A_t during iteration value; a' prime is the reward for the optimal solution in the S_{t+n} state.

When the update is stored in the experience pool, the priority experience value playback is used, and the weight p_t of the sampling is determined according to the loss function:

$$p_t \propto \left| r_{t+1} + \gamma \max_{a'} q_{\overline{\theta}}\left(S_{t+1}, A'\right) - q_\theta(S_t, A_t) \right|^w \tag{10}$$

In the formula, p_t will be obtained from the loss function; w is the priority factor of priority experience playback. Based on the above improvements and other extensions, in the DDPG proposed in this paper, it is necessary to redefine the state space, action space and reward function according to the system requirements [24], and introduce weights into the reward function to better fit the actual operating scenario and optimize serial task scheduling strategy.

In the DDPG algorithm, when the MEC server receives the task unloading request sent by the user equipment, it obtains the current system state, obtains the weight vector through calculation, and can obtain the optimal unloading strategy output according to the current state. Combining the above models [25], the DDPG algorithm is as follows.

Algorithm 1 DDPG algorithm
Randomly initialize critic network $Q(s, a \mid \theta^Q)$ and actor $\mu(s \mid \theta^\mu)$ with weight sand actor
Initialize target network Q' and μ' with weights $\theta^{Q'} \leftarrow \theta^Q, \theta^{\mu'} \leftarrow \theta^\mu$
Initialize replay buffer R
1   for episode = 1, M do
2   Initialize a random process $\mathcal{N}$ for action exploration
3   Receive initial observation state s_1
4   for t = 1, T do
5   Select action $a_t = \mu(s_t \mid \theta^\mu) + \mathcal{N}_t$ according to the current policy and exploration noise
6   Execute action a_t and observe reward r_t and observe new state s_{t+1}
7   Store transition (s_t, a_t, r_t, s_{t+1}) in R
8   Sample a random minibatch of N transitions (s_i, a_i, r_i, s_{i+1}) from R
9   Set $y_i = r_i + \gamma Q'(s_{i+1}, \mu'(s_{i+1} \mid \theta^{\mu'}) \mid \theta^{Q'})$
10   Update critic by minimizing the loss: $L = \frac{1}{N} \sum_i (y_i - Q(s_i, a_i \mid \theta^Q))^2$
11   Update the actor policy using the sampled policy gradient: $$\nabla_{\theta^\mu} J \approx \frac{1}{N} \sum_i \nabla_a Q(s, a \mid \theta^Q)\big|_{s=s_i, a=\mu(s_i)}$$
12   Update the target networks: $$\theta^{Q'} \leftarrow \tau \theta^Q + (1-\tau)\theta^{Q'}$$ $$\theta^{\mu'} \leftarrow \tau \theta^\mu + (1-\tau)\theta^{\mu'}$$
13   end for
14   end for

The overall time complexity of the DDPG algorithm mainly depends on the process of network update, experience playback and interaction with the environment. Generally speaking, as the number of neural networks and samples increases, the complexity of the algorithm gradually increases. Specifically, the time complexity of the DDPG algorithm is usually linear, that is, $O(N)$, while the space complexity is relatively high, usually $O(N^2)$ or $O(N^3)$ level (Table 1).

Table 1. Symbol summary

Symbol	Definition
s	The initial state
a	The perform action
θ^Q	The neural network parameters of critic
θ^μ	The neural network parameters of actor
M	Total number of training epochs
$\mathcal{N}_t$	A random process
T	The number of time steps in each episode
R	The experience replay buffer
r	The reward value
N	The random mini-batch size
Q'	The target critic network
μ'	The target actor network
γ	The discount factor
τ	The soft update rate
y	The target Q value

4 Experimental Results and Analysis

Based on the python programming language, this paper uses the PyCharm platform to build an experimental environment for edge-cloud collaborative serial task offloading, and simulates to estimate its performance. The simulation environment consists of a wireless base station with MEC server, a cloud server and multiple user equipment. The performance of the algorithm is evaluated by comparing the latency, energy consumption, and service quality of different algorithms on local computing, cloud computing, and edge server computing. In the experiment, the environment configuration given in Table 2 is used, and 5 user devices are used to generate serial tasks, a total of 50 serial tasks, each serial task consists of 4 micro-tasks, by adjusting the computational complexity of serial tasks The degree and generation rate are compared.

The DDPG algorithm is an extension and optimization of the DQN algorithm, so that the DQN is extended to a continuous action space. After the serial task is disassembled into multiple microtasks, it is necessary to process the numerical standardization and the frequency of reward value acquisition. After experimentally testing the performance of different hyperparameter combinations, this paper sets the learning rate to $r = 0.01$, the step size to 5, the discount factor $\gamma = 0.95$, the noise network $\sigma = 0.09$, and the experience playback $\alpha = 0.4$, $\beta = 0.5$. It converges when the number of steps is 15,000. The DDPG algorithm uses a greedy strategy, which also fluctuates when the number of steps is high.

Table 2. The experimental parameters of the simulation environment

Experimental parameters	Value
Number of applications running on end devices	[2, 6]
The application contains is the number of tasks	5
CPU frequency of the end device	0.5
CPU frequency of the MEC server	5
Cloud CPU frequency	15
CPU cycles required for task computation	[0.1, 0.9]
Task size	[0.5, 1]
Task output data	[0.01, 0.03]
Transmission rate between terminal equipment and MEC server	[3.5, 5]
Transmission rate between MEC servers	[10, 20]
Transfer rate between server and cloud	[2, 3]

In Fig. 3, the horizontal axis represents the interval time between serial task request unloading, and the unit time is 10 ms, and the vertical axis represents the reward value of the objective function. It can be seen that when the task calculation pressure is low and the generation interval is large, the offloading effect of the edge server is the best, and the edge server cannot bear the situation that the calculation transmission volume increases in a short period of time. The DDPG algorithm used in this paper has certain advantages compared with the Q-learning algorithm and the DQN algorithm in various situations.

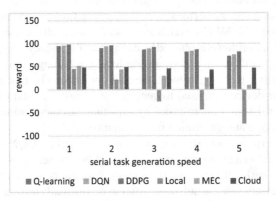

Fig. 3. The change of objective function value with the generation speed of serial tasks.

In addition, in the case of the same task unloading time interval, change the proportion of higher computational complexity in the serial task, Fig. 4. Reflects the change of the reward value of the objective function, with the increase of task computational complexity, the computational power is weak Local devices cannot complete tasks, and edge servers with limited carrying capacity will experience task accumulation, while operations with high network latency and high computing power can run normally. Figure 5 and Fig. 6 respectively reflect the performance in terms of delay and energy consumption. In the case of high computational complexity, the weight allocation strategy of serial tasks effectively reduces system delay and energy consumption. Compared with other algorithms, the DDPG algorithm proposed in this paper effectively reduces the delay and energy consumption, and provides better service quality.

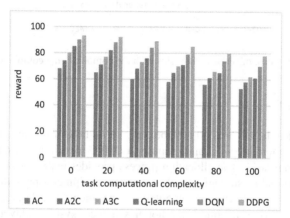

Fig. 4. Variation of objective function value with task computational complexity.

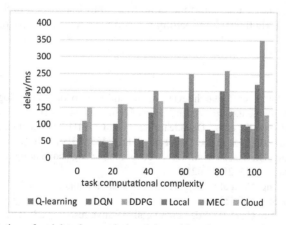

Fig. 5. Variation of serial task completion delay with task computational complexity.

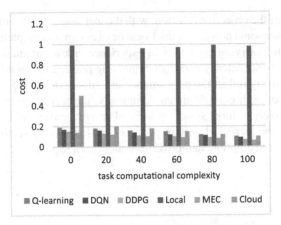

Fig. 6. The energy cost of serial tasks varies with the computational complexity of the tasks.

5   Conclusion

This paper studies the edge-cloud collaborative serial task offloading algorithm based on deep reinforcement learning, and proposes a DDPG algorithm to optimize the characteristics of serial tasks. The allocation process provides approximately optimal task allocation and offloading strategies for different user equipment applications. The effectiveness of the algorithm is proved by simulation experiments, and the algorithm has great advantages under various parameters. It not only reduces system delay and energy consumption, but also improves user service quality. This paper does not fully consider the problem of device mobility. In future research work, we will introduce the multi-device task offloading strategy under mobile conditions into the device mobility prediction mechanism, and study the task offloading method for device mobility prediction.

References

1. Hu, H., Jin, F., Lang, S.: Research review of computing offloading technology in mobile edge computing environment. Comput. Eng. Appl. **57**(14), 60–74 (2021)
2. Lv, Z., Li, J., Dong, C., et al.: Deep learning in the COVID-19 epidemic: a deep model for urban traffic revitalization index. Data Knowl. Eng. **135**, 101912 (2021)
3. Liang, G., Wang, Q., Xin, J., et al.: Overview of mobile edge computing resource allocation. J. Inf. Secur. **6**(03), 227–256 (2021)
4. Lv, Z., Li, J., Dong, C., et al.: DeepSTF: a deep spatial–temporal forecast model of taxi flow. Comput. J. **66**, 565–580 (2021)
5. Yu, B., Li, X., Pan, C., et al.: Edge-cloud collaborative resource allocation algorithm based on deep reinforcement learning. Comput. Sci. **49**(07), 248–253 (2022)
6. Shi, J., Du, J., Wang, J., et al.: Priority-aware task offloading in vehicular fog computing based on deep reinforcement learning. IEEE Trans. Veh. Technol. **69**(12), 16067–16081 (2020)
7. Zhang, L., Zhang, Z.Y., Min, L., et al.: Task offloading and trajectory control for UAV-assisted mobile edge computing using deep reinforcement learning. IEEE Access **9**, 53708–53719 (2021)

8. Chen, Y., Gu, W., Li, K.: Dynamic task offloading for internet of things in mobile edge computing via deep reinforcement learning. Int. J. Commun. Syst. e5154 (2022)

9. Cao, Z., Zhou, P., Li, R., et al.: Multiagent deep reinforcement learning for joint multichannel access and task offloading of mobile-edge computing in industry 4.0. IEEE Internet Things J. **7**(7), 6201–6213 (2020)

10. Lv, Z., Li, J., Dong, C., et al.: DeepPTP: A deep pedestrian trajectory prediction model for traffic intersection. KSII Trans. Internet Inf. Syst. (TIIS) **15**(7), 2321–2338 (2021)

11. Zhang, F., Zhao, J., Liu, D., et al.: Edge-cloud collaborative serial task offloading algorithm based on deep reinforcement learning. J. Univ. Electron. Sci. Technol. China **50**(03), 398–404 (2021)

12. Xu, Z., Lv, Z., Li, J., et al.: A novel perspective on travel demand prediction considering natural environmental and socioeconomic factors. IEEE Intell. Transp. Syst. Mag. **15**, 136–159 (2022)

13. Liu, W., Huang, Y., Du, W., et al.: Resource-constrained serial task offloading strategy in mobile edge computing. J. Softw. **31**(06), 1889–1908 (2020)

14. Xu, Z., Li, J., Lv, Z., et al.: A graph spatial-temporal model for predicting population density of key areas. Comput. Electr. Eng. **93**, 107235 (2021)

15. Xu, Z., Li, J., Lv, Z., et al.: A classification method for urban functional regions based on the transfer rate of empty cars. IET Intell. Transp. Syst. **16**(2), 133–147 (2022)

16. Zhang, H., Li, H., Chen, S., et al.: Task offloading and resource optimization based on mobile edge computing in ultra-dense networks. J. Electron. Inf. Technol. **41**(05), 1194–1201 (2019)

17. Lv, Z., Wang, X., Cheng, Z., et al.: A new approach to COVID-19 data mining: a deep spatial–temporal prediction model based on tree structure for traffic revitalization index. Data Knowl. Eng. **146**, 102193 (2023)

18. Li, H., Lv, Z., Li, J., et al.: Traffic flow forecasting in the COVID-19: a deep spatial-temporal model based on discrete wavelet transformation. ACM Trans. Knowl. Discov. Data **17**, 1–28 (2022)

19. Wang, Y., Fan, J., Wang, C.: A two-stage task migration strategy based on game theory in the cloud edge environment. Comput. Appl. **41**(05), 1392–1398 (2021)

20. Zhao, H., Zhang, T., Chen, Y., et al.: Task distribution and offloading algorithm for in-vehicle edge network based on DQN. J. Commun. **41**(10), 172–178 (2020)

21. Tang, M., Wong, V.W.S.: Deep reinforcement learning for task offloading in mobile edge computing systems. IEEE Trans. Mob. Comput. **21**(6), 1985–1997 (2020)

22. Shen, H., Jiang, Y., Deng, F., et al.: Task unloading strategy of multi UAV for transmission line inspection based on deep reinforcement learning. Electronics **11**(14), 2188 (2022)

23. Wang, J., Hu, J., Min, G., et al.: Dependent task offloading for edge computing based on deep reinforcement learning. IEEE Trans. Comput. **71**(10), 2449–2461 (2021)

24. Wang, J., Hu, J., Min, G., et al.: Fast adaptive task offloading in edge computing based on meta reinforcement learning. IEEE Trans. Parallel Distrib. Syst. **32**(1), 242–253 (2020)

25. Zhao, N., Ye, Z., Pei, Y., et al.: Multi-agent deep reinforcement learning for task offloading in UAV-assisted mobile edge computing. IEEE Trans. Wireless Commun. **21**(9), 6949–6960 (2022)

Intelligent Internet of Things

WiKnow: A Human Activity Recognition Method in Office Scene with Coordinate Attention from WiFi Channel State Information

Ping Wang[1,2]($\boxtimes$), Tao Yin[1,2], Zhenya Zhang[1,2], Wenkai Wang[1,2], and Jiaojiao Gao[1,2]

[1] Anhui Province Key Laboratory of Intelligent Building and Building Energy Saving, Anhui Jianzhu University, Hefei 230022, China
wangping@ahjzu.edu.cn
[2] School of Electronics and Information Engineering, Anhui Jianzhu University, Hefei 230601, China

Abstract. In the modern information society, people spend more and more time in the office. Therefore, understanding the various human activities of users in office scenarios is important to enable health monitoring, smart home, and human-computer interaction. Current human activity recognition (HAR) approaches for office scenarios are often characterized by privacy invasiveness, high cost, insufficient accuracy, or the need for additional wearable devices. To this end, we propose WiKnow, a non-contact radio frequency (RF) human activity recognition system based on WiFi channel state information (CSI), which is based on denoising CSI amplitude data and converting it into a 3D tensor based on the CSI data characteristics, inputting it into a designed convolutional neural network (CNN), and improving the performance of the network through the coordinated attention (CA) mechanism, to understand the corresponding human activities. We conducted experiments on our dataset and a public dataset, and the accuracy reached 98.61% and 97.92%, respectively, and the experimental results verified the effectiveness of the method in recognizing human activities.

Keywords: human activity recognition (HAR) · channel state information (CSI) · convolutional neural network (CNN) · coordinate attention (CA)

1 Introduction

With the rapid development of artificial intelligence, big data, cloud computing, the Internet of Things, and other technologies, the Internet of Everything is rapidly evolving in the direction of the intelligence of everything [1]. HAR is a part of human-computer interaction that aims to detect and determine human actions to provide valuable information about the person being detected.

In today's society, people are spending more and more time working in buildings, especially at their desks. Some data suggests that people spend an average of 66% of their working time at their desktops. HAR in office scenarios has significant application value, e.g., health monitoring, smart home, etc. Long-term desktop office naturally causes the problem of sedentary behavior, which is precisely one of the triggers of other major diseases [2]. The realization of HAR can record what human activities are carried out by the monitored person in front of the desk, to indirectly assess the physical health condition of the person; it can also realize the control of other electrical equipment through human activity so that we can have a more comfortable and intelligent living environment.

In this paper, we propose a HAR method based on WiFi CSI in office scenarios. We designed a set of filters to efficiently handle the noise in the CSI data, which includes environmental noise as well as noise from other unrelated activities (that we are not interested in); a CNN structure is designed to process CSI amplitude data, and the CA mechanism is introduced to optimize the network, which is relied upon to obtain a higher recognition accuracy for HAR in office scenes. Thus, the main contributions of this study can be summarized as follows.

- We propose a deep learning model (WiKnow) that eliminates the need for subcarrier selection and automatically recognizes human activities in office scenes with very high accuracy.
- In the WiKnow model, we have designed an efficient neural network and innovatively introduced the CA mechanism, which greatly improves our accuracy in HAR.
- The system is generic and can be easily extended to other CSI activity recognition datasets by focusing only on the format of the acquired CSI data and making simple adjustments to the input matrix.

2   Related Work

There are currently three mature approaches in the field of HAR: vision-based HAR, wearable device-based HAR, and WiFi-based HAR.

2.1   Vision-Based HAR

For computer vision-based recognition methods, the main way of recognition still relies on specialized equipment, such as cameras and camcorders. Nagarajan et al. [3] developed a physical space detection model across multiple relevant environments and experimentally demonstrated that the system can accurately predict the next human action in long video learning scenarios. Qiu et al. [4] proposed a skeleton-based action recognition model named STTFormer, and the method yielded a cross-view performance result of 89.2% on the NTU RGB+D 120 dataset. Overall, computer vision-based recognition methods have already possessed a wider range of application scenarios, but various factors significantly affect vision-based activity recognition, such as the extremely high requirements on the number of data collected, the influence of light, angle, and other factors, and the difficulty of guaranteeing the privacy and security of users.

2.2   Wearable Device-Based HAR

Recognition methods based on wearable devices currently rely heavily on wearable sensor devices. By deploying integrated or multiple decentralized sensors, motion state sensing can be achieved at one or more points. Common sensing devices are such as inertial guides, barometers, and accelerometer needles. One often collects data from sensing devices through relevant modules, based on which data features are extracted and then HAR is realized. In conclusion, the recognition method based on wearable devices has certain advantages in terms of motion sensing latency, but at present, wearable devices generally have the disadvantages of not being lightweight, not having high experimental convenience, and relatively expensive equipment, and it is easy to lose or blur the key information in the process of data extraction, with a large difference in the stability of the recognition, unstable data, and the overall user experience is not friendly [5, 6].

2.3 WiFi-Based HAR

WiFi-based recognition method has many advantages, such as the ubiquity of WiFi devices, non-intrusiveness, protection of user's privacy and identity, and NLOS communication. WiFi signals to achieve the behavioral The mechanism of recognition is because WiFi signals are easily affected by human behavior, and different activities of the human body can cause different degrees of signal changes, so the corresponding behavior can be identified according to the changes in CSI. Existing WiFi-based human behavior recognition usually uses two metrics: RSSI (Received Signal Strength Indicator) and CSI [7, 8].

Sigg et al. [9] proposed a device-less HAR system that uses a mobile phone to collect RSSI and selects the best features to accomplish the recognition of 11 gestures with 52% accuracy and 4 gestures with 72% accuracy. Gu et al. [10] proposed an online HAR system that explores WiFi RSSI fingerprints of different human activities. Sigg et al. [11] proposed a hardware device USRP for collecting RSSI from WiFi devices. They used RSSI to recognize four activities: standing, walking, lying down, and crawling, and achieved more than 80% accuracy. The disadvantage is that RSSI contains only signal strength, which is one-dimensional data and tends to have coarse perceptual granularity on environment perception, and due to the inevitable existence of various noises in real environments, RSSI is not an effective metric for complex multi-dimensional information superimposed on multiple paths, and path differentiation is even more difficult to realize. Therefore, the robustness and effectiveness of RSSI-based recognition systems are not ideal in complex real environments. Compared to RSSI, CSI is a fine-grained signal, and existing studies have shown that CSI signals outperform RSSI signals in complex environments.

Wang et al. [12] proposed WiFall in 2017, which utilizes CSI to detect falls and the most common daily activities of the elderly such as walking, sitting, standing, etc., and can achieve better fall detection accuracy with an average experimental accuracy of 87%. Zhang et al. [13] proposed a non-contact sensing theory based on the Fresnel zone, and the proposed model characterizes the relationship between the target motion and the corresponding signal changes when the target is close to and far from the wireless transceiver. Shi et al. [14] proposed MatNet-eCSI, which implements the original model's good performance on a new dataset, improves the recognition accuracy in new environments, and the training complexity greatly reduced. Jia et al. [15] proposed to visualize channel data affected by human actions as time-series heatmap images, which are processed by CNN, based on which the user's behavior is discriminated and understood, and can achieve an accuracy of 94.4%. Alsaify et al. [16] proposed a CSI-based multi-environment HAR system. They extracted several statistical features from their own collected dataset and selected the best subset of features to achieve 91.27% accuracy with the SVM classifier, but the method requires a lot of preprocessing operations and has relatively low performance. Shalaby et al. [17] proposed four deep learning models and tested them on two publicly available datasets, and all of them achieved good recognition accuracy but did not consider signal preprocessing. However, signal preprocessing and the use of phase information were not considered.

Our system, WiKnow, eliminates the need for subcarrier selection, which can be input into an already designed CNN based on signal processing, which is utilized to obtain spatial information in the data, and introduces a CA mechanism to improve the recognition accuracy of HAR.

3 Background of CSI

According to the IEEE 802.11 protocol, WiFi signals are transmitted using OFDM modulation, which makes the channel between each transceiver antenna pair consist of multiple subcarriers. Since the human body changes the distribution of multipath when performing different activities and produces the Doppler effect, these factors affect the propagation of the signal. When the number of antennas at the transmitting end is m and the number of antennas at the receiving end is n, the frequency response of the received signal of the kth subcarrier in the ith antenna pair, which is transmitted from the transmitting end and arrives at the receiving end through several different paths, can be expressed as follows:

$$h_i^{(k)}(\theta, t) = e^{-j \cdot 2\pi \Delta \theta t} \sum_{l=1}^{L} \varpi_l(\theta, t) \cdot e^{-j \cdot 2\pi \theta \tau_l(t)} \tag{1}$$

where j denotes the imaginary unit, $e^{-j \cdot 2\pi \Delta \theta t}$ denotes the phase shift due to the subcarrier frequency difference between the transceiver devices, θ denotes the frequency of the kth subcarrier, $\varpi_l(\theta, t)$ denotes the complex numerical representation of the attenuation and the initial phase shift for the lth path, and $e^{-j \cdot 2\pi \theta \tau_l(t)}$ is the phase shift on the lth path with a propagation delay of $\tau_l(t)$. Meanwhile, this $h_i^{(k)}$ can be also expressed as

$$h_i^{(k)} = \|h_i^{(k)}\| e^{-j \cdot \angle h_i^{(k)}} \tag{2}$$

where $\|h_i^{(k)}\|$ denotes the amplitude of the kth subcarrier of the ith antenna pair and $\angle h_i^{(k)}$ denotes the phase of the kth subcarrier of the ith antenna pair. Therefore, the human body will cause the length of the communication path to change when performing different activities, which will cause the phase change and amplitude change of the WiFi signal. In a MIMO system, when the number of subcarriers is, then the CSI measured at the moment can be expressed as

$$H(t) = [H_1, H_2, \cdots, H_K] \tag{3}$$

$$H_i = \begin{pmatrix} h_{11} & \cdots & h_{1n} \\ \vdots & \ddots & \vdots \\ h_{m1} & \cdots & h_{mn} \end{pmatrix} \tag{4}$$

Since the human body contains many sampling points in its activity progression, there is when the sampling time is T, the amplitude is denoted as *amp*, and the amplitude sequence data of the kth subcarrier of the ith antenna pair is denoted as X:

$$X_{(num)} = \left\{ amp_i^k(1), amp_i^k(2), \cdots, amp_i^k(T) \right\} \tag{5}$$

$$amp_i^k(t) = \left\| h_i^k(t) \right\| \tag{6}$$

In the experiment of this paper, there are 6 antenna pairs with 30 subcarrier signals on each antenna pair, so the value of *num* is taken as $[1, 2, \cdots, 180]$.

4   System Design

In this section, we present the system design of WiKnow.

4.1   System Overview

As shown in Fig. 1, we built an experimental environment to capture six everyday human activities in an office scenario, details about the dataset are presented in Sect. 5. We analyzed the raw CSI data collected and extracted the amplitude information in the CSI data as the base signal for HAR. In the signal preprocessing module, we used various filters to denoise the data. Due to the instability of wireless signals in the propagation process, there are some outliers, i.e., outliers, in the CSI amplitude data that fluctuate a lot, so in this paper, we first use the Hampel filter to process the outliers in the data. Second, there is noise caused by the environment in the data, this paper uses a Butterworth low-pass filter to denoise. Again, the Savitzky-Golay filter is used to smooth the data. In the CSI data reconstruction module, we convert the CSI amplitude data into a 3D tensor based on the characteristics of CSI amplitude data and the duration of various human activities. In the HAR classification module, we use the 3D tensor as the input data for subsequent processing, design a convolutional neural network structure suitable for HAR in office scenarios, and importantly, introduce the CA mechanism to improve the network performance. From the experimental results, we achieve higher accuracy for HAR.

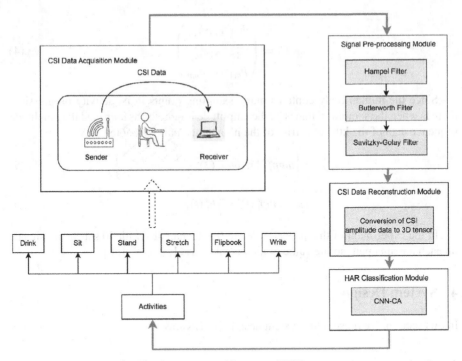

Fig. 1. System architecture of WiKnow

4.2 Signal Pre-processing Module

Hampel Filter. In this paper, to reduce the effect of outlier data on the accuracy of HAR, the CSI amplitude data obtained from each action acquisition is processed using a Hampel filter.

$$X_{(num)} = \left\{ amp_i^k(1), amp_i^k(2), \cdots, amp_i^k(T) \right\} \tag{7}$$

$$X'_{num} = hampel(X_{num}) \tag{8}$$

For each piece of CSI data, the Hampel filter will generate an observation window for each element in it. We choose an observation window consisting of the element itself and 7 elements on each side of the element. After that, the median value of the data within the observation window is calculated. In this paper, if the difference between the element to be processed and the median value is more than 3 standard deviations, then the data is recognized as an outlier, and the median value is used instead of the element.

Butterworth Filter. In the CSI data collected in the office scene, due to the multipath effect, equipment, and other factors, there is still some high-frequency noise after the outlier processing. Considering that the fluctuation of CSI data caused by the action occurs in the low-frequency part, and the change frequency of CSI amplitude caused by the action is mainly lower than 60 Hz, this paper chooses the 5th-order Butterworth low-pass filter to denoise the data, which is expressed as follows:

$$|H(\omega)|^2 = \frac{1}{1 + \left(\frac{\omega}{\omega_c}\right)^{2\gamma}} = \frac{1}{1 + \varepsilon^2 \left(\frac{\omega}{\omega_p}\right)^{2\gamma}} \tag{9}$$

where $|H(\omega)|^2$ denotes the value of the passband edge, γ denotes the order of the Butterworth filter, ω_c denotes the cutoff frequency, and ω_p denotes the passband edge frequency.

Savitzky-Golay Filter. The Savitzky-Golay filter is based on the idea of a sliding window to process the data. Compared with other smoothing methods, it is more effective in retaining information about the variation of the signal, such as distributional features like relative great and small values in the original data. In this paper, for each CSI amplitude data, the Savitzky-Golay filter will process the data according to the length of the sliding window until all data points are fitted. The sliding window length of the filter in this paper is set to 250.

4.3 CSI Data Reconstruction Module

In some existing works on HAR based on WiFi CSI, some works linearly sum and average the subcarriers to generate a one-dimensional sequence to process the data, and some works utilize principal component analysis to select a portion of the subcarriers to be used as subsequent data processing. Although these works take into account the correlation between subcarriers and reduce the complexity of data computation, they do not fully utilize the variability in CSI data. In this paper, based on the characteristics of the collected CSI data, a 3D tensor of A*B*C will be constructed for each action, where A denotes the number of antenna pairs consisting of the transmitting antenna and the receiving antenna, B denotes the number of CSI packets collected by the current action, and C denotes the number of subcarriers. The values of A, B, and C in the data for which experiments were conducted in this paper are 6, 4000, and 30, respectively.

4.4 HAR Classification Module

In this paper, to solve the problem of HAR in office scenarios, a CNN is designed and the CA mechanism is introduced. The network structure is shown in Fig. 2.

According to the processing in Sect. 4.3, we will get reconstructed CSI data, i.e., a 3D tensor. In Conv2d, we have a kernel size of 5 and a stride of 1, using 'same' for padding. In AvgPool2d, the kernel size is 2 and the stride is 2, using '0' for padding. In Dropout2d, we take the value of p to be 0.6.

The attention mechanism is currently one of the mainstream methods and research hotspots in the field of deep learning, in which SENet [18], and CBAM [19] are typical representatives of the attention mechanism, in the processing of the data, they generally take the average pooling and global maximum pooling practice, but this practice ignores the spatial information in the data. CA mechanism [20] is based on the principle of average pooling in the input data in the width and height directions to generate feature

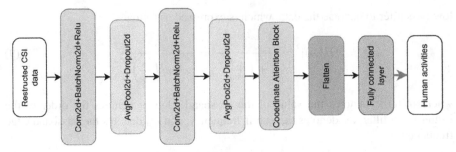

Fig. 2. Structure of CNN-CA

data in their respective directions, followed by splicing of the two data, channel scaling, batch normalization, nonlinear transformations, and other operations, and then continue to segment the data, converted to the format before splicing and processed by the Sigmoid function, respectively, to finally generate the output data. The structure of the CA Block is shown in Fig. 3.

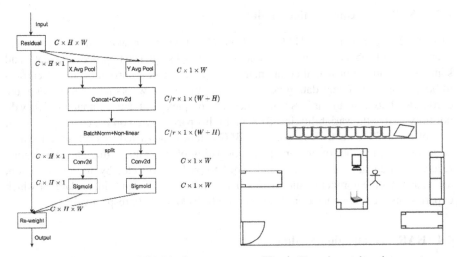

Fig. 3. Structure of CA Block   **Fig. 4.** Experimental environment

5   Dataset

5.1   Own Dataset

We conducted the data acquisition experiments in a room the size of $8.5 \times 6 \, m^2$, which is a complex environment with sofas, computers, tables, chairs, cabinets, and other items. The transmitting end of the experiment was an ordinary home router with 2 antennas, and the receiving end was a small Hewlett-Packard desktop mainframe computer, specifically model HP 288 Pro G3, with an Intel 5300 NIC installed and 3 receiving antennas. The router operates in the 5 GHz band, and the desktop host has an operating system of

Ubuntu 14.04.01 with the open-source tool CSI Tool [21], which is used to collect CSI data, installed.

During the data acquisition process, the transmitter and receiver devices were placed on a table and spaced 1 m apart with a table height of 0.75 m. Volunteers performed predefined 6 human activities in front of the table, and the experimental environment is shown in Fig. 4. The six human activities are drinking water, sitting still, standing, stretching, flipping through a book, and writing. Eight volunteers were invited to collect the data, and each volunteer needed to complete these six activities, each activity needed to be performed 30 times, and the time for each activity collection was 4 s, which resulted in 1440 data samples. The transmitter sends data packets to the receiver at a frequency of 0.001, and each activity will collect data of size 4000 × 2 × 3 × 30, where 4000 is the number of data packets. 2 is the number of transmitting antennas, 3 is the number of receiving antennas, and 30 is the number of subcarriers.

5.2 StanWiFi

To verify the validity of the method, this paper also conducts experiments on a publicly available dataset. The University of Toronto and Stanford University made a CSI dataset publicly available in 2017 [22], which includes raw information of magnitude and phase, The collected data were participated by six volunteers and contained six activities, which are lying, falling, walking, running, sitting down, and getting up, and the dataset has a size of about 4 GB. In this paper, the CSI amplitude information of the six actions in the dataset was selected for the experiment.

6 Performance Evaluation

To test the effectiveness of HAR, in this paper, we use Accuracy, Precision, Recall, and F1 Score as evaluation metrics.

$$Accuracy = \frac{TP + TN}{TP + TN + FP + FN} \tag{10}$$

$$\Pr ecision = \frac{TP}{TP + FP} \tag{11}$$

$$\mathrm{Re}call = \frac{TP}{TP + FN} \tag{12}$$

$$F1 - score = 2 \times \frac{\Pr ecision \times \mathrm{Re}call}{\Pr ecision + \mathrm{Re}call} \tag{13}$$

Here, TP classifies the positive class as positive, FP classifies the positive class as negative, TN classifies the negative class as negative, and FN classifies the negative class as positive.

To verify the effectiveness of the algorithm proposed in this paper, the data collected were subjected to an experimental study, in which the data were processed on a computer with the following configurations: Windows 10, PyTorch 1.13, AMD Ryzen

7 5800H processor, 16G of memory, and NVIDIA GeForce RTX3050Ti graphics card, The graphics card is NVIDIA GeForce RTX3050Ti with 4G of video memory.

In this section, we present numerous experimental results obtained from the WiKnow model, including an analysis of the study on the attention mechanism; an analysis of the comparative study with other state-of-the-art models; an analysis of the length of time to collect CSI actions; and experimental results obtained on StanWiFi.

6.1 Experimental Results on Own Dataset

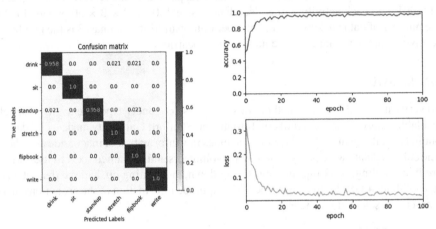

Fig. 5. Confusion matrix of the proposed model on own dataset

Fig. 6. Accuracy and loss graph of the CNN-CA model

We conducted experiments on our own actual collected data. In this paper, our CNN structure can also be used for classification, but its discriminative accuracy is not as good as the best, so we introduced the CA attention mechanism. Table 1 shows our experimental results, where CNN-CA indicates the results with the addition of the CA mechanism, i.e., the network model designed in this paper; CNN indicates the experimental results without the addition of the attention mechanism; SENet and CBAM are also widely used attention mechanisms, so we also conducted experiments in combination with them. From the experimental results, the incorporation of the attention mechanism can improve the recognition accuracy of the model, in which the CA mechanism improves the most, followed by CBAM, and SENet. They can improve 3.12%, 1.73%, and 0.69%, respectively, relative to the model without the attention mechanism.

As shown in Fig. 5, for the six activities, our model can achieve an overall 98.61% accuracy. The actions of sitting still, stretching, turning the pages of a book, and writing can achieve 100% accuracy, while the two actions of drinking water and standing can also achieve more than 95% accuracy. And Precision is 98.65%, Recall is 98.6% and F1 Score is 98.62%. For misclassification, this may be due to similarities between human activities. Figure 6 shows the loss and accuracy changes during training.

For the six human activities, we also used three learning algorithms (LSTM, SVM, and RF) for classification. The experiments proved that among these three algorithms, the LSTM algorithm obtained a higher accuracy (LSTM: 0.9514; SVM: 0.8854; RF:

Table 1. Comparison of various attention mechanisms

Model	Accuracy	Precision	Recall	F1 Score
CNN-CA	98.61%	98.65%	98.6%	98.62%
CNN-CA (without signal pre-process)	95.14%	95.35%	95.13%	95.24%
CNN	95.49%	95.52%	95.47%	95.47%
CNN-SENet	96.18%	96.28%	96.18%	96.13%
CNN-CBAM	97.22%	97.38%	97.23%	97.3%

0.8125), but there is still a gap with the recognition accuracy of CNN-CA (0.9861). The experimental results are shown in Table 2. The experimental results show that our model has a better recognition effect.

Table 2. Comparison of different classification models

Model	Accuracy	Precision	Recall	F1 Score
CNN-CA	98.61%	98.65%	98.6%	98.62%
LSTM	95.14%	95.2%	95.13%	95.16%
SVM	88.54%	88.83%	88.55%	88.69%
RF	81.25%	82.38%	81.25%	81.81%

Through CSI data collection, we found that the timing of human activities varies depending on individual habits. After conducting experiments centered on the number of data packets collected, we found that a decrease in the number of data packets leads to a decrease in the accuracy of the model. This is because the information on human activities during this period is not complete. The results of our study are shown in Table 3. It is worth noting that longer training time requires more computational resources. In the follow-up work, we will address the conflict between recognition accuracy and consumption of computational resources.

Table 3. Comparison of different CSI collection time

Time (ms)	Accuracy	Precision	Recall	F1 Score
4000	98.61%	98.65%	98.6%	98.62%
3000	93.4%	94%	93.42%	93.71%
2000	90.63%	91.08%	90.62%	90.85%
1000	86.46%	88.77%	86.43%	87.58%

6.2 Experimental Results on StanWiFi

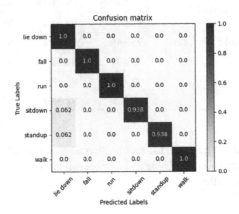

Fig. 7. Confusion matrix of the proposed model on StanWiFi

We also conducted experiments on the publicly available dataset StanWiFi, for which we were able to achieve an average accuracy of 97.92% for the six actions included in that data. The experimental results are shown in Fig. 7. For two actions, standing up and sitting down, 100% accuracy was not achieved and the model misidentified them as lying down.

In the original paper, RF, HMM, and LSTM were used to train the data, and the experimental results indicated that LSTM was the most effective, and was able to achieve an average accuracy of 90.5%. We similarly compared it with more representative articles from recent years, Chen et al. [23] proposed an attention-based bi-directional LSTM. They utilized attention to obtain more basic features. Their proposed ABLSTM model provided 97.3% accuracy on the StanWiFi dataset. Salehinejad et al. [24] proposed a lightweight HAR method called the LiteHAR model. The model achieved 93% accuracy on the StanWiFi dataset without training. The method in this paper can obtain 97.92% accuracy on the StanWiFi dataset with a Precision of 98.15%, Recall of 97.93%, and F1 Score of 98.04%.

7 Conclusion and Future Work

In this paper, we design a HAR method based on WiFi CSI in office scenes. For the collected CSI data, we need to perform a series of filtering processes to remove the noise contained in the data; we do not need to select the subcarriers, but directly convert the CSI data into a 3D tensor based on the characteristics of the CSI data for the subsequent processing of the data; in the predefined structure of convolutional neural network, we introduce the CA mechanism to improve the performance, so that we can effectively and accurately recognize the human activities in the office scene. Compared with other attentional mechanisms and other classification methods, the method in this paper performs well and achieves an average recognition accuracy of over 98% for the six common human activities in the office scenario. This paper also explores the effect of the length of acquisition time on the experimental results. In the end, we also conducted experiments on StanWiFi, which proved the effectiveness of WiKnow.

However, in this paper, we only recognized human activities in one scene and did not consider the cross-domain performance of the model; we also did not take full advantage of the phase information in the CSI data, which is a limitation; and the system has a high demand on computational resources. In our next work, we will further investigate the performance of the model in more complex office scenes; utilize both CSI magnitude and phase information data for human activity recognition; and optimize the model's demand for computational resources. Based on this, we will accomplish real-time human activity recognition in office scenarios.

Acknowledgement. This work is partially supported by the Discipline (Major) Top-notch Talent Academic Funding Project of Anhui Provincial University and College (gxbjZD2021067, gxyq2022030), Key Project of Natural Science Research of Universities of Anhui Province (KJ2020A0470), the Innovative Leading Talents Project of Anhui Provincial Special Support Program ([2022]21), the director foundation of the Anhui Province Key Laboratory of Intelligent Building & Building Energy Saving (No. IBES2022ZR01).

References

1. Lu, Y., Lv, S., Wang, X., Zhou, X.: A survey on WiFi based human behavior analysis technology. Chin. J. Comput **41**, 1–22 (2018)
2. Tremblay, M.S., et al.: Sedentary behavior research network (SBRN) - terminology consensus project process and outcome. Int. J. Behav. Nutr. Phys. Act. **14**, 75 (2017)
3. Nagarajan, T., Li, Y., Feichtenhofer, C., Grauman, K.: Ego-topo: environment affordances from egocentric video. In: Proceedings of the IEEE/CVF Conference on Computer Vision and Pattern Recognition, pp. 163–172 (2020)
4. Qiu, H., Hou, B., Ren, B., Zhang, X.: Spatio-temporal tuples transformer for skeleton-based action recognition. arXiv preprint arXiv:2201.02849 (2022)
5. Chen, L., Zhang, Y., Peng, L.: METIER: a deep multi-task learning based activity and user recognition model using wearable sensors. Proc. ACM Interact. Mob. Wearable Ubiquit. Technol. **4**, 1–18 (2020)
6. Pei, L., et al.: MARS: Mixed virtual and real wearable sensors for human activity recognition with multidomain deep learning model. IEEE Internet Things J. **8**, 9383–9396 (2021)
7. Moshiri, P.F., Shahbazian, R., Nabati, M., Ghorashi, S.A.: A CSI-based human activity recognition using deep learning. Sensors **21**, 7225 (2021)
8. Yang, Z., Zhou, Z., Liu, Y.: From RSSI to CSI: indoor localization via channel response. ACM Comput. Surv. (CSUR) **46**, 1–32 (2013)
9. Sigg, S., Blanke, U., Tröster, G.: The telepathic phone: frictionless activity recognition from WiFi-RSSI. In: 2014 IEEE International Conference on Pervasive Computing and Communications (PerCom), pp. 148–155. IEEE (2014)
10. Gu, Y., Ren, F., Li, J.: PAWS: passive human activity recognition based on WiFi ambient signals. IEEE Internet Things J. **3**, 796–805 (2015)
11. Sigg, S., Shi, S., Buesching, F., Ji, Y., Wolf, L.: Leveraging RF-channel fluctuation for activity recognition: active and passive systems, continuous and RSSI-based signal features. In: Proceedings of International Conference on Advances in Mobile Computing & Multimedia, pp. 43–52 (2013)

12. Wang, Y., Wu, K., Ni, L.M.: WiFall: device-free fall detection by wireless networks. IEEE Trans. Mob. Comput. **16**, 581–594 (2016)
13. Zhang, D., Zhang, F., Wu, D., Xiong, J., Niu, K.: Fresnel zone based theories for contactless sensing. In: Ahad, M.A.R., Mahbub, U., Rahman, T. (eds.) Contactless Human Activity Analysis. ISRL, vol. 200, pp. 145–164. Springer, Cham (2021). https://doi.org/10.1007/978-3-030-68590-4_5
14. Shi, Z., Zhang, J.A., Xu, R.Y., Cheng, Q.: Environment-robust device-free human activity recognition with channel-state-information enhancement and one-shot learning. IEEE Trans. Mob. Comput. **21**, 540–554 (2020)
15. Jia, L., Gu, Y., Cheng, K., Yan, H., Ren, F.: BeAware: convolutional neural network (CNN) based user behavior understanding through WiFi channel state information. Neurocomputing **397**, 457–463 (2020)
16. Alsaify, B.A., Almazari, M.M., Alazrai, R., Alouneh, S., Daoud, M.I.: A CSI-based multi-environment human activity recognition framework. Appl. Sci. **12**, 930 (2022)
17. Shalaby, E., ElShennawy, N., Sarhan, A.: Utilizing deep learning models in CSI-based human activity recognition. Neural Comput. Appl. **34**, 1–18 (2022)
18. Hu, J., Shen, L., Sun, G.: Squeeze-and-excitation networks. In: Proceedings of the IEEE Conference on Computer Vision and Pattern Recognition, pp. 7132–7141 (2018)
19. Woo, S., Park, J., Lee, J.-Y., Kweon, I.S.: CBAM: convolutional block attention module. In: Ferrari, V., Hebert, M., Sminchisescu, C., Weiss, Y. (eds.) ECCV 2018. LNCS, vol. 11211, pp. 3–19. Springer, Cham (2018). https://doi.org/10.1007/978-3-030-01234-2_1
20. Hou, Q., Zhou, D., Feng, J.: Coordinate attention for efficient mobile network design. In: Proceedings of the IEEE/CVF Conference on Computer Vision and Pattern Recognition, pp. 13713–13722 (2021)
21. Halperin, D., Hu, W., Sheth, A., Wetherall, D.: Tool release: gathering 802.11 n traces with channel state information. ACM SIGCOMM Comput. Commun. Rev. **41**, 53–53 (2011)
22. Yousefi, S., Narui, H., Dayal, S., Ermon, S., Valaee, S.: A survey on behavior recognition using WiFi channel state information. IEEE Commun. Mag. **55**, 98–104 (2017)
23. Chen, Z., Zhang, L., Jiang, C., Cao, Z., Cui, W.: WiFi CSI based passive human activity recognition using attention based BLSTM. IEEE Trans. Mob. Comput. **18**, 2714–2724 (2018)
24. Salehinejad, H., Valaee, S.: LiteHAR: lightweight human activity recognition from WiFi signals with random convolution kernels. In: ICASSP 2022-2022 IEEE International Conference on Acoustics, Speech and Signal Processing (ICASSP), pp. 4068–4072. IEEE (2022)

DRL-Based Scheduling Scheme with Age of Information for Real-Time IoT Systems

Jianhui Wu, Hui Wang[✉], Zheyan Shi, and Sheng Pan

School of Computer Science and Technology, Zhejiang Normal University,
Jinhua 321004, China
hwang@zjnu.cn

Abstract. With the rapid development of Mobile Edge Computing (MEC) and the Internet of Things (IoT) technology, real-time monitoring applications have become a part of our daily life. However, these applications rely on the timeliness of collecting environmental information. Therefore, we introduce the emerging metric of Information Age (AoI) to measure the freshness of information. In this article, Due to the simultaneous requests from multiple devices in an IoT system, we consider the data update sampled by the device can be computed by the device or offloaded directly to the destination for computing, jointly design offloading and scheduling policies in sequential time frames to minimize the average weighted sum of AoI and energy consumption. We first formulate the optimization problem as multi-stage non-linear integer programming (NLP) problem. Secondly, to reduce the computational complexity, we develop a learning-based algorithm based on emerging deep reinforcement learning (DRL) to reduce the dimensionality of state space and utilize a late experience storage method to train a heterogeneous deep neural networks (DNNs) synchronously during the training process. Meanwhile, one exploration policy is designed to obtain multiple candidate actions based on single real-number output of neural network. The proposed policy method provides higher diversity in the generated actions and the performance is near-optimal.

Keywords: Age of Information (AoI) · Deep reinforcement learning · Exploration policy

1 Introduction

With the further development of wireless communication and Internet of Things (IoT), due to the limited process- ing capacity of IoT devices and data processing locally is time consuming. Therefore, we should further processing before the embedded information. However, Most wireless devices (WDs) are unable to provide substantial computing power. For this issue, MEC [1,2] has been become a promising computing paradigm that can offload the real-time data to an edge server for reducing the computation latency and improving the Quality of Experience (QoE). Extensive works have been focused on studying computation offloading and task scheduling algorithms that minimize the latency of tasks or maximize the utilization of system resources. However, [3] points out that optimize these performance metrics does not necessarily optimize the information as timely as possible even in the simplest queueing systems.

To solve above-mentioned problem, AoI has recently been proposed to measure the freshness of information [3,4]. After that, numerous works optimize AoI by studying update policies. [5] proposes a scheduling algorithm to minimize the average AoI under time-varying channels. [6] considers such multi-time slot transmissions with heterogeneous sizes of the status updates under noisy channels, sampling and scheduling policies were jointly designed to minimize the average AoI.

However, in many real IoT systems, the limited processing capacity of IoT devices will lead to data processing locally is time consuming. To address this issue, We can leverage edge computing to offload real-time data to edge servers for quick processing to guarantee the freshness of data. The offloading modes with respect to AoI have been preliminarily studied in [7] and [8].

Despite the extensive works relate to joint offloading and scheduling algorithms for AoI under deterministic channels have been studied, the policies of making make online optimal decisions in real time under fast-varying channel fading and dynamic task arrivals to minimize AoI in multidevice IoT systems have not been developed. In this paper, we consider a multidevice IoT system with an edge server in time-varying channel, and jointly develop online binary offloading and scheduling algorithms to minimize the average weighted sum of AoI and energy consumption. Our main contributions of the paper can be summarized as follows.

1) Considering data arrivals, we extend the AoI definition based on the [9] and formulate the average weighted sum of AoI and energy consumption minimization problem as a multi-stage NLP problem.
2) To reduce the computational complexity and support to the continuous action space, we propose a novel deep reinforcement learning(DRL)-based Online offloading framework, which uses an actor network to learn the optimal binary offloading action and a critic network to evaluates the binary offloading action [10]. To improve the running efficiency, we design a exploration policy to generate candidate actions.
3) We validate the performance of our algorithm with extensive simulations. Numerical results demonstrate that our algorithm is highly efficient and outperforms the other baseline algorithms.

the rest of this paper are organized as follows. In Sect. 2, we describe the system model and formulate the average weighted sum of AoI and energy consumption minimization problem. In Sect. 3, the online algorithm design based on deep reinforcement learning is presented. Section 4 illustrates the performance of the proposed algorithms, and compares it with other baseline algorithms. Section 5 concludes this work in our paper.

2   System Model and Problem Formulate

In this section, as shown in Fig. 1, we consider the system model is an IoT system, and it comprises of N calculable devices and a destination node. we assume the destination node is integrated with an edge server. Meanwhile, Similar to [11], we assume that the system is frame and is divided into T time slots. At the beginning of every frame,each device $i \in \{1, 2, \ldots, \mathcal{N}\}$ samples the surrounding environment by the sensor and generates a computation task containing related raw data when a change of status occurs. The task can be processed locally or offloaded to the edge server. Similar to [12], we consider deliver the task in each slot via wireless channel. the previous status update will be replaced by the new status update when the status update in the previous frame is undelivered completely.

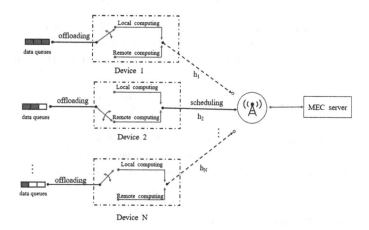

Fig. 1. The multi-devices network in IoT system

2.1   Network Model

At the beginning of every frame, when a new status occurs, each device needs to determine the offloading mode. For local processing, the devices have limitation of computing power. Therefore, it will take several slots for data processing. For remote processing, We assume the computation capability of destination node is much stronger than that of calculable devices. Hence, the computation data offloaded to the destination node can be processed within one time frame. At the beginning of each slot, the device will make scheduling decision. Consider the time-varying fading channels [13], we denote the channel gain between the ith calculable device and the destination node as $h_i(k)$. All channels follow quasistatic flat-fading, i.e. the channel gain remains constant during each time frame, but can vary at the boundary of neighboring slots.

Let k be the index of frame, $\mu_i(k) \in \{0, 1\}$be the offloading decision of device i at frame k. If $\mu_i(k) = 1$, the device will process the data locally, otherwise, it will process the data for remote computing. We divide frame k into T time slots of equal length t. Let (k, t) be the index of a slot, where $t \in \{1, 2, \ldots, T\}$.

For local computing decision, According to the results in [14], let $f_i(k)$ be the CPU frequency of calculable device i at frame k. $\delta > 0$ denotes the number of computation cycles required to process one bit of data, the amount of data processed locally within the each time slot(k,t) is

$$d^l_{i,k}(t) = \frac{f_i(k)t}{\delta}. \tag{1}$$

the energy consumption per CPU cycle is $\gamma f_i^2(k)$, which is proportional to the square of the frequency, where γ is the energyefficiency factor. Combining with (1), the consumed energy within the each time slot(k,t) given by

$$e^l_{i,k}(t) = \gamma \delta f_i^2(k) d^l_{i,k}(t) = \frac{\gamma \delta^3}{t^2} \left(d^l_{i,k}(t) \right)^3. \tag{2}$$

For remote computing decision, we adopt the TDMA manner to deliver the task data to the destination,i.e. the offloading calculable devices share a common bandwidth W. According to the Shannon's capacity formula, the transmission rate can be formulated as

$$r_i(k) = W \log_2 \left(1 + \frac{P_i(k)h_i(k)}{\sigma^2} \right). \tag{3}$$

where $P_i(k)$ is the transmission power of calculable device i. σ^2 denotes the noise power at the destination node. Due to follow quasistatic flat-fading, the amount of data offloaded from calculable device i to the destination node is

$$d^o_{i,k}(t) = r_i(k)t. \tag{4}$$

By substituting (3),the corresponding energy consumption is

$$e^o_{i,k}(t) = P_i(k)t = \left(2^{\frac{d^o_{i,k}(t)}{Wt}} - 1 \right) \frac{\sigma^2 t}{h_i(k)}. \tag{5}$$

Let $d_{i,k}(t)$ denotes the total amount of data within the each time slot(k,t), then the total amount of data processed is

$$d_{i,k}(t) = d^l_{i,k}(t) + d^o_{i,k}(t). \tag{6}$$

Let $e_{i,k}(t)$ denotes the total energy consumption within the each time slot(k,t), then the energy consumption is

$$e_{i,k}(t) = e^l_{i,k}(t) + e^o_{i,k}(t). \tag{7}$$

Let $q_{i,k}(t)$ denotes the number of queueing tasks on calculable device i at time slot(k,t). Meanwhile,we assume that $q_i(k) \geq d_i(k)$, Then the queue dynamics can be modeled as

$$q_{i,k}(t+1) = q_{i,k}(t) - d_{i,k}(t) + a_{i,k}(t) \tag{8}$$

where $a_{i,k}(t)$ denotes the raw task data computed at the data queue of the ith calculable device, and it follows a exponential distribution.

2.2 AoI Model

In the IoT real-time monitoring system, the freshness of information is of great importance. Therefore,we use AoI to quantify the freshness of information, which represent the time since the latest update received by the destination was generated. In this article, Different from the policy that the device's AoI is updated to T when the status update of device i is successfully delivered in a frame [17], we embed the status information into the computation tasks. Similar to [17], we also use the frame as the unit of AoI. Let $g_i(k)$ be a positive integer representing the number of frames since the destination receives the most recently whole task update from device i. Then the update formula of $g_i(k)$ is

$$g_i(k+1) = \begin{cases} 1, & q_{i,k}(T+1) = 0 \\ g_i(k) + 1, & \text{otherwise.} \end{cases} \tag{9}$$

2.3 Problem Formulation

In this paper, we aim to design an online algorithm to jointly minimize the average weighted sum of AoI and energy consumption of all the calculable devices under the data queue stability and limited energy consumption. Then, the long-term average AoI for device i is given by

$$\bar{A}_i = \lim_{K \to \infty} \frac{T}{K} \sum_{k=1}^{K} g_i(k) \tag{10}$$

and the long-term average energy consumption for device i is

$$\bar{e}_i = \lim_{K \to \infty} \frac{1}{KT} \left[\sum_{k=1}^{K} \sum_{t=1}^{T} \mu_i(k) e_{i,k}^l(t) + (1 - \mu_i(k)) e_{i,k}^o(t) \right] \tag{11}$$

Hence, we construct the optimization objective by formula (9) and (10) as follows

$$\min \sum_{i=1}^{N} \bar{A}_i + \alpha_i \bar{e}_i \tag{12}$$

$$s.t. \quad 0 < \alpha_i \leq \mathcal{N}, \quad \forall i \in \mathcal{N} \tag{12a}$$

$$\lim_{K \to \infty} \frac{1}{K} \cdot \sum_{k=1}^{K} \mathbb{E}\left[q_i(k)\right] < \infty, \quad \forall i \in \mathcal{N} \tag{12b}$$

$$0 \leq f_i(k) \leq f_i^{max}, \quad \forall i \in \mathcal{N}, \quad \forall k \in K \tag{12c}$$

$$0 \leq P_i(k) \leq P_i^{max}, \quad \forall i \in \mathcal{N}, \quad \forall k \in K \tag{12d}$$

Constraint (12a) is the weighted factor of average energy consumption for device i described above. Constraint (12b) is the data queue stability constraints. The potential values of all decision variables are defined in constraints (12c)and(12d).

3   Online Algorithm Design Based on DRL

In this section, for the case where the prior knowledge of the probability of successful data delivery is unknown, we develop an algorithm called DRLA to solve minimize the average weighted sum of AoI and energy consumption by deep reinforcement learning. Similar algorithm to [9], we also divide algorithm into four main modules. However, The minimization problem and the exploratory policy we are considering is different from this work. Compared with traditional reinforcement learning (RL) methods, neural networks is utilized to reduce the dimensionality of state space while learning the optimal policy.

In order to address the optimization problem mentioned above, we observe $\theta^k \triangleq \{h_i(k), g_i(k), q_i(k), e_i(k)\}_{i=1}^{\mathcal{N}}$ in the kth time frame, including the channel gains $\{h_i(k)\}_{i=1}^{\mathcal{N}}$, the number of frames $\{g_i(k)\}_{i=1}^{\mathcal{N}}$since the destination receives the most recently whole status update of device i, the system queue states $\{q_i(k)\}_{i=1}^{\mathcal{N}}$and the total energy consumption $\{e_i(k)\}_{i=1}^{\mathcal{N}}$. Here, we denote $G(\mu^k, \theta^k)$ as the optimal value of given the optimization problem. Then, the best scheduling decision $(\mu^k)^*$ can be expressed as

$$\left(\mu^k\right)^* = \arg\min_{\mu^k} \quad G\left(\mu^k, \theta^k\right) \tag{13}$$

Due to the consideration that binary offloading decision may enumerate $2^{\mathcal{N}}$ offloading decisions. we construct a policy π that maps from the input θ^k to the optimal action $(\mu^k)^*$(i.e.$(\mu^k)^* = \pi(\theta^k)$) to reduce complexity. Starting from the initial values θ, the time average expectation of device's AoI energy consumption under policy $\pi \in \Pi$ are defined as

$$\bar{A}_i^\pi(\theta) = \lim_{K \to \infty} \frac{T}{K} \mathbb{E}_\pi \left[\sum_{k=1}^{K} g_i(\theta^k, \pi(\theta^k)) \mid \theta^0 = \theta \right] \tag{14}$$

and

$$\bar{e}_i^\pi(\theta) = \lim_{K \to \infty} \frac{1}{KT} \mathbb{E}_\pi \left[\sum_{k=1}^{K} \sum_{t=1}^{T} \mu_i(\theta^k, \pi(\theta^k)) e_{i,k}^l(t) + (1 - \mu_i(\theta^k, \pi(\theta^k))) e_{i,k}^o(t) \mid \theta^0 = \theta \right] \tag{15}$$

where Π be the set of all possible offloading policies. Hence, jointly minimize the average weighted sum of AoI and energy consumption (12) can be transformed into the following equivalent formulation

$$\min_{\pi \in \Pi} \sum_{i=1}^{N} \bar{A}_i^\pi(\theta) + \alpha_i \bar{e}_i^\pi(\theta) \quad s.t. \quad (12a), (12b), (12c), (12d), \theta \in \theta^k \tag{16}$$

As shown in Fig. 2, DRLA comprises four main modules. an actor module which accepts the input θ^k and outputs candidate actions $\{\mu_i^k\}$, a critic module evaluates $\{\mu_i^k\}$ to select offloading decision, a policy update module improves the strategy of the actor module over time, and a queueing module updates the

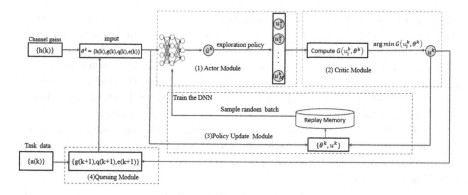

Fig. 2. The scheme of the DRLA algorithm

energy,AoI and queue states $\{g_i(k), q_i(k), e_i(k)\}_{i=1}^{\mathcal{N}}$ after executing the action. Through interactions with the environment $\{h_i(k), a_i(k)\}_{i=1}^{\mathcal{N}}$, these four modules run repeatedly as follows.

(1) Actor Module: The actor module comprises a DNN that has a parameter δ^k at kth time frame, and an exploration policy that obtains $\mathcal{M}$ feasible offloading decisions. The network parameter initialization follows a standard Gaussian distribution when $k = 1$. Then, the input θ^k will output a offloading probability $\hat{\mu}^k \in [0,1]^{\mathcal{N}}$ by the neural network. The offloading probability will be quantized into binary actions. The input-output relation is $\theta^k \mapsto \hat{\mu}^k$. the authors in [15] studied that a multi-layer perceptron with a sufficient number of neurons can accurately approximate any continuous mappings if proper activation functions are applied at the neurons (e.g. Sigmoid, ReLU and Tanh functions). Here, we use ReLU activation function at the hidden layers and a sigmoid activation function at the output layer.

Based on the continuous offloading probability $\hat{\mu}^k$, the exploration policy obtains $\mathcal{M}$ feasible offloading decisions and can be expressed as

$$\Pi_M : \hat{\mu}^k \mapsto \Omega^k = \{\mu_j^k, j = 1, \cdots, \mathcal{M}\} \tag{17}$$

where $\mu_j^k \in \{0,1\}$ denotes binary offloading decision and Ω^k denotes the set of candidate offloading modes in the tth time frames.Π_M represents an exploration policy that generates $\mathcal{M}$ modes. μ_j^k may be far from the $\hat{\mu}^k$ and lead to premature convergence to suboptimal solutions. Hence, we should design an exploration policy to ensure good training convergence.

Based on the above-mentioned issues, we design the following strategy. We set the value of the largest item in $\hat{\mu}^k$ to 1 and the other items to 0, mean while we use it as a backup decision and consider the decision have been used. Calculate whether the backup decision is feasible(whether the task data or equal to 0). if the backup decision is feasible, we use it as a candidate decision until the number of candidate decisions reach $\mathcal{M}$. The value of $\mathcal{M}$ can be adjusted dynamically during the training. we use an example to illustrate the exploration policy. Suppose that $\hat{\mu}^k = [0.1, 0.3, 0.5, 0.8]$, $\mathcal{N} = 4$ and $\mathcal{M} = 3$. Firstly, we set the largest value to 1 and others to 0 and obtain a decision $[0,0,0,1]$ that means the task data of third calculable device should be scheduled to destination node. Then, we need to check whether the decision is feasible (i.e., whether the task data has not been processed in third calculable device). if the decision is feasible, we set μ_1 as $[0,0,0,1]$. Similarly, we the secondly largest value to 1 and others to 0 and obtain a decision μ_2 as $[0,0,1,0]$ if the decision is feasible.

(2) Critic Module: The critic module evaluates Ω^k and select the optimal decision in time frame k. Through interaction with the system environment, we can minimize the objective value. The optimal decision μ^k is represented by the following expression.

$$\mu^k = \arg \min_{\mu_j^k \in \Omega^k} G\left(\mu_j^k, \theta^k\right). \tag{18}$$

Compared to the traditional actor-critic module, We directly calculate the target value in the critic module.

(3) Policy Update Module: we maintain a replay memory that stores ν data samples. the critic module selects the optimal decision μ^k and (θ^k, x^k) will be placed inside the replay memory. When new data samples arrive and the storage is full, we will remove the oldest data sample from it. Meanwhile, We will retrain the samples every η time intervals to avoid model over-fitting. When $\mathrm{mod}(k, \eta) = 0$, we randomly select a batch of data samples from replay memory.we then update the parameters of DNN by minimizing average cross-entropy loss function by the Adam algorithm [16].

(4) Queuing Module: The decision selected based on the output of the critic module, the queuing module updates the AoI,data and energy queues $\{g_i(k + 1), q_i(k+1), e_i(k+1)\}$ using formula (9) and (8) and (7) at the beginning of time frame $k + 1$. Meanwhile, based on the channel gains observation $h_i(k + 1)$,the system inputs $\theta^k \triangleq \{h_i(k + 1), g_i(k + 1), q_i(k + 1), e_i(k + 1)\}$ into the DNN and starts a new iteration.

Through the continuous iteration of the above steps, the DNN can learn state-action pairs to approximate the optimal solution. The actor module consists of a DNN and an exploration strategy with computational complexity linear to the number of calculable devices. we calculate it using Eq. (16) with a complexity of O(N) For each candidate decision. Therefore, the complexity of the critic module is $O(N)$. As a result, the overall complexity of DRLA is O(N). The pseudocode for DRLA is summarized in Algorithm 1.

4   Simulation Results

In this section, we evaluate the performance of the proposed algorithms. Here, we consider a MEC network with $\mathcal{N} = 10$ calculable devices and each device is equipped with a processor with a maximum frequency of $f_i^{max} = 1\,\mathrm{GHz}$. The channel gains is $h_i = \Gamma \psi^2 l_i^{-\nu}$, where $\Gamma = 0.2$ is the signal power gain at a reference distance of $1\,\mathrm{m}$, ψ^2 follows exponentially distributed with unit

---

Algorithm 1 DRLA Algorithm

Require: Joint state $\theta^k = \{h(k), g(k), q(k), e(k)\}$ at each time frame k
Ensure: Execute action $\{\mu^k\}_{k=1}^K$
 1: Initialize the DNN with random parameters δ^k and clean up the replay memory
 2: Set the number of iterations K,the training interval η,the AoI queue $g_i(1) = 1$,the
    data queue $q_i(1) = 0$, and energy queue $e_i(1) = 0$ for each device i
 3: **for** k=1 to K **do**
 4:     Generate offloading action $\hat{\mu}^k = f_{\delta^k}(\theta^k)$
 5:     Quantize $\hat{\mu}^k$ into $\mathcal{M}$ binary actions $\{\mu_j^k\}$
 6:     **for** j=1 to $\mathcal{M}$ **do**
 7:         Compute $G\left(\mu_j^k, \theta^k\right)$
 8:     **end for**
 9:     Select the best action $\mu^k = \arg\min G\left(\mu_j^k, \theta^k\right)$
10:     Update the replay memory by adding (μ^k, θ^k)
11:     **if** mod(k,η)= 0 **then**
12:         Uniformly sample a batch of data set (μ^k, θ^k) from the replay memory
13:         Train the DNN with the sampled data set
14:         use theAdam algorithm to update DNN δ^k
15:     **end if**
16: $k \leftarrow k + 1$
17: Obtain $\{g(k),q(k),e(k)\}$ based on action by using (7),(8) and (9).
18: **end for**

---

mean. $l_i^{-\nu}$ represents standard power law path-loss with exponent $\nu = 2$. the noise power is $\sigma^2 = 10^{-9}$. The maximum transmission power is $P_i^{max} = 1\text{W}$ for each device and all devices share $W_i^{max} = 20\,\text{MHz}$ bandwidth. Every bit of data requires $\delta = 1\text{K}$ CPU cycles and the energy efficiency of calculable device's processor is $\gamma = 5 \times 10^{-28}$. The task data size of all the devices follow exponential distribution in 3 Kb. Each simulation result is obtained by running 800 frames for all policies. the DNN of the actor module is fully connected DNN. The input layer has $4\mathcal{N}$ input nodes, the first hidden layer has 120 nodes, the second hidden layer has 80 nodes, and the output layer has $\mathcal{N}$ nodes. The hidden layers use ReLU activation function and output layer uses Sigmoid activation function.

To demonstrate the superiority of our algorithm, we conducted a comparison with the following benchmarks:

- Local Processing (LP): the computation data are always processed locally on calculable devices.
- Remote Offloading (RO): the computation tasks are fully offloaded to the destination node.
- KNN-based exploration policy (KEP): same as the proposed algorithm except that the exploration policy.

The time-average AoI and energy consumption of all algorithms in the runtime is presented in Fig. 3 and Fig. 4. As shown in Fig. 3, we compare the average AoI under the same conditions and see that the other algorithms are superior to the proposed algorithm(DRLA) at the beginning. However, time-average AoI is smaller than that of the other algorithms as the time frames increases. During the whole running process, the AoI of keeps growing. This is because the task data is still not processed completely. In Fig. 4, we also the compare average energy consumption of two algorithms under the different weighting factor $\alpha_i = \{2, 4\}$, Although the energy consumption is larger at the begining, It suggests that the performance of the DRLA algorithm is close to the KEP algorithm and outperforms the KEP algorithm under the same weighting factor. Combine Fig. 3 and Fig. 4, we can see that the average AoI increases while the average energy consumption decreases under the DRLA algorithm and KEP algorithm.

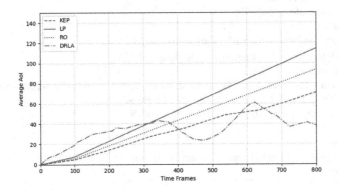

Fig. 3. The average AoI of the different algorithms.

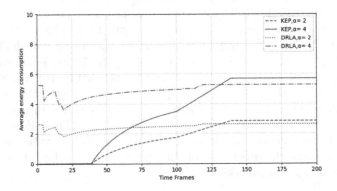

Fig. 4. The average energy consumption of the different algorithms.

In Fig. 5, we show average weighted sum AoI and average energy consumption of two algorithms under the different weighting factor $\alpha_i = \{2, 4\}$. It suggests that the performance of two algorithms with same weighting factor and the different weighting factor. We can see that the average AoI and average energy consumption increases with the weighting factor α_i under the same policy. Under the different policy, the DRLA is optimal with the same weighting factor with the running of the algorithm. However, the performance gap increases with the weighting factor increases.

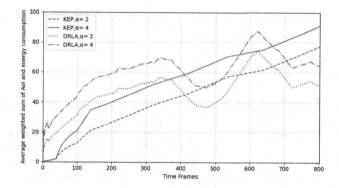

Fig. 5. The Average weighted sum of AoI and energy consumption of the two algorithms with different weighting factor α_i

In Fig. 6, we evaluates the algorithms under different frame lengths. We set $T \in \{4, 5, \ldots, 7\}$ and $\alpha_i = 1$. Since the DRLA algorithm considers the effect of the frame length on decision-making, its performance is better than the traditional algorithms and achieves a close performance to the KEP algorithm. we can see that the resluts is not linearly increasing or decreasing. This is because the increase of frame length leads to the reduce the period of update generation.

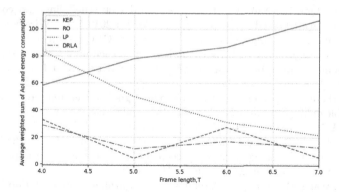

Fig. 6. The Average weighted sum of AoI and energy consumption wiht different frame length

5   Conclusion

In this paper, we investigate that a multidevice IoT system with an edge server under time-varying channels and task data arrivals. we first amend the AoI concept to accommodate the data arrivals. After that, we formulate the average weighted sum of AoI and energy consumption minimization problem as a multistage NLP problem and develop a exploration policy to reducing prediction errors and obtain the optimum. the simulations demonstrate that our algorithm is highly efficient. In future work, we will consider the coupling problem in the decisions of different time frames.

Acknowledgments. This research was supported by the National Natural Science Foundation of China under Grant Nos. 62171413.

References

1. Mao, Y., You, C., Zhang, J., et al.: A survey on mobile edge computing: the communication perspective. IEEE Commun. Surv. Tutor. **19**(4), 2322–2358 (2017)
2. Mach, P., Becvar, Z.: Mobile edge computing: a survey on architecture and computation offloading. IEEE Commun. Surv. Tutor. **19**(3), 1628–1656 (2017)
3. Kaul, S., Yates, R., Gruteser, M.: Real-time status: how often should one update?. In: 2012 Proceedings IEEE INFOCOM, pp. 2731–2735. IEEE (2012)
4. Kosta, A., Pappas, N., Angelakis, V.: Age of information: a new concept, metric, and tool. Found. Trends® Netw. **12**(3), 162–259 (2017)
5. Tang, H., Wang, J., Song, L., et al.: Minimizing age of information with power constraints: multi-user opportunistic scheduling in multi-state time-varying channels. IEEE J. Sel. Areas Commun. **38**(5), 854–868 (2020)
6. Zhou, B., Saad, W.: Minimum age of information in the Internet of Things with non-uniform status packet sizes. IEEE Trans. Wirel. Commun. **19**(3), 1933–1947 (2019)
7. Kuang, Q., Gong, J., Chen, X., et al.: Analysis on computation-intensive status update in mobile edge computing. IEEE Trans. Veh. Technol. **69**(4), 4353–4366 (2020)
8. Song, X., Qin, X., Tao, Y., et al.: Age based task scheduling and computation offloading in mobile-edge computing systems. In: 2019 IEEE Wireless Communications and Networking Conference Workshop (WCNCW), pp. 1–6. IEEE (2019)
9. Kadota, I., Sinha, A., Uysal-Biyikoglu, E., et al.: Scheduling policies for minimizing age of information in broadcast wireless networks. IEEE/ACM Trans. Netw. **26**(6), 2637–2650 (2018)
10. Bi, S., Huang, L., Wang, H., et al.: Lyapunov-guided deep reinforcement learning for stable online computation offloading in mobile-edge computing networks. IEEE Trans. Wirel. Commun. **20**(11), 7519–7537 (2021)
11. Yan, J., Bi, S., Zhang, Y.J.A.: Offloading and resource allocation with general task graph in mobile edge computing: a deep reinforcement learning approach. IEEE Trans. Wirel. Commun. **19**(8), 5404–5419 (2020)
12. Xie, X., Wang, H., Weng, M.: A reinforcement learning approach for optimizing the age-of-computing-enabled IoT. IEEE Internet Things J. **9**(4), 2778–2786 (2021)
13. Hsu, Y.P., Modiano, E., Duan, L.: Age of information: design and analysis of optimal scheduling algorithms. In: 2017 IEEE International Symposium on Information Theory (ISIT), pp. 561–565. IEEE (2017)
14. He, X., Wang, S., Wang, X., et al.: Age-based scheduling for monitoring and control applications in mobile edge computing systems. In: IEEE INFOCOM 2022-IEEE Conference on Computer Communications, pp. 1009–1018. IEEE (2022)
15. Marsland, S.R.: Machine Learning: An Algorithmic Perspective, Second Edition (2014)
16. Kingma, D.P., Ba, J.: Adam: a method for stochastic optimization. arXiv preprint arXiv:1412.6980 (2014)
17. Kadota, I., Sinha, A., Uysal-Biyikoglu, E., et al.: Scheduling policies for minimizing age of information in broadcast wireless networks. IEEE/ACM Trans. Networking **26**(6), 2637–2650 (2018)

Reverse Multidimensional Auction Based Vehicle Selection and Resource Allocation for IoV

Jianxi Chen, Zhipeng Tang, Zhaohui Li, and Yongmin Zhang[✉]

Central South University, Changsha, China
{8208200119,8208201411,lizhaohui,zhangyongmin}@csu.edu.cn

Abstract. Federated Learning (FL) is gaining popularity in the Internet of Vehicles (IoV), which has led to a rise in demand for high-quality communication and computation resources. To address the communication and computation issues, we formulate the vehicle selection and channel allocation problem in the IoV as a social welfare optimization problem. We propose an efficient reverse multi-dimensional auction-based vehicle selection and channel allocation scheme, called RAFS, to enhance the overall performance of FL in the IoV. Simulation results demonstrate the efficacy of RAFS in improving social welfare and constructing higher quality virtual global datasets.

Keywords: Internet of vehicles · Federated learning · Incentive mechanism

1 Introduction

The availability of perception data, along with communication and computing capabilities of Internet of Vehicles (IoV) terminals, has enabled the development of AI models for various applications [1]. As a collaborative learning approach, Federated Learning (FL) is widely used in IoV due to its high utilization of computing resources and effective data privacy protection. However, FL for IoV faces challenges in training efficiency and model accuracy due to the different data collected from vehicles and unstable communication conditions in high-mobility environment. Additionally, unprofitable training services may lead to low participation, which further decrease the amount of collected data and negatively impact the performance of the FL model. To address these challenges, it is necessary to design an effective incentive mechanism that considers both data heterogeneity and unstable communication cost.

This work has been supported in part by the National Natural Science Foundation of China under Grant No. 62172445, by the Young Talents Plan of Hunan Province, and Major Project of Natural Science Foundation of Hunan Province under Grant No. 2021JC0004.

Generally, most existing work primarily focuses on designing mechanisms from the perspective of data heterogeneity or unstable communication. Considering data heterogeneity, researchers have proposed a terminal active selection system based on homomorphic encryption where the data distribution information guides whether the terminal participates in training [2] to improve the global data heterogeneity. Considering unstable communication cost in the IoV, researchers have proposed a method that increases the number of participants in each round of global iteration and requires them to conduct more rounds of local training to reduce communication cost [3]. Others update the model based on parameter importance. In each round of communication, only a portion of important parameters are selected and transmitted to the central server for update [4]. For example, the CMFL algorithm only uploads local model updates with higher correlation by comparing the correlation between local and global updates to reduce communication cost [5]. Concurrently, lower participation of vehicles results in a smaller amount of training data, ultimately affecting training efficiency and model accuracy.

Unlike existing works, this paper focuses on exploring an efficient FL-based vehicle selection and resource allocation mechanism. We consider both heterogeneous data and the cost in dynamic communication scenario. Then, we formulate the vehicle selection and channel allocation as a social welfare optimization problem. To account for the selfish behaviour of participants, we design an efficient reverse multi-dimensional auction-based mechanism that derives optimal solutions and improves participation while maximizing social welfare. Our main contributions can be summarized as follows:

- By jointly considering the cost in dynamic communication scenario and the impact of heterogeneous data, we formulate the vehicle selection and channel allocation as a social welfare maximization problem.
- To ensure the participation of training vehicles, we propose an efficient reverse multi-dimensional auction-based vehicle selection and channel allocation scheme that can improve the performance of FL in IoV.
- Through extensive simulations, we demonstrate that our proposed scheme effectively improves social welfare and the quality of virtual global data in various communication scenarios.

The rest of the paper is organized as follows: Sect. 2 introduces the system model and problem definition. Section 3 presents the reverse multi-dimensional auction mechanism. Section 4 provides performance analysis based on simulation results. Finally, Sect. 5 summarizes our work.

2   System Model and Problem Formulation

In this section, we explore a FL-based IoV environment where edge servers can incentivize vehicle participation in FL training to enhance AI application performance in IoV. Since the coverage of any two edge servers is typically unique and non-overlapping, we can independently design the incentive mechanism for each edge server. Thus, we consider a scenario with one edge server and N vehicles, where the vehicle set is denoted as $\mathcal{N} = \{1, \ldots, N\}$. Each vehicle i has a local dataset D_i, which can be represented as $D_i = \{D_{i,1}, \ldots, D_{i,J}\}$, where J is the number of data classes and $D_{i,j}$ is the j-th type of dataset on vehicle i with data amount $d_{i,j}$. The total data amount on vehicle i is denoted as d_i. The edge server has M channels allocated to individual vehicles. To account for data heterogeneity and training cost in dynamic communication scenarios, we develop a heterogeneous data model and training cost model. Using these models, we propose an auction model and formulate a social welfare optimization problem, which will be discussed in the following subsections.

2.1   Heterogeneous Data Model

Previously, distributed machine learning separated datasets in an unbiased and Independent Identically Distribution (IID) manner, distributing them to homogeneous computing devices to accelerate training [6]. However, in the IoV environment, sensor-collected data varies in location, sensor types, and storage capacity. Thus, there are differences in content and data quantity, leading to varying sample sizes, feature distributions and class distributions. This data greatly affects the performance of the globally trained model. Based on the relationship between data amount and model accuracy under the IID [7], the accuracy, denoted as A, can be expressed as:

$$A = \tau\sqrt{D}, \tag{1}$$

where τ is the system parameter and D is the total data amount.

However, Eq. (1) is constructed based on balanced data distribution and can't assess the impact of heterogeneous data on model performance. Thus, considering the effect of heterogeneous data on the performance of the global model, motivated by [8], this paper redefines Eq. (1) as:

$$A = \tau\frac{\sum_{j=1}^{J}\sqrt{d_j^{total}}}{\sqrt{J}}, \tag{2}$$

where d_j^{total} is the total amount of jth class data.

2.2   Training Cost Model

Here, we formulate the training cost and packet error rate based on dynamic communication. Since vehicles incur training cost by utilizing their computing and communication resources during local training, we divide the training cost into computational cost and communication cost. The computational cost (c_i^{comp}) of vehicle i is calculated based on the required local model accuracy (ε) and the number of local iterations needed to achieve that accuracy ($\log\frac{1}{\varepsilon}$), i.e.,

$$c_i^{comp} = \delta log\left(\frac{1}{\varepsilon}\right)k_i\alpha_i d_i f_i^2, \tag{3}$$

where k_i represents the effective capacitance switch coefficient of vehicle i, α_i denotes the number of CPU cycles required for vehicle i, f_i represents the computing power allocated to model training and δ represents the cost of energy consumption per unit of computation, respectively.

As for communication cost, we assume that the transmission is based on the Orthogonal Frequency Division Multiple Access (OFDMA) protocol, which can prevent interference between different communication pairs. The transmission rate of the vehicle denoted as r_i^{comm} can be expressed as

$$r_i^{comm} = Blog_2\left(1 + \frac{\rho_i h_i}{I + BN_0}\right), \tag{4}$$

where B represents the channel transmission rate, I denotes the channel interference caused by other areas using the same channel, ρ_i represents the communication power of vehicle i, and N_0 denotes the noise power spectral density, respectively. We denote the channel gain between the vehicle and the server as h_i, which is a function of the relative distance Δd_i between the vehicle and the server, and the Rayleigh fading parameter o_i. The cost of transmission, denoted as c_i^{comm}, can be calculated as follows:

$$c_i^{comm} = \eta \frac{s\rho_i}{r_i^{comm}}. \tag{5}$$

Here, η represents the energy consumption per unit of distance travelled. It is assumed that each vehicle uploads model parameters of the same size. Based on this, the total energy consumption cost, denoted by c_i, can be calculated as follows:

$$c_i = c_i^{comp} + c_i^{comm} \tag{6}$$

Since Ensuring the communication quality of vehicles is difficult due to the unreliable vehicle-to-server transmission channels and various factors, it is hard to guarantee the transmission rate and other communication quality metrics for vehicles, as noted in [5]. To address this issue, [9] has been noted that communication factors like packet errors and limited wireless resources can seriously affect training quality. Thus, in this paper, the error rate of the training vehicle depends on its transmission power and channel gain, denoted by e_o, which can be expressed as:

$$e_i = 1 - exp(-\frac{\vartheta(I + BN_0)}{\rho_i h_i}). \tag{7}$$

Here, h_i denotes the channel gain of the training vehicle i, which is a function of the distance d_i between the vehicle and the server, the Rayleigh fading parameter o_i, and the transmission power p of the vehicle. The waterfall threshold of the OFDMA protocol is denoted by m.

Based on the above assumption, the vehicle sends its local model parameters to the edge server in a single packet. Packet error rate e_i of vehicle i can be derived by Eq. (7). After receiving parameters, the edge server checks for errors in the data packet. If errors are found, the server will discard the parameters and use the remaining correct local parameters for global update. Vehicles that upload erroneous parameters won't receive rewards. Besides, all vehicles must finish training and parameter uploading before deadline.

2.3   Auction Model

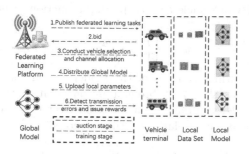

Fig. 1. FL Auction Framework

To reduce transmission error rates and improve training effectiveness in the training cost model, we construct an auction model to derive the optimal vehicle selection. Figure 1 shows the auction framework proposed in this paper. According to the platform publishing rules and task-related information, vehicle i selects the dataset $Q_i \subseteq D_i$ based on personal privacy preferences and calculates its transmission error rate μ_i after receiving the information. Then the vehicle places a bid on the platform. The total bid set is denoted by $L = \{l_1, \ldots, l_N\}$, where the bids from vehicle i is given by $l_i = \{e_i, q_i, b_i\}$. Here b_i is vehicle i's price and $q_i = \{q_{i,1}, \ldots, q_{i,J}\}$ is the number of each type of data, denoted by $q_{i,j}$ for the jth data type.

Note that the auction mechanism is incentive compatible when the asking price b_i equals its true training cost on the dataset q_i. We assume that there are no malicious attackers and the vehicles will report μ_i and conduct model training based on q_i [10], where $\mu_i = 1 - e_i$ represents the probability that vehicle i's parameters will be used.

Besides, when the platform selects winning bids from the vehicles, which is denoted as W where $W \subseteq \mathcal{N}$, rewards are given to each winning vehicle i, denoted by p_i where $i \in W$ and $p_i \geq 0$, which are determined by the payment rule. The platform sends the model to select the winning vehicles after auction and conduct local training. Once the training is complete, the winning vehicles send their parameters to the platform, which gives rewards to the winners without transmission errors.

2.4   Problem Formulation

We can derive the platform utility based on the above models. The auction model determines the training reward for datasets p that successfully transmit during communication, using the heterogeneous data model and auction model. Then, we subtract the total training cost c from the reward to obtain the platform utility for a winning participant i denoted by $u_{i,i\in W}$, which can be given by

$$u_{i,i\in W} = \begin{cases} p_i - c_i, & \text{with probability } \mu_i \\ -c_i, & \text{with probability } 1 - \mu_i \end{cases} \tag{8}$$

The expected utility of vehicle i participating in auction, denoted by u_i can be expressed as:

$$u_i = \begin{cases} \mu_i p_i - c_i, & i \in W \\ 0, & i \notin W \end{cases} \tag{9}$$

Since the platform utility consists of the model revenue and vehicle incentive cost, denoted as φ as the profit brought by one unit of accuracy and $A(W)$ as the expected model accuracy when the winner set is W, and $\varphi A(W)$ as the model revenue, the expected platform utility denoted as $\psi(W)$ can be given by:

$$\psi(W) = \varphi\tau\frac{\sum_{j=1}^{J}\sqrt{\sum_{i=1}^{W} q_{i,j}\mu_i}}{\sqrt{J}} - \sum_{i=1}^{W}\mu_i p_i \tag{10}$$

Based on this, the maximizing expected social welfare problem can be given by

$$\max_{W, W \subseteq \mathcal{N}} S(W) = \psi(W) + \sum_{i=1}^{W} u_i, \tag{11}$$

$$\text{s.t. } |W| \leq M, \tag{12}$$

$$u_i \geq 0, \forall i \in \mathcal{N}, \tag{13}$$

$$u_i(l_i) \geq u_i(l_i'), \forall i \in \mathcal{N}. \tag{14}$$

The objective is to maximize social welfare, subject to constraints such as the size of the winning vehicle set, non-negative incentives, and monotonicity of incentives. To solve this problem, we will propose an auction-based mechanism in the next section.

3   Algorithm Design and Theorem Analysis

In this section we propose a two-stage reverse auction mechanism (RAFS) to solve the social welfare maximization problem. The rationality of the algorithm is verified through theoretical analysis. The first stage determines the winners based on bidding information and the second stage uses a payment rule to determine rewards.

3.1   Algorithm Design

To solve the vehicle selection and channel allocation problem, we employ a greedy algorithm. Given $\mathcal{N}$ vehicles, the total bid set L and M channels, the algorithm outputs a set W^* of selected vehicles.

We propose an algorithm for selecting the best vehicle in each round to maximize the expected social welfare. After receiving the bidding information, RAFS creates a winning set W^* and a candidate set U. Initially, $W^* = \emptyset$ and $U = \mathcal{N}$. To maximize the expected social welfare, we define the expected marginal welfare to describe the contribution of each vehicle. The expected marginal welfare for vehicle i denoted as $V_i\left(w^*_{m-1}\right)$ is

$$V_i\left(w^*_{m-1}\right) = S\left(w^*_{m-1} \cup \{i\}\right) - S\left(w^*_{m-1}\right) = \psi_i\left(w^*_{m-1}\right) - b_i$$

$$= \varphi\tau \frac{\sum_{j=1}^{J}\left(\sqrt{\sum_{n\in w^*_{m-1}\cup\{i\}} \mu_i q_{n,j}} - \sqrt{\sum_{n\in w^*_{m-1}} \mu_i q_{n,j}}\right)}{\sqrt{J}} - b_i, \qquad (15)$$

where, w^*_{m-1} represents the winning set from the first $m-1$ rounds, with $w^*_0 = \emptyset$. $S\left(w^*_{m-1}\right)$ denotes the sum of expected social welfare from the winning vehicles in the first $m-1$ rounds, while $V_i\left(w^*_{m-1}\right)$ represents the expected social welfare increase when vehicle i is selected as a winner in the mth round. Additionally, $\psi_i\left(w^*_{m-1}\right)$ denotes the expected revenue that vehicle i can bring to the platform when it is selected as a winner in the mth round.

The greedy algorithm determines vehicle selection and channel allocation using Eq. (15). After initializing the winning and candidate sets, it initiates vehicle selection. In each round, the vehicle with the highest positive marginal welfare is chosen from the candidate set and added to the winning set. If multiple vehicles have the same highest welfare, one is chosen randomly. The selection process ends when M channels are allocated or there is no vehicle with a positive expected marginal welfare in the current round.

3.2   Payment Confirmation

After the execution of the greedy algorithm, the platform obtains the winner set W^*. For each $j \in W^*$, the platform determines the reward. The payment determination algorithm for RAFS is shown below:

To determine the payment for winner j, RAFS re-executes the greedy algorithm on the set $\mathcal{N}_{-j} = \mathcal{N}\backslash j$ to obtain a new set of winners, denoted as W^*_{-j}. When the number of winners in W^*_j reaches M, the channel allocation is complete. In round m, let $k_{j,m}$ denote the vehicle selected from the set $\mathcal{N}_{-j}$. Then, the critical bid of vehicle j is $b^{max}_{j,m}$, which is the highest bid that vehicle j is willing to pay to win vehicle $k_{j,m}$ in round m:

$$b^{max}_{j,m} = \left(arg_{b_j} V_j\left(w^*_{-j,m-1}\right) = V_{k_{j,m}}\left(w^*_{-j,m-1}\right)\right) \qquad (16)$$

Here, $w^*_{-j,m-1}$ represents the set of winners selected in the first $m-1$ iterations on the set $\mathcal{N}_{-j}$ according to Algorithm 1. Thus, if vehicle j wants to win the auction on the set $\mathcal{N}-j$, its highest bid is given by $b^{max}_j = max\left(arg_{b_j} V_j\left(w^*_{-j}\right)\right) = (0, b^{max}_{j,1}, \ldots, b^{max}_{j,E})$.

If the number of winners in W^*_{-j} is E and $E < M$, the channel allocation is not complete. If vehicle j wants to win the auction, its highest bid is given by

---

Algorithm 1. Payment Determination Algorithm

Input: $W^*, \mathcal{N}, L, M$

Output: P

1: Initialize $P \leftarrow \emptyset$, $p_i \leftarrow 0$, $b_i{}^{\max} \leftarrow 0, \forall i \in \mathcal{N}$

2: **for all** $j \in W^*$ **do**

3:      $\mathcal{N}_{-j} \leftarrow \mathcal{N} \backslash j$, $W^*_{-j} \leftarrow \emptyset$, $C \leftarrow \mathcal{N}_{-j}$, $m \leftarrow 1$, $b_j^{\max} \leftarrow 0$

4:      **for** $m = 1$ to M **do**

5:          Select vehicle j in candidate set C with the highest expected marginal welfare according to Eq.(15)

6:          **if** $V_j\left(w^*_{m-1}\right) < 0$ **then**

7:              $b_j^{\max} = \max(b_j^{\max}, \arg\max_{b_j} V_j\left(w^*_{-j}\right) = 0)$

8:          **else**

9:              Calculate $b_{j,m}^{\max}$ according to Eq.(16)

10:         $W^*_{-j} \leftarrow W^*_{-j} \cup \{j\}, C \leftarrow C \backslash \{j\}, b_j^{\max} \leftarrow \max(b_j{}^{\max}, b_{j,m}^{\max})$

11:          **end if**

12:          **if** $C = \emptyset$ **then**

13:              break

14:          **end if**

15:      **end for**

16:      $p_j \leftarrow \frac{b_j^{\max}}{\mu_j}$

17:      $P \leftarrow P \cup \{p_j\}$

18: **end for**

$\mathcal{N}_{-j}$, its highest bid is given by $b_j^{max} = max\left(\arg_{b_j} V_j\left(w^*_{-j}\right) = 0, b_{j,1}^{max}, \ldots, b_{j,E}^{max}\right)$. RAFS uses the highest bid $b_j^{m\tilde{a}x}$ as the expected payment to winner j. Thus, when winner j uploads the correct parameters, its payment is $p_j = \frac{b_j^{max}}{\mu_j}$.

3.3 Theoretical Analysis

Based on the truthful ascending auction mechanism proposed in [11], we present the following theorem:

Theorem 1. *In a single-parameter reverse auction, when the allocation rule is monotonic and the expected payment received by seller is its critical value, the auction mechanism is incentive compatible.*

Monotonicity: When the bids of other participants are fixed, for two asking prices b_i and b'_i for bid l_i where $b'_i \leq b_i$, if l_i wins the auction with asking price b_i, then l_i can win the auction with a lower price b'_i. In this case, allocation rule is monotonic.

Critical value: Under a monotonic allocation rule, when the bids of other participants are fixed, if bid l_i wants to win the auction, its asking price b_i can't exceed z_i. The value z_i is defined as critical value for bid l_i.

The following will prove that the auction mechanism RAFS satisfies incentive compatibility, individual rationality and computational traceability:

Incentive-compatible

Proof. Considering two asking prices b_i and b_i', where $b_i' \leq b_i$ and other bids are fixed, then if vehicle i is selected as the winner with asking price b_i in the jth iteration, according to Eq. (15), the expected marginal welfare of vehicle i in the first j rounds is higher when using asking price b_i' compared to b_i. Thus, vehicle i can win in the jth round with a bidding price no higher than b_i', meeting the defined monotonicity.

We can prove that the expected payment $\mu_i p_i = b_i^{max}$ obtained by Algorithm 1 is the critical value. When the number of winners selected from the set $\mathcal{N}_{-i}$ is M, we have: $b_i^{max} = max(arg_{b_i} \ V_i(w_{-i,m-1}^*) = V_{k_{i,m}}(w_{-i,m-1}^*), m = 1, \ldots, M)$. If the asking price $b_i > b_i^{max}$, then $V_i(w_{-i,m-1}^*) < V_{k_{i,m}}(w_{-i,m-1}^*)$, and vehicle i will not be selected as a winner. When the number of winners selected from the set $\mathcal{N}_{-i}$ is E and $E < M$, $b_i^{max} = max(max(arg_{b_i} \ V_i(w_{-i,e-1}^*) = V_{k_{j,m}}(w_{-i,E-1}^*), e = 1, \ldots, E), arg_{b_i} \ V_i(w_{-i,E}^*) = 0)$. If the asking price $b_i > b_i^{max}$, then $V_i(w_{-i,e-1}^*) < V_{k_{i,e}}(w_{-i,e-1}^*), \forall e \in 1, 2, \ldots E$, thus vehicle i will not win in the first E rounds. Moreover, since $V_i(w_{-i,E}^*) < 0$, even if channels are not fully allocated, vehicle i still won't be selected as a winner. Thus, the expected payment b_i^{max} determined by Algorithm 1 is the critical value, hence the auction mechanism is incentive compatible.

Individual Rationality

Proof. If vehicle i wins in the jth round, its expected marginal benefit is $V_i(w_{j-1}^*)$, and vehicle $k_{i,j}$ with the second-highest benefit wins in round j on the set $\mathcal{N}_{-i}$ with an expected marginal benefit $V_{k_{i,j}}(w_{-i,j-1}^*)$. Thus, we have $V_{k_{i,j}}(w_{-i,j-1}^*) = V_{k_{i,j}}(w_{j-1}^*)$, $V_i(w_{j-1}^*) = V_i(w_{-i,j-1}^*)$, and $V_i(w_{-i,j-1}^*) \geq V_{k_{i,j}}(w_{-i,j-1}^*)$.

The critical value for vehicle i in the jth round of iteration on the set $\mathcal{N}_{-i}$ is given by $b_{i,j}^{max} = arg_{b_i} V_i(w_{-i,j-1}^*) = V_{k_{i,j}}(w_{-i,j-1}^*)) = \psi_i(w_{-i,j-1}^*) - \psi_{k_{i,j}}(w_{-i,j-1}^*) + b_{k_{i,j}}$. Since $b_{i,j}^{max} - b_i = V_i(w_{-i,j-1}^*) - V_{k_{i,j}}(w_{-i,j-1}^*) \geq 0$, we have $b_i^{max} \geq b_{i,j}^{max} \geq b_i = c_i$. Thus, the expected utility of vehicle i when winning the auction is $u_i = b_i^{max} - c_i \geq 0$ and this applies when vehicle i wins in any round.

The expected utility of vehicle i is non-negative, which implies that the auction mechanism satisfies individual rationality.

Calculate Traceability

Proof. The greedy Algorithm can perform up to M rounds, with a time complexity of $O(M|\mathcal{N}|)$ to determine the winning set W^*. For Algorithm 1, the time complexity to determine the reward payment P is $O(M|\mathcal{N}|^2)$. Overall, the auction mechanism can determine the winning set and pay rewards in polynomial time with a total time complexity of $O(M|\mathcal{N}|^2)$. ∎

4   Performance Evaluation

We conduct simulations in this section to compare our algorithm with existing works, focusing on social welfare to validate its effectiveness. We analyze the impact of channel number, system data heterogeneities, and the number of vehicles.

In our experiments, we consider N vehicles, M channels and J data classes. The dataset that vehicular vehicle i is willing to contribute is denoted as Q_i, and the total data amount in Q_i is q_i. The value of q_i follows a uniform distribution. The imbalance degree of the data in Q_i is measured by the Earth Mover's Distance (EMD) value, denoted as σ_i. To simplify the analysis without loss of generality, we assume that the local iteration times of all vehicles are the same and equal to $log(\frac{1}{\varepsilon})$. So the computation cost function of vehicle i can be transformed into a linear function of data volume q_i. The other parameters can be shown in Table 1

Table 1. System Communication Parameter Settings

Parameter	Meaning	Value
N_0	Noise power spectral density	$-174\,\mathrm{dBm/hz}$
B	Bandwidth	$1\,M\mathrm{hz}$
ϑ	Waterfall threshold	$0.023\,\mathrm{dB}$
p_i	Transmission power of vehicle i	$(0,1]\,\mathrm{w}$
h_i	Channel gain of vehicle i	$[-90,-100]\,\mathrm{dB}$

4.1   Comparison of Social Welfare

We compared RAFS with Greedy-DB and Random-SW under various conditions. Random-SW is a benchmark mechanism that randomly selects vehicles until channel allocation is complete. Greedy-DB is based on DQRQA proposed in [12], which sets an EMD threshold σ_{max} to exclude vehicles with high EMD values and greedily selects vehicles with the largest $\frac{q_i}{c_i}$. Since RAFS and DQRQA calculate vehicle contribution differently, we do not directly compare them. We set σ_{max} to 1.4, as in [12]. In the ideal scenario, vehicle parameters are transmitted correctly. In the practical scenario, the transmission error rate is calculated using Eq. (7).

In the first experiment, we compare social welfare with different vehicle numbers, where $M = 12$ and $N \in [5, 100]$. Meanwhile, EMD values follow a uniform distribution. The social welfare comparison of three mechanisms under ideal and practical communication situations is shown in Fig. 2 for both scenarios.

RAFS outperforms Greedy-DB and Random-SW by adjusting vehicle selection and balancing data distribution, volume, and cost. When there are few vehicles and many channels, all mechanisms increase social welfare by adding vehicles. When channels are equal to vehicles, Random-SW's social welfare fluctuates, while others increase social welfare until convergence. As the number of vehicles increases, Greedy-DB selects vehicles with larger data volume and lower cost. In contrast, RAFS builds a balanced data distribution and larger virtual global dataset with more vehicles. However, Greedy-DB removes vehicles based on EMD values above σ_{max}, leading to fewer vehicles and less data volume, resulting in worse performance when the number of vehicles is small.

Next, we compare social welfare with different channel numbers, where $M \in [1, 20]$, $N = 100$, and EMD values follow a uniform distribution. Figure 3 shows the comparison of social welfare among RAFS, Greedy-DB and Random-SW.

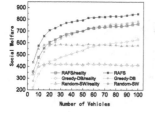 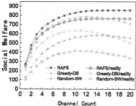 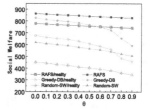

Fig. 2. Comparison of Social Welfare with Different Number of Vehicles

Fig. 3. Comparison of Social Welfare with Different Channel Numbers

Fig. 4. Comparison of Social Welfare with Different System Data Heterogeneities

In both scenarios, all mechanisms initially increase social welfare with channel numbers due to higher data volume. Among all mechanisms, RAFS outperforms others by prioritizing balanced data distribution and increasing social welfare with channel numbers in both scenarios. However, when the number of channels increases to 12, the social welfare brought by increasing data volume is not enough to offset training cost. Other mechanisms decrease social welfare by selecting more vehicles, while RAFS doesn't select vehicles when marginal welfare is less than training cost.

We also compare social welfare under different system data heterogeneities, where $M = 12$ and $N = 100$. To measure the impact of data heterogeneity on RAFS, we reconstruct the EMD value distribution, where σ_i takes values in the range of $[1.0, 1.2, 1.4, 1.6, 1.8]$. We define vehicles with EMD values greater than σ_{max} and highly imbalanced data distribution as strong non-IID vehicles. θ represents the proportion of strong non-IID vehicles, where a higher θ indicates a stronger non-IID data degree. We test the social welfare under different θ values, shown in Fig. 4.

Social welfare decreases as the system data heterogeneity increases. However, RAFS performs better by balancing the virtual global dataset and maintaining social welfare even as system data heterogeneity increases. Greedy-DB reduces the impact of data heterogeneity by removing vehicles with high EMD values, but as the level of data heterogeneity increases, the number of available vehicles decreases, leading to a decrease in social welfare. If the number of selectable vehicles is fewer than the number of channels, the social welfare will drop sharply.

4.2   Virtual Global Dataset Quality Comparison

We evaluate the quality of the virtual global dataset built by RAFS, DQRQA, and Random-SW in various environments with different data heterogeneity to assess the learning performance. After removing vehicles with high EMD values, DQRQA calculates the marginal contribution of vehicle i based on Eq. (1) and selects the vehicle with the largest $\frac{mc_i}{c_i}$ in a greedy manner. The EMD threshold σ_{max} of DQRQA is set to 1.4, which is identical to Greedy-DB's setting.

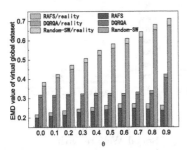

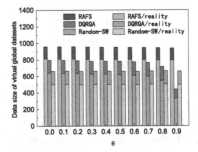

Fig. 5. EMD values of virtual global datasets with different heterogeneity of system data

Fig. 6. Data volume of virtual global datasets with different heterogeneity of system data

Figure 5 shows EMD values of the virtual global dataset under different system data heterogeneities. Random-SW increases EMD values as data heterogeneity strengthens, whereas DQRQA removes high EMD vehicles, resulting in low and stable EMD values. However, when $\theta = 0.9$, the imbalance level increases sharply with DQRQA because there aren't many vehicles with EMD values less than σ_{max} and the limited number of vehicles may cause the absence of categories. RAFS considers both the data amount and the current data distribution's balance, resulting in a more balanced virtual global dataset. In actual situations, transmission errors can lead to a decrease in data volume and an increase in data imbalance.

Figure 6 shows the data volume in the virtual global dataset under different system data heterogeneities. Transmission errors can lead to a decrease in data volume. RAFS outperforms DQRQA and Random-SW by selecting cost-effective vehicles over those with larger marginal contributions.

5   Conclusion

This paper focuses on vehicle selection and channel allocation for FL in the IoV environment. We model vehicle selection and channel allocation as a social welfare maximization problem in a reverse multi-dimensional auction. Then, we analyze the relationship between vehicle channel states and dataset features and design a greedy method. Theoretical analysis proves that the proposed mechanism RAFS matches individual rationality, incentive compatibility, and computational traceability. Simulations show that the algorithm can improve social welfare.

References

1. Lim, W.Y.B., et al.: Towards federated learning in UAV-enabled internet of vehicles: a multi-dimensional contract-matching approach. IEEE Trans. Intell. Transp. Syst. **22**(8), 5140–5154 (2021)
2. Zhang, S., Li, Z., Chen, Q., Zheng, W., Leng, J., Guo, M.: Towards data unbiasedness with homomorphic encryption in federated learning client selection. In: 50th International Conference on Parallel Processing, pp. 1–10 (2021)
3. McMahan, B., Moore, E., Ramage, D., Hampson, S., y Arcas, B.A.: Communication-efficient learning of deep networks from decentralized data. Artif. Intell. Stat. 1273–1282 (2017)
4. Ström, N.: Scalable distributed DNN training using commodity GPU cloud computing (2015)
5. Luping, W., Wei, W., Bo, L.C.: CMFL: mitigating communication overhead for federated learning. In: 2019 IEEE 39th International Conference on Distributed Computing Systems (ICDCS), pp. 54–964 (2019)
6. Shimizu, R., Asako, K., Ojima, H., Morinaga, S., Hamada, M., Kuroda, T.: Balanced mini-batch training for imbalanced image data classification with neural network. In: 2018 First International Conference on Artificial Intelligence for Industries (AI4I), pp. 27–30 (2018)
7. Zhan, Y., Li, P., Qu, Z., Zeng, D., Guo, S.: A learning-based incentive mechanism for federated learning. IEEE Internet Things J. **7**(7), 6360–6368 (2020)
8. Wang, S., Liu, F., Xia, H.: Content-based vehicle selection and resource allocation for federated learning in IoV. In: 2021 IEEE Wireless Communications and Networking Conference Workshops (WCNCW), pp. 1–7 (2021)
9. Chen, M., Yang, Z., Saad, W., Yin, C., Poor, H.V., Cui, S.,: A joint learning and communications framework for federated learning over wireless networks. IEEE Trans. Wirel. Commun. **20**(1), 269–283 (2020)
10. Kairouz, P., et al.: Advances and open problems in federated learning. Found. Trends® Mach. Learn. **14**(1–2), 1–210 (2021)
11. Nisan, N.: Algorithmic mechanism design: through the lens of multiunit auctions. Handb. Game Theory Econ. Appl. **4**, 477–515 (2015)
12. Fan, S., Zhang, H., Zeng, Y., Cai, W.: Hybrid blockchain-based resource trading system for federated learning in edge computing. IEEE Internet Things J. **8**(4), 2252–2264 (2020)

Universal Handwriting Recognition for Mobile Devices via Acoustic Sensing

Huanpu Yin[1,3,4], Le Kang[2], and Haisheng Li[1,3,4(✉)]

[1] School of Computer and Artificial Intelligence, Beijing Technology and Business University, Beijing 100048, China
{yinhuanpu,lihsh}@btbu.edu.cn
[2] School of Computer Science, Beijing University of Posts and Telecommunications, Beijing 100876, China
Kangle@bupt.edu.cn
[3] Beijing Key Laboratory of Big Data Technology for Food Safety, Beijing 100048, China
[4] National Engineering Laboratory for Agri-product Quality Traceability, Beijing 100048, China

Abstract. Handwriting input is essential for efficient human-computer interaction on small-screen mobile devices, as it provides a more intuitive and convenient method compared to soft keyboard typing. One promising approach for handwriting recognition is based on passive acoustic sensing, which offers advantages such as low cost, universal availability, and robustness to various factors. However, its performance on cross-user problem still needs to be further improved, especially for free-style lowercase input. In this paper, we propose *TransWriter*, an acoustic-based handwriting recognition system suitable for mobile devices. It utilizes the built-in microphone to collect acoustic signals generated by the pen scratch on the surface. We perform data augmentation based on the key factor of writing speed to enhance the diversity of the training dataset. Furthermore, we propose a deep network architecture combining LSTM and transformer models, which can capture local features and global features, retain more spatial information, and models the temporal relationship between time frames. To validate the effectiveness of *TransWriter*, we implement a prototype system on a mobile phone and conduct an extensive experimental evaluation. The results of our experiments demonstrate that *TransWriter* achieves an accuracy of 80.77% for unseen users, across various practical scenarios.

Keywords: Handwriting recognition · Acoustic signal · Passive sensing · Transformer

1 Introduction

The increasing popularity of mobile devices, including smartwatches and smart bands, has brought convenience to our daily lives. However, efficient text input on it is still a great challenge. As the primary input form, the soft keyboard on the screen is limited by the size of the touchscreen, which is extremely inconvenient [20]. In order to solve this problem, some works propose methods such as handwriting recognition [16] and gesture tracking [6] to interact with small-screen devices, bringing users a new input experience. Handwriting recognition, as a common daily human-computer interaction method, is more socially acceptable than traditional speech recognition, does not cause social embarrassment, and has a broader prospect.

Existing handwriting recognition solutions are mainly divided into two types: sensor-based, and acoustic-based. Sensor-based solutions usually utilize sensors such as gyroscopes and inertial sensors for in-air or on-surface handwriting recognition [11,19]. For example, AirContour [17] proposes a contour-based gesture model, which converts gestures into contours in 3D space, and then recognizes the contours as characters to realize in-air handwriting recognition. However, they require sensors and lack generality and portability for mobile devices [13].

As for acoustic-based solutions, some methods actively emit and receive acoustic signals and distinguish written texts through signal changes caused by finger movements [23]. For example, EchoWrite2.0 [22] exploits the Doppler shift in the received signal to realize in-air finger input. Different from them, some passive sensing methods leverage built-in microphone to capture the typing or handwriting sound generated by the pen/finger writing on the table, and then recognizes the handwriting content using signal processing and machine learning techniques [5,12,15]. For example, WritingRecorder [16] designs a deep neural network, which extracts the depth information to build a user-independent model for handwriting recognition. Compare with the above solutions, the passive acoustic-based handwriting recognition method has the salient advantage of low cost and ubiquitous availability, and is robust to the movement of surrounding objects. However, its performance on cross-user problem still needs to be further improved, especially for free-style lowercase input.

Similar to WritingRecorder [16], in this work, we also follow a passive sensing route with a microphone to capture finger-writing activities. But the critical difference from WritingRecorder lies in the novel model training strategy proposed in this work. In order to provide enough training samples at a low cost to build an effective classification model, we perform data augmentation based on the key factor of writing speed to add diversity to the training dataset. Moreover, we propose a LSTM-transformer deep network, in which the long short-term memory (LSTM) module models the temporal relationship of the acoustic signal, and the transformer module can not only capture local features, but also capture global features through the self-attention layers, retaining more spatial information compared with convolutional neural network (CNN).

In short, the main contributions of this paper are as follows.

- We propose a novel model training strategy that combines data augmentation and LSTM-transformer network, in order to improve data diversity and capture the deep local and global features, and enhance the generalization ability of the model.
- We implement a prototype on the Android phone. The experimental results show that, as for users without training, we can achieve 80.77% of lowercase letter accuracy with much fewer training samples.

The remainder of this paper is organized as follows. In Sect. 2 we introduce the work related to handwriting recognition and in Sect. 3, we give the details and algorithms of system design. Section 4 describes implementation and performance evaluation. We present the discussion and future work in Sect. 5 and conclude the paper in Sect. 6.

2   Related Works

In this section, we discuss the existing handwriting recognition works, which can be roughly divided into two categories:

2.1   Sensors-Based Handwriting Recognition

Sensor-based methods typically recognize handwriting by capturing motion information of the hand [1,3,11,14,17,19]. For example, Chen *et al.* leverage collect six-degree-of-freedom hand motion data and incorporate context information to achieve air-writing character recognition. However, it requires the extra hardware [1]. To solve this problem, GyroPen *et al.* capture angular trajectory of phone's corner for text entry by built-in gyroscope and accelerometer sensors, but it need the user to hold the device [3]. Meanwhile, UbiTouch senses the user's finger movements through the phone's proximity and ambient light sensors to extend a virtual touchpad on the desktop. *Compare with sensors-based methods, TransWriter is an acoustic-based approach that is universality, low cost, and does not require no additional hardware.*

2.2   Acoustic-Based Handwriting Recognition

In recent years, the most widely acoustic-based methods are mainly divided into two types according to the signal generation method: active sensing and passive sensing.

Active Sensing Methods. Similar to sensor-based methods, these methods actively send the acoustic signal and track the motion of the user's hand according to reflection signal, and use handwriting recognition tools to recognize characters [21–23]. For example, Nandakumar *et al.* track the motion object by calculating the cross-correlation change of echo' two consecutive frames [7]. Yun *et al.* [18] and Vernier [21] measure the phase shift and Doppler shift of the received signal respectively to estimate the moving distance. However, these methods are sensitive to the movement of surrounding objects.

Passive Sensing Methods. In contrast to active sensing, these methods capture the scratch sounds generated by handwriting on the table through the microphone for handwriting recognition. For example, Du *et al.* [5] extracts the short-time feature and feeds it as an image into a deep neural network, which extracts the depth information to recognize print-style capital letters. However, this method requires specifying the order of strokes.

Additionally, some studies explore the recognition of other characters. For example, Chen *et al.* [2] apply CNN to recognize 46 different characters and limits the need for pauses between two characters when writing. And Schrapel *et al.* [8] capture writing sound and pen motion information from microphones and inertial measurement units, and feeds different modal information into multiple neural networks for voting selection. The above methods are not suitable for most daily situations that require free-style input. For example, Chen *et al.* [2] apply CNN to recognize 46 different characters and limits the need for pauses between two characters when handwriting.

To solve this problem, Yin *et al.* incorporate a series techniques including dynamic time wrapping based letter alignment, k-Nearest Neighbor letter classification to achieve free-style handwriting recognition [15]. But it require training a new model for each new user. To solve this problem, they design the Inception-LSTM network, which extracts the depth information to build a user-independent model for free-style lowercase letter recognition [16]. However, its performance on cross-user problem still needs to be further improved, especially for free-style lowercase input. *In this paper, we focus on a user-independent model for free-style handwriting recognition, and achieve a better recognition accuracy than previous methods.*

3   System Design

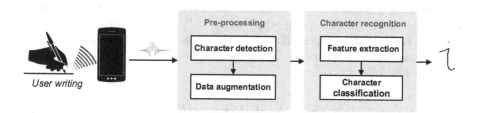

Fig. 1. The system architecture of *TransWriter*.

Figure 1 illustrates the architecture of *TransWriter*, which consists of two main components: pre-processing and character recognition. Next, we will describe each component in detail below.

3.1   Pre-processing

Character Detection. Character detection is designed to accurately extract each handwritten character segment from the acoustic signal. We apply the dual-threshold stroke segment detection method [15] to detect each stroke segment, and merge these segments into character fragments.

In detail, we first use the Wiener filter to reduce the effect of noise generated from the background environment and device, then apply a Hanning window

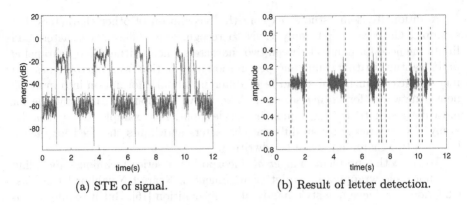

(a) STE of signal.   (b) Result of letter detection.

Fig. 2. Character detection of 'soft'

with size L on the time domain to split the signal $x(t)$ into frames, and compute the short-time energy (STE) for each frame as follows:

$$E(i) = \sum_{n=0}^{L-1} x_i(n)^2. \tag{1}$$

In order to detect the stroke segment, as shown in Fig. 2(a), we first roughly consider that a stroke segment is detected if $E(i) > \Gamma_2$ (the green dotted line) satisfied on this segment, where i means ith frame. The exact start/end point of this segment is the first point which $E(i) \leqslant \Gamma_1$ (the red dotted line) on the left/right side of this segment. If the length of a segment is less than threshold T_2, we remove it as burst noise. The high threshold Γ_2 and low threshold Γ_1 s are defined as follows:

$$\Gamma_2 = \frac{1}{t_{noise}} \sum_{t=1}^{t_{noise}} E(t) + max(E(t)) * c_1, \tag{2}$$

$$\Gamma_1 = \max_{t \in [1, t_{noise}]} E(t) + c_2, \tag{3}$$

where $max(E(t))$ denotes the maximum STE of all frames, c_1 is a constant value in the range $[0.3, 0.5]$, and $c_2 = 4$. Then, we combine the stroke segments as a character if the time interval between continuous burst segments is shorter than threshold T_1. Thus, the start point of a character is the start point of the first burst segment, and the end point of this character is the end point of the last burst segment. The character detection result is as shown in Fig. 2(b).

Data Augmentation. In general, large-scale data helps to optimize the performance of deep neural networks. However, it is difficult to collect a sufficient amount of handwriting samples in practice. Data augmentation is a common strategy to deal with this problem. Since speed is a key factor in inducing user diversity [22], we adopt time-scale modification (TSM) techniques [10] to enrich the training data. TSM can speed up or slow down a sound without affecting the frequency domain information. Specifically, we divide the signal $x(t)$ into multiple frames, and perform stretching or compression by a factor α ($\alpha \in [0.5, 0.75, 1.25, 1.5]$) for each frame, and finally combine these frames into a new signal.

3.2 Character Recognition

Feature Extraction. For non-stationary signals, such as handwriting signals, the time-frequency information cannot be obtained directly by fast Fourier transform. Therefore we perform a short-time Fourier transform on the signals to extract power spectral density, *i.e.*, short-time power spectral density (stPSD). Specifically, we use the Hanning window for framing in which the length of the window and overlap part is set to 0.02 s, 0.01 s receptively, and the FFT length is equal to the window size. Besides, we remove the useless high-frequency part (i.e. higher than 10 kHZ) of stPSD in order to reduce the calculation cost of the network [16].

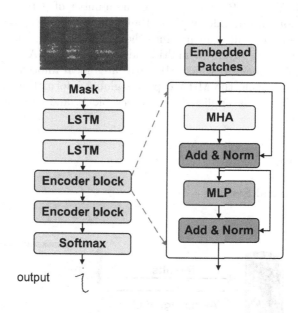

Fig. 3. The network structure of *TransWriter*.

Character Classification. Due to the variation in writing speed and device sampling rate, the extracted stPSD features usually have different lengths in the time dimension. Therefore, before character classification, we require padding the input features to regularize them to a uniform length.

We propose an LSTM-transformer deep network for character classification. Our initial motivation is to adopt the transformer model for further deep feature extraction. Transformer [9] is commonly used to process sequence data and is widely used in many fields such as speech recognition, natural language processing, and language translation. It mainly consists of an encoder and a decoder, in this paper, we only use its encoding module for classification tasks. It can not only capture local features, but also capture global features through the self-attention mechanism, which retains more spatial information than CNN. As shown in Fig. 3, the network includes a mask layer, two LSTM layers, two encoder blocks, and a softmax layer, where the mask layer is used to offset the negative impact of the filling operation; the LSTM layer is used to model the temporal relationship between the features of each frame; the softmax layer is used for classification.

Also, since stPSD is a two-dimensional feature, we use the encoder structure of vision transformer (ViT) [4] as the encoder block. The input of the encoder block is the deep feature map ($H \times W \times C$) through the LSTM layers, where H, W, C are the height, width, and number of channels, respectively. As for embedded patches, the feature map is divided into small patches and reshaped into a patch sequence. Note that unlike ViT, the size of the patch is $(M \times N), M \neq N$. And $P = HW/MN$ is the number of patches. At the same time, the position encode information of all patches is added to the sequence, to obtain the actual input sequence into the encoder block. The encoder block consists of alternating layers of multi-head attention (MHA) and multi-layer perception (MLP) block, in which MLP captures local information and translation equivariant, while the MHA captures global information. Besides, layer normalization (Norm) is applied before every block, and residual connections after every block.

4 Evaluation

4.1 Experimental Setting

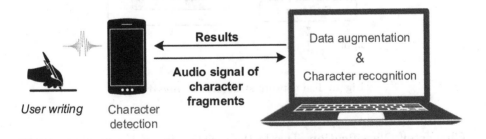

Fig. 4. The implementation of *TransWriter*.

Hardware Platform. To evaluate *TransWriter*, we implement it as a prototype system follows the app-server architecture. Specifically, the *character detection* is implemented on the *OPPO R17* phone with Android 8.1 OS, while *data augmentation* and *character recognition* are implemented on a Lenovo laptop (Intel Core i7-9750 CPU@2.6 GHz and 16 GB RAM) as the cloud server. They are connected via the WiFi channel.

Figure 4 illustrates the architecture and workflow of the prototype. The phone receives the handwritten signal in real time and detects the character one after one. When a character fragment is detected, the phone sends the audio signal of a character to the server. The server recognizes the current character and gives the result word back to the phone, while the user writes the next character at the same time. Note that *data augment* belongs to the off-line training process, *i.e.*, before running *TransWriter*.

Parameter Setting. As for character detection, we set the Hanning window length $L = 0.02$ s and the overlap length is 0.01 s. Besides, T_1, T_2 are set to 0.04 s, 0.6 s, respectively, according to related papers [15].

As for the LSTM-Transformer network, each LSTM layer has 128 hidden cells; the number of attention heads is set to 4, and the size of the patch is $M = 30$, $N = 16$. We use the batch size of 128 for 40 epochs. Moreover, we use AdamW optimizer with a learning rate of 0.001 and weigh decay of 0.0001 to optimize the network. The loss function is the mean squared error (MSE).

Dataset. We recruit 24 volunteers (14 males and 10 females) that use different pens to write the lowercase letters on the wooden table. The mobile phone is placed about 15 cm away from the writing position. Note that, for calculation convenience, we set the default sampling rate to 44.1 kHz. Handwritten sounds with a sampling rate of 48 kHz will be re-sampled. The training set consists of 3952 letter samples from 19 volunteers, each writing 8 times per letter. To evaluate the performance of character recognition, we ask the remaining 5 volunteers to write the letters 8 times to build the test set.

4.2 Overall Recognition Performance

Character Classification. In this experiment, we mainly focus on the user without training. Figure 5 illustrates the average recognition accuracy of 80.77% for 26 lowercase letters. The accuracy of some letters such as 'm', 'f' reaches up to 100%, while the accuracy of 'b' is only 50%. We analyze the result and find that 29% probability of 'b' is recognized as 'p', far exceeding the correct probability. The main reason is possible that users' free-style handwriting habits lead to the indistinguishable writing trajectory of the two letters. In the future, we will combine active sensing to obtain the position information of strokes to distinguish the writing trajectories of two similar letters.

Compare with Other Methods. We compare *TransWriter* with WritingRecorder [16], Ipanel [2], WordRecorder [5] and Pentelligence [8]. Table 1 shows

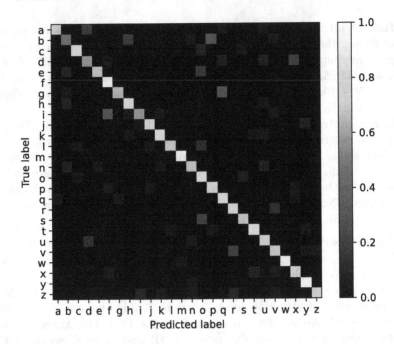

Fig. 5. Confusion matrix of lowercase letter recognition.

the comparison results. As for users without training data, *TransWriter* has the highest accuracy, followed by WritingRecorder, Ipanel and WordRecorder, and Pentelligence is the worst. The main reason is our deep network can extract both local and global depth information of time frames and model the relationship of time frames. As a result, it achieves higher recognition accuracy.

Table 1. Compare with other methods.

Method	*TransWriter*	WritingRecorder	Ipanel	WordRecorder	Pentelligence
Accuracy	80.77%	73.8%	59.45%	47.25%	32.98%

4.3   Impact Factors

The Parameters of LSTM-Transformer Network. We investigate the impact of the training epoch by comparing the loss and recognition accuracy of training and testing under various settings of the epoch number. The result is shown in Fig. 6, which demonstrates that as the epoch increases, the accuracy of training and testing quickly increases, and its loss quickly decreases. In particular, the training accuracy and loss gradually converges after 40 training epochs, while the test accuracy decreases slightly, since too much training epochs will cause over-fitting. Therefore, we set the default epochs to 40. In addition, we also conduct experiments on various learning rates and optimizer combinations. Experiments show that the learning rate of 0.001 and MSE loss function leads to the most accurate recognition.

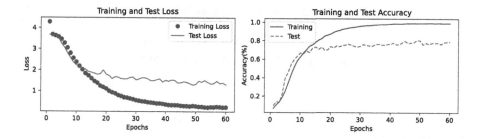

Fig. 6. The effect of training epochs.

The Training Dataset Size. We evaluate the effect of training dataset size. Specifically, we change the number of users collecting training data from 5 to 19 with step 2. Figure 7 presents the letter accuracy for different training user numbers. We can see that when the number of trained users is 5, the accuracy of the letters is approximately 50.9%. When the number of trained users is 13, the accuracy rate significantly improves to over 75%. In addition, after the number of training samples exceeded 13, the accuracy remained stable, ranging from 75% to 80%.

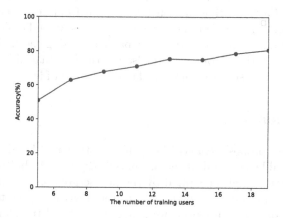

Fig. 7. The effect of training dataset size.

Phone Location. In this part, we explore the effect of variation of writing position on recognition accuracy. We ask volunteers to write the letters when the phone is placed on the top, below, left, and right of the handwriting position, respectively. As depicted in Table 2, the result shows that the average accuracy is 79.65%. Thus, we can conclude that *TransWriter* is robust to location variation.

Table 2. The effect of phone locations.

Location	Above	Below	Left	Right
Accuracy	80.77%	78.24%	79.89%	79.7%

5   Discussion

Extend to Other Characters. This paper mainly describes the recognition of English free0-style lowercase letters, mainly considering non-word recognition without semantic information such as password eavesdropping. As for digit and capital letters, highly differentiated writing trajectories make them not difficult to recognize and thus outside the scope of this paper's discussion. As for the word, we can further leverage the N-Gram language model or connectionist temporal classification to recognize the word [16]. In the future, we can also extend to recognize the Chinese language. Since Chinese characters are composed of multiple strokes, more complex network models should be considered or combined with language models for recognition.

Further Improve the Accuracy. At present, *TransWriter* can achieve about 80.77% accuracy for users without training, but the accuracy needs to be further improved. Incorporating motion information from active acoustic sensing may achieve higher recognition performance than using audio alone. Therefore, we plan to combine acoustic active and passive sensing methods together for handwriting recognition. Moreover, we also use the fact that different users have different handwriting styles for user authentication and identification.

6   Conclusion

In this paper, we propose *TransWriter*, an acoustic-based handwriting recognition system suitable for mobile devices. *TransWriter* uses the built-in microphone to collect acoustic signals generated by the pen scratch on the surface. We perform data augmentation based on the key factor of writing speed to add diversity to the training dataset. Moreover, we propose an LSTM-transformer deep network to build a universal model, which can capture local features and global features, retain more spatial information, and models the temporal relationship between time frames. The experiment results show that *TransWriter* can achieve

80.77% accuracy for unseen users under a series of practical scenarios, *etc.* In future work, we plan to further improve recognition accuracy and extend to other characters' recognition.

Acknowledgements. This work was supported in part by the Scientific and Technological Innovation 2030 - "New Generation Artificial Intelligence" Major Project (2022ZD0119502), the Beijing Science Foundation (9232005), National Natural Science Foundation of China (No. 62277001), and the Scientific Research Program of Beijing Municipal Education Commission (KZ202110011017).

References

1. Chen, M., AlRegib, G., Juang, B.: Air-writing recognition-part i: modeling and recognition of characters, words, and connecting motions. IEEE Trans. Hum. Mach. Syst. **46**(3), 403–413 (2016)
2. Chen, M., et al.: Your table can be an input panel: acoustic-based device-free interaction recognition. Proc. ACM Interact. Mob. Wearable Ubiquitous Technol. **3**(1), 3:1–3:21 (2019)
3. Deselaers, T., Keysers, D., Hosang, J., Rowley, H.A.: Gyropen: gyroscopes for pen-input with mobile phones. IEEE Trans. Hum. Mach. Syst. **45**(2), 263–271 (2015)
4. Dosovitskiy, A., et al.: An image is worth 16 × 16 words: transformers for image recognition at scale. CoRR abs/2010.11929 (2020)
5. Du, H., Li, P., Zhou, H., Gong, W., Luo, G., Yang, P.: Wordrecorder: accurate acoustic-based handwriting recognition using deep learning. In: IEEE INFOCOM 2018 - IEEE Conference on Computer Communications, pp. 1448–1456 (2018)
6. Liu, Y., et al.: Vernier: accurate and fast acoustic motion tracking using mobile devices. IEEE Trans. Mob. Comput. **20**(2), 754–764 (2021)
7. Nandakumar, R., Iyer, V., Tan, D., Gollakota, S.: Fingerio: using active sonar for fine-grained finger tracking. In: Proceedings of the 2016 CHI Conference on Human Factors in Computing Systems, pp. 1515–1525. ACM, New York, NY, USA (2016)
8. Schrapel, M., Stadler, M.L., Rohs, M.: Pentelligence: combining pen tip motion and writing sounds for handwritten digit recognition. In: Proceedings of the 2018 CHI Conference on Human Factors in Computing Systems, pp. 131:1–131:11. CHI '18, ACM, New York, NY, USA (2018)
9. Vaswani, A., et al.: Attention is all you need. In: Guyon, I., Luxburg, U.V., Bengio, S., Wallach, H., Fergus, R., Vishwanathan, S., Garnett, R. (eds.) Advances in Neural Information Processing Systems, vol. 30. Curran Associates, Inc. (2017)
10. Verhelst, W., Roelands, M.: An overlap-add technique based on waveform similarity (WSOLA) for high quality time-scale modification of speech. In: 1993 IEEE International Conference on Acoustics, Speech, and Signal Processing, vol. 2, pp. 554–557 (1993)
11. Vu, T.H., Misra, A., Roy, Q., Wei, K.C.T., Lee, Y.: Smartwatch-based early gesture detection 8 trajectory tracking for interactive gesture-driven applications. Proc. ACM Interact. Mob. Wearable Ubiquitous Technol. **2**(1) (2018)
12. Wang, L., Zhang, X., Jiang, Y., Zhang, Y., Xu, C., Gao, R., Zhang, D.: Watching your phone's back: gesture recognition by sensing acoustical structure-borne propagation. Proc. ACM Interact. Mob. Wearable Ubiquitous Technol. **5**(2) (2021)
13. Wang, L., Zhang, J., Li, Y., Wang, H.: Audiowrite: a handwriting recognition system using acoustic signals. In: 2022 IEEE 28th International Conference on Parallel and Distributed Systems (ICPADS), pp. 81–88 (2023)

14. Wen, E., Seah, W., Ng, B., Liu, X., Cao, J.: Ubitouch: ubiquitous smartphone touchpads using built-in proximity and ambient light sensors. In: Proceedings of the 2016 ACM International Joint Conference on Pervasive and Ubiquitous Computing, pp. 286–297. ACM, New York, NY, USA (2016)

15. Yin, H., Zhou, A., Liu, L., Wang, N., Ma, H.: Ubiquitous writer: robust text input for small mobile devices via acoustic sensing. IEEE Internet Things J. **6**(3), 5285–5296 (2019)

16. Yin, H., Zhou, A., Su, G., Chen, B., Liu, L., Ma, H.: Learning to recognize handwriting input with acoustic features. Proc. ACM Interact. Mob. Wearable Ubiquitous Technol. **4**(2) (2020)

17. Yin, Y., Xie, L., Gu, T., Lu, Y., Lu, S.: Aircontour: building contour-based model for in-air writing gesture recognition. ACM Trans. Sens. Netw. **15**(4) (2019)

18. Yun, S., Chen, Y.C., Zheng, H., Qiu, L., Mao, W.: Strata: fine-grained acoustic-based device-free tracking. In: Proceedings of the 15th Annual International Conference on Mobile Systems, Applications, and Services, pp. 15–28. MobiSys '17, ACM, New York, NY, USA (2017)

19. Zhang, Q., Wang, D., Zhao, R., Yu, Y.: Myosign: enabling end-to-end sign language recognition with wearables. In: Proceedings of the 24th International Conference on Intelligent User Interfaces, pp. 650–660. IUI '19, Association for Computing Machinery, New York, NY, USA (2019)

20. Zhang, Q., Wang, D., Zhao, R., Yu, Y., Jing, J.: Write, attend and spell: streaming end-to-end free-style handwriting recognition using smartwatches. Proc. ACM Interact. Mob. Wearable Ubiquitous Technol. **5**(3) (2021)

21. Zhang, Y., Wang, J., Wang, W., Wang, Z., Liu, Y.: Vernier: accurate and fast acoustic motion tracking using mobile devices. In: IEEE INFOCOM 2018 - IEEE Conference on Computer Communications, pp. 1709–1717, April 2018. https://doi.org/10.1109/INFOCOM.2018.8486365

22. Zou, Y., Xiao, Z., Hong, S., Guo, Z., Wu, K.: Echowrite 2.0: a lightweight zero-shot text-entry system based on acoustics. IEEE Trans. Hum.-Mach. Syst. **52**(6), 1313–1326 (2022)

23. Zou, Y., Yang, Q., Han, Y., Wang, D., Cao, J., Wu, K.: Acoudigits: enabling users to input digits in the air. In: 2019 IEEE International Conference on Pervasive Computing and Communications (PerCom), pp. 1–9 (2019)

Reinforcement-Learning-Based 2D Flow Control for Logistics Systems

Mingrui Yin[1(✉)], Chenxin Cai[1], and Jie Liu[2]

[1] Faculty of Computing, Harbin Institute of Technology, Harbin 150001, China
`Mingrui.Yin@hotmail.com`
[2] International Research Institute for Artificial Intelligence,
Harbin Institute of Technology, Shenzhen 518055, China

Abstract. To address large-scale challenges in current logistics systems, we present an logistics system employing a multi-agent framework grounded on an actuator network named Omniveyor. This design ensures real-time responsiveness and scalability in flow operations. Under the premise of centralized control, we employ Reinforcement Learning (RL) to efficiently control omni-wheel conveyors. Different from traditional path planning, our approach considers the entire platform as an agent, using the package state for observation. Proximal Policy Optimization (PPO) proves to be an effective algorithm for platform-wide control planning. Experimental results demonstrate the system's capability to accurately deliver packages. Therefore, the RL algorithm allows the omni-wheel platform to autonomously learn and optimize package paths, circumventing the need for traditional controls or path planning methods.

Keywords: Logistics system · Reinforcement Learning · Centralized control system

1 Introduction

In contemporary logistics and transportation sectors, the conventional belt conveyor system remains predominant. While its structure suits various industrial applications, the linear conveying methodology suffers from a series of problems such as low efficiency, poor durability, and insufficient flexibility, and cannot meet transport requirements. To address the limitations of standard belt conveyor systems, scholars and industry professionals have developed advanced intelligent logistics systems, such as Automated Guided Vehicles (AGVs) and Robotic Material Flow Systems (RMFS).

Corresponding to those distributed transportation methods, 2D conveyor surfaces (2D-CS) are proposed as a new type of logistics system, such as Celluveyor and Gridsorter. Notably, the Celluveyor is a prime example of a conveyance tool within distributed platforms. Compared with traditional logistics systems, 2D-CS usually uses distributed components as the core of the system, with these advantages: flexibility, robustness, and compactness.

In logistics systems, an optimal control method that can save consumption is very important. In distributed systems, reinforcement learning is widely recognized as a potent solution. Its principle involves identifying the current state of

© The Author(s), under exclusive license to Springer Nature Singapore Pte Ltd. 2024
L. Wang et al. (Eds.): CWSN 2023, CCIS 1994, pp. 257–270, 2024.
https://doi.org/10.1007/978-981-97-1010-2_19

the environment that the agent seeks to control, selecting appropriate actions, and receiving rewards from the environment based on the effectiveness of the actions taken by the agent [4].

Drawing inspiration from the 2D-CS, we propose a multi-agent system characterized by an actuator network-based structure called Omniveyor. Meanwhile, under the premise of centralized control, we address the control challenge of omni-wheel platforms via reinforcement learning.

This study offers the following contributions:

(1) Omniveyor is discrete, possesses scalability, and ensures real-time performance. We have integrated the strengths of previous 2D-CS systems by combining the omni-wheel with the square modules, to avoid the possibility of slipping while saving costs. On the basis of the platform, we propose a multi-dimensional spatio-temporal graph of process operations, and formulate a mathematical model based on it.
(2) In contrast to traditional path planning, we regard the entire platform rather than the package as an agent, and employee the state of the package as the observation. We execute control planning across the entire platform, comparing different RL algorithm on it. Experimental results confirm the successful delivery of goods to their destinations under the conditions we established.

The paper is structured as follows: Sect. 2 briefly introduces the relevant literature and works. Section 3 details the system structure we proposed, abstracting it into a spatio-temporal graph, and establishing the mathematical model. The reinforcement learning algorithm and the environment established are in Sect. 4. Section 5 shows the experimental results, and Sect. 6 summarizes the conclusions and points out the future research direction.

2   Related Works

2.1   Logistics System Problems

With market and e-commerce developments, there is an increased interest in automation for order picking. For example, AGV is an unmanned material handling equipment used for horizontal movement of packages, but the application scope of AGV-assisted picking is narrow, and it is only suitable for picking small and heavy items [14]. RMFS is a new type of automated storage and retrieval system. Because of its more flexible layout and easier hardware installation, RMFS can provide higher productivity in practical applications [1].

The Institute of Production and Logistics of the University of Bremen in Germany proposed an intelligent transportation system called Celluveyor [10], which is a modular transmission and positioning system. It is highly scalable and adaptable in terms of range and throughput adjustments. Celluveyor consists of several small hexagonal transport modules, each with three omni wheels. Thanks to the connectors between the modules, they can be combined into any kind of layout. And due to the special arrangement of the wheels and the individual control of each wheel, the transported goods can move independently on the platform in any path. With this modular hardware, the sorting efficiency of material flow warehousing can be improved from many aspects [11].

However, the hexagonal design is not stable enough for transportation in actual tests, grid-based design can effectively improve this problem. GridSorter is a grid-based transportation system, which consisted of several grid platforms with decentralized control and logical time scheme [8]. Packages could enter the platform through any conveyor module on either side, and exit through the designated [9].

2.2 Reinforcement Learning Theories

In reinforcement learning, an agent is given a state and a reward from the environment. The agent's task is to determine an appropriate action [5]. Different from machine learning, the reinforcement learning algorithm does not rely on labeled data, but focuses on the interaction between agent and environment.

Nowadays, multi-agent systems is widely used in industrial production [6], and RL research progress and achievements based on which have attracted much attention. Typical deep reinforcement learning (DRL) algorithms have been proposed one after another, with diversified algorithms and high application flexibility. Taking a single agent as an example, according to whether the algorithm depends on the model, RL can be divided into two types: model-free reinforcement learning (MFRL) and model-based reinforcement learning (MBRL).

As for the application, reinforcement learning has been widely used in discrete systems and logistics systems. For example, Q-learning algorithm and Deep Q-learning is been applied into omnidirectional-wheel conveyor [12], PPO algorithm is been applied into flexible job-shop scheduling problem [13]. Considering the multi-agent reinforcement learning in the path planning problem, AGVs have received more extensive attention. Multi-Agent Deep Deterministic Policy Gradient has been used in AGVs conflict prevention, and scholars focus more on multi-agent path and delivery problems [2].

2.3 Technical Challenges

Although reinforcement learning has achieved certain results in path finding and system control, existing results based on logistics platforms does not conform to the traditional logic. In the system mentioned above, researchers regard the packages rather than controllers as agents, but in practice, the controllers are what we should focus on. Therefore, we propose a corresponding solution on this problem.

3 Structure of Omniveyor and Model Definition

3.1 Structure of the Omniveyor

Omniveyor employs a platform equipped with omni-directional wheels for the transportation of parcels.

Omni-directional wheels are distinguished by having rollers oriented perpendicularly to their rotational axis. The platform constructed with omni-directional wheels enables the multi-directional movement of packages without necessitating alterations to the platform's structure, thereby addressing the limitations of unidirectional transportation.

In addition, the system issues basic control commands based on distributed multi-agent equipment, and locates the parcel location through the visual positioning module.

Figure 1 illustrates the design of the transmission module.

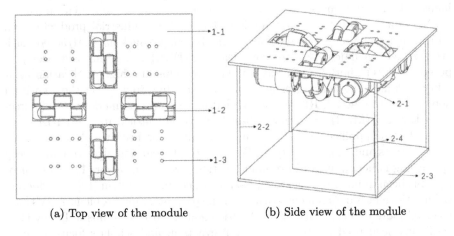

| (a) Top view of the module | (b) Side view of the module |

Fig. 1. The structure of controller model, including top and side views.

This module comprises a rectangular load-bearing plate (1-1). At its center are several mounting holes (1-3), around which omni-directional wheels (1-2) are affixed, and the transport platform could be extended to the specified width by adding modules. Each wheel is powered by a motor (2-1) featuring an integrated Hall encoder. These motors are secured to the underside of the load-bearing plate (1-1) via a support frame.

Each motor (2-1) independently modulates the velocity and direction of its corresponding wheel (1-2). Omni-directional wheels (1-2) interact with the package via the slot in the load-bearing plate (1-1), and the entire transmission module is firmly attached to the base platform (2-3) through brackets (2-2). A single drive board (2-4) regulates the motors (2-1) across the transmission modules. These drive boards are governed by a distributed edge device, with multiple such devices being supervised by a central server control. The distribution of control commands and feedback between distributed edge devices and servers is carried out through wireless local area networks.

In the follow-up sections, we will treat the drive board and its accompanying motor components as an entity for study.

3.2   Spatio-Temporal Graph

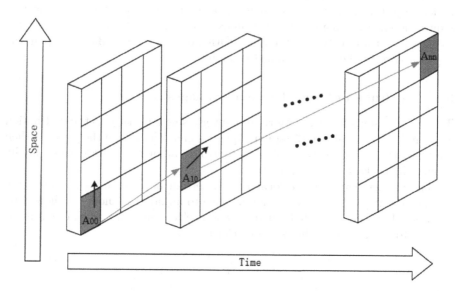

Fig. 2. The spatio-temporal graph of the entire platform.

In contrast to traditional logistics projects, which tend to concentrate solely on controllers without comprehensively modeling the entire system, our intelligent logistics platform necessitates the consideration of the interplay between packages and controllers. In this section, we propose a new spatio-temporal graph model for the platform, which exploits the interaction between objects across both time and space, providing an explicit basis for subsequent algorithmic research.

The system has different actions in different spatial and temporal domains. The purpose of the spatial graph is to capture the state of the package relative to the controller in space. In this representation, the logistics platform can be reconfigured as a grid map. To simplify the problem description, we propose the following constraints here: acceleration and deceleration during package transit are disregarded, each package adheres strictly to control instructions to reach the designated location, and the size of each package could completely overlaps the built platform.

But in spatial diagram, we cannot point out the continuity in time, which means it cannot model the transformation of the system over time. Thus, to account for this aspect, it's essential that we incorporate a temporal graph into our model.

In conclusion, we propose the spatio-temporal graph depicted in Fig. 2, which is constructed based on the grid platform. The spatio-temporal graph simultaneously captures the system's states in both time and space. The underlying grid represents the actions of the controller, while the color-coded grid cells indicate the state of the box. For illustrative purposes, we consider a single box: at time A, the object is situated at the node A_{00} as indicated in the figure. In the subsequent moment, owing to the interconnectivity among agents, it is constrained to move either upwards or to the right. Ultimately, over a specific time span, the object arrives at the predetermined endpoint A_{nn}.

3.3   The Rules of Controllers and Packages

The primary steps for the platform to deliver a single package to the destination are as follows: first, obtain the starting point and destination of the package, then plan the control instructions of each controller at predetermined time, finally convey the package to its destination.

The package can only be located at a certain node at any time, and stay at the current position at any time or move to an adjacent node as allowed by the rules. Each node can hold at most one package one time. Packages are not allowed to move outside the whole platform.

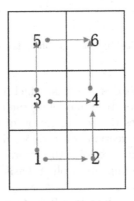

Fig. 3. The rules for package drives on six controller.

Within the mathematical model, the forward direction of the package is constrained according to the instruction rules of the controller. Specifically, the package can only run upwards or to the right. To represent this constraint, we proposed a corresponding adjacency matrix, with 1 indicating that it is feasible for the package to achieve from controller A to B, otherwise it is 0. For instance, considering the platform depicted in Fig. 3, and accounting for the controllers at nodes 1–4, the adjacency matrix is presented below:

$$
\begin{array}{c c c c}
 & \mathbf{1} & \mathbf{2} & \mathbf{3} & \mathbf{4} \\
\mathbf{1} & \begin{bmatrix} 1 & 1 & 1 & 0 \\ \mathbf{2} & 0 & 1 & 0 & 1 \\ \mathbf{3} & 0 & 0 & 1 & 1 \\ \mathbf{4} & 0 & 0 & 0 & 1 \end{bmatrix}
\end{array}
$$

3.4 Mathematical Model Definition

The index, sets, parameters of the problem and decision variables of the model are as follows:

Index and Sets:

i, j, k: the index of agents.

p: the index of packages.

t: the index of time steps.

K: the set of agents.

P: the set of packages.

T: the set of time steps, $T = \{1, 2, ..., t_{max}\}$

Parameters of the problem:

a_p^s: the starting point of package, $p \in P$

a_p^e: the end point of package, $p \in P$

β: an adjacent matrix with K * K dimension. If agent i and j are adjacent in the platform, and packages can move from i to j by the controller, then the β_{ij} equals 1, otherwise 0

Decision variables:

s_{pkt}: a binary variable, equals 1 if package p is at agent a_k at time t, otherwise 0

C_{kt}: a binary variable, equals 1 if the agent k have an action at time t, otherwise 0

On this basis, we define the mathematical model under centralized control state:

$$min \quad \sum_{k \in K} \sum_{t \in T} C_{kt} \tag{1}$$

subject to:

$$s_{pa_p^s 0} = 1, \forall p \in P \tag{2}$$

$$s_{pa_p^e t} = 1, \forall p \in P, t \in T \tag{3}$$

$$\sum_{k \in K} s_{pkt} \leqslant 1, \forall p \in P, t \in T \tag{4}$$

$$\sum_{p \in P} s_{pkt} \leqslant 1, \forall k \in K, t \in T \tag{5}$$

$$s_{pi(t+1)} \leqslant \sum_{j \in K} \beta_{ij} \cdot s_{pjt}, \forall p \in P, i \in K, t \in T \tag{6}$$

$$s_{pkt} \in \{0,1\}, \forall p \in P, k \in K, t \in T \tag{7}$$

$$C_{kt} \in \{0,1\}, k \in K, t \in T \tag{8}$$

Objective (1) is to minimize the total cost of all agents. Constrains (2) and (3) ensure that all packages should be positioned at its start agent at time 0, and must each their respective end points before end time. Constrains (4) means that each package can be assigned to only one agent. (5) dictates that for each agent, it can only hold an package at same time. Constrains (6) guarantee that each package can only move to adjacent agent or remain stationary. Constrains (7) and (8) and the integer restrictions of the decision variables.

4   The System Using Reinforcement Learning

Different from the traditional scenario that focuses on the operation of packages, we focus more on the integration of the controller and the packages. Most of the usual logistics systems build multi-objective decision-making models through simulation or heuristic algorithms to complete the delivery of packages. The above decision models usually ignore the actual operation effect of the controllers. In response to the above problems, we propose a decision-making method based on deep reinforcement learning. As the first stage of the experiment, we can regard the entire logistics platform as a unified agent and only consider the case of a single package.

4.1   Algorithms Introduction

Reinforcement learning constitutes a subdomain within machine learning, which focuses on formulating actions in response to environmental conditions with the goal of optimizing expected rewards [3]. We mainly consider Advantage Actor Critic (A2C) and PPO algorithms in this paper.

Algorithm 1: A2C Algorithm

---

1. Observing the current state s_t, make a decision according to the policy network: $a_t \sim \pi(\cdot|s_t; \theta_t)$, and let the agent perform the action a_t.

2. Observe the reward r_t and the new state s_{t+1} from the environment.

3. Make decision according to the policy network: $\tilde{a}_{t+1} \sim \pi(\cdot|s_{t+1}; \theta_{now})$, but do not let the agent perform the action $\tilde{a}_{t+1}$.

4. Let the value network score: $\hat{q}_t = q(s_t, a_t; \omega_{now})$ and $\hat{q_{t+1}} = q(s_{t+1}, a_{t+1}; \omega_{now})$

5. Calculate TD target and TD error: $\hat{y}_t = r_t + \gamma \cdot \hat{q_{t+1}}$ and $\delta_t = \hat{q}_t - \hat{y}_t$

6. Update value network: $\omega_{new} \leftarrow \omega_{now} - \alpha \cdot \delta \cdot \nabla_\omega q(s_t, a_t; \omega_{now})$

7. Update policy network: $\theta_{new} \leftarrow \theta_{now} + \beta \cdot \delta \cdot \nabla_\theta ln\pi(a_t|s_t; \theta_{now})$

Q-learning is a value iteration method, while policy gradient is a strategy iteration method, and A2C uses both methods. In practice, the actor network in A2C employs the TD error when computing the gradient, which is an unbiased estimate of the advantage function. Therefore, the update formula of the actor network shows in Algorithm 1.

PPO is a policy optimization method that uses multiple epochs for random gradient ascent to update the policy. This method has the stability and reliability, is suitable for more general settings and has better overall results [7].

Algorithm 2 is the PPO algorithm for the logistics system:

Algorithm 2: Optimization method based on PPO

---

1. Initial policy parameters θ^0 and generate a simulated logistics environment for training
2. For iteration = 1,2,...,N do
3. Reset the simulated logistics environment
4. For actor = 1,2,...,T do
5. Observe the package state s_t of the environment
6. Run policy $\pi(\cdot|s_t; \theta_{now})$ to choose action a_t based on the environment state s_t
7. After the action a_t is executed, the environment feeds back a reward value r_t to the system and converts to a new state $s_{(t+1)}$
8. End for
9. Compute the value of advantage function $A^{\theta^k}(s_t, a_t)$
10. Find θ optimizing the loss function $J_{ppo}(\theta)$
11. Replace the parameters of actor network $\theta_{old} \leftarrow \theta$
12. End for

The loss function $J_{ppo}(\theta)$ used to update and optimize the weight parameters of $\pi(a_t|s_t; \theta_{now})$ is computed by Eq. (9) and (10):

$$J_{ppo}^{\theta^k} = J^{\theta^k}(\theta) - \beta KL(\theta, \theta^k) \tag{9}$$

$$J^{\theta^k}(\theta) \approx \sum_{(s_t, a_t)} \frac{\pi_\theta(a_t|s_t)}{\pi_{\theta......k}(a_t|s_t)} A^{\theta^k}(s_t, a_t) \tag{10}$$

$A^{\theta^k}(s_t, a_t)$ is the estimator of advantage function, and $KL(\theta, \theta^k)$ is a constrain means KL divergence between θ and θ^k, β could be adaptive during calculating KL penalty.

4.2   Environment Creation

Markov decision process (MDP) is a common model in reinforcement learning. In the control problem of the smart logistics platform, the task of each controller could be described as an MDP. However, since our problem focuses on centralized planning and control, we regard the entire platform as an MDP in actual experiments.

A standard tuple MDP consists of (S, A, R, S'), where S is the state, A is the action, R is the reward, and S' is the next state. The platform environment constructed in this paper is discrete, so we discretized the action space.

State: The state is determined by the x-y axis coordinates of each package and is represented as an M * N two-dimensional matrix. If there is a package at agent a_{ij}, the corresponding element in the matrix is set to 1; otherwise, it is 0.

Reward: Rewards and penalties are determined based on the location of the package. If the action makes the package arrive at the specified destination, the system will get a reward of +50. If the package goes out of bounds, the system receives a penalty of -3 and the state remains unchanged.

The reward $r_t(s_t, a_t)$ represents the immediate reward of the system when it takes an action at time t:

$$r_t(s_t, a_t) = \begin{cases} 50 & \text{when package arrives} \\ -3 & \text{when package out of platforms} \end{cases} \tag{11}$$

Action: It is represented by a one-dimensional discrete array with a length of M * N, equals to the total number of actuators. For each actuator, there are five discrete actions - up, down, left, right, or stay still - which correspond to 0, 1, 2, 3, and 4 respectively (see Fig. 4).

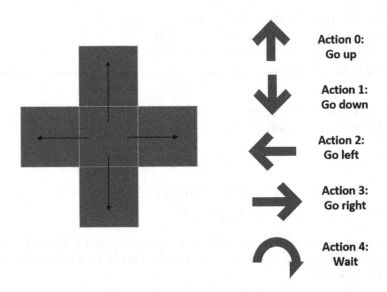

Fig. 4. The actions of each controller.

5   Experiment Results

In this section, experiment is set to evaluate the effectiveness of the proposed environment and solution method.

5.1   Experiment Environment

All experiments in this article are conducted on a Windows 10 system with a CPU, the CPU core model is Intel(R) Core(TM) i5-10400F. The version of Python used is 3.7.8. All the models in this section employ MLP as the policy network. For the A2C algorithm, we use the RMSProp optimizer to update the network parameters with an initial learning rate of 0.0007, while for the PPO algorithm, we employ the Adam optimizer with an initial learning rate of 0.0003.

We have created an environment with a grid map, and all algorithms are evaluated within this environment. The size of the platform and the number of actuators in the environment can be adjusted through parameters.

In a 7×7 environment, the algorithms are run for 100,000 rounds, while in a 10×10 environment, they are run for 200,000 rounds. For the PPO algorithm, the batch size is set at 64. In the experiment, the reward is used as indicator, and the calculation is performed every 100 rounds. The model is updated every round, and the reward of 100 rounds near the current round is used as the indicator.

5.2   Experiment Result

This experiment is carried out under the set environment. On a smaller platform, the A2C algorithm converges more rapidly than the PPO algorithm. However, as the platform size and number of actuators increase, the A2C algorithm falls short in effectively accomplishing our task.

In an environment with 49 actuators and a single package, the PPO algorithm can successfully reach convergence within 100k iterations, which A2C shows better performance. The results of the experiments are presented in Fig. 5.

When the environment is scaled up to a platform of size 10 * 10, with the number of actuators increased to N = 100, the experimental results are depicted in Fig. 6. As can be observed from the figure, within 200,000 rounds, the PPO algorithm converges to approximately 50 rewards, signifying that the agent has fully learned to accomplish the task set by the environment. In contrast, the A2C algorithm converges to an incorrect reward in about 40,000 epochs, indicating that the agent fails to learn relevant information and successfully deliver the package to its destination.

Table 1 further demonstrates the results of our experimental. We evaluate the model by calculating the mean reward and the standard deviation (std) of reward per episode. The results reveal that PPO maintains stability in both environments, whereas A2C exhibits instability on the 10 * 10 platform.

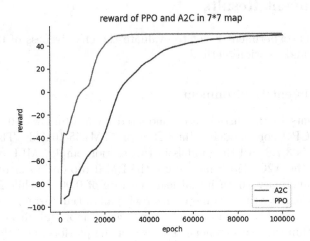

Fig. 5. The reward of PPO and A2C in 7 * 7 map, A2C have better performance than PPO.

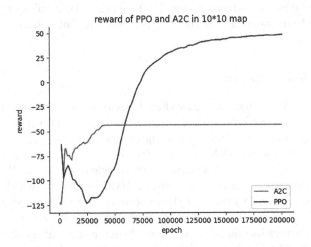

Fig. 6. The reward of PPO and A2C in 10 * 10 map, PPO converges to correct reward.

Table 1. Evaluate of PPO and A2C in different size platform.

mean, std	PPO	A2C
7 * 7	50,0	50,0
10 * 10	50,0	−150,450

6   Conclusion

This paper mainly focus on the application of reinforcement learning in real industrial scenarios. We design a process-oriented multi-agent collaboration system: Omniveyor, including cloud and edge multi-agent devices, which has certain scalability and can transport packages to designated locations through a platform built with omnidirectional wheels.

Furthermore, based on this system, this paper proposes a corresponding spatio-temporal graph to describe the problem, and establishes a corresponding mathematical model.

Unlike traditional path planning problems, our research focuses on how to control the actuators directly, employing reinforcement learning to solve this model. In this paper, we build the environment corresponding to the model and use two different reinforcement learning methods to test their performance as theoretical algorithms in smart logistics system. The simulation results indicate that the PPO algorithm can accomplish our proposed problem and is as effective as the traditional control algorithm.

For the future research: when the platform size is further expanded, the training time of reinforcement learning will be extended. In addition, since not all actuators can obtain global perception, we plan to introduce local observations to better simulate real situations, and aim to experiment with multi-agent reinforcement learning methods in subsequent steps.

References

1. Bozer, Y.A., Aldarondo, F.J.: A simulation-based comparison of two goods-to-person order picking systems in an online retail setting. Int. J. Prod. Res. **56**(11), 3838–3858 (2018)
2. Hu, H., Yang, X., Xiao, S., Wang, F.: Anti-conflict AGV path planning in automated container terminals based on multi-agent reinforcement learning. Int. J. Prod. Res. **61**(1), 65–80 (2023)
3. Hu, J., Niu, H., Carrasco, J., Lennox, B., Arvin, F.: Voronoi-based multi-robot autonomous exploration in unknown environments via deep reinforcement learning. IEEE Trans. Veh. Technol. **69**(12), 14413–14423 (2020)
4. Kim, K., Hong, Y.G.: Industrial general reinforcement learning control framework system based on intelligent edge. In: 2020 22nd International Conference on Advanced Communication Technology (ICACT), pp. 414–418. IEEE (2020)
5. Ladosz, P., Weng, L., Kim, M., Oh, H.: Exploration in deep reinforcement learning: a survey. Inf. Fusion **85**, 1–22 (2022)
6. Lu, Z., Zhuang, Z., Huang, Z., Qin, W.: A framework of multi-agent based intelligent production logistics system. Procedia CIRP **83**, 557–562 (2019)
7. Schulman, J., Wolski, F., Dhariwal, P., Radford, A., Klimov, O.: Proximal policy optimization algorithms. arXiv preprint arXiv:1707.06347 (2017)
8. Seibold, Z., Furmans, K.: Gridsorter-Logische Zeit in dezentral gesteuerten Materialflusssystemen. Logist. J. Proc. **2014**(01) (2014)
9. Seibold, Z., Furmans, K., Gue, K.R.: Using logical time to ensure liveness in material handling systems with decentralized control. IEEE Trans. Autom. Sci. Eng. **19**(1), 545–552 (2020)

10. Uriarte, C., Rohde, A., Kunaschk, S., Schenk, M., Zadek, H., Müller, G.: Celluveyor-ein hochflexibles und modulares förderund positioniersystem auf basis omnidirektionaler antriebstechnik, pp. 237–247
11. Uriarte, C., Thamer, H., Freitag, M., Thoben, K.D.: Flexible automatisierung logistischer prozesse durch modulare roboter. Logist. J. Proc. **2016**(05) (2016)
12. Zaher, W., Youssef, A.W., Shihata, L.A., Azab, E., Mashaly, M.: Omnidirectional-wheel conveyor path planning and sorting using reinforcement learning algorithms. IEEE Access **10**, 27945–27959 (2022)
13. Zhang, Y., Zhu, H., Tang, D., Zhou, T., Gui, Y.: Dynamic job shop scheduling based on deep reinforcement learning for multi-agent manufacturing systems. Robot. Comput.-Integr. Manuf. **78**, 102412 (2022)
14. Zhen, L., Li, H.: A literature review of smart warehouse operations management. Front. Eng. Manag. **9**(1), 31–55 (2022). https://doi.org/10.1007/s42524-021-0178-9

A Survey of Deep Learning-Based Multimodal Vehicle Trajectory Prediction Methods

Xiaoliang Wang, Lian Zhou, and Yuzhen Liu[✉]

School of Computer Science and Engineering, Hunan University of Science and Technology, Xiangtan 411201, China
21182240@qq.com

Abstract. With the rapid development of deep learning, an increasing number of researchers have paid attention to and engaged in research in the field of autonomous driving, achieving numerous remarkable achievements. The paper aims to explore the current status and methods of trajectory prediction for autonomous vehicles, and reviews some commonly used trajectory prediction techniques and algorithms. The existing vehicle trajectory prediction tasks mainly involve extracting and modeling the historical trajectory sequences of the target vehicle and the surrounding environmental information features, to infer multimodal trajectories for a certain future time duration. The paper focuses on deep learning-based multimodal trajectory prediction methods, including traditional convolutional neural networks, recurrent neural networks, graph neural networks, attention mechanisms, and the latest research results of mixed models composed of multiple network structures. Additionally, two large-scale publicly available datasets in the field of autonomous driving, the Argoverse dataset and the nuScenes dataset are introduced, and the performance of existing evaluation metrics is analyzed. Finally, through the analysis and comparison of these methods, the paper summarizes and deduces the possible future directions of vehicle trajectory prediction and the existing technological bottlenecks, aiming to provide useful assistance and prospects for future research and application of autonomous vehicle trajectory prediction.

Keywords: Multimodal · Vehicle trajectory prediction · Deep learning · Argoverse dataset · nuScenes dataset

1 Introduction

Vehicle trajectory prediction, as the most crucial research direction in autonomous driving, provides essential decision-making for the operation and control of vehicles. Trajectory prediction aims to accurately forecast the driving path of vehicles by analyzing their current state and environmental information, ensuring effective interaction with the surrounding environment. Previous work has laid a solid foundation in this area (As shown in Fig. 1 search for the number of Web of Science papers published based on deep learning related keywords). Jin et al. [1] introduce an interactive multiple-model algorithm based on optimal autoregressive and an exchange Kalman filter physical model as early as 2014. J. Chen et al. [2] propose a deep Monte Carlo tree search (deep-MCTS) method for visual-based vehicle trajectory prediction. Lim Q [3], S. Mosharafian [4], and others utilize Gaussian processes to establish dynamic models of vehicles. R. S. Tomar [5], R. Izquierdo [6], and others employ support vector machine (SVM) methods for vehicle trajectory prediction. However, traditional physical or machine learning models often suffer from issues such as low prediction accuracy, low robustness, and high latency.

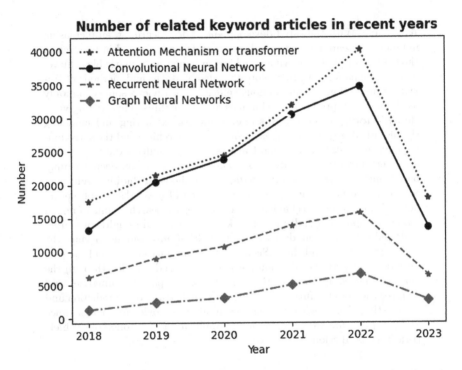

Fig. 1. Retrieve the number of Web of Science papers published based on deep learning related keywords. By observing the chart, we can see that with the rapid development of deep learning, the number of published papers has been steadily increasing year by year (data collected up to July 2023). Particularly noteworthy is the significant quantity of papers related to attention mechanisms.

With the popularity of deep learning and the improvement of device computing performance, there are increasingly more methods using deep learning for trajectory prediction. Deep learning typically utilizes past trajectory information of vehicles and surrounding environmental information as inputs. Through various network models, it outputs future multimodal predicted trajectories (as shown in Fig. 2.), we will focus on investigating and comparing models proposed in recent years, summarizing the methods used by each model, and exploring their commonalities. Therefore, our main contributions are as follows:

1) We investigate the trajectory prediction directions of typical deep learning models in recent years, briefly introduce each model, and compare the impact of model structures on their prediction metrics.
2) We summarize the methods of each model to facilitate researchers in the field to choose the most suitable model for experiments and applications.
3) Based on the characteristics of each model, we boldly predict and speculate on possible research trends for future vehicle trajectory prediction.

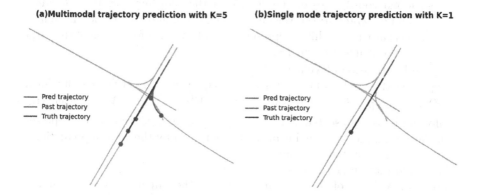

Fig. 2. Results of future trajectory prediction based on the historical trajectory sequence of the target agent. In the left panel, we present the results of multimodal trajectory prediction with a mode count (k) of 5, while in the right panel, we show the results of unimodal trajectory prediction with a mode count (k) of 1. The predicted trajectories are depicted in green, representing the future trajectories derived from the historical trajectory sequence of the target agent. The red trajectories indicate the past trajectory of the target agent, and the blue trajectories represent the actual future paths taken by the target agent. It is evident that in the left panel, the predicted trajectories align more closely with the real trajectories. (Color figure online)

Our paper is divided into the following sections: In Sect. 2, we represent the trajectory prediction task using mathematical expressions. Next, in Sect. 3, we mainly introduce high-performance trajectory prediction models and methods in recent years. In Sect. 4, we evaluate and summarize the performance of various models based on commonly used trajectory prediction datasets, such as Argoverse [7] and nuScenes [8]. Finally, in Sect. 5, we provide an outlook on future research directions.

2   Problem Description

Currently, vehicle trajectory prediction is mainly based on modeling using large datasets. In order to formalize the representation of vehicle prediction problems, the vehicle's motion trajectory and surrounding environmental information need to be preprocessed. This allows obtaining relevant information such as the vehicle's spatial coordinates and the surrounding environment at different time intervals. Then, based on this premise, the problem can be defined:

1) Vehicle History Information $(V_{tar/sur}^{(p)})$

   Display the trajectory information of the vehicle at the past $(T+1)$ time step. That is to say, $V_{tar/sur}^{(p)} = \{V_{-T}^{(p)}, V_{-T+1}^{(p)}, \cdots, V_0^{(p)}\}$, each state is represented as $V_t^{(p)} = \{x_t, y_t, v_t, a_t, \theta_t, c\}$, x_t and y_t respectively represent the lateral and longitudinal coordinates of the vehicle in the coordinate system at time t. v_t, a_t and θ_t represent the velocity, acceleration, and yaw angle information of a vehicle at time t, while c represents the identifier information of the target vehicle or surrounding vehicles.

2) Future Information of Vehicles $(V_{tar}^{(f)})$

   Represent the predicted trajectory state sequence of target vehicles for future (H) time steps. That is to say, $V_{tar}^{(f)} = \{V_1^{(f)}, V_2^{(f)}, \cdots, V_H^{(f)}\}$, each state information is represented as $V_h^{(f)} = [x_h, y_h]$, x_h and y_h respectively represent the lateral and longitudinal coordinates obtained by the vehicle prediction in the coordinate system at time h.

3) Lane Information (L^N)

   Provides N lanes of information indicating the impact of the surrounding environment on the target vehicle. That is to say, $L^N = \{L^1, L^2, \cdots, L^N\}$.

Therefore, the common vehicle trajectory prediction can be expressed as follows: given the historical vehicle information and lane information, the posterior distribution of the target vehicle can be obtained, which can be represented as $P(V_{tar}^{(f)}|V_{tar}^{(p)}, V_{sur}^{(p)}, L^{(N)})$, Fig. 3 shows an example diagram of a driving scenario for reference terminology. In the diagram, vehicles are categorized into target agents V_{tar}, surrounding agents V_{sur}, and regular agent V based on a distance-based criterion.

3   Method

In this section, we review five common deep learning trajectory prediction based methods from shallow to deep focus and detail the existing research progress of the method:

3.1   Traditional Convolutional Neural Network (CNN)

Convolutional neural network [9] is a deep learning model that consists of input layers, convolutional layers, pooling layers and fully connected layers connected

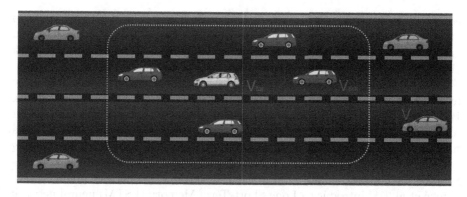

Fig. 3. Based on a distance-based vehicle partitioning graph, vehicles are categorized into surrounding agents V_{sur} and regular agents V according to the distance criteria around the target agent V_{tar}.

in multiple layers and similar to the structure of the network, which is often used in the direction of image recognition, natural language processing and so on.

In trajectory prediction tasks, agent state information and environmental feature maps are generally used as inputs to different CNN modules. In [10], Bojarski et al. create the PilotNet CNN system, which uses road images and manually collected driving data to predict steering angles and output appropriate steering angles. N. Lee et al. [11] use agent's historical trajectory information and interaction information between agents as inputs to the CNN model to generate multimodal trajectory information, which is then refining and sorting through the ranking refinement module. H. Cui et al. [12] introduce raster maps as inputs to the MobileNet-v2 module of the CNN model and created the MTP model, which concatenates the extracted features with vehicle state information. T. Phan-Minh et al. [13] improve the MTP model by using a set of trajectories that approximate all possible motions and focusing on the trajectory output. They also define multimodal trajectory prediction as a classification problem to avoid the "mode collapse" issue associated with regression methods. N. Deo et al. [14] replace the fully connected layers with convolutional and max-pooling layers for the tensor encoding of the agent's LSTM-encoded tensor, enabling robust learning of interdependencies between vehicles. J. Hong et al. [15] use CNN models to model semantic environment maps to integrate contextual information. The above methods can extract and model trajectory information to a certain extent, but CNN lacks understanding of detailed information.

3.2   Recurrent Neural Network (RNN)

Recurrent neural network (RNN) is a neural network structure for processing sequential data [16], the basic principle of which lies in the presence of recurrent connections in the network, which gives the network the ability to memorise and capture the dependencies in the time series. However, pure RNN is difficult to capture long-term temporal correlations because it cannot deal with the problem of exponential explosion of weights or gradient disappearance with recursion, and the variant of recurrent neural network, Long Short-Term Memory Network (LSTM) can solve this problem very well.

The trajectory of vehicles is serialized data with a temporal order. To some extent, LSTM demonstrates good applicability in predicting vehicle trajectories. B. Kim et al. [17] obtain a large amount of motion trajectory data from sensor measurements during vehicle driving processes. They input the trajectory data into an LSTM network to learn complex motion information of surrounding vehicles and predict their future positions. The method marked a new beginning for the application of LSTM in the field of vehicle trajectory prediction. F. Altché et al. [18] introduce a Long Short-Term Memory (LSTM) neural network and propose the first step of consistent trajectory prediction. The model accurately predicts the lateral and longitudinal trajectories of vehicles on highways. A. Zyner et al. [19] propose a multimodal trajectory prediction method based on uncertainty by using a recursive neural network combining with a mixture density network output layer. The method predicts the driving intentions at urban intersections. B. Kim et al. [20] consider lane information that previous researchers had overlooked. They focus on the lane information in the semantic map and propose a new lane-aware prediction (LaPred) network. LaPred uses an LSTM network to fuse the candidate lane features of the target agent with the joint features of adjacent agents. It further combines all candidate lane features with attention weights learned through self-supervised learning tasks to determine the candidate lane that the target agent may follow. In [21], N. Deo et al. propose a high-speed highway vehicle interaction-aware motion prediction model based on an LSTM network. The model consists of an LSTM trajectory encoder, maneuver classes branch, and LSTM trajectory decoder, forming a typical encoder-decoder structure. A. Ip et al. [22] verify the high performance and low computation time advantages of LSTM network models through experiments. In [23] and [24], K. Wang and L. Lin respectively model trajectory in terms of time and space. RNN can effectively model the time dimension of trajectory sequences to a certain extent, but it is often easy to overlook the impact of spatial dimensions on prediction.

3.3   Graph Neural Networks (GNN)

In the task of vehicle trajectory prediction, there is significant social interaction between vehicles and between lanes, which has a large impact. By utilizing the characteristics of graph structures, and modeling the complex relationship between vehicles and roads can lead to more accurate future trajectory predictions. Graph neural networks can consider a wider range of contextual information, such as traffic flow, road topology, and intersections. In the task of vehicle trajectory prediction, there is significant social interaction between vehicles and between lanes, which has a large impact. By utilizing the characteristics of graph structures, and modeling the complex relationship between vehicles and roads can lead to more accurate future trajectory predictions. Currently, Graph neural networks can consider a wider range of contextual information, such as traffic flow, road topology, and intersections.

Currently, a large number of methods use Graph Neural Networks (GNNs) and Graph attention networks (GAT) for modeling and extracting spatiotemporal information. Salzmann et al. [25] propose a model that integrates intelligent agent motion states and heterogeneous data (such as semantic graphs) to predict multimodal vehicle trajectories. Deo et al. [26] introduce a new trajectory prediction method called Policy-guided Prediction (PGP), which consists of a lane graph encoder, a policy header, and a trajectory decoder. The policy header ensures lateral changes (lane changes, turns, etc.) of the vehicle, while the latent variable z ensures longitudinal changes (acceleration, deceleration, etc.). LaneR-CNN [27] uses GNNs to capture the mapping relationship between participants and map information for map perception. J. Li et al. [28] design a general neural network system (STG-DAT) for multi-agent trajectory prediction. This system incorporates a graph dual-attention network to extract features from spatiotemporal dynamic graphs. Singh et al. [29] focus on road information, representing road entities as nodes and their relationships as edges. The graph structure is input to temporal and spatial convolutional blocks for GNN modeling to capture spatiotemporal correlations. J. Chen et al. [30] utilize spatiotemporal graphs to extract vehicle interaction information and design an end-to-end Variational Autoencoder (VAE) for generating multimodal prediction information. Z. Sheng et al. [31] propose a graph-based Spatiotemporal Convolutional Network (GSTCN) that predicts future trajectory states of all adjacent vehicles based on historical trajectory information. Z. Li et al. [32] introduce a hierarchical GNN framework combined with an LSTM model to predict trajectories of different types of traffic participants. Park et al. [33] improve upon previous trajectory prediction methods by using GNNs to model the relationships between vehicles and addressing the limitations in modeling vehicle relationships. GNN enables effective interaction between multiple agents and the environment, and appropriate graph structure design will lead to computational accuracy and complexity.

3.4   Attention Mechanism (AM)

In vehicle trajectory prediction, the use of attention mechanisms allows adaptive focusing on the most relevant parts of the trajectory during the prediction process. By encoding the historical trajectories and environmental information and weighting them using attention mechanisms [34], the model can better capture crucial temporal and spatial contexts. Vehicle trajectory prediction methods based on attention mechanisms demonstrate excellent accuracy and robustness.

Bhat et al. [35] design an end-to-end vehicle trajectory prediction model called Trajformer, which uses a self-attention-based backbone to learn social interactions and generate multimodal prediction distributions. K. Messaoud et al. [36] employ attention mechanisms to emphasize the influence of adjacent vehicles on their future trajectory prediction. In [37], Y. Cai et al. propose an environmental-attention Network model (EA-Net) to extract social interaction information between vehicles and the surrounding environment. The model primarily uses modules composed of Graph Attention Networks (GAT) embedded in LSTM encoders-decoders and Convolutional Social Pooling to extract environmental feature information, similar to the pedestrian trajectory prediction method in [38]. [39] uses transformer sequence representation to model both time and social dimensions simultaneously. Y. Liu et al. [40] also use Transformers with map and historical trajectory information for trajectory prediction. X. Chen et al. [41,42] two propose a vehicle trajectory prediction method based on a spatiotemporal dynamic attention network, and introduce a feature fusion mechanism based on driving intent to incorporate the extracted spatiotemporal and social interaction information into the multimodal vehicle trajectory prediction task. Liu et al. [43] develop an end-to-end attention-based trajectory prediction model called LAformer, which takes historical trajectories and HD maps as input and outputs a set of multimodal predicted trajectory distributions. A large amount of previous research has demonstrated the effectiveness of using attention mechanisms for spatiotemporal modeling of trajectories, modeling their interdependence by calculating the attention values between agents.

3.5   Mixed Model

Due to the complexity of the vehicle trajectory prediction scenario, there is a certain one-sidedness in the extraction of features by a single model, while the mixed model uses a combination of multiple models according to the needs of the actual situation to more comprehensively utilise the information of temporal and spatial features to effectively improve the accuracy and robustness of the trajectory prediction task. Common mixed models include the use of long short term memory (LSTM) networks combined with graph neural networks and so on.

   Cheng et al. [44] propose a trajectory prediction model called GATraj, based on graph attention model (GAT), which uses attention mechanism to extract trajectory features and implements interactions between agents using graph neural networks (GNN), thus improving the speed of trajectory prediction. Y. Wang et al. [45] combine attention mechanism with generative adversarial networks (GANs) to improve the effective extraction and utilization of trajectory information. Y. Liu et al. [46] propose a trajectory prediction framework based on a multi-agent, multimodal graph attention isomorphic network (GAIN) to improve the interaction capabilities and computational efficiency among multiple agents. The mixed model requires significant computational overhead, and by combining the advantages of multiple models, the model has high accuracy and multimodality.

4   Evaluation

Each method has its unique characteristics, and Table 1 shows typical methods based on deep learning. In this part, we will first introduce the commonly used

experimental datasets in vehicle trajectory prediction. And, we propose existing
metrics to evaluate experiments. Finally, we compare existing methods using the
evaluation metrics.

Table 1. The mainstream methods based on deep learning

Model	Classification	Year	Encoder	Interaction Module	Decoder
Desire [11]	CNN+RNN	2017	GRU	Social Pooling	GRU
MTP [12]	CNN	2019	CNN	-	Trajectory Set Generator
Deo [14]	CNN+RNN	2018	LSTM	Convolutional Social Pooling	LSTM
Deo [21]	RNN	2018	LSTM	Maneuver Encoder	LSTM
LaPred [20]	RNN	2021	LSTM	Lane Attention Block	CNN
PGP [26]	GNN	2022	GNN	Policy Header	Trajectory Decoder
GSTCN [31]	GNN	2022	GCN	Temporal Dependency	GRU
Messaoud [36]	Attention	2021	LSTM	Multi-Head Attention	LSTM
LAformer [43]	Attention+GNN	2023	GRU	Attention+GNN	Refinement module

4.1   Dataset

Argoverse [7]: The dataset is the first autonomous driving car dataset that
includes "HD maps" (high-definition maps). We are interested in the Motion
Forecasting dataset within Argoverse, which consists of 327,790 valuable scenes
extracted from over 1,000 h of driving data. Each scene includes the 5-second trajectory of the autonomous vehicle, along with tracking of all other participants
(such as cars, pedestrians).

nuScenes [8]: The nuScenes dataset, launched in 2019, is the first dataset to
include a suite of sensors for autonomous driving. The dataset consists of 1000
driving scenes (in the cities of Boston and Singapore), each lasting 20 s. Among
them, 850 scenes are for training and validation, while 150 scenes are for testing.
The dataset allows predicting the future motion trajectory of an agent for up to
6 s based on the agent's past 2 s of historical trajectory.

4.2   Evaluation Indicators

Average Displacement Error (ADE): Average Displacement Error is obtained by
calculating the Euclidean distance between the predicted position at each time
step in the predicted trajectory and the corresponding position in the ground
truth trajectory, and then averaging the distances across all time steps. The
formula for Average Displacement Error is shown as follows.

$$ADE = \frac{1}{k} \sum_{i=1}^{k} \frac{1}{t_h} \sum_{t=1}^{t_h} \sqrt{(y_{i,t}^{(f)} - y_{i,t})^2 + (x_{i,t}^{(f)} - x_{i,t})^2} \tag{1}$$

where, $x_{i,t}^{(f)}$ and $y_{i,t}^{(f)}$ respectively represent the predicted horizontal and vertical coordinates of the target agent at future time t, while $x_{i,t}$ and $y_{i,t}$ denote the actual horizontal and vertical coordinates of the target agent at future time t.

Final Displacement Error (FDE): The Final Displacement Error refers to the difference or deviation between the predicted trajectory and the actual trajectory at the last time step (typically at the end of the predicted time range). The formula for Final Displacement Error is shown as follows.

$$FDE = \frac{1}{k} \sum_{i=1}^{k} \sqrt{(y_i^{(f)} - y_i)^2 + (x_i^{(f)} - x_i)^2} \qquad (2)$$

where, $x_i^{(f)}$ and $y_i^{(f)}$ respectively represent the predicted horizontal and vertical coordinates of the target agent at a future endpoint, while x_i and y_i denote the actual horizontal and vertical coordinates of the target agent at the same moment.

Table 2. Trajectory prediction performance on the Argoverse dataset test set.

Model	ADE_5	FDE_5	ADE_6	FDE_6
GAI [46]	0.83	1.52	–	–
LaneRCNN [27]	0.77	1.19	–	–
Lapred [20]	0.76	1.55	0.71	1.44
MMtTrans [40]	–	–	0.71	1.15
FRM [33]	–	–	0.68	0.99
LAformer [43]	–	–	0.64	0.92
Singh [29]	**0.53**	**0.87**	–	–

Table 3. Trajectory prediction performance on the test set based on the nuScenes dataset.

Model	ADE_5	ADE_{10}	FDE_{10}
Trajectron++ [25]	1.88	1.51	9.52
GATraj [44]	1.87	1.46	–
AgentFormer [39]	1.86	1.45	–
Lapred [20]	1.53	1.12	8.37
PGP [26]	1.30	1.00	7.17
LAFormer [43]	1.19	0.93	–
FRM [33]	**1.18**	**0.88**	**6.59**

4.3   Existing Main Results

In this section, we compare the results of the aforementioned paper methods based on the Argoverse and nuScenes datasets. Based on the characteristics of experimental data and existing literature, we evaluated the Average Displacement Error (ADE) and Final Displacement Error (FDE) on the Argoverse dataset using mode counts (k) 5 and 6. For the nuScenes dataset, we employed mode counts (k) 5 and 10 for ADE evaluation, and mode count (k) 10 for FDE evaluation. We have chosen to present experimental results from papers that currently demonstrate superior performance, and all data were sourced from published papers, and the performance results are shown in Table 2 and Table 3, respectively.

Comparing the experimental results with the experimental processing flow mentioned above, it is common to establish relatively ideal conditions in experiments to enhance prediction performance. However, in real driving scenarios, the complexity and specificity of traffic scenes may significantly impact prediction performance. This constitutes a challenge for current technology and potentially indicates future directions for development.

5   Outlook

In this section, we will analyze the shortcomings of the current vehicle trajectory prediction and autonomous driving field based on the above experimental results and the real situation, so that subsequent researchers can explore the technical bottlenecks of the future trajectory prediction direction based on the following shortcomings. (As shown in Table 4: Comparison of advantages and disadvantages of deep learning methods).

Modeling Complex Traffic Environments: Vehicle trajectory prediction requires understanding and modeling of complex traffic environment information such as interaction between vehicles and road topology. Existing studies often use Attention Mechanisms (AM), Graph Neural Networks (GNN), etc. to establish interaction-aware module modeling, but still face the difficulties of insufficient understanding of real complex traffic scenarios, and the prediction accuracy needs to be improved.

Real-time and Efficiency: For the real driving environment, vehicles need to make instant predictions and decisions based on the existing environmental conditions, and more efficient algorithms and system design are the key research directions in the future.

Inter-Vehicle Communication: Efficient inter-vehicle communication can provide more information about the behaviour of the surrounding vehicles, thus increasing the accuracy of inter-vehicle interactions to improve trajectory prediction. In the future, inter-vehicle communication techniques can be further researched and explored in conjunction with Telematics to enable inter-vehicle collaboration and sharing of prediction results.

Table 4. Comparison of advantages and disadvantages based on deep learning methods.

Deep Learning Method	Advantages	Disadvantages
Convolutional Neural Network (CNN)	- Suitable for processing trajectories with regular structures	- Not suitable for handling variable-length sequences
	- Possesses local perception ability, capturing local features	- Difficulties in handling long-term dependencies
Recurrent Neural Network (RNN)	- Suitable for processing sequential data, good at modeling time dependencies	- Prone to vanishing/exploding gradient problems
	- Capable of handling variable-length sequences, suitable for variable-length trajectory data	- May suffer from information forgetting in long-term dependency tasks
Graph Neural Network (GNN)	- Able to capture social interaction information among traffic participants	- More complex in graph construction and processing, computationally expensive
	- Suitable for dealing with complex relationships in traffic scenarios	- Requires more computational resources for larger-scale graphs
Attention Mechanism	- Adaptive focus on important parts of trajectories	- Possibility of uneven attention weight distribution, introducing uncertainties
	- Suitable for extracting the importance of specific interaction relationships	- May still encounter information forgetting in long-term dependency tasks
Mixed Model	- Combines advantages of multiple models, providing a more comprehensive trajectory modeling	- More complex model design, requiring more tuning and optimization
	- Has advantages in handling multimodal data and complex traffic scenarios	- May require more data and computational resources

6   Conclusions

In this paper, we first provide a comprehensive review of existing methods for vehicle trajectory prediction using deep learning algorithms. We classify mainstream algorithms for vehicle trajectory prediction into Convolutional Neural Networks (CNN), Recurrent Neural Networks (RNN), Graph Neural Networks (GNN), Attention Mechanisms (AM), and Mixed Models, and summarize the commonalities in the literature from these perspectives. Additionally, we show the current research progress in trajectory prediction based on the nuScenes and Argoverse datasets. Finally, we provide an outlook on the future development trend of trajectory prediction for researchers to achieve greater breakthroughs.

References

1. Jin, B., Jiu, B., Su, T., Liu, H., Liu, G.: Switched Kalman filter-interacting multiple model algorithm based on optimal autoregressive model for manoeuvring target tracking. IET Radar Sonar Navig. **9**(2), 199–209 (2015)
2. Chen, J., Zhang, C., Luo, J., Xie, J., Wan, Y.: Driving maneuvers prediction based autonomous driving control by deep Monte Carlo tree search. IEEE Trans. Veh. Technol. **69**(7), 7146–7158 (2020)
3. Lim, Q., Johari, K., Tan, U.X.: Gaussian process auto regression for vehicle center coordinates trajectory prediction. In: TENCON 2019–2019 IEEE Region 10 Conference (TENCON), pp. 25–30. IEEE (2019)
4. Mosharafian, S., Razzaghpour, M., Fallah, Y.P., Velni, J.M.: Gaussian process based stochastic model predictive control for cooperative adaptive cruise control. In: 2021 IEEE Vehicular Networking Conference (VNC), pp. 17–23. IEEE (2021)
5. Tomar, R.S., Verma, S., Tomar, G.S.: SVM based trajectory predictions of lane changing vehicles. In: 2011 International Conference on Computational Intelligence and Communication Networks, pp. 716–721. IEEE (2011)
6. Izquierdo, R., Parra, I., Muñoz-Bulnes, J., Fernández-Llorca, D., Sotelo, M.: Vehicle trajectory and lane change prediction using ANN and SVM classifiers. In: 2017 IEEE 20th International Conference on Intelligent Transportation Systems (ITSC), pp. 1–6. IEEE (2017)
7. Chang, M.F., et al.: Argoverse: 3D tracking and forecasting with rich maps. In: Proceedings of the IEEE/CVF Conference on Computer Vision and Pattern Recognition, pp. 8748–8757 (2019)
8. Caesar, H., et al.: nuscenes: a multimodal dataset for autonomous driving. In: Proceedings of the IEEE/CVF Conference on Computer Vision and Pattern Recognition, pp. 11621–11631 (2020)
9. Gu, J., et al.: Recent advances in convolutional neural networks. Pattern Recogn. **77**, 354–377 (2018)
10. Bojarski, M., et al.: Explaining how a deep neural network trained with end-to-end learning steers a car. arXiv preprint arXiv:1704.07911 (2017)
11. Lee, N., Choi, W., Vernaza, P., Choy, C.B., Torr, P.H., Chandraker, M.: DESIRE: distant future prediction in dynamic scenes with interacting agents. In: Proceedings of the IEEE Conference on Computer Vision and Pattern Recognition, pp. 336–345 (2017)
12. Cui, H., et al.: Multimodal trajectory predictions for autonomous driving using deep convolutional networks. In: 2019 International Conference on Robotics and Automation (ICRA), pp. 2090–2096. IEEE (2019)
13. Phan-Minh, T., Grigore, E.C., Boulton, F.A., Beijbom, O., Wolff, E.M.: CoverNet: multimodal behavior prediction using trajectory sets. In: Proceedings of the IEEE/CVF Conference on Computer Vision and Pattern Recognition, pp. 14074–14083 (2020)
14. Deo, N., Trivedi, M.M.: Convolutional social pooling for vehicle trajectory prediction. In: Proceedings of the IEEE Conference on Computer Vision and Pattern Recognition Workshops, pp. 1468–1476 (2018)
15. Hong, J., Sapp, B., Philbin, J.: Rules of the road: predicting driving behavior with a convolutional model of semantic interactions. In: Proceedings of the IEEE/CVF Conference on Computer Vision and Pattern Recognition, pp. 8454–8462 (2019)
16. Yu, Y., Si, X., Hu, C., Zhang, J.: A review of recurrent neural networks: LSTM cells and network architectures. Neural Comput. **31**(7), 1235–1270 (2019)

17. Kim, B., Kang, C.M., Kim, J., Lee, S.H., Chung, C.C., Choi, J.W.: Probabilistic vehicle trajectory prediction over occupancy grid map via recurrent neural network. In: 2017 IEEE 20Th International Conference on Intelligent Transportation Systems (ITSC), pp. 399–404. IEEE (2017)
18. Altché, F., de La Fortelle, A.: An LSTM network for highway trajectory prediction. In: 2017 IEEE 20th International Conference on Intelligent Transportation Systems (ITSC), pp. 353–359. IEEE (2017)
19. Zyner, A., Worrall, S., Nebot, E.: Naturalistic driver intention and path prediction using recurrent neural networks. IEEE Trans. Intell. Transp. Syst. **21**(4), 1584–1594 (2019)
20. Kim, B., et al.: LaPred: lane-aware prediction of multi-modal future trajectories of dynamic agents. In: Proceedings of the IEEE/CVF Conference on Computer Vision and Pattern Recognition, pp. 14636–14645 (2021)
21. Deo, N., Trivedi, M.M.: Multi-modal trajectory prediction of surrounding vehicles with maneuver based LSTMs. In: 2018 IEEE Intelligent Vehicles Symposium (IV), pp. 1179–1184. IEEE (2018)
22. Ip, A., Irio, L., Oliveira, R.: Vehicle trajectory prediction based on LSTM recurrent neural networks. In: 2021 IEEE 93rd Vehicular Technology Conference (VTC2021-Spring), pp. 1–5. IEEE (2021)
23. Wang, K., Qian, Y., An, T., Zhang, Z., Zhang, J.: LSTM-based prediction method of surrounding vehicle trajectory. In: 2022 International Conference on Artificial Intelligence in Everything (AIE), pp. 100–105. IEEE (2022)
24. Lin, L., Li, W., Bi, H., Qin, L.: Vehicle trajectory prediction using LSTMs with spatial-temporal attention mechanisms. IEEE Intell. Transp. Syst. Mag. **14**(2), 197–208 (2021)
25. Salzmann, T., Ivanovic, B., Chakravarty, P., Pavone, M.: Trajectron++: dynamically-feasible trajectory forecasting with heterogeneous data. In: Vedaldi, A., Bischof, H., Brox, T., Frahm, J.M. (eds.) ECCV 2020. LNCS, vol. 12363, pp. 683–700. Springer, Cham (2020). https://doi.org/10.1007/978-3-030-58523-5_40
26. Deo, N., Wolff, E., Beijbom, O.: Multimodal trajectory prediction conditioned on lane-graph traversals. In: Conference on Robot Learning, pp. 203–212. PMLR (2022)
27. Zeng, W., Liang, M., Liao, R., Urtasun, R.: LaneRCNN: distributed representations for graph-centric motion forecasting. In: 2021 IEEE/RSJ International Conference on Intelligent Robots and Systems (IROS), pp. 532–539. IEEE (2021)
28. Li, J., Ma, H., Zhang, Z., Li, J., Tomizuka, M.: Spatio-temporal graph dual-attention network for multi-agent prediction and tracking. IEEE Trans. Intell. Transp. Syst. **23**(8), 10556–10569 (2021)
29. Singh, D., Srivastava, R.: Graph neural network with RNNs based trajectory prediction of dynamic agents for autonomous vehicle. Appl. Intell. **52**(11), 12801–12816 (2022). https://doi.org/10.1007/s10489-021-03120-9
30. Chen, J., Chen, G., Li, Z., Wu, Y., Knoll, A.: Multimodal vehicle trajectory prediction based on graph convolutional networks. In: 2022 International Conference on Advanced Robotics and Mechatronics (ICARM), pp. 605–610. IEEE (2022)
31. Sheng, Z., Xu, Y., Xue, S., Li, D.: Graph-based spatial-temporal convolutional network for vehicle trajectory prediction in autonomous driving. IEEE Trans. Intell. Transp. Syst. **23**(10), 17654–17665 (2022)
32. Li, Z., Lu, C., Yi, Y., Gong, J.: A hierarchical framework for interactive behaviour prediction of heterogeneous traffic participants based on graph neural network. IEEE Trans. Intell. Transp. Syst. **23**(7), 9102–9114 (2021)

33. Park, D., Ryu, H., Yang, Y., Cho, J., Kim, J., Yoon, K.J.: Leveraging future relationship reasoning for vehicle trajectory prediction. arXiv preprint arXiv:2305.14715 (2023)
34. Vaswani, A., et al.: Attention is all you need. In: Advances in Neural Information Processing Systems, vol. 30 (2017)
35. Bhat, M., Francis, J., Oh, J.: Trajformer: trajectory prediction with local self-attentive contexts for autonomous driving. arXiv preprint arXiv:2011.14910 (2020)
36. Messaoud, K., Yahiaoui, I., Verroust-Blondet, A., Nashashibi, F.: Attention based vehicle trajectory prediction. IEEE Trans. Intell. Veh. **6**(1), 175–185 (2020)
37. Cai, Y., et al.: Environment-attention network for vehicle trajectory prediction. IEEE Trans. Veh. Technol. **70**(11), 11216–11227 (2021)
38. Zhou, X., Zhao, W., Wang, A., Wang, C., Zheng, S.: Spatiotemporal attention-based pedestrian trajectory prediction considering traffic-actor interaction. IEEE Trans. Veh. Technol. **72**(1), 297–311 (2022)
39. Yuan, Y., Weng, X., Ou, Y., Kitani, K.M.: AgentFormer: agent-aware transformers for socio-temporal multi-agent forecasting. In: Proceedings of the IEEE/CVF International Conference on Computer Vision, pp. 9813–9823 (2021)
40. Liu, Y., Zhang, J., Fang, L., Jiang, Q., Zhou, B.: Multimodal motion prediction with stacked transformers. In: Proceedings of the IEEE/CVF Conference on Computer Vision and Pattern Recognition, pp. 7577–7586 (2021)
41. Chen, X., Zhang, H., Zhao, F., Hu, Y., Tan, C., Yang, J.: Intention-aware vehicle trajectory prediction based on spatial-temporal dynamic attention network for internet of vehicles. IEEE Trans. Intell. Transp. Syst. **23**(10), 19471–19483 (2022)
42. Chen, X., Zhang, H., Zhao, F., Cai, Y., Wang, H., Ye, Q.: Vehicle trajectory prediction based on intention-aware non-autoregressive transformer with multi-attention learning for internet of vehicles. IEEE Trans. Instrum. Meas. **71**, 1–12 (2022)
43. Liu, M., et al.: LAformer: trajectory prediction for autonomous driving with lane-aware scene constraints. arXiv preprint arXiv:2302.13933 (2023)
44. Cheng, H., Liu, M., Chen, L., Broszio, H., Sester, M., Yang, M.Y.: GATraj: a graph-and attention-based multi-agent trajectory prediction model. arXiv preprint arXiv:2209.07857 (2022)
45. Wang, Y., Chen, W., Wang, C., Wang, S.: Vehicle trajectory prediction based on attention mechanism and GAN. In: 2021 7th International Conference on Systems and Informatics (ICSAI), pp. 1–6. IEEE (2021)
46. Liu, Y., Qi, X., Sisbot, E.A., Oguchi, K.: Multi-agent trajectory prediction with graph attention isomorphism neural network. In: 2022 IEEE Intelligent Vehicles Symposium (IV), pp. 273–279. IEEE (2022)

Predicting Turning Points in Air Quality: A Dual-Guided Denoising Teacher-Student Learning Approach

Jinxiao Fan[✉], Pengfei Wang, Liang Liu, and Huadong Ma

Beijing University of Posts and Telecommunications, Beijing, China
{jinxiaofan,wangpengfei,liangliu,mhd}@princeton.edu

Abstract. The increasing application of IoT technology has facilitated the widespread deployment of air quality stations, making accurate air quality prediction increasingly essential for ensuring the stability of our daily lives and work environments. In this task, predicting abrupt changes or turning points is of utmost significance, as it helps to mitigate risk and prevent losses. However, the problems of future information deficiency and irrelevant sequence noise mislead the result to suboptimal performance. To overcome this problem, we propose a **D**ual-guided **D**enoising **T**eacher-**S**tudent learning approach (named TS-D^2) to predict turning points in air quality. Since the complete distribution of turning points encompasses past and future data, we design a teacher network that integrates future data to guide the student network's learning process that relies solely on the historical sequence. To only absorb credibly relevant features, the teacher network adds a Gumbel-enhanced denoising strategy for optimizing sequence. Based on this well-trained teacher, our student network employs a dual-guided learning mechanism to adaptively excavate important and salient knowledge for training and optimization purposes. Finally, we validate the effectiveness of our proposed TS-D^2 through extensive experiments conducted on three real-world datasets. The results demonstrate that our approach outperforms existing state-of-the-art baselines.

Keywords: IoT sensing data · Air quality monitoring · Time-series analysis · Deep learning

1 Introduction

Air quality significantly impacts various human outdoor activities, such as work, socializing, and travel. A recent report from the World Health Organization (WHO) reveals that nearly all of the global population (99%) is exposed to air containing high levels of pollutants that exceed the WHO guideline limits. Therefore, to facilitate prompt and informed decision-making, it has become increasingly necessary to predict and analyze air quality [12,33]. In particular, predicting abrupt changes or turning points in air quality data holds significant

© The Author(s), under exclusive license to Springer Nature Singapore Pte Ltd. 2024
L. Wang et al. (Eds.): CWSN 2023, CCIS 1994, pp. 286–300, 2024.
https://doi.org/10.1007/978-981-97-1010-2_21

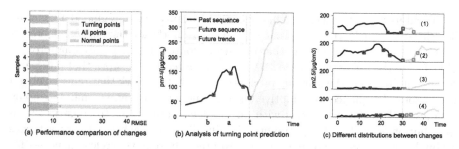

Fig. 1. A motivating sample to analyze turning point prediction. (a) The performance of LSTM for air quality prediction, measured by RMSE, differs among change points, normal points, and all points. The PM$_{2.5}$ data is sampled eight times, revealing that predicting change points is still more challenging. (b) Analysis of turning point prediction. Given the PM$_{2.5}$ time series containing historical and future data that draws boundaries by dashed lines. Three future trends affect the changing state at time t. (c) Different distributions between changes. The target predictions of (1) and (2) are turning points, (3) and (4) are normal points, and their relevant points are marked with red circles. (Color figure online)

importance as it is conducive to mitigating risks and preventing losses. Unfortunately, existing air quality prediction methods primarily focus on estimating the overall accuracy of time series, often neglecting the analysis of turning points in particulate matter concentrations, despite their small proportion but significant impact [8, 25]. As shown in Fig. 1(a), the disparity in performance between predicting turning points and normal points emphasizes the urgent challenge of achieving more precise predictions for turning points.

Turning point prediction is an analytical method that aims to forecast series changes associated with abrupt and significant increases (or decreases) transitioning to decreasing (or increasing) trends. Figure 1(c) demonstrates the distinguishable distribution or shape patterns between turning points and normal points. Utilizing these differences in modeling can help improve prediction accuracy. However, it may be affected by low data quality. (1) **Future information deficiency**. In contrast to traditional air quality prediction tasks that use DNN-based models (e.g., GRU [3], DeepAir [30]) to predict the next point directly from the historical sequence, determining whether the current point represents a turning point requires considering both its historical and future nearby points to understand its complete trend. This comprehensive analysis also aligns with retrospective change point detection methods like KL-CPD [7]. Under the circumstances, we can exploit a teacher model that grasps the complete structural information to supervise the learning of the student model inspired by [29]. (2) **Irrelevant sequence noise**. While some existing methods attempt to explore the inconsistency in distribution with the assumption of known future [7, 10], they often suffer from a deficiency. These methods tend to consider all points within a fixed window, which can introduce potential noise and complicate the learning process of local distribution. As shown in Fig. 1(c), the relevant features for the target prediction are indicated by the parts marked with red circles.

To address these issues, in this paper, we propose a **D**ual-guided **D**enoising **T**eacher-**S**tudent learning approach (TS-D^2 for short) for turning point prediction in air quality. Considering that the future context is practically unapproachable during the prediction phase [31], we design a teacher network that integrates future data to guide the learning process of a student network that relies solely on the historical sequence. In adaptive teacher-student learning, we mainly employ a series of Transformer blocks with an input encoding layer to construct local distribution regarding target points. Specifically, the teacher network attaches a Gumbel-enhanced denoising strategy to precisely remove irrelevant noises for optimizing sequence. Based on this well-trained teacher, the student network uses a dual-guided learning mechanism to learn and excavate valuable knowledge for training and optimization. Finally, we evaluate the effectiveness of our proposed model based on four air quality datasets. In total, the contributions of our work are as follows:

- We focus on a novel task in air quality – Turning points prediction. And for that, we propose an adaptive teacher-student learning to solve the two problems: future information deficiency and irrelevant sequence noise.
- To address this, a well-trained teacher network integrates future data and implements a Gumbel-augmented denoising strategy to construct an accurate local distribution. Furthermore, the student network is designed to leverage a dual-guided learning mechanism, enabling it to extract comprehensive and precise knowledge during training and optimization.
- We conducted extensive experiments on three real-world datasets collected from air quality stations. Our proposed method helped the model achieve better forecast performance over time series forecasting and detection methods.

2   Related Work

In this section, we first compare existing works of anomalies, change points, and turning points. And then, we provide a brief overview of air quality prediction.

2.1   Anomalies, Change Points, and Turning Points

Detecting and identifying the emergence of abrupt changes and anomalies in time series have been intensively studied over the past several decades, which leads to three analogous concepts: anomalies, change points, and turning points. They are usually rare and hidden by a large number of normal points, thus making data labeling and sequence analysis difficult. Specifically:

Anomalies (also known as outliers) are the measurable consequences of the changes in time series, which are outside of their local or global patterns [6]. Plenty of approaches have been proposed for the anomaly detection task. The common unsupervised algorithms, such as MAD-GAN [18] and Anomaly Transformer [28], usually forecast or reconstruct multivariate time series and compares a predefined threshold with prediction error or reconstruction error to detect anomalies respectively. Additionally, the existing supervised learning approaches [21,27] extract features from time series and use well-extracted feature vectors to detect anomalies.

Change points are abrupt variations in time series data. Unlike anomalies, change points can represent transitions between two normal states due to external events or internal changes [20]. Therefore, most existing methods generally detect change points based on their temporal continuity, curve shape, and data distribution [19]. Specifically, unsupervised methods generally find change points according to particular features by segmenting time series, which have combined the Bayesian [1], the Gaussian process [4], and two-sample test [7] with some success. In addition, many supervised methods [5,13] have been employed and designed for change point detection. These approaches possess a more straightforward training phase as binary classifiers while providing more adequate training data for each category.

Turning points are points in the time series where there are significant changes from increasing (decreasing) to decreasing (increasing). It characterizes changes in trend patterns, as shown in Fig. 1(b). Many traditional efforts mainly focused on the issue of next-value prediction [22,35], which does not lay particular emphasis on predicting rare turning points. In addition, the research correlated with turning point forecasting has some progress in stock analysis. [24] integrated piecewise linear representation and weighted support vector machine for predicting turning points. And [9] utilizes the chaos theory to analyze time series and model the nonlinear dynamic system to predict turning points. However, these methods in regression prediction tasks heavily depend on historical observations, which can be restrictive in their effectiveness. In this work, we introduce a novel learning approach that integrates future data without any data leakage, thereby enabling precise and reliable turning point predictions.

2.2 Air Quality Forecasting

Air quality forecasting has a good study history in the literature, and extensive research indicates that air quality forecasting methods can be broadly divided into two categories: (1) Statistical model. These models generally fuse air quality or meteorological data to build forecasting models based on statistics, such as Regression [23], ARIMA [11]. (2) Deep neural network model. DNN-based models are frequently used to extract spatial-temporal features of data and then perform fusion analysis to tackle prediction problems. For instance, RNNs [16] has also been successfully applied to air quality forecasting problems. Subsequently, deep learning-based methods that combine convolutional layers and recurrent layers, such as LSTnet [17] and TPA-LSTM [22], have also demonstrated excellent empirical performance. In addition, the potential of Transformer gets developed, which can perform long sequence air quality prediction. It constructs a self-attention map to obtain the temporal association of each time point. Its variants, Informer [35] achieves better improvement on quadratic complexity and serial correlation. And TimesNet [26] captures intricate temporal patterns based on the observation of multi-periodicity to analyze various time-series analysis

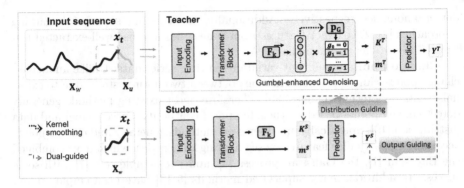

Fig. 2. Over architecture of our Dual-guided Denoising Teacher-Student learning approach (TS-D²). The teacher network incorporates future data and utilizes Gumebed-enhanced denoising strategy to capture highly relevant features and construct precise local distribution for the target points. With the historical sequence provided, the student network learns valuable knowledge using a dual-guided learning mechanism, which involves distribution and output guiding.

tasks. In this paper, we adopt adaptive teacher-student learning, which effectively models the distribution inconsistency between turning points and normal points for the specific task of air quality.

3 Design

3.1 Problem Formulation

In this paper, we focus on turning point prediction in air quality. Let $x_t \in \mathbb{R}^M$ denote the value of a M-dimension variables at time step $t(t \in N)$, with $x_t[i]$ representing i^{th} air quality indicator. Our goal is to predict whether the value of $y_t \in \{0, 1\}$ at t-step is a turning point based on a sequence of w previous observations $X_w = x_{t-w+1}, ..., x_{t-1}, x_t$. Here, we learn a mapping $f(\cdot)$ from X_p to Y by teacher-student learning, where we incorporate future data $X_u = \{x_{t+1}, x_{t+2}..., x_{t+u}\}$ as auxiliary information for teacher network. Specifically, we utilize the cross-entropy loss $\mathcal{L}_{task}$ as the objective function for our teacher network and as the base loss for our student network. We differentiate the teacher and student networks using the superscripts T, S, respectively.

3.2 Adaptive Teacher-Student Learning

As shown in Fig. 2, the well-trained teacher network processes a sequence of training samples $[X_W, X_u]$ to predict the class label y_t. In contrast, the to-be-guided student network only considers the historical sequence $[X_w]$, where $w(w < W)$ denotes the commonly used length of input time series of TS-D². At the core of our method lies a series of Transformer blocks with an input encoding layer. Specifically, the input encoding layer comprises a positional projection and causal convolution block, effectively incorporating sequential information and local dependence. Within each transformer block, layer normalization is applied after computing self-attention and the feed-forward layer, generating hidden features H, which help construct the parameters necessary for the target distribution. Subsequently, the teacher network employs a Gumbel-enhanced denoising strategy to optimize this distribution by removing irrelevant features, followed by inputting a predictor composed of a multi-layer perceptron module. Moreover, given the limited information available about the target distribution, the student network employs a dual-guided learning mechanism to learn valuable knowledge for training and optimization purposes adaptively.

3.3 Gumbel-Enhanced Denoising Strategy

This strategy aims to construct a local distribution by leveraging the kernel smoothing of observed parts, while further denoising to mitigate prediction bias caused by irrelevant features.

We utilize a Radial Basis Function kernel [2] to learn the nonlinear mapping of high-dimensional features, and for the target point t:

$$K_{i,t} = \exp\left(-\gamma \|h_i - h_t\|^2\right) \tag{1}$$

where $i \in [1, W + u]$, and γ is a learnable parameter for controlling the smoothness. While this soft-coding kernel smoothing mechanism mitigates the adverse effects of irrelevant features to some extent, it may introduce some perturbations to the construction of an accurate target prediction distribution. However, traditional hard-coding methods, such as top-k and sampling, are non-differentiable, posing optimization challenges.

To this end, we exploit a Gumbel-Softmax trick [15] for the teacher network to help construct a precise distribution. Intuitively, this trick reparameterizes kernel smoothing as a 2-way categorical variable, which cases for on-off gates and learns two logits G^0, G^1 for each gate. Specifically, our Gumbel-enhanced denoising strategy can be expressed as follows:

$$G_{i,t} = \frac{\exp\left((log(p_{G,i}) + \epsilon_i)/\tau\right)}{\sum_{l=0}^{1} \exp\left((log(p_{G,i}^l) + \epsilon_i^l)/\tau\right)}, \text{where } p_{G,i} = \text{softmax}\left(\text{MLP}(K_{i,t})\right). \tag{2}$$

Here, ϵ_i denotes the two-dimensional noise vector sampled from $Gumbel(0,1)$ distribution to introduce randomness for the selection process. τ is a learned temperature parameter that dynamically adjusts the sharpness of features, and when it approaches 0, $G_{i,t}$ approximates a one-hot vector.

For the student network, denoising the sequence with incomplete structural features poses a challenge as it cannot capture future interactions while learning kernel smoothing. In order to match the knowledge transferred by the teacher network during the dual-guided learning process, we directly integrate the soft-coding information into the student model via Eq. 1. Last, we extrapolate the

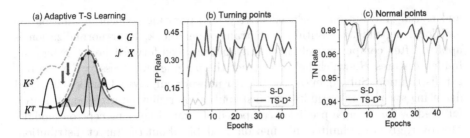

Fig. 3. The training process of my TS-D². (a) Adaptive adjustment of local distribution in teacher-student learning. (bc) Recall curves of TS-D and TS-D² between turning points(true positive rate) and normal points(true negative rate) respectively in varying training epochs.

results by leveraging smooth trends and temporal intensities of the given windows: $y_t = f(K_{:,t} \cdot H)$, where $f(\cdot)$ is a multi-layer perceptron that maps to predictive steps. The student network Adaptively adjusts the local distribution regarding the target points under the guidance of the teacher network, as illustrated in Fig. 3(a).

In terms of the model's computational efficiency, while we haven't introduced specific speed-up modules, it's important to note that due to our sequence length w being significantly smaller than the feature dimension h, the overall complexity can be approximated as $\mathcal{O}(w^2 h) \approx \mathcal{O}(h)$. This means that the computational requirements of our model are effectively controlled by the feature dimension, and we benefit from a favorable computational efficiency given the characteristics of our datasets.

3.4 Dual-Guided Learning

In our work, we aim to obtain a reliable and precise distribution of the target points. We accomplish this by extracting valuable knowledge from the well-trained teacher network using cross-entropy loss. Meanwhile, considering the incomplete structure and unreliable distribution constructed solely from the historical sequence, we recast the knowledge distillation from our teacher network as a multi-objective optimization problem to supervise the student network effectively. To this end, we employ a dual-guided learning mechanism to determine a better optimization direction for the training stage of our student network.

Output Guiding. We first train our student network to learn proper responses from the well-trained teacher network. This is achieved by minimizing the Kullback-Leibler (KL) divergence between the output distributions of the teacher and student networks given pair-wise class probability distribution. And the output-guided loss $\mathcal{L}_{out}$ is expressed as:

$$\mathcal{L}_{out} = \frac{1}{N} \sum_{i=1}^{N} \mathrm{KL}\big(\sigma(\frac{y_i^S}{\tau'}) \parallel \sigma(\frac{y_i^T}{\tau'})\big), \tag{3}$$

where y_i^S, y_i^T represent the class probabilities predicted by the student and teacher networks for the i-th time step change, respectively. The temperature parameter τ' is introduced to achieve the soft labels by scaling the increase of small probabilities. Here, considering these logits of the last layer as conditional targets is advantageous for improving the model's generalization and preventing over-fitting.

Distribution Guiding. Besides applying distillation in the final outputs, we encourage the student network to emulate the precise distribution from the teacher network. By transferring kernel vectors in feature-level granularity, we encourage the student network to compensate for the imperfection in future information deficiency and irrelevant sequence noise. Drawing inspiration from the work in [32], we define the following distribution-guided loss:

$$\mathcal{L}_{disb} = \frac{1}{N \times w} \sum_{i=1}^{N} \sum_{j=1}^{w} \| \frac{G_{j,i}^T}{\|G_{j,i}^T\|_2} - \frac{\Phi(K_{j,i}^S)}{\|\Phi(K_{j,i}^S)\|_2} \|_2, \tag{4}$$

where $\phi(\cdot)$ is respectively the transition functions that are used to align and match their dimensions.

Finally, we summarize our optimization objective using a dual-guided learning mechanism to train the student model. We employ the conventional step-wise cross-entropy loss $\mathcal{L}_{task}$ as our base loss. So, the overall loss is formulated as follows:

$$\mathcal{L}_{ours} = \mathcal{L}_{task} + \beta\mathcal{L}_{out} + \lambda\mathcal{L}_{disb}. \tag{5}$$

Here, β and λ are the weights coefficients of each guiding loss. We set $\beta \in [2, 10]$ and $\lambda \in [10, 100]$ to adapt to different datasets. Within the process of dual-guided learning, our TS-D^2 is designed to acquire proficient decision-making skills while concurrently improving its exploration capabilities.

4   Experiments

4.1   Datasets

We perform experiments on three real-world air quality datasets from Beijing, London, Tianjin, Guangzhou and Shenzhen, as shown in Table 1.

MEMC: This dataset are crawled from Beijing Municipal Ecological and Environmental Monitoring Center[1] from January 1, 2020, to December 31, 2020, in Beijing, China. Each record contains a total of six air quality observations (*i.e.*, PM2.5, PM10, NO2, SO2, O3, and CO).

KDDCUP: This dataset comes from KDD CUP 2018[2], from January 1, 2017, to December 31, 2017, in London, England. Each record contains three quality observations (*i.e.*, PM2.5, PM10, and NO2).

---

[1] http://www.bjmemc.com.cn/.
[2] https://www.biendata.xyz/competition/kdd_2018/data/.

UCTM: This dataset is from the Urban Computing Team in Microsoft Research[3] [34] ranging from May 1, 2014 to April 30, 2015. It covers four major Chinese cities (Beijing, Tianjin, Guangzhou, and Shenzhen) and 39 adjacent cities within 300 km of them. And it has the same six air quality observations as MEMC.

Table 1. Description on three real-world air quality datasets.

Datesets	Samples	Change rate	Stations	Cities
MEMC	59,568	4.92%	34	Beijing
KDDCUP	26,195	5.09%	24	London
UCTM	573,218	5.42%	437	Beijing, Tianjin, Guangzhou, Shenzhen

4.2 Experimental Setup

Baselines. To evaluate the effectiveness of our approach, We compare TS-D^2 against two types of baselines, which are time series forecasting (TSF) methods and time series detection (TSD) methods, respectively.

Table 2. Performance on the MEMC, KDDCUP and UCTM datasets between diferent methods (all the values in the table are percentage numbers with % omited). The best performance in each row is in bold font.

Datasets		MEMC			KDDCUP			UCTM		
Evaluation Metric		AUC	Micro-F1	G-Mean	AUC	Micro-F1	G-Mean	AUC	Micro-F1	G-Mean
TSF	GRU	67.8	71.2	63.1	65.9	69.3	62.1	68.2	74.7	66.8
	DeepAir	70.5	72.1	67.2	68.9	72.4	65.4	71.8	75.9	69.2
	Informer	71.1	72.5	68.3	70.1	72.9	66.5	72.9	76.5	70.1.
	TimesNet	71.7	72.9	68.7	70.0	73.1	67.1	73.2	76.8	69.8
TSD	KL-CPD	60.7	63.3	52.3	60.6	61.8	52.1	58.2	64.1	52.1
	MAD-GAN	65.1	68.6	56.2	63.4	67.8	56.6	66.4	70.6	60.5
	Anomalyformer	71.5	72.6	68.5	69.3	71.1	63.5	72.7	75.9	69.5
TS-D^2		**73.2**	**74.3**	**70.1**	**71.2**	**73.8**	**68.9**	**74.3**	**77.7**	**71.85**

TSF methods primarily focus on capturing sequential dependencies as follows:

1) GRU [3] is a type of recurrent neural network to tackle long-term memory problems.
2) DeepAir [30] is a DNN-based air quality prediction approach that considers direct and indirect factors have different effects on air quality.

---

[3] http://research.microsoft.com/apps/pubs/?id=246398.

3) Informer [35] is an efficient transformer-based model for long sequence time-series forecasting, which achieves $\mathcal{O}(l \log l)$ in time complexity and memory usage.
4) TimesNet [26] extends the analysis of temporal variations into the 2D space to extract both intra-period and inter-period temporal features.

TSD methods include change point detection and anomaly detection:

1) KL-CPD [7] a novel kernel learning framework that combines the latent space of RNNs with RBF kernels to detect change points.
2) MAD-GAN [18] is an anomaly detection method using both the GAN-trained generator and discriminator to model the complex multivariate correlations.
3) Anomalyformer [28] is an anomaly detection method using an Anomaly-Attention mechanism to model the prior-association and series-association.

Evaluation Metrics. We employ the commonly used AUC (Area Under ROC), Macro-F1 (macro F1 score) and G-Mean (geometric mean) to assess the results. We perform significant tests using the paired t-test. Differences are considered statistically significant when the p-value is lower than 0.05.

Parameter Settings. For a fair comparison, the batch size is fixed to 128, and the latent dimension for all models is tuned in the range of [32, 64, 128, 256]. The parameters are initialized with a mean of 0, using normal initializers with a standard deviation of 0.01. We label turning points using a second-order difference strategy [14], and make a simple single-step prediction according to the past 24 (window size) hours records. And we divide the training set, validate set, and test set with a ratio of 7 : 1 : 2. We optimize these methods according to the validation sets and implement them based on the PyTorch framework. All methods are conducted on a Linux server with 4 NVIDIA P100 GPUs. For the teacher network, the future window size is set to 6. The temperature τ is annealed using the schedule $\tau = \max(0.5, \tau \exp(-rt))$ of the global training step t, where r represents the decay rate. We anneal the temperature based on it after 500 steps.

4.3   Experimental Results

Table 2 presents a summary of the experimental outcomes obtained using various methods. These methods have been verified across diverse cities and datasets of varying scales, collectively showcasing the effectiveness and versatility of our approach. Specifically, our observations are as follows:

1) Analysis of TSF methods. We observe that the GRU model had the poorest performance. This can be attributed to its simplicity, as the basic GRU model solely focuses on capturing sequential dependencies in the air quality series without incorporating any auxiliary functions to identify turning points.

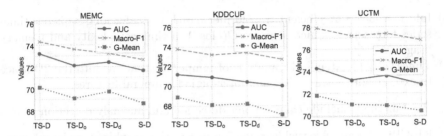

Fig. 4. Comparisons between TS-D^2 and its three variant models TS-D_o, TS-D_d, S-D in term of AUC, Macro-F1, G-Mean metrics on all datasets.

In contrast, the DeepAir model, which captures domain knowledge, outperformed the GRU model regarding prediction accuracy. This outcome underscores the effectiveness of leveraging local distributions to discern crucial patterns and fluctuations that indicate turning points within the air quality data. Furthermore, the transformer-based models, Informer and TimesNet demonstrated superior performance. Both methods employ an attention mechanism to highlight the significance of individual features within the sequence, which are proven to be effective in enhancing the prediction accuracy of turning points.

2) Analysis of TSD methods. We find that Anomalyformer outperforms both KL-CPD and MAD-GAN by effectively leveraging the distinction between local and global dependencies to identify turning points. This approach empowers the model to recognize changes in the data that deviate from historical trends, leading to more precise and dependable predictions. The relatively poorer performance of KL-CPD stems from its inability to access future data. Without complete structural knowledge, its predictive capabilities are limited, highlighting the necessity of incorporating future data for achieving higher accuracy in predictions. In addition, the unsatisfactory performance of MAD-GAN can be attributed to its focus on reconstructing future data while lacking the ability to identify turning points. This limitation emphasizes the significance of explicitly distinguishing changes to enhance predictive performance.

3) Analysis of our TS-D^2. Our proposed TS-D^2 demonstrates superior performance compared to all other methods across all three datasets. This outcome highlights the importance of two critical factors in turning point prediction: integrating future knowledge and constructing distributional inconsistencies. By introducing teacher-student learning, we can achieve precise modeling of the target distribution based on sequence correlation, which effectively enhances the accuracy of turning point prediction without any data leakage.

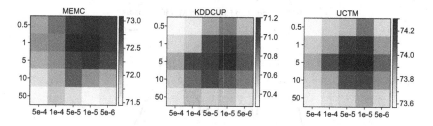

Fig. 5. Heatmap on all datasets. The x-axis denotes the temperature τ, and the y-axis denotes decay rates r. Darker colors indicate better performance on AUC.

4.4 Further Analysis

To validate the effectiveness of our proposed TS-D^2, we conduct further analysis on its parameters and components in the following two aspects.

Analysis on Dual-Guided Learning Mechanism. To verify the effectiveness of dual-learning of the student network, we conduct the following ablation experiments on all datasets, and three variants of TS-D^2 are designed.

- TS-D$_o$: Multi-objective optimization with only output guiding;
- TS-D$_d$: Multi-objective optimization with only distribution guiding;
- S-D: Basic prediction target optimization without any external guidance.

The results, depicted in Fig. 4, clearly illustrate the superior performance of our TS-D^{2}compared to other variants. This advantage can be attributed to the effectiveness of its dual-guided learning mechanism, which facilitates the alignment and exploration of soft targets and intermediate processes, resulting in improved predictive capabilities. The unsatisfactory performance of TS-D$_o$ with only output guiding reinforces the former point, contributing to its poor results. And the performance of S-D with only basic optimization is also inferior to the TS-D$_o$, as it cannot consider local distribution inconsistency. Additionally, the result of TS-D$_d$, without classification knowledge transfer, highlights the significance of output guiding in enhancing the model's predictive capabilities.

Analysis on Gumble-Enhanced Denoising Strategy Effectiveness Analysis. One significant advantage of our TS-D^2 is its ability to address the prediction bias problem caused by irrelevant features. Moreover, using a Gumble-enhanced denoising strategy, the model effectively constructs accurate local distributions. To this end, we introduce a variant of TS-D^2 called TS-D by simplifying the model using a basic soft-encoding, which allows us to assess the impact of our denoising optimization on the model's training capabilities. Here in Fig. 3(bc), we represent the recall curves of TS-D^{2}and TS-D between turning points and normal points, respectively, in various training epochs, *i.e.*, true positive rate and true negate rate. It is easy to see that, in comparison to TS-D, our TS-D^2 exhibits superior convergence during the entire training process.

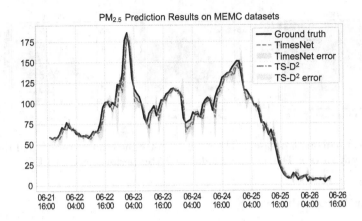

Fig. 6. The comparison of prediction results between our model and TimesNet.

Furthermore, it achieves higher prediction accuracy, notably in improving the prediction of turning points.

Hyper-parameters Analysis. The temperature (τ) and decay rate (r) are two critical hyper-parameters in our Gumble-enhanced denoising process. In this analysis, we explore various combinations of τ and r on all datasets and evaluate how they affect prediction performance. The results, as shown in Fig. 5, revealed that increasing τ initially improves the performance of TS-D^2, emphasizing the significance of a larger initial temperature for a broader sampling range in Eq. 2. However, excessively increasing τ eventually leads to overall performance degradation due to the increased difficulty for the model to converge. On the other hand, fixing τ and using low decay rates r make TS-D^2 difficult to converge, while higher r restrict its ability to explore a broader sampling space. Based on these observations, in our experiments, we set the initial temperature $\tau \in [1, 10]$ and the decay rate $r \in [5e-5, 1e-5]$ to strike a suitable balance between convergence and exploration capabilities.

4.5   Case Study

Here we select PM$_{2.5}$ from the MEMC datasets to conduct a case study. As Fig. 6 shows, the single-step prediction results of TS-D^2 are remarkably closer to the ground truth than TimesNet. Under normal circumstances, our model generates smooth predictions, effectively filtering out small oscillations to combat noise. However, when an abrupt change occurs, TS-D^2 demonstrates a rapid response to adapt it. The superiority of TS-D^2 handling different states can be attributed to its ability to utilize the inconsistency of local distribution to analyze changes effectively. In contrast, TimesNet primarily focuses on multi-periodic temporal features to overlook changes and result in unstable performance.

5   Conclusion

Turning point prediction is an exciting and crucial task in the air quality field, which has not been well explored. In this paper, we formalize this task into a TS-D^2 with adaptive teacher-student learning. Specifically, the teacher network integrates future data and is designed to employ a Gumbel-enhanced denoising strategy to construct a comprehensive and accurate local distribution regarding the target points. The student network merely considers the historical sequence and is designed to imitate the well-trained teacher network by a dual-guided learning mechanism. Empirical results on three real-world datasets demonstrate the feasibility of our proposed model.

References

1. Adams, R.P., MacKay, D.J.: Bayesian online changepoint detection. arXiv preprint arXiv:0710.3742 (2007)
2. Al-Shedivat, M., Wilson, A.G., Saatchi, Y., Hu, Z., Xing, E.P.: Learning scalable deep kernels with recurrent structure. J. Mach. Learn. Res. **18**(1), 2850–2886 (2017)
3. Athira, V., Geetha, P., Vinayakumar, R., Soman, K.: Deepairnet: applying recurrent networks for air quality prediction. Procedia Comput. Sci. **132**, 1394–1403 (2018)
4. Caldarelli, E. et al.: Adaptive gaussian process change point detection. In: ICML, pp. 2542–2571. PMLR (2022)
5. Camci, F.: Change point detection in time series data using support vectors. Int. J. Pattern Recognit. Artif. Intell. **24**(01), 73–95 (2010)
6. Chandola, V., Banerjee, A., Kumar, V.: Anomaly detection: a survey. ACM Comput. Surv. (CSUR) **41**(3), 1–58 (2009)
7. Chang, W.C., Li, C.L., Yang, Y., Póczos, B.: Kernel change-point detection with auxiliary deep generative models. arXiv (2019)
8. Chen, F., et al.: Data mining for the internet of things: literature review and challenges. Int. J. Distrib. Sensor Netw. **11**(8), 431047 (2015)
9. Chen, J., Yang, S., Zhang, D., Nanehkaran, Y.A.: A turning point prediction method of stock price based on RVFL-GMDH and chaotic time series analysis. Knowl. Inf. Syst. **63**(10), 2693–2718 (2021)
10. Deldari, S., Smith, D.V., Xue, H., Salim, F.D.: Time series change point detection with self-supervised contrastive predictive coding. In: WWW, pp. 3124–3135 (2021)
11. Díaz-Robles, L.A., et al.: A hybrid ARIMA and artificial neural networks model to forecast particulate matter in urban areas: the case of Temuco, Chile. Atmos. Environ. **42**(35), 8331–8340 (2008)
12. Godish, T., Fu, J.S.: Air Quality. CRC Press, Boca Raton (2019)
13. Han, M., et al.: Comprehensive context recognizer based on multimodal sensors in a smartphone. Sensors **12**(9), 12588–12605 (2012)
14. Hu, J., Zheng, W.: A deep learning model to effectively capture mutation information in multivariate time series prediction. Knowl.-Based Syst. **203**, 106139 (2020)
15. Jang, E., Gu, S., Poole, B.: Categorical reparameterization with gumbel-softmax. arXiv (2016)
16. Karevan, Z., et al.: Transductive LSTM for time-series prediction: an application to weather forecasting. Neural Netw. **125**, 1–9 (2020)

17. Lai, G., Chang, W.C., Yang, Y., Liu, H.: Modeling long-and short-term temporal patterns with deep neural networks. In: SIGIR, pp. 95–104 (2018)
18. Li, D., Chen, D., Jin, B., Shi, L., Goh, J., Ng, S.K.: MAD-GAN: multivariate anomaly detection for time series data with generative adversarial networks. In: Tetko, I., Kůrková, V., Karpov, P., Theis, F. (eds.) ICANN 2019. LNCS, vol. 11730, pp. 703–716. Springer, Cham (2019). https://doi.org/10.1007/978-3-030-30490-4_56
19. Matteson, D.S., James, N.A.: A nonparametric approach for multiple change point analysis of multivariate data. J. Am. Stat. Assoc. 109(505), 334–345 (2014)
20. Montanez, G., Amizadeh, S., Laptev, N.: Inertial hidden Markov models: modeling change in multivariate time series. In: Proceedings of the AAAI Conference on Artificial Intelligence, vol. 29 (2015)
21. Ren, H., et al.: Time-series anomaly detection service at Microsoft. In: KDD, pp. 3009–3017 (2019)
22. Shih, S.Y., Sun, F.K., Lee, H.Y.: Temporal pattern attention for multivariate time series forecasting. Mach. Learn. 108(8), 1421–1441 (2019)
23. Singh, K., et al.: Linear and nonlinear modeling approaches for urban air quality prediction. Sci. Total Environ. 426, 244–255 (2012)
24. Tang, H., Dong, P., Shi, Y.: A new approach of integrating piecewise linear representation and weighted support vector machine for forecasting stock turning points. Appl. Soft Comput. 78, 685–696 (2019)
25. Weigend, A.S.: Time Series Prediction: Forecasting the Future and Understanding the Past. Routledge, Milton Park (2018)
26. Wu, H., Hu, T., Liu, Y., Zhou, H., Wang, J., Long, M.: Timesnet: Temporal 2d-variation modeling for general time series analysis. arXiv preprint arXiv:2210.02186 (2022)
27. Wu, J., et al.: Multi-task learning based encoder-decoder: a comprehensive detection and diagnosis system for multi-sensor data. Adv. Mech. Eng. 13(5), 16878140211013138 (2021)
28. Xu, J., Wu, H., Wang, J., Long, M.: Anomaly transformer: time series anomaly detection with association discrepancy. arXiv (2021)
29. Yang, C., Xie, L., Su, C., Yuille, A.L.: Snapshot distillation: teacher-student optimization in one generation. In: CVPR, pp. 2859–2868 (2019)
30. Yi, X., Zhang, J., Wang, Z., Li, T., Zheng, Y.: Deep distributed fusion network for air quality prediction. In: Proceedings of the 24th ACM SIGKDD International Conference on Knowledge Discovery & Data Mining, pp. 965–973 (2018)
31. Yuan, F., et al.: Future data helps training: modeling future contexts for session-based recommendation. In: Proceedings of The Web Conference 2020, pp. 303–313 (2020)
32. Zagoruyko, S., Komodakis, N.: Paying more attention to attention: improving the performance of convolutional neural networks via attention transfer. arXiv (2016)
33. Zhang, Y., et al.: Real-time air quality forecasting, part i: history, techniques, and current status. Atmos. Environ. 60, 632–655 (2012)
34. Zheng, Y., et al.: Forecasting fine-grained air quality based on big data. In: KDD, pp. 2267–2276 (2015)
35. Zhou, H., et al.: Informer: beyond efficient transformer for long sequence time-series forecasting. In: AAAI (2021)

SymRecorder: Detecting Respiratory Symptoms in Multiple Indoor Environments Using Earphone-Microphones

Zhiyuan Li[1], Feng Hong[1(✉)] , Yan Xue[2], Qingbin Li[1], and Zhongwen Guo[1]

[1] Ocean University of China, Qingdao 266000, China
{lizhiyuan,liqingbin}@stu.ouc.edu.cn, {hongfeng,guozw}@ouc.edu.cn
[2] Qingdao University, Qingdao 266100, China
xueyan0512@qdu.edu.cn

Abstract. Respiratory symptoms associated with sound frequently manifest in our daily lives. Despite their potential connection to illness or allergies, these symptoms are often overlooked. Current detection methods either depend on specific sensors that must be deliberately worn by the user or are sensitive to environmental noise, limiting their applicability to specific settings. Considering that indoor environments vary, we propose SymRecorder, an earphone microphone-based application, for detecting respiratory symptoms across a range of indoor settings. By continuously recording audio data through the earphone's built-in microphone, we can detect the four common respiratory symptoms: cough, sneeze, throat-clearing, and sniffle. We have developed a modified ABSE-based method to detect respiratory symptoms in noisy environments and mitigate the impact of noise. Additionally, a Hilbert transform-based method is employed to segment the continuous respiratory symptoms that users may experience. Based on selected acoustic features, the four symptoms are classified using the residual network and the multi-layer perceptron. We have implemented SymRecorder on various Android devices and evaluated its performance in multiple indoor environments. The evaluation results demonstrate SymRecorder's dependable ability to detect and identify users' respiratory symptoms in various indoor environments, achieving an average accuracy of 92.17% and an average precision of 90.04%.

Keywords: respiratory symptoms · ear-phone · signal process · deep-learning

1 Introduction

Respiratory symptoms are associated with illnesses, infections or allergies. For example, cough is the main symptom of asthma. When the patient has pneumonia (e.g., COVID-19), it is often accompanied by throat-clearing (t-c) and

L. Wang et al. (Eds.): CWSN 2023, CCIS 1994, pp. 301–315, 2024.
https://doi.org/10.1007/978-981-97-1010-2_22

nasal aspiration symptoms. Currently, patients commonly use subjective reporting methods when seeking medical care [6]. This has been shown to be inefficient and inaccurate.

In recent years, works have focused on the detection of specific types of respiratory symptoms, such as cough [13], sneeze [1], and snore [15]. PulmoTrack-CC [14] uses a combination of sound recorded from the neck and a motion sensor placed on the chest to achieve a sensitivity of approximately 96% when calculating cough events. All of the above systems require the user to wear special sensors and are not practical enough. With the increasing power of smartphones, many studies have emerged on the use of smartphones to improve the quality of healthcare services [10,11,17,18]. A cough detection system [19] uses a local Hu matrix and a k-nearest neighbor (KNN) algorithm to achieve 88.51% sensitivity (SE) and 99.72% specificity (SP). SymDectector [12] is a smartphone-based application that implements the detection of sound-related respiratory symptoms in office and home scenarios. SymListener [16] implements three types of respiratory symptom detection in driving environments with strong interior noise. However, SymDetector and SymListener do not consider continuous symptoms. The popularity of earphones provides an opportunity to detect respiratory symptoms in multiple indoor environments. When users wear earphones, their relative position to the human body does not change and they are able to receive the acoustic signals generated by the user more stably.

Driven by these circumstances, we propose an earphone-microphone based system, called SymRecorder, for detecting sound-related respiratory symptoms in a variety of indoor environments. SymRecorder uses the earphone microphone connected to a smart device to sense the environment and detects and recognizes sound-related respiratory symptoms, including cough, sneeze, t-c and sniffle. To achieve the above objective, we face the following challenges: (1) the indoor environment where the user is located may be noisy, which can lead to a lower signal-to-noise ratio and make it difficult to detect sound events; (2) the user may experience continuous respiratory symptoms, especially continuous cough, at very short intervals, SymRecorder needs to accurately subdivide these continuous symptoms.

To address the above challenges, we design a sound event detection method combining dual threshold and Adaptive Band-partitioning Spectral Entropy (ABSE) [3], named RA-ABSE to detect sound-related events occurring in different indoor environments. RA-ABSE uses dual thresholds to detect sound event endpoints in quiet environments. While in the noisy environment, ABSE is used as a feature to detect the endpoints of sound-related events and is combined with Berouti power spectrum subtraction to remove the effect of noises on sound events. With the help of the RA-ABSE, segments of the audio containing sound events are filtered out. After acquiring the sound event fragments, we design a Hilbert Transform (HT) based method to subdivide the possible continuous symptoms. Then we use a combination of features based on Mel Frequency Cepstrum Coefficients (MFCC), Gammatone Frequency Cepstrum Coefficients (GFCC) and spectrogram. SymRecorder adopts the Residual Network (ResNet) and Multi-layer Perceptron (MLP) to classify the four types of respiratory symptoms. We also incorporate the attention mechanism into the ResNet to highlight the unique features of the same respiratory symptoms and reduce the influence of different environments and different populations.

To evaluate the performance of SymRecorder, we collect data from a total of 20 volunteers over 4 months using earphones to build the system model. We implement SymRecorder on the Android platform and comprehensively evaluate its performance. The experimental results show that SymRecorder is effective in four indoor environments: home, office, canteen, and shopping mall. Our contributions are summarized as follows:

- We propose a detection system, called SymRecorder to detect sound-related respiratory symptoms in different indoor environments. Through acoustic sensing, SymRecorder only uses a pair of earphones and a mobile device to detect and differentiate between cough, sneeze, t-c, and sniffle.
- We design a dual threshold and ABSE-based sound event detection method, called RA-ABSE, to detect sound events in different indoor environments, and use Berouti power spectrum subtraction to eliminate the environmental noises. We also design a HT based method to subdivide possible continuous respiratory symptoms.
- We design a combination of features based on the spectrogram, MFCC, and GFCC, and use a deep learning model combining ResNet, attention mechanism, and MLP for classification. The evaluation results show that SymRecorder has an average accuracy of 92.17% and an average precision of 90.04%.

The rest of this article is organized as follows: In Sect. 2, we describe The detailed description of the SymRecorder design. Experimental details and future work on SymRecorder are presented in Sect. 3. Section 4 discusses related work, and finally, we draw our conclusion in Sect. 5.

2 System Design

This section describes the system architecture of SymRecorder. As shown in Fig. 1, the whole system consists of six modules. First, the original microphone audio recording is split into frames and windows, and the frames and windows are sent to the sound event detection module. This module first determines the current environment type and detects sound events using the RA-ABSE method. Next, the sound events are passed through the continuous symptom detection module to subdivide the possible continuous symptoms. Next, features are extracted for each filtered sound event and a deep learning network is used to classify the sound events. Finally, respiratory symptoms are recorded. The design details of each module are described in detail below.

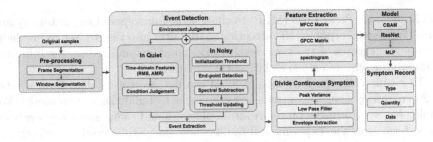

Fig. 1. System overview.

2.1   Sampling and Pre-processing

Existing earphones are capable of sampling audio signals at a variety of sampling rates. We choose 20000 Hz as the sampling rate. The sampled audio stream is then segmented into $10ms$ non-overlapping frames, which are used to extract time-domain features. The VocalSound [7] dataset contains recordings of 3365 subjects performing six physiological activities: laugh, sigh, cough, t-c, sneeze, and sniffle. We count the distribution of all symptom durations. As seen in Fig. 2a, respiratory symptoms typically last for hundreds of milliseconds and cover multiple frames. Therefore, we group a fixed number of consecutive frames into a single window for processing. In addition, the user may also experience continuous respiratory symptoms, especially continuous cough. To determine the window size, we also count the number of possible occurrences of continuous respiratory symptoms. As shown in Fig. 2b, continuous respiratory symptoms tend to last 1 to 3 times, while reference [5] states that during continuous respiratory symptoms, subsequent symptoms will not include an inspiratory period except for the first symptom, and the duration of each symptom will not exceed 0.5 s. Therefore, the window size is set to 2 s, which can cover any respiratory symptoms. To avoid double counting, there is no overlaph between windows. When a user experiences consecutive symptoms, they are distributed in a maximum of two windows.

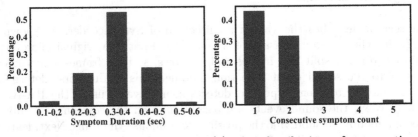

(a) the distribution of symptom dura- (b) the distribution of consecutive
tion   symptom count

Fig. 2. The distribution of symptom.

2.2   Sound Event Detection

We utilize the short-time power (STE) to determine the user's environment. Specifically, SymRecorder stores data from the current window and the past 4 windows, totaling 5 windows (i.e., 10 s). Subsequently, the STE of the frames within each window is computed. Only when 80% of the frames' STE in each window are below the STE threshold (i.e., 10), the current environment is classified as a quiet environment. Otherwise, it is considered as a noisy environment. Following this, we design a sound event detection method called RA-ABSE. In quiet indoor environments, the method employs dual-threshold time-domain features for sound event detection, while in noisy indoor environments, ABSE is used as a feature to detect sound events.

Quiet Indoor Environment. In a quiet indoor environment, the energy of the audio signal received by the earphone microphone is typically low except for sound events. Figure 3a illustrates an earphone audio recording in an office scenario with a subject's speech signal and several respiratory symptoms. It can be observed that the energy of the environmental noise is very low except for the sound events. Furthermore, in addition to discrete sound events containing respiratory symptoms, continuous sound events (e.g., speech or music) are included, which need to be filtered out. In the following, we introduce the employed time-domain features and elucidate how these features can be used to filter out continuous sound events.

Root Mean Square (RMS): Suppose l denotes the frame consisting of N samples, and $x(l, n)$ denotes the amplitude value of the n sample in l, then the RMS [8] of the l frame is

$$rms\,(l) = \sqrt{\frac{1}{N} \sum_{n=1}^{N} x\,(l, n)^2} \tag{1}$$

The RMS measures the energy level contained in the current acoustic frame so that the RMS can distinguish between acoustic and non-acoustic event frames.

Above α-Mean Ratio (AMR): Assuming that w represents a window consisting of m frames, the AMR of the window w is calculated as

$$amr\,(\alpha, w) = \frac{\sum_{i=1}^{m} ind\,[rms\,(l_i) > \alpha \cdot \overline{rms}\,(w)]}{m} \tag{2}$$

where $\overline{rms}\,(w)$ is the mean RMS of all frames in window w and $ind\,(\cdot)$ indicates the indicator function that returns 1 when the condition is true and 0 otherwise. α is the given parameter. AMR measures the ratio of high-energy frames in the window and the experimental parameter α is jointly set with the mean RMS of the window to distinguish between high-energy and low-energy windows. Given an appropriate value of α, windows containing discrete sound events, continuous sound events, and environmental noise return different AMR. Therefore, this feature can be used to filter windows with discrete sound events. In SymRecorder, α is set to 0.6.

RMS is first used to find the endpoints of sound events. As shown in Fig. 3b, sound events usually have higher energy, and therefore the RMS of the sound event frames is also significantly larger than the surroundings. Specifically, when the RMS of three consecutive frames is above the RMS threshold β (i.e., 0.005), the beginning of the first frame is considered the start point of the sound event. The end point is obtained when the RMS of three consecutive frames below the threshold. And the AMR is used to filter out continuous sound events, especially the user's speech signals. As shown in Fig. 3c, windows contain discrete sound events typically have lower AMR due to the windows contain fewer frames of sound events, while the sound events contain much more energy than environmental noise frames. The AMR of the speech event window typically ranges from 0.3 to 0.5, since the voiced frames occupy about 30% to 50% [9] in a fluent speech. Therefore, when the AMR of the window where the current sound event is less than 0.3 and the duration of the sound event is greater than 0.2 s, the sound event is considered as a valid sound event, otherwise, the sound event is discarded.

Finally, we consider the situation when the user experiences continuous symptoms. We observe that when most of the continuous symptoms are distributed across two windows, the AMR of the window containing more symptom parts will be slightly higher, but still below the threshold of 0.3, so that the continuous symptoms are preserved. However, when continuous symptoms are concentrated within a single window, the AMR of that window becomes similar to the AMR of the continuous speech windows, which means that the continuous symptoms will be discarded. Therefore, if the AMR of the window containing the sound event is higher than 0.3 but the duration of that sound event is lower than the window size (i.e., 2 s), the sound event is still preserved.

Noisy Indoor Environment. In a noisy indoor environment, the earphone microphone continuously receives audio signals with higher energy. Figure 4a shows an audio recording in a canteen scene, where it can be observed that the environmental noise in the canteen makes it challenging to accurately detect respiratory symptoms by time-domain features. Therefore, we employ the ABSE as a feature parameter to detect sound events in noisy environments. ABSE divides the spectrum into multiple frequency bands and calculates the spectral entropy within each frequency band, thus avoiding dependence on the entire spectral amplitude variance. The ABSE for the l frame is calculated as

$$H_b(l) = \sum_{m=1}^{N_b} W(m,l) \cdot H_b(m,l) \tag{3}$$

where $W(m,l)$ and $H_b(m,l)$ are the weight and spectral entropy value of the m sub-band, respectively. Then an adaptive signal threshold T_s is set to classify

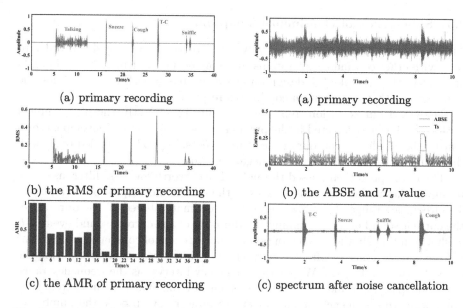

(a) primary recording

(a) primary recording

(b) the RMS of primary recording

(b) the ABSE and T_s value

(c) the AMR of primary recording

(c) spectrum after noise cancellation

Fig. 3. Example of audio recording in office.

Fig. 4. Example of audio recording in canteen.

event segment or noise-only segment according to the mean μ and variance θ of the logarithmic ABSE value of detected noise-only segments. Formally, $T_s = \mu + \gamma \cdot \sigma$, and γ (i.e., 0.005) is an experimental coefficient. This threshold is compared to the value of the current frame. Whenever the difference surpasses a specified threshold, event segment is detected. If a given segment is detected as a noise-only segment, then the signal threshold is updated. Figure 4b illustrates the trend of the ABSE of Fig. 5(a) and T_s. It can be observed that T_s is constantly updated during the pure noise and remains unchanged when a sound event is detected.

After the sound events endpoints are detected, it is necessary to separate the noise components from the sound events. We employ the Berouti spectral subtraction method to reduce the noise components in the sound events. Suppose $Y(e^{jw})$, $S(e^{jw})$ and $N(e^{jw})$ denote the Fourier Transform (FT) result of the mixed noisy signal, the pure signal and the additive noise, then we have $|Y(e^{jw})|^2 = |X(e^{jw})|^2 + |N(e^{jw})|^2$. As for the additive noise can not be obtained directly, we use the average power spectral E of several beginning frames to approximately replace $|N(e^{jw})|^2$. Finally, $|S(e^{jw})|$ can be calculated by $|S(e^{jw})| = \sqrt{|Y(e^{jw})|^2 - E}$. Figure 4c illustrates the processed result, it can be seen that most of the environmental noise has been eliminated, and the sound events can be effectively extracted from the time domain.

2.3   Subdivision of Continuous Symptom

Although continuous symptoms mainly refer to continuous cough, in order to cope with other continuous symptoms that may occur, all detected sound events are sent to this module. We design an algorithm based on HT to subdivide the sound events that may contain continuous respiratory symptoms.

The algorithm execution steps are shown in Fig. 5. Firstly, the HT is applied to the sound events detected in the previous stage to extract the envelope, representing the amplitude contour of the sound events. The HT is applied to smooth the sound signal and eliminate the negative values [4].

The envelope is then passed through a Butterworth low-pass filter, as a way to obtain the fundamental frequencies of the continuous respiratory symptoms. The frequency range of the low-pass filter is estimated based on the duration of the current sound event. Assuming the duration of the current sound event is t, as shown in Fig. 2b, the number of possible occurrences of consecutive symptoms is from 1 to 4. Thus, the frequency interval of the current symptom during the time of t is $(1/t, 4/t)$ Hz. We set this frequency interval as the frequency range of the low-pass filter and iteratively increment 0.1 Hz. When the filter frequency approaches the frequency of the current respiratory symptoms, the number of peaks on the filtered envelope corresponds to the number of occurrence counts of the current symptom. Thus, when the criteria for the number of peaks are met, the variance of all peaks is recorded until the iteration process concludes. The set of peaks with the minimum variance is subsequently selected, and the subdivision of sound events is achieved by the distance differences between the peaks. In the algorithm design process, additional conditional statements are incorporated to handle specific situations:

(a) Since the number of peaks in the filter envelope corresponds to the number of times during the filter frequency change, only one peak can be detected for a sound event that contains only one respiratory symptom. If only one peak is still detected when the filter frequency iterates to $4/t$Hz, the current sound event is not processed in the current module.

(b) Some single symptoms can have two stages of energy bursts, with the first phase being sharper and containing higher energy, while the second stage is relatively flat and has lower energy. Therefore, two peaks may appear during the filter frequency iterations, indicating the subdivision of a single symptom. To differentiate it from two consecutive symptoms, the values of the two peaks are compared after the set of peaks with the lowest variance is obtained. For two consecutive symptoms, the peaks on the filtered envelope will be evenly distributed. Suppose the first peak value is $Peak_1$ and the second peak value is $Peak_2$. If $0.8 \cdot Peak_1 < Peak_2$ is satisfied, the sound event is subdivided according to the distance between the peaks, otherwise the current sound event is output directly.

(c) Two stages of energy bursts may also occur during continuous symptoms. The variance of the peak set can help filter out such case. During the iteration of the filter frequency, when a smaller peak appears, the variance of the set of peaks increases, and therefore the current peak set is not selected. So, if the number of selected peak set is more than two, the current sound event is subdivided directly according to the distance between the peaks.

Finally, we perform alignment processing on each subdivided sound event to facilitate the next step of feature extraction. Specifically, the duration of the sound event is denoted as d, if $d < 0.2\,\mathrm{s}$, the sound event is discarded; if $0.2\,\mathrm{s} < d < 0.5\,\mathrm{s}$, then the sound event is zero-padded to $0.5\,\mathrm{s}$; if $d > 0.5\,\mathrm{s}$, then the middle part of the sound event is taken, and the part before and after the length of $1/2 \cdot (d - 0.5)$ is deleted.

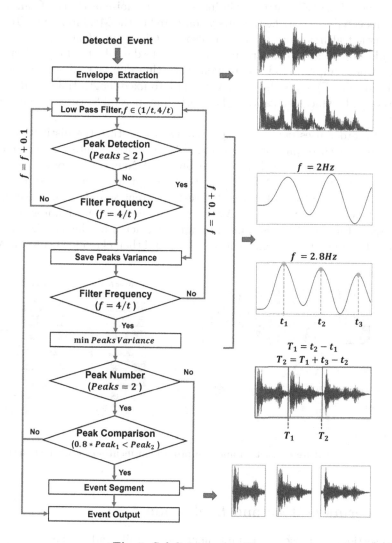

Fig. 5. Subdivision algorithm.

2.4   Feature Extraction and Classified Model

Respiratory symptoms are abnormal manifestations related to the respiratory system, typically emitted from the nasal cavity or throat, presented in the acoustic form of specific audio signals. Many features exist for identifying specific types of audio signals, and one of the most commonly used features is the MFCC. MFCC takes into account the non-linear response of the human ear on the audio spectrum, and is obtained through a frequency transformation of the logarithmic spectrum.

Although MFCC is widely used as a feature in audio signal processing, the performance of MFCC is strongly influenced by the noise level. The Gammatone filter bank can provide higher accuracy compared to the Mel filter bank. To make the acoustic features more robust, we also use GFCC as a feature.

In addition, SymRecorder requires a feature to describe the local information of respiratory symptoms in both frequency and time domains. Short-term Fourier Transform (STFT) splits the original signal into fixed-length time windows and applies the FT, which can capture the short-time spectral features in the original signal.

SymRecorder uses deep learning networks to capture the distinctive representations of each respiratory symptom. The network architecture is shown in Fig. 6. The learning network uses Convolutional Neural Network (CNN) and ResNet as the backbone, MFCC matrix, GFCC matrix, and spectrogram as inputs. To enhance the differences between different sound event features, the lightweight Convolutional Block Attention Module (CBAM) is integrated into the ResNet. Finally, the fine-grained features extracted by the learning network are concatenated into the same feature vector and then classified using the MLP.

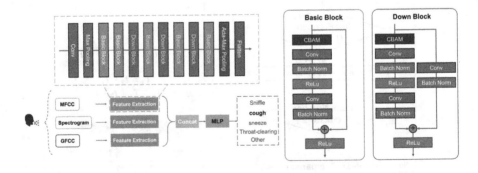

Fig. 6. Finer feature extraction and symptom identification network structure.

3   Experimentation and Evaluation

In this section, we present the implementation details and evaluates the performance of SymRecorder based on the data collected from experiments. We also conclude with a discussion on the future work of SymRecorder.

3.1   Experimental Setup

The training set used is derived from two datasets. The first dataset is from VocalSound [7]. We get 2013 cough, 1310 sneeze, 1764 t-c, and 2341 sniffle samples. These samples are utilized to investigate the features extracted from respiratory symptoms and enable deep learning networks to learn the distinctions between different respiratory symptom characteristics.

The second dataset comes from 14 participants we recruited, consisting of 4 females and 10 males. The participants' ages range from 12 to 58 years. Three participants are from the same family and spend much of their time at home; the remaining 11 participants are graduate students who frequented the office and canteen almost every day. Additionally, they spend one day per week shopping at the mall. Over a period of four months, we collect 2,873 cough, 2,008 sneeze, 2,577 t-c, and 3,135 sniffle samples under the four different environmental conditions. In addition, we also gathered non-symptomatic sound events (e.g., door closing), which are labeled as "other" categories.

To test the performance of SymRecorder, a prototype is developed and installed on Honor-10 and Xiaomi 12Pro smartphones. Four volunteers who participate in data collection are joined by an additional 6 volunteers for evaluation purposes. The evaluation scenarios included home, office, canteen, and shopping mall. Over the course of nearly three months of evaluation, we collect 1331 cough, 797 sneeze, 916 t-c, and 1054 sniffle samples. Table 1 presents detailed information about the utilized dataset. We compare the performance of SymRecorder with the following methods, which also focus on detecting respiratory symptoms through acoustic sensing:

SymDetector [12]: This work classifies cough, sneeze, sniffle, and t-c symptoms using the SVM classifier using time-domain features and frequency-domain features such as symptom length, the center of mass, bandwidth, etc.

SymListener [16]: This work uses MFCC and GFCC features to classify cough, sniffle, and sneeze using Long Short Term Memory (LSTM) networks.

3.2   System Performance

Overall Performance. We first compare the overall performance of SymRecorder with the baseline methods realized in an offline manner. Figure 7a shows the confusion matrix of SymRecorder, indicating that 93.18% of respiratory symptoms are correctly classified. Sniffle has a probability of being classified as "other", but is less likely to be classified as cough. Cough has a probability of being classified as t-c, while sneeze has a probability of being classified as sniffle. Figure 7b illustrates the overall performance of SymRecorder compares to the two baseline methods. It can be observed that SymRecorder achieved the highest average recall and precision, which are 92.17% and 90.04%, respectively. Due to SymDetector relying only on audio amplitude and RMS to detect sound-related events, it is less robust to the interference of noisy environments, such as canteens and malls. This may result in SymDetector missing sound events in noisy environments. Although SymListener can adapt to strong driving noise, it

Table 1. Setup of Datasets.

dataset	cough	sneeze	t-c	sniffle	days	source
train set	2013	1310	1764	2341	–	vocalsound
	2873	2008	2577	3135	120	1st–14th
testset	1331	797	916	1054	85	11th–20th

does not consider the impact of consecutive symptoms, treating them as individual occurrences. Furthermore, both SymDetector and SymListener do not differentiate the source of symptoms, and symptoms generated by other people also lead to overall performance degradation. For SymRecorder, the detection accuracy for cough and sneeze is relatively high. This can be attributed to the high energy density and long symptom duration associated with these two symptoms. In contrast, the detection accuracy for sniffle is relatively low due to its lower energy density and shorter symptom duration.

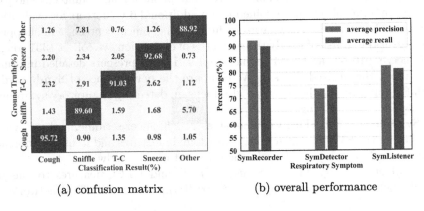

(a) confusion matrix   (b) overall performance

Fig. 7. The overall performance of SymRecorder.

Influence of Indoor Scenario. Figure 8a and Fig. 8b illustrate the recall and precision in different indoor scenarios. In this context, the term "mall" refers to a comprehensive commercial complex where the environmental noise tends to be more pronounced compared to other scenarios. It can be observed that SymRecorder performs the best in office environments, as offices are typically characterized by relatively quiet surroundings. Across various scenarios, the detection performance for cough and sneeze is consistently good. However, in canteen and mall scenarios, the recall and precision for sniffle are relatively low. This is because these scenarios often feature short and high-frequency sound events such as tray handling noises and buzzing sounds, which can either mask sniffle sounds or be misclassified as sniffle. Additionally, the category of "other" sound events exhibits a lower recall rate but higher precision in the evaluation. This suggests that sound events tend to be classified as respiratory symptoms, while respiratory symptoms are difficult to classify as "other". This phenomenon may be attributed to the fact that certain sound events can generate acoustic characteristics similar to respiratory symptoms.

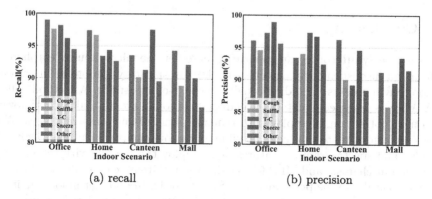

(a) recall   (b) precision

Fig. 8. The performance of different scenarios.

3.3   Discussion and Future Work

Although we introduce a subdivision algorithm to handle potential instances of continuous cough events, the subdivision algorithm cannot handle all continuous cough events. The algorithm can fail when the second burst stage of a cough symptom resembles the first stage. Furthermore, if multiple individuals cough simultaneously, causing overlapping cough sounds, the subdivision algorithm may also produce errors. We will subsequently improve the subdivision algorithm and consider acquiring dual-channel signals from headphones to distinguish between different users.

4   Related Work

The audio-based approach has an excellent track record in detecting respiratory health. PulmoTrack-CC [14] achieved 94% overall specificity and 96% overall sensitivity in detecting cough events. VitaloJAKTM [2] proposes to capture signal regions with high energy and high spectral mass to automatically count coughs from recordings. However, all of the above work requires the user to wear a recording device or acoustic sensor, which is extremely inconvenient to use.

In many previous works, smartphones started to be used to collect respiratory health information. iSleep [8] is a smartphone-based sleep monitoring system that detects snoring sounds from the user, but it has high environmental requirements. symDetector [12] is a smartphone-based application that detects sneeze, cough, sniffle, and t-c sounds in a home or office environment, and has high ambient noise requirements. SymListener [16] is also a smartphone-based application that detects sneeze, cough, and sniffle sounds in the driving environment, with a high level of environmental robustness, but without considering the effects of continuous symptoms.

5   Conclusion

We propose SymRecorder, an application based on the microphone of earphones, which can inconspicuously detect user-related respiratory symptoms in various indoor environments, including cough, sneeze, t-c, and sniffle. A method called RA-ABSE is designed to detect the endpoints of sound events, and Berouti power spectral subtraction is employed to remove potential environmental noise. We devise an algorithm to subdivide possible continuous symptoms, utilizing MFCC, GFCC, and spectrogram as features, and employ the ResNet with the stacked attention mechanism and MLP for classification. Extensive experiments are conducted to evaluate the performance of SymRecorder in different indoor environments, and the results demonstrate that SymRecorder can detect respiratory symptoms with high accuracy.

References

1. Akhil, S., et al.: A novel approach for detection of the symptomatic patterns in the acoustic biological signal using truncation multiplier. In: ICICICT 2019, pp. 49–53 (2019). https://doi.org/10.1109/ICICICT46008.2019.8993389
2. Barton, A., Gaydecki, P., Holt, K., Smith, J.A.: Data reduction for cough studies using distribution of audio frequency content. Cough **8**, 12 (2012). https://doi.org/10.1186/1745-9974-8-12
3. Wu, B.-F., Wang, K.-C.: Robust endpoint detection algorithm based on the adaptive band-partitioning spectral entropy in adverse environments. IEEE Trans. Speech Audio Process. **13**, 762–775 (2005). https://doi.org/10.1109/TSA.2005.851909
4. Chauhan, J., Hu, Y., Seneviratne, S., Misra, A., Seneviratne, A., Lee, Y.: BreathPrint: breathing acoustics-based user authentication. In: MobiSys 2017, pp. 278–291 (2017). https://doi.org/10.1145/3081333.3081355
5. Chung, K.F., et al.: Cough hypersensitivity and chronic cough. Nat. Rev. Dis. Primers. **8**, 45 (2022). https://doi.org/10.1038/s41572-022-00370-w
6. French, C.T., Irwin, R.S., Fletcher, K.E., Adams, T.M.: Evaluation of a cough-specific quality-of-life questionnaire. Chest **121**, 1123–1131 (2002). https://doi.org/10.1378/chest.121.4.1123
7. Gong, Y., Yu, J., Glass, J.: Vocalsound: A dataset for improving human vocal sounds recognition. In: ICASSP 2022, pp. 151–155 (2022). https://doi.org/10.1109/ICASSP43922.2022.9746828
8. Hao, T., Xing, G., Zhou, G.: iSleep: unobtrusive sleep quality monitoring using smartphones. In: Sensys 2013, pp. 1–14 (2013). https://doi.org/10.1145/2517351.2517359

9. Korpáš, J., Sadloňová, J., Vrabec, M.: Analysis of the cough sound: an overview. Pulm. Pharmacol. **9**, 261–268 (1996). https://doi.org/10.1006/pulp.1996.0034

10. Lu, H., Pan, W., Lane, N.D., Choudhury, T., Campbell, A.T.: SoundSense: scalable sound sensing for people-centric applications on mobile phones. In: MobiSys 2009, Kraków, Poland, pp. 165–178 (2009). https://doi.org/10.1145/1555816.1555834

11. Qian, K., et al.: Acousticcardiogram: monitoring heartbeats using acoustic signals on smart devices. In: INFOCOM 2018, pp. 1574–1582 (2018). https://doi.org/10.1109/INFOCOM.2018.8485978

12. Sun, X., Lu, Z., Hu, W., Cao, G.: SymDetector: detecting sound-related respiratory symptoms using smartphones. In: UbiComp 2015, pp. 97–108 (2015). https://doi.org/10.1145/2750858.2805826

13. Vhaduri, S., Kessel, T.V., Ko, B., Wood, D., Wang, S., Brunschwiler, T.: Nocturnal cough and snore detection in noisy environments using smartphone-microphones. In: ICHI 2019, pp. 1–7 (2019). https://doi.org/10.1109/ICHI.2019.8904563

14. Vizel, E., et al.: Validation of an ambulatory cough detection and counting application using voluntary cough under different conditions. Cough **6**, 3 (2010). https://doi.org/10.1186/1745-9974-6-3

15. Wang, C., Peng, J., Song, L., Zhang, X.: Automatic snoring sounds detection from sleep sounds via multi-features analysis. AUST. Phys. Eng. Sci. **40**, 127–135 (2017). https://doi.org/10.1007/s13246-016-0507-1

16. Wu, Y., Li, F., Xie, Y., Wang, Y., Yang, Z.: SymListener: detecting respiratory symptoms via acoustic sensing in driving environments. ACM Trans. Sens. Netw. **19**, 1–21 (2023). https://doi.org/10.1145/3517014

17. Xie, Y., Li, F., Wu, Y., Wang, Y.: HearFit: fitness monitoring on smart speakers via active acoustic sensing. In: INFOCOM 2021, pp. 1–10 (2021). https://doi.org/10.1109/INFOCOM42981.2021.9488811

18. Xie, Y., Li, F., Wu, Y., Yang, S., Wang, Y.: D^3-guard: acoustic-based drowsy driving detection using smartphones. In: INFOCOM 2019, pp. 1225–1233 (2019). https://doi.org/10.1109/INFOCOM.2019.8737470

19. You, M., et al.: Novel feature extraction method for cough detection using NMF. IET Signal Process. **11**, 515–520 (2017). https://doi.org/10.1049/iet-spr.2016.0341

Author Index

© The Editor(s) (if applicable) and The Author(s), under exclusive license
to Springer Nature Singapore Pte Ltd. 2024
L. Wang et al. (Eds.): CWSN 2023, CCIS 1994, pp. 317–318, 2024.
https://doi.org/10.1007/978-981-97-1010-2

Printed in the United States
by Baker & Taylor Publisher Services